Contemporary Social Work Practice

Series Editor
Christina E. Newhill

For further volumes:
http://www.springer.com/series/8853

Helen Cahalane

Editor

Contemporary Issues
in Child Welfare Practice

 Springer

Editor
Helen Cahalane
Child Welfare Education
    and Research Programs
School of Social Work
University of Pittsburgh
Pittsburgh, PA, USA

ISBN 978-1-4614-8626-8   ISBN 978-1-4614-8627-5 (eBook)
DOI 10.1007/978-1-4614-8627-5
Springer New York Heidelberg Dordrecht London

Library of Congress Control Number: 2013953256

Printed on acid-free paper

Springer is part of Springer Science+Business Media (www.springer.com)

Preface

Child welfare is the oldest specialization within social work practice and the only specialty area in which social work is the host profession. Following the creation of agencies devoted to child protective services across the country, the recognition of battered child syndrome, and the initiation of state and federal mandatory child abuse and neglect reporting laws, child welfare entered into a period beginning in the 1970s where the need to provide child protection required a workforce greater than the number of social work practitioners with a specialization in child welfare services. High personnel vacancy and turnover rates, less-than-desirable educational levels of staff, court determinations of inadequate service, and a dearth of evidence-based practice models have contributed to the challenges experienced in the child welfare system. At the same time, the need to educate child welfare professionals has been acknowledged for several decades. Increased recognition has been given to the provision of services that result in measurable outcomes. There is also increasing demand for the implementation of practice models that are driven by evidence and for child welfare policies and practices to be informed by, and responsive to, the youth and families who are served by the child protection system. The recognition of organizational factors in influencing child welfare service delivery; the retention of staff; and the outcomes achieved by children, youth, and families have also resulted in a greater emphasis on effective organizational functioning and the importance of larger systems-level intervention in child welfare.

Child welfare practice is at a critical period of re-professionalization. Driving forces in child welfare services reform include professional education of the workforce, training and effective skill transfer to the field, the implementation of evidence-informed practices, demonstration of measurable outcomes and cost effectiveness, attainment of performance standards, organizational excellence and continuous quality improvement, and the provision of community-based, client-informed models of service. Increased attention has been directed toward supervisory practices and the importance of effective supervision in supporting a workforce challenged by continual exposure to trauma; compliance with a myriad of policy mandates; staff shortages due to worker turnover; position freezes or eliminations;

and financing that is inadequate, inflexible, and geared toward institutional forms of care. Clearly, the child welfare profession is at a critical juncture. Prior models of practice and service delivery; the education, training, supervision, and support provided to the workforce; and the organizational structure and effectiveness of child welfare agencies are being challenged by the demand for outcome measurement, evidence-based practice, and youth- and family-driven policies and services.

Few practice-oriented books are written for social workers who specialize in child welfare services. This volume fills the gap by providing a unique and comprehensive overview of contemporary practice issues relevant to child welfare professionals who are entering the field, as well as those already working in direct service and management positions. This book can be used not only by undergraduate and graduate students in social work but also by researchers and practitioners who have an interest in intervention related to child abuse and neglect at the individual, family, community, and organizational level. The emphasis is placed upon systemic, integrated, and evidence-driven practices that are in keeping with child welfare's core mission of child protection, child and family well-being, family support, and permanency for youth. Case examples are provided to connect theory with practice and to incorporate the voice and perspective of youth, families, caregivers, and child welfare caseworkers. Both challenges and opportunities are addressed within the context of the contemporary practice environment that is increasingly driven by fiscal limitations, the attainment of defined outcomes, and the need for an informed, professionalized child welfare workforce.

This volume begins with foundational material related to child-serving systems of care by placing child welfare within the spectrum of community-based services and supports for children and youth with or at risk for challenges across a range of life domains. In Chap. 1, "Child Welfare Practice in a Systems of Care Framework," Marlo Perry and Rachel Fusco highlight the evolution of an integrated approach to providing services to children and families across categorical systems. They focus on the challenges and opportunities unique to the child welfare system in maintaining the core values of a child-centered, community-based, and linguistically and culturally competent approach to care that includes partnership with families. This theme of partnership and inclusion is taken up by Fusco and Mary Elizabeth Rauktis in Chap. 2, "They Brought Me in Like I Was Their Own Kid: Youth and Caregiver Perceptions of Out-of-Home Care." The authors provide powerful, firsthand accounts from parents and children who have experienced separation and loss as result of out-of-home care, prompting social workers and other helping professionals to recognize that home and family are critical to one's identity. Fusco and Rauktis remind us that when placement is unavoidable, we must ensure that youth and their families are being nurtured, supported, and connected.

In keeping with an increased emphasis on strengths-based and family-centered approaches to care, the child welfare field has become more focused on effective engagement strategies. In Chap. 3, "Family Engagement Strategies in Child Welfare Practice," Helen Cahalane and Carol Anderson focus on the unique opportunity for engaging with families in a partnership focused on solutions and change, despite the involuntary nature of involvement with the child welfare system. Practical engagement strategies are provided for child welfare professionals who are faced with the complex task of forming a therapeutic relationship that will help families make difficult changes. The origin, theoretical base, key elements, method of delivery, and evidence base of two models of child welfare intervention, Family Group Decision Making and Family Finding, are summarized to illustrate practices that effectively engage youth and families by facilitating connections between children and their family network.

Transformation of the child welfare system from one of legal authority over youth and families to one of partnership and collaborative decision making is further examined by exploring best practices related to establishing permanency and the successful transition of youth to adulthood. Caroline Donohue, Cynthia Bradley-King and Helen Cahalane tackle the various forms that permanency may take for children and youth receiving child welfare services in Chap. 4, "Permanency." They consider options involving biological family members, relatives, fictive kin, adoptive families, and/or long-term foster families. While recognizing that reunification, legal guardianship, and adoption all provide opportunities for a long-term sense of connectedness, Donohue, Bradley-King and Cahalane argue that no placement, service, or effort at larger scale community building can thrive in the absence of a committed federal effort to reorganize child welfare financing.

In Chap. 5, "Transitioning into Adulthood: Promoting Youth Engagement, Empowerment, and Interdependence Through Teaming Practices," Rauktis, Ben Kerman, and Chereese Phillips provide a synthesis of family and youth teaming models. They describe the important leadership role of youth and the essential need for a supporting cast of family members as young persons transition into adulthood, using the case illustration of a story not unusual among the 254,162 children who entered foster care in 2012. Highlighting the growing evidence that suggests that family and youth teaming practices such as Family Group Decision Making, Team Decision Making, and Lifelong Family Connections offer a variety of options for building secure interdependence for youth and a lasting support network to draw on in the future, Rauktis, Kerman, and Phillips illustrate the ways in which teaming practices that respect youth voice, promote emerging autonomy, and engage a broad support system represent a needed step beyond traditional life skills curricula, which focus on transitioning youth in isolation.

Child welfare systems must be equipped with a competent workforce that is capable and ready for the difficult work of child protection. The effectiveness of child welfare services is dependent in large part upon the skills and acumen of the caseworkers who work with youth and families. Chapters 6 and 7 provide cutting-edge information to build cultural competence and cultural humility with specific youth populations receiving child protective services. Elizabeth Winter elucidates the elevated risks to the safety, well-being, and permanency of sexual minority youth in Chap. 6, "Lesbian, Gay, Bisexual, Transgendered, Questioning, and Queer Youth: The Challenge for Child Welfare." She begins with the definitions of each of the LGBTQ groups and then presents a thorough and comprehensive review of the relevant literature to highlight particular challenges experienced by LGBTQ youth both generally and in the child welfare system. Winter then explores the myths, misperceptions, and facts of LGBTQ culture in child welfare and discusses the need for an LGBTQ-inclusive organizational culture within the child welfare system. In Chap. 7, "Race, Disparity, and Culture in Child Welfare," Bradley-King, Perry, and Donohue survey the empirical literature and emphasize the central issue of racial disproportionality in child welfare. They begin by reviewing relevant terms and providing an overview of racial demographics in the USA and in the child welfare system, then provide a historical context, and finally, review different positions in a debate about disproportionality. The authors conclude with a discussion of cultural competence and cultural humility, calling upon caseworkers to thoughtfully consider how race and culture intersect with social and economic risk factors that contribute to child welfare outcomes.

Professional development of the child welfare workforce is discussed by Anita Barbee and Marcia Martin in their overview of the knowledge and skills a child welfare worker must possess. In Chap. 8, "Skill-Based Training and Transfer of Learning," these seasoned and experienced child welfare academicians and researchers recognize the critical importance of preparing the child welfare workforce to address the complexities of achieving safety, permanency, and well-being for children and families who present with multiple needs and a host of challenges involving concrete resources, social support, and personal autonomy. Barbee and Martin point out that classroom training builds a foundation that must be reinforced in the field through coaching, mentoring, and specific feedback on key practice behaviors. They also elucidate the fact that simply possessing knowledge and skills is insufficient; child welfare workers must be able to translate a sense of knowing and doing into distinct situations by transferring learning as they engage with each new client and each new situation.

Child welfare work is extraordinarily rewarding and full of opportunities to make a critical difference in the lives of children and families. With this also comes the difficulty of dealing with the stressful aspects of the job and exposure to the details of the suffering of maltreated children and their families. Added to the mix for both individuals and organizations are environmental stressors, such as a lack of understanding of the work of child welfare and the ambivalence of a society that recognizes the need to safeguard vulnerable children on one hand while also viewing child welfare intervention with suspicion and mistrust. In Chap. 9, "Stress and Child Welfare Work," Winter describes the individual and organizational exposure to traumatic events that is an ongoing reality in child protective services. She details the significant distress that can affect individuals, their quality of work, and the atmosphere within child welfare organizations and provides an overview of suggested ways that agencies, administrators, supervisors, and caseworkers can work toward self-care within a trauma-informed culture. Likewise, supervision is an important factor in creating an agency culture that is responsive and attuned to the needs of child welfare workers. A number of studies have confirmed that supervision not only is critical for worker satisfaction and retention but also has an impact on the quality and outcomes of services provided to children and families. Rauktis and Tammy Thomas address the challenge of keeping committed, compassionate, and well-educated workers in the field of child protection in Chap. 10, "Reflective

Practices in Supervision: Why Thinking and Reflecting Are as Important as Doing."
Using examples from a qualitative study of caseworker decision making, they
describe reflective supervision and other reflective practices that offer the potential
to move child welfare work beyond a narrow focus on investigation of abuse and
compliance with procedural mandates. Rauktis and Thomas propose that reflective
supervision practices help workers manage the stressful nature of child welfare
work by providing a space to reflect on their own thoughts and feelings. Thus, child
welfare practice can move to a point where thinking, problem solving, and exploring emotions are part of standard practice, ultimately improving the decisions that
are made when working with children and families.

Child welfare practice occurs within the context of dynamic, multifaceted organizational systems that are ripe with opportunities to positively impact children,
families, and the professionals who dedicate their careers to improving the lives of
young persons. As with all complex, hierarchical social structures, child welfare
agencies can vary in performance and efficiency. In Chap. 11, "Organizational
Effectiveness Strategies for Child Welfare," Phil Basso, Helen Cahalane, Jon Rubin,
and Kathy Jones Kelley describe a practice model for enhancing agency functioning, capacity, and ability to meet client outcomes. Drawing on applied work in organizational development, performance management, quality improvement,
organizational learning, and leadership, the authors delineate a set of key strategies
for helping child welfare agencies leverage their strengths, address performance
gaps, and continuously improve across all areas of work. The parallels between
intervention with individuals, groups, families, and communities and the process of
organizational effectiveness within child welfare agencies are highlighted through
the use of case examples that illustrate both micro and macro practice. Megan Good,
Erin Dalton, and Marc Cherna demonstrate the critical connection between casework practice and organizational performance in Chap. 12, "Managing for Outcomes
in Child Welfare." These authors provide social workers with a greater understanding of how performance is measured and monitored in child welfare, first describing
the process of federal accountability and then discussing the principles necessary to
implement continuous quality improvement within a child welfare framework.
A case study demonstrates that performance tools and data serve a purpose beyond
simply reporting and monitoring. Good, Dalton, and Cherna argue that agencies
with cultures that embrace continuous quality improvement and feedback from all
levels of the organization are those most able to utilize information to their advantage in improving the lives of children and families.

In sum, this volume is designed to enhance the knowledge, skills, and competence of social workers who practice in the field of child welfare. Given the enormous responsibility for protecting children, supporting families, and assuring
permanency for youth, the authors hope that this volume contributes to increased
knowledge and effectiveness in child welfare practice, a field described as one of the
toughest jobs you will ever love.

Pittsburgh, PA, USA   Helen Cahalane

Contents

Contributors

Carol M. Anderson Western Psychiatric Institute and Clinic, School of Medicine, University of Pittsburgh Medical Center, Pittsburgh, PA, USA

Anita P. Barbee Kent School of Social Work, University of Louisville, Louisville, KY, USA

Phil Basso Organizational Effectiveness Department, American Public Human Services Association, Washington, DC, USA

Cynthia Bradley-King Child Welfare Education and Research Programs, School of Social Work, University of Pittsburgh, Pittsburgh, PA, USA

Helen Cahalane Child Welfare Education and Research Programs, School of Social Work, University of Pittsburgh, Pittsburgh, PA, USA

Marc Cherna Allegheny County Department of Human Services, Pittsburgh, PA, USA

Erin Dalton Allegheny County Department of Human Services, Pittsburgh, PA, USA

Caroline Donohue Child Welfare Education and Research Programs, School of Social Work, University of Pittsburgh, Pittsburgh, PA, USA

Rachel A. Fusco School of Social Work, University of Pittsburgh, Pittsburgh, PA, USA

Megan Good Allegheny County Department of Human Services, Pittsburgh, PA, USA

Kathy Jones Kelley Merced County Human Services Agency, Merced, CA, USA

Ben Kerman Strategic Learning and Evaluation, The Atlantic Philanthropies, New York, NY, USA

Marcia L. Martin Graduate School of Social Work and Social Research, Bryn Mawr College, Bryn Mawr, PA, USA

Marlo A. Perry Child Welfare Education and Research Programs, School of Social Work, University of Pittsburgh, Pittsburgh, PA, USA

Chereese M. Phillips School of Social Work, University of Pittsburgh, Pittsburgh, PA, USA

Mary Elizabeth Rauktis Child Welfare Education and Research Programs, School of Social Work, University of Pittsburgh, Pittsburgh, PA, USA

Jon Rubin Organizational Effectiveness Department, American Public Human Services Association, Washington, DC, USA

Tammy L. Thomas School of Social Work, University of Pittsburgh, Pittsburgh, PA, USA

Elizabeth A. Winter Child Welfare Education and Research Programs, School of Social Work, University of Pittsburgh, Pittsburgh, PA, USA

Chapter 1
Child Welfare Practice in a Systems of Care Framework

Marlo A. Perry and Rachel A. Fusco

Abstract A systems of care (SOC) framework is an approach to service delivery that works cooperatively across systems to create an integrated process for meeting the many needs of families. Based on the principles of interagency collaboration, community-based services, strength-based practices, cultural competence, and full participation of families and youth, a SOC framework requires that multiple systems serving children and families come together to create and offer coordinated programs and services. This is particularly crucial for child welfare, as families often have multiple, complex needs that are better served by agencies and organizations typically seen as "outside" the child welfare system (e.g., substance abuse programs and domestic violence counseling).

The families entering the child welfare system are frequently dealing with poverty, substance abuse issues, mental health issues, and health problems. Children in the child welfare system sometimes have educational needs and interaction with the juvenile justice system. Using a systems of care framework in the child welfare system allows workers to best meet the needs of families with multiple issues by providing a coordinated system of services for all family members. A SOC approach exemplifies the non-categorical system reform necessary to ensure that the goals of safety, permanency, and well-being are achieved for all children and families across child-serving systems.

Keywords Systems of care • Child-centered • Community-based • Culturally competent • Evidence-based • Population-driven

M.A. Perry (✉)
Child Welfare Education and Research Programs, School of Social Work,
University of Pittsburgh, Pittsburgh, PA, USA
e-mail: map225@pitt.edu

R.A. Fusco
School of Social Work, University of Pittsburgh, Pittsburgh, PA, USA

H. Cahalane (ed.), *Contemporary Issues in Child Welfare Practice*,
Contemporary Social Work Practice, DOI 10.1007/978-1-4614-8627-5_1,
© Springer Science+Business Media New York 2013

Mr. Ryan, a ninth-grade teacher, made a report about Ricky Garza, a 14-year-old male Latino youth, to Children's Protective Services (CPS). Mr. Ryan made the call because Ricky came to school with a welt on his left cheek; additionally, over the last sixth months, Mr. Ryan had observed other marks on the boy's arms and legs. The CPS investigator went to Ricky's home and met with his mother, Sofia Garza. Sofia admitted that she caused the mark on Ricky's face when she disciplined him with a belt and he tried to get away from her. She said that she had a difficult time getting Ricky to listen to her and said she had no choice but to punish him with a belt or a paddle "to get his attention".

Further discussion revealed that the Garza family was dealing with many challenges. Sofia's husband had been arrested for manufacturing and selling crystal methamphetamine 2 years earlier and was incarcerated. Sofia had had to take on a second job to make ends meet. Ricky had a 4-year-old brother, Michael, who had been diagnosed with autism a month before. Ricky had been arrested twice the previous year for shoplifting and vandalism.

Sofia explained that she had been having a difficult time taking care of her boys. Ricky had been having problems in school, not completing work, and fighting with other kids. He had been diagnosed with dyslexia at age eight and continued to struggle with his work. He received support in school through his Individualized Education Program (IEP), but Sofia struggled to help him with homework since she dropped out of school in ninth grade.

She felt that the boys really needed a male role model and worried that Ricky would end up in jail like his father. She believed she had to discipline her sons harshly to maintain control of them. Sofia seemed baffled by Michael's diagnosis, and she believed that his problems were really behavioral. She described him as "defiant" and said, "There is nothing wrong with that child except that he will not listen!"

During further investigation the worker learned that Sofia had type 2 diabetes and needed to give herself insulin shots daily. She was so tired in the evenings that she frequently fed the kids and herself fast-food dinners. She also drank to the point of passing out on occasional weekend evenings. Sofia was able to earn enough to basically support the family, but she was at risk of losing her second job.

Sofia reported that Ricky cut his wrists the month before but claimed the cuts were not even deep enough to take him to a doctor. Ricky expressed a lot of grief and anger about his father's incarceration. He only got to see his father about three times a year, because the family lived in a semirural area with poor bus service and had an unreliable car. Sofia owned the family home, but it was in poor physical condition.

The Garza's story is not an uncommon one in the child welfare system. Although the family came into the system because of suspected physical abuse, there are clearly other overlapping issues. Ricky has learning problems and is struggling in school. He has some mental health concerns and may have made a suicide attempt. He clearly has some grief about his separation from his father.

Michael is also at risk. He was very recently diagnosed with autism, and his mother may still be adjusting to this diagnosis. He has a much older brother who is acting out and a mother who may have substance abuse problems. Although there is no evidence that Michael is currently being maltreated, his family stress and his autism diagnosis place him at high risk for abuse or neglect.

Sofia seems to love her children and is doing her best to parent them under difficult circumstances. However, she is working 50–60 h a week and is a single mother. She has only a ninth-grade education and may not have a strong understanding of child development. Sofia has a chronic disease that requires diligent maintenance, but there are indications that she has a poor diet. She is also using alcohol to cope with her life stress.

The Garzas need services from not only the child welfare system but the education and early intervention systems, the mental health system, the healthcare system, and the juvenile and criminal justice systems. For the child welfare system to best meet its goals of safety, permanency, and well-being, it needs to effectively partner with these other systems. A systems of care (SOC) framework is an approach to service delivery that works cooperatively across systems to create an integrated process for meeting the many needs of families. This approach is based on the principles of interagency collaboration, community-based services, strengths-based practices, cultural competence, and full participation of families and youth.

The SOC framework was developed as a response to growing recognition that children with serious mental health disorders were not receiving needed help and services (Knitzer 1982; Stroul and Friedman 1986). In the early 1980s the Children's Defense Fund published *Unclaimed Children* (Knitzer 1982), which exposed the inadequate care received by youth with mental health problems and the consequences of such care. The report was based on interviews across the states' mental health departments, as well as interviews with providers, parents, and public officials. Findings showed that many states did not prioritize child and adolescent mental health despite a relatively high prevalence of problems in this population, and few had staff specifically trained to work with this population. Knitzer also reported that, while children and adolescents were underserved overall, a few subpopulations were disproportionately underserved. This included abused or neglected children. Other work further supported these findings by highlighting the fragmentation of mental health services, a lack of coordination among agencies serving children with overlapping problems (e.g., child welfare, juvenile justice, education), the placement of children away from their families and communities, and the lack of recognition of cultural differences (Burchard et al. 1993; Stroul 1996).

These concerns led to the development of the Child and Adolescent Service System Program (CASSP), funded by the National Institute of Mental Health (NIMH). The CASSP provided funds and technical assistance to all 50 states for planning and developing community-based services for children with serious emotional or mental health disturbances. CASSP was a SOC framework that mandated state mental health collaboration between state mental health departments and other public systems serving children (Knitzer 1993). The CASSP integrated principles developed by Stroul and Friedman (1986), who coined the term "community-based system of care for seriously emotionally disturbed children" (p. iv). As originally defined, a system of care is "a comprehensive spectrum of mental health and other necessary services which are organized into a coordinated network to meet the multiple and changing needs of children and their families" (Stroul and Friedman 1986).

Two of the core principles of SOC are that services must be *child-centered* and *community-based* (Stroul and Friedman 1986). Child-centered refers to the need for the SOC to be guided by the specific needs of the child. Typically, before SOC were introduced services took more of a "one size fits all" approach, with the expectation that children and families would select and use an existing set of programs and services. The notion of child-centered services allowed for more individually tailored combinations of services that could work in harmony with a family's needs, goals, and strengths. Similarly, community-based care was a relatively novel approach to working with children and families at the time when a SOC framework was first introduced. Historically, services for children with severe mental health disorders were hospital- and/or institution-based. The SOC approach called for a network of services provided in less restrictive environments in a child's home and community.

Expanding a SOC Framework to Child Welfare

In recent years, researchers and policymakers have called for a SOC framework to be applied to populations beyond children and youth with mental health concerns (Fluke and Oppenheim 2010; Pires 2010; Stroul and Blau 2010). In the spirit of the original concept, but noting the need for an updated definition, Stroul and Blau (2010) offer the following broadened definition of systems of care:

> A spectrum of effective, community-based services and supports for children and youth with or at risk for mental health or other challenges and their families, that is organized into a coordinated network with a supportive infrastructure, builds meaningful partnerships with families and youth, and addresses their cultural and linguistic needs, in order to help them to function better at home, in school, in the community, and throughout life (p. 61).

This updated definition maintains the core values of child-centered and community-based, but broadens the scope of child-centered to include partnerships with families and also includes the need for culturally and linguistically competent care. These three components (child-centered and family-focused, community-based, and linguistically and culturally competent) are congruent with the tenets of child welfare philosophy and are critical to ensure positive outcomes for children and families involved with the child welfare system.

Child-Centered and Family-Focused

Child-centered refers to having the child's needs at the forefront and tailoring services to a child's individual set of strengths and needs. Child welfare has historically been very child-centered; however, the field has often advocated for protecting the child at the expense of the family (Sandau-Beckler et al. 2002). Early legislation (i.e., Public Law 93–247, the Child Abuse Prevention and Treatment Act) focused solely on the safety of the child, mandating reporting of abuse and often blaming the family for the abuse without implementing any supports or services for the family. However, if work with the Garza family focused only on Ricky, without looking at the challenges faced by all members of the family system, it wouldn't address the larger issues that contributed to Ricky's behavior problems and likely wouldn't result in positive outcomes related to his safety, permanency, and well-being. More recent legislation has made efforts to balance the safety and well-being of the child with family-engagement strategies and family supports that will, ideally, result in family preservation or at least permanence for the child (Fluke and Oppenheim 2010).

There are several challenges related to a family-centered SOC that are unique to the field of child welfare. For example, unlike involvement with other systems (e.g., education, mental health), families are typically not involved with the child welfare system voluntarily; instead, involvement is mandated due to allegations of maltreatment (Fluke and Oppenheim 2010; Williamson and Gray 2011). Historically, child welfare has taken a deficit-based approach with families, with practitioners assuming that they know what is best for the family without giving the family a voice or including the family in the decision-making process. Families may feel angry, scared, disempowered, and/or isolated; they may not have the skills to advocate for themselves and become actively involved in the planning process. A SOC approach is strengths-based and requires that practitioners actively engage parents in all phases of the planning process and give them the tools with which to do so (some family-engagement practice models, such as Family Group Decision Making, are highlighted below and described in more detail in Chaps. 3 and 5).

As the example of the Garzas demonstrates, families involved with the child welfare system typically have multiple, complex needs, further complicating the provision of family-centered care. Many parents involved with child welfare services have addiction or mental health issues, which can limit their decision-making abilities regarding their families (Fluke and Oppenheim 2010). Issues such as these can also hinder parents' ability to engage in the process and advocate for themselves and their child(ren), and these families may need more active direction on the part of the caseworker in order to set and meet appropriate and attainable goals (Fluke and Oppenheim 2010). Practitioners will need to find a careful balance between letting parents take the lead on planning and services and knowing how and when to take a more directive approach.

Finally, in order for a family-centered approach to be successful, "family" needs to be defined more broadly (Fluke and Oppenheim 2010). The notion of family should include not only the primary caregivers but also fictive kin, including extended family, godparents, and perhaps foster parents (Fluke and Oppenheim 2010). The Garzas have close friends in their neighborhood who provide support for Sophia and the children, and they should be viewed as part of the extended family system. Sofia is also very close to her grandmother, who provides occasional respite care for the boys. Kin networks should be critical components of family-centered care, particularly since kin and/or fictive kin may be responsible for caring for the child, on either a temporary or a long-term basis.

While each family will bring its own set of skills, resources, and challenges, a SOC approach demands that families are involved to the greatest extent possible given their set of skills, resources, and needs. The level of involvement will vary depending on safety concerns, availability of extended kin and other social supports, the ability of the parents to recognize the needs of their child(ren), and the parents' ability and willingness to engage with the agency. In this way, family-centered care works in harmony with the strengths and needs of children and families served by the child welfare system and facilitates the child welfare system truly operating as a SOC (Fluke and Oppenheim 2010).

Community Based

A SOC for child welfare needs to be community-based. This is also a strengths-based approach, in that a family's community (i.e., home, school, neighborhood) is seen as a collection of assets that can be utilized to support the child and family (Child Welfare Information Gateway 2008; Stroul et al. 2010). A community-based approach capitalizes on natural supports in a family's environment, which can include nonprofit agencies, faith-based organizations, educational programs, and neighbors. These supports and services will vary greatly from family to family. The Garzas, for example, have strong ties within their community, including their membership at a local church and after-school and preschool programs at the community YMCA. Ideally, these community-based services will work collaboratively with one another and provide complementary (instead of duplicate) services.

A community-based approach allows children to remain in their homes, schools, and/or neighborhoods, which can have beneficial impacts for both children and their families. Children are therefore able to maintain crucial relationships with friends and families, as well as teachers, neighbors, and/or members of their religious community. Further, this type of arrangement allows for the continuation of support after formal child welfare services are terminated or removed, because relationships and structures are already in place that allow for more informal supports for the child and family (Child Welfare Information Gateway 2008).

Linguistically and Culturally Competent

Although national demographic data are not available for all children and families who have contact with the child welfare system, statistics do show that racial and ethnic minority children are disproportionately placed in out-of-home care in this country. In 2010, 53 % of children aged 0–18 in the general population were white, 14 % were black, 24 % were Hispanic, 4 % were Asian-American/Pacific Islander, 1 % were American Indian/Alaskan Native, and 4 % were children of other races and ethnicities. Comparatively, in the same year, 41 % of children in out-of-home care were white, 29 % were black, 21 % were Hispanic, 1 % were Asian-American/Pacific Islander, 2 % were American Indian/Alaskan Native, and 7 % were of other races and ethnicities (Kids Count Data Center 2012). Again, although national data are not available showing the racial and ethnic background of child welfare caseworkers, there is some evidence that the majority of caseworkers are white, indicating that there are often racial, ethnic, and cultural mismatches between families and their caseworkers (Courtney et al. 1996; Ryan et al. 2006). A SOC approach demands that practitioners within those systems demonstrate cultural and linguistic competence with the populations with whom they work; this is consistent with the SOC strengths-based approach. The underlying assumption of culturally and linguistically competent care is that children and families should receive services that are consistent with and that support the integrity and strengths of their culture

(McPhatter 1997). A culturally competent professional is one who works in a manner that is consistent with the behavior and expectations that members of a particular cultural group see as normative among themselves (Green 1999; McPhatter 1997). Interventions and services must therefore be congruent with cultural norms; providers need to understand the cultural lens through which families see the provider, the agency, and the plan of care (Child Welfare Information Gateway 2008).

In the Garzas' case, the family identifies as Latino, and Sofia's parents emigrated from Mexico. Sofia and her sons speak both English and Spanish fluently, but some members of her extended family prefer to speak Spanish. It is important for social workers who work with the Garza family to have some understanding of their culture, including parenting practices. Ideally, the worker should speak Spanish or have access to an interpreter so communication with extended kin will not be impeded. This cultural awareness helps to form an alliance with the family and to build on family strengths.

By making efforts to understand the needs of families within a cultural framework, providers convey respect and dignity to all involved in the system; by addressing issues of culture, practitioners and systems increase the likelihood of family engagement and a successful outcome (Child Welfare Information Gateway 2008). Issues related to child maltreatment are common across many cultures and communities; a system's and/or practitioner's willingness and ability to understand the unique needs and strengths that a family brings to the process will not only increase the families' willingness to participate but will also help to improve the system's ability to provide effective services (Child Welfare Information Gateway 2008).

Congruence of Systems of Care Principles with Child and Family Services Reviews

Amendments to the Social Security Act authorized the US Department of Health and Human Services to review each state's child welfare system to ensure adherence with the requirements for child protective care, foster care, adoption, family preservation and family support, and independent living services (Children's Bureau 2011). Federally mandated Child and Family Services Reviews (CFSRs) are conducted by the Children's Bureau to help improve safety, permanency, and well-being outcomes for children and families who receive services through the child welfare system. They are also intended to assist states in building and enhancing their capacity to provide better services to children and families. CFSRs evaluate the effectiveness of the entire child welfare delivery system, which includes other systems it commonly interacts with, such as mental health providers, the justice system, and substance abuse treatment, to ensure positive outcomes for children and their families. CFSRs look at whether or not a child welfare agency made concerted efforts to provide or arrange for appropriate services, such as those needed to ensure a child's safety and enhance the parents' ability to provide care and supervision.

In recent years, CFSRs have found that child welfare systems need to improve the practice of effectively engaging families to participate meaningfully in ensuring good outcomes for children (Pires 2008). Another finding is that these improved outcomes for children and their families cannot be realized in the absence of strong working relationships between child welfare agency staff and a full range of community partners; in other words, CFSRs call for a SOC approach to child welfare.

The SOC approach is congruent with the goals and values of the CFSRs, including the focus on providing family-centered practice, basing services in the community, strengthening the capacity of families, and individualizing services to best fit the needs of children and families. As a way of meeting these goals, state and local child welfare agencies have implemented a number of evidence-informed practices to address the mental health needs of children and to support and build positive parenting practices to help achieve permanency. Further, these practices promote partnerships between various child- and family-serving systems.

Examples of Evidence-Informed Practices and How They Fit Within a SOC Framework

In order for a SOC to facilitate successful outcomes for children and families, services that agencies provide must be based on evidence-informed practices. Evidence-informed practice refers to the application of the best available research evidence to the provision of services in order to enhance outcomes (Chaffin and Friedrich 2004). Evidence-informed practice originated in the medical field, where thousands of randomized controlled trials have been conducted, but it has been challenging to incorporate many of these findings into direct practice with clients. More recently, disciplines such as social work have embraced the evidence-informed practice movement as a nationwide effort to build quality and accountability.

In child welfare, several evidence-informed practices are in common use. A few of these will be discussed within the framework of systems of care. These programs are focused on maintaining the safety, permanency, and well-being of children in care and demonstrate collaboration across systems to meet these goals.

Family Group Decision Making

Family Group Decision Making (FDGM) is an innovative approach that positions the family as leaders in decision making about their children's safety, permanency, and well-being. FGDM brings together a broad group of family, community, and agency supports to develop a plan to safeguard the child (Crampton and Natarajan 2005). Cultural competence is one of FGDM's core principles (Pennell 2003). The practice aims to reduce the power imbalance between families and child welfare agencies through a process of shared decision making and mutual respect (Garcia et al. 2003). FGDM strives to help children maintain kinship and cultural connections and to contribute to culturally competent policies and procedures in child welfare services (American Humane Association 2009; Pennell 2003). FGDM could be a positive practice to use with the Garzas as it would build on their existing community supports and incorporate extended kin who play a strong role in the family, and also because it views their ethnic heritage as a strength for building change in the family.

Multisystemic Therapy

Multisystemic Therapy (MST) is an intensive family- and community-based treatment for children with externalizing behavioral issues and their families. The primary goals of MST are to decrease youth antisocial behavior and out-of-home placements (Henggeler and Borduin 1990). The model also aims to build parent discipline practices, to improve family communication, and to develop family support networks to help maintain positive change. MST is guided by a theory of change rooted in Bronfenbrenner's (1979) ecological theory, and the approach views individuals as being within a complex network of interconnected systems that encompass individual, family, and community (e.g., peer, school, neighborhood) factors. Services are targeted toward the entire family and are offered either in home or in the family's community (Henggeler et al. 1998). In randomized control trials comparing MST to standard practices for children and families, MST was found to reduce social problems experienced by the family and improve parent–child relations (Brunk et al. 1987), decrease children's externalizing symptoms (Henggeler et al. 1999), reduce criminal and violent activity among youth (Henggeler et al. 1996), and result in fewer days in out-of-home care (Schoenwald et al. 1996). MST could be an effective treatment model for the Garzas, since Ricky is having issues across contexts (such as fighting in school as well as vandalism in the neighborhood) and is displaying some antisocial behaviors. Sofia has also expressed a need for building her parenting practices with both children.

Parent–Child Interaction Therapy

Parent–Child Interaction Therapy (PCIT) was developed for young children (2–10 years) with emotional and behavioral problems and their families (Schuhmann et al. 1998). It has two main foci: (1) to improve parent–child interactions and (2) to increase child compliance through developing stronger parenting skills. Therapists coach parents during interactions with their children to teach new parenting skills. These skills are designed to strengthen the parent–child bond, decrease harsh and ineffective discipline control tactics, improve child social skills and cooperation, and reduce negative or maladaptive child behaviors. PCIT outcome research has demonstrated significant improvements in parent–child relationships and a reduction of disruptive behavior in children. Although Ricky is now too old for PCIT, it could have been a powerful intervention option for the Garzas if problems had been detected earlier. PCIT could have addressed the antisocial behaviors that were starting to emerge with Ricky and helped Sofia develop firm and appropriate discipline practices.

Multidimensional Treatment Foster Care

Multidimensional Treatment Foster Care (MTFC) is focused on children who demonstrate disruptive behaviors and their families (Fisher and Chamberlain 2000). This program exists for both preschool-aged children (MTFC-P) and adolescents (MTFC-A). MTFC-P is effective at promoting secure attachments in foster care and facilitating successful permanent placements. It is delivered through a treatment team approach in which foster parents receive training and ongoing consultation and support, children receive individual skills training and participate in therapeutic playgroups, and permanent caregivers receive family therapy (Fisher et al. 2009). MTFC-P emphasizes the use of encouragement for pro-social behavior and consistent and appropriate limit setting to address disruptive behavior. In addition, the MTFC-P intervention employs a developmental framework in which preschoolers in foster care are viewed as having a delayed developmental trajectory.

If a determination was made that Ricky Garza needed to be removed from his home, MTFC-A could be helpful in moving him toward permanency. MTFC-A aims to create opportunities for youths to successfully live in families rather than in group or institutional settings and to simultaneously prepare their caregivers to effectively parent (Chamberlain 2003). Four key elements of treatment include providing youth with a consistent environment where they are mentored and encouraged to develop academic and positive living skills; daily structure with clear expectations and limits, with well-specified consequences delivered in a teaching-oriented manner; close supervision of youths' whereabouts; and helping the youth avoid deviant peer associations while providing them with the support and assistance to establish pro-social peer relationships.

Triple P-Positive Parenting Program

The Triple P-Positive Parenting Program is a system of parenting and family support that aims to prevent severe behavioral, emotional, and developmental problems in children and to prevent child maltreatment. The program is multidisciplinary, with a focus on enhancing the knowledge, skills, and confidence of parents; both individual and group formats are utilized (Sanders 1999). Intervention is tailored to the child's developmental stage, from infancy to adolescence. Encouraging outcomes have been found for both children and their parents in randomized control trials comparing Triple-P to standard practices. Parents reported increased parental competence and decreased dysfunctional parenting (Bor et al. 2002) and showed more realistic expectations for their children, fewer negative attributions for their children's misbehavior, and reduced child abuse potential (Sanders et al. 2004). Children in the program showed fewer disruptive behaviors and decreased inattention and hyperactivity (Bor et al. 2002). Triple-P could be beneficial for Sofia Garza as she has two children of different ages and seems unaware of unique developmental challenges at each stage of life. The Triple P-Positive Parenting Program focuses on both communities and individuals and includes a universal media information campaign that targets all parents in a community.

High-Fidelity Wraparound

Wraparound is a team-based planning process intended to provide individualized and coordinated family-driven care. It is designed to meet the complex needs of children who are involved with several child and family-serving systems (e.g., child welfare, mental health, juvenile justice) who are at risk of placement in institutional settings and who experience emotional, behavioral, or mental health difficulties (Burns and Goldman 1999). The wraparound process builds on existing support available to a family by strengthening interpersonal relationships and utilizing other resources available in the family's network of social and community relationships. The process requires that families, providers, and members of the family's social support network collaborate to build an individualized plan that responds to the particular needs of the child and family. Team members then implement the plan and continue to monitor progress and make adjustments to the plan as necessary (VanDenBerg and Grealish 1996). The team continues its work until members reach a consensus that a formal wraparound process is no longer needed. Wraparound would be a good program for the Garzas as they have identified issues in the education and juvenile justice systems, and they need to work with the mental health system. The Garzas also have strong community supports upon which they can build.

Overview of Systems that Should Be Involved with a Child Welfare SOC

A SOC framework requires that multiple systems serving children and families involved with child welfare come together to create and offer more coordinated programs and services. This is particularly crucial for child welfare, as families involved with this system often have multiple, complex needs that are better served by agencies and organizations typically seen as "outside" the child welfare system (e.g., substance abuse programs, domestic violence counseling). A unique aspect of a SOC approach is that it is a non-categorical system reform (Pires 2008). Most system reforms are categorical, in that each is restricted to its own individual system (e.g., deinstitutionalization in mental health, inclusion reforms in special education). However, a SOC approach utilizes a shared population focus, in that a target group (e.g., youth aging out of foster care, minority children disproportionately represented in child welfare, young children in care with special health needs) is selected, and then all systems who may serve that target population engage collaboratively in a reform agenda (Pires 2008).

In this way, it is the particular set of strengths and needs of the target population that will dictate the types of programs and strategies that will be needed in the SOC (Pires 2008). For example, if the target population is young children of mothers with mental health needs, then organizations and services in the system of care may include Head Start, child care, and/or early intervention services, as well as community-based mental health services and parenting programs. Alternatively, if the target population is adolescents aging out of foster care, then organizations and services in the system of care may include the education system, job training programs, the mental health system, the criminal justice system, and the health system.

There is no definitive list of programs and services that can be involved in a SOC. The mental health, addictions, and juvenile and criminal justice systems are perhaps most frequently involved in systems of care, because they commonly overlap with child welfare in terms of the populations they serve. However, there are several other systems that are frequently overlooked but that should be part of a successful SOC if the target population warrants it. These include domestic violence services, the education system (including early childhood education programs such as Head Start, as well as special education and/or vocational/technical programs), early intervention programs, and the health system.

Case Example: Cuyahoga Tapestry System of Care

One example of a successful systems of care approach is the Cuyahoga Tapestry System of Care in Cuyahoga County, Ohio. Originating through a grant received from the United States Substance Abuse and Mental Health Services Administration (SAMHSA) in 2003 to develop a system of care, Tapestry now serves more than 600 families each year (Cuyahoga Tapestry System of Care 2009). Tapestry was set up as a partnership between county child-serving systems of care and collaboratives of neighborhood provider agencies. The collaboratives utilize wraparound strategies to work with families, advocates, and professionals to improve access to mental health services and nontraditional supports for children and families (Munson et al. 2009). Tapestry has been successful in reducing recidivism in both the juvenile justice and child welfare systems, as well as in improving child and family functioning (Cuyahoga Tapestry System of Care 2009).

Conclusion

Using a systems of care framework in the child welfare system allows workers to best meet the needs of families with multiple issues. The families entering the child welfare system are frequently dealing with poverty, substance abuse issues, mental health issues, and health problems. Children in the child welfare system sometimes have educational needs and interaction with the juvenile justice system. Providing a coordinated system of services for all family members can best ensure we meet the goals of safety, permanency, and well-being.

> Fortunately, the Garza family lives in an area that utilizes a systems of care approach to serving children and families. Over the next year, the Garzas were able to access and utilize multiple community-based services that have helped to address many of the challenges they were facing. The Garzas participated in Multisystemic Therapy, which helped Sofia strengthen her parenting skills and helped Ricky develop coping skills that decreased his externalizing behaviors. Additionally, Sofia enrolled Ricky in Big Brothers Big Sisters, so that he could build a positive relationship with a male role model. Ricky is also receiving therapy from a community-based mental health clinic; the work he is doing there is helping him work through some of the depression and anger he has related to his father's incarceration.
>
> The family's case manager assisted Sofia in enrolling Michael in early intervention services. With the help of a Therapeutic Staff Support (TSS) worker, Michael now participates in a full day Head Start program. The TSS worker has also been able to occasionally offer support to Sofia at home. Sofia is coming to terms with Michael's autism diagnosis and is learning more about the disorder and how she can better meet Michael's needs.
>
> Sofia's parent advocate also helped connect Sofia to a diabetes management support group and to some GED classes; Sofia's friends and grandmother agreed on a schedule to help care for the children so that Sofia can participate in these activities. Although Sofia's job situation is still precarious, she is working with a job placement agency to try to find one full-time position that will allow her to financially support her family. She also feels optimistic about other potential job opportunities once she completes her GED.

Questions for Discussion

1. Describe how the three main tenets of a SOC framework (family-focused, community-based, and culturally and linguistically appropriate) are crucial to successful outcomes for children and families. How might the Garzas have fared if their services weren't congruent with this model?
2. Think about a specific target population (e.g., LGBT youth in out-of-home care or young children with special health care needs). What systems would need to be involved in a SOC approach to that target population? Why?
3. The final vignette discusses multiple services that the Garzas were able to access and utilize through a systems of care approach. What different and/or additional services might have been helpful for this family? What other systems would need to engage in the process? How are each of your suggested systems family-focused, community-based, and culturally and linguistically appropriate?
4. Even if your agency and/or county doesn't participate in a SOC approach to serving children and families, how can you incorporate a SOC philosophy into your work with children and families?

References

American Humane Association. (2009). *Cultural appropriateness of child welfare agencies.* Washington, DC: Child Protection Position Statements.
Bor, W., Sanders, M. R., & Markie-Dadds, C. (2002). The effects of the Triple P-Positive Parenting Program on preschool children with co-occurring disruptive behavior and attentional/hyperactive difficulties. *Journal of Abnormal Child Psychology, 30,* 571–587.
Bronfenbrenner, U. (1979). *The ecology of human development: Experiments by nature and design.* Cambridge, MA: Harvard University Press.
Brunk, M. A., Henggeler, S. W., & Whelan, J. P. (1987). Comparison of multisystemic therapy and parent training in the brief treatment of child abuse and neglect. *Journal of Consulting and Clinical Psychology, 55*(2), 171–178.
Burchard, J. D., Burchard, S. N., Sewell, R., & VanDenBerg, J. (1993). *One kid at a time: Evaluative case studies and description of the Alaska Youth Initiative Demonstration Project.* Washington, DC: Georgetown University Press.
Burns, B. J., & Goldman, S. K. (Eds.). (1999). *Promising practices in wraparound for children with serious emotional disturbance and their families. Systems of Care: Promising Practices in Children's Mental Health, 1998 Series* (Vol. 4). Washington, DC: Center for Effective Collaboration and Practice, American Institutes for Research.
Chaffin, M., & Friedrich, B. (2004). Evidence-based treatments in child abuse and neglect. *Children and Youth Services Review, 26,* 1097–1113.
Chamberlain, P. (2003). The Oregon Multidimensional Treatment Foster Care model: Features, outcomes, and progress in dissemination. *Cognitive and Behavioral Practice, 10*(4), 303–312.
Child Welfare Information Gateway. (2008). *Systems of care: Bulletin for professionals.* Washington, DC: Author.
Children's Bureau (2011). *Child welfare monitoring.* Retrieved from http://www.acf.hhs.gov/programs/cb/cwmonitoring/.
Courtney, M. E., Barth, R. P., Berrick, J., Brooks, D., Needell, B., & Park, L. (1996). Race and child welfare services: Past research and future directions. *Child Welfare, 75*(2), 99–137.
Crampton, D., & Natarajan, A. (2005). Connections between group work and family meetings in child welfare practice: What can we learn from each other? *Social Work with Groups, 28,* 65–79.
Cuyahoga Tapestry System of Care. (2009). *Project Summary: 2003–2009.* Cleveland, OH: Author.
Fisher, P. A., & Chamberlain, P. (2000). Multidimensional Treatment Foster Care: A program for intensive parenting, family support, and skill building. *Journal of Emotional and Behavioral Disorders, 8,* 155–164.
Fisher, P. A., Kim, H. K., & Pears, K. C. (2009). Effects of Multidimensional Treatment Foster Care for Preschoolers (MTFC-P) on reducing permanent placement failures among children with placement instability. *Children and Youth Services Review, 31,* 541–546.
Fluke, J. D., & Oppenheim, E. (2010). Getting a grip on systems of care and child welfare using opposable thumbs. *Evaluation and Program Planning, 33,* 41–44.
Garcia, J. A., Sivak, P., & Tibrewal, S. (2003). Transforming relationships in practice and research: What is the Stanislaus model? *Protecting Children, 18,* 22–29.
Green, J. W. (1999). *Cultural awareness in the human services.* Needham Heights, MA: Allyn & Bacon.
Henggeler, S. W., Cunningham, P. B., Pickrel, S. G., Schoenwald, S. K., & Brondino, M. J. (1996). Multisystemic therapy: An effective violence prevention approach for serious juvenile offenders. *Journal of Adolescence, 19,* 47–61.
Henggeler, S. W., Rowland, M. D., Randall, J., Ward, D. M., Pickrel, S. G., Cunningham, P. B., & Santos, A. B. (1999). Home-based multisystemic therapy as an alternative to the hospitalization of youths in psychiatric crisis: Clinical outcomes. *Journal of the American Academy of Child & Adolescent Psychiatry, 38,* 1331–1339.

Henggeler, S. W., Schoenwald, S. K., Borduin, C. M., Rowland, M. D., & Cunningham, P. B. (1998). *Multisystemic treatment of antisocial behavior in children and adolescents*. New York: Guilford.

Henggeler, S. W., & Borduin, C. M. (1990). *Family therapy and beyond: A multisystemic approach to treating the behavior problems of children and adolescents*. Pacific Grove, CA: Brooks/Cole.

Kids Count Data Center. (2012). Data across states: Retrieved from http://datacenter.kidscount.org/data/acrossstates/Default.aspx.

Knitzer, J. (1982). *Unclaimed children: The failure of public responsibility to children and adolescents in need of mental health services*. Washington, DC: Children's Defense Fund.

Knitzer, J. (1993). Children's mental health policy: Challenging the future. *Journal of Emotional and Behavioral Disorders, 1*, 8–16.

McPhatter, A. R. (1997). Cultural competence in child welfare: What is it? How do we achieve it? What happens without it? *Child Welfare, 76*, 255–278.

Munson, M. R., Hussey, D., Stormann, C., & King, T. (2009). Voices of parent advocates within the systems of care model of service delivery. *Children and Youth Services Review, 31*, 879–884.

Pennell, J. (2003). Are we following key FGC practices? Views from conference participants. *Protecting Children, 18*, 16–21.

Pires, S. A. (2008). *Building systems of care: A primer for child welfare*. Washington, DC: National Technical Assistance Center for Children's Mental Health.

Pires, S. A. (2010). How states, tribes, and localities are re-defining systems of care. *Evaluation and Program Planning, 33*, 24–27.

Ryan, J. P., Garnier, P., Zyphur, M., & Zhai, F. (2006). Investigating the effects of caseworker characteristics in child welfare. *Children and Youth Services Review, 28*, 993–1006.

Sandau-Beckler, P., Salcido, R., Beckler, M. J., Mannes, M., & Beck, M. (2002). Infusing family-centered values into child protection practice. *Children and Youth Services Review, 24*, 719–741.

Sanders, M. R. (1999). Triple P-Positive Parenting Program: Towards an empirically validated multilevel parenting and family support strategy for the prevention of behavior and emotional problems in children. *Clinical Child and Family Psychology Review, 2*, 71–90.

Sanders, M. R., Pidgeon, A. M., Gravestock, F., Connors, M. D., Brown, S., & Young, R. W. (2004). Does parental attributional retraining and anger management enhance the effects of the Triple-P Positive Parenting Program with parents at risk of child maltreatment? *Behavior Therapy, 35*, 513–535.

Schoenwald, S. K., Ward, D. M., Henggeler, S. W., Pickrel, S. G., & Patel, H. (1996). Multisystemic therapy treatment of substance abusing or dependent adolescent offenders: Costs of reducing incarceration, inpatient, and residential placement. *Journal of Child and Family Studies, 5*(4), 431–444.

Schuhmann, E. M., Foote, R., Eyberg, S. M., Boggs, S., & Algina, J. (1998). Parent–child interaction therapy: Interim report of a randomized trial with short-term maintenance. *Journal of Clinical Child Psychology, 27*, 34–45.

Stroul, B. A. (1996). *Children's mental health: Creating systems of care in a changing society*. Baltimore: Paul H. Brookes.

Stroul, B. A., & Blau, G. M. (2010). Defining the system of care concept and philosophy: To update or not to update? *Evaluation and Program Planning, 33*, 59–62.

Stroul, B. A., Blau, G. M., & Friedman, R. M. (2010). *Issue brief: Updating the system of care concept and philosophy*. Washington, DC: National Technical Assistance Center for Children's Mental Health.

Stroul, B., & Friedman, R. (1986). *A system of care for children and youth with severe emotional disturbances* (Rev ed.). Washington, DC: Georgetown University Child Development Center, CASSP Technical Assistance Center.

VanDenBerg, J. E., & Grealish, E. M. (1996). Individualized services and supports through the wraparound process: Philosophy and procedures. *Journal of Child and Family Studies, 5*, 7–21.

Williamson, E., & Gray, A. (2011). New roles for families in child welfare: Strategies for expanding family involvement beyond the case level. *Children and Youth Services Review, 33*, 1212–1216.

Chapter 2
"They Brought Me in Like I Was Their Own Kid": Youth and Caregiver Perceptions of Out-of-Home Care

Rachel A. Fusco and Mary Elizabeth Rauktis

Abstract The child welfare system usually becomes involved with families when there are child safety concerns as a result of child abuse or neglect, serious parent–child conflict, physical or behavioral health conditions, or family violence. As part of their practice, child welfare workers must make every reasonable effort to safely maintain children within their families, including providing supports and services. However, for some families these preservation services are insufficient and when this is the case, children are placed in out-of-home care.

Removing children from their homes is difficult for everyone involved. Even when there is serious maltreatment of children, and removal is necessary for safety, lives are still disrupted. Children are moved into a new home or shelter, may not know the people who will be caring for them, and may have to go to a different school. Siblings may be separated, family connections and friendships are disrupted, and everything that is familiar to the child or older youth is taken away. In addition, the separation from parents, siblings, and grandparents may generate feelings of helplessness, anger, and fear.

It is never easy when children are placed into an out-of-home setting. Children, youth, and parents face challenges that include living in someone else's home, losing contact with family, or trying but not succeeding in keeping the family together. When placement is unavoidable, social workers and other helping professionals must keep in mind that home and family are critical to identity and ensure that both children and adults are being nurtured, supported, and connected to their families.

Keywords Youth perception • Out-of-home care • Parent perception • Residential • Foster care

R.A. Fusco (✉)
School of Social Work, University of Pittsburgh, Pittsburgh, PA, USA
e-mail: raf45@pitt.edu

M.E. Rauktis
Child Welfare Education and Research Programs, School of Social Work,
University of Pittsburgh, Pittsburgh, PA, USA

H. Cahalane (ed.), *Contemporary Issues in Child Welfare Practice*,
Contemporary Social Work Practice, DOI 10.1007/978-1-4614-8627-5_2,
© Springer Science+Business Media New York 2013

Dante, a young Hispanic man, entered the child welfare system at age 15 when his parents told a child welfare worker that they could no longer "handle him." It wasn't immediately clear what was fueling Dante's angry outbursts at his stepfather, but later he revealed that both parents were abusing alcohol and his father was physically abusive to his mother and sister. Dante also began carrying a gun and hanging out with a gang that had been known to engage in illegal activities. During his time in out-of-home care, Dante received several diagnoses such as conduct disorder and oppositional defiant disorder. During his first 3 years in the system, he moved from a residential treatment center to a group home, a wilderness camp, and, lastly, an independent living facility until he aged out at 18.

Dante's mother, Louisa, had some level of understanding that child welfare involvement might result in Dante leaving home, but she certainly didn't think he would be leaving for good. Louisa believed that her own life was out of control. She was not very happy in her marriage, but she told herself that Dante's stepfather was a good man with a bad temper. She knew that his treatment of Dante was wrong—Dante had hit his stepfather, but only as a way of defending Louisa against her husband's beatings. But she was afraid that if she spoke up for Dante, the tension in the home would only get worse. She wanted to stop drinking but tried unsuccessfully, and the more she drank, the worse she felt about herself and her life; this resulted in her feeling hopeless about her situation. Even worse was the realization that she was repeating her own family history: Louisa's mother had problems with alcohol abuse and was frequently assaulted by her husband, and Louisa and her siblings ended up in foster care. She comforted herself with the thought that Dante's leaving was only temporary, until "things got better at home—he'll be fine."

In a second case, 13-year-old Leah and her 5-year-old sister Cecelia, both African-American females, were known to child welfare because their mother, Paula, had a long history of serious mental illness that necessitated child welfare's intermittent involvement. Paula was diagnosed with recurrent major depression with psychotic features, and when she took her medicine, she was a loving parent. Unfortunately, she occasionally stopped taking her medication, and the resultant reoccurrence of symptoms leads to disastrous outcomes: in the past the family had become homeless, and now Leah was reported as truant since she stayed home from school to take care of her sister and mother. The caseworker who had been assigned to this family was unsuccessful in finding family members who were willing to foster Leah and Cecelia, since Paula had "burned her bridges" with her family as her mental illness had progressed. Lacking the supports to keep them safe with their mother, the worker placed Leah into a group home for girls and Cecelia into nonrelative foster care.

Paula knew that she needed to take medication, but she got tired of the side effects. It made her feel tired and unable to concentrate. She just wanted to "have a normal life, like everyone else." Why did it have to be different for her? When she stopped taking her medicine, Paula believed there were ghosts in the walls of the apartment, and she was afraid to sleep there or to let the children out of her sight. When the caseworker got involved after Leah was cited for truancy, Paula was shocked and upset—she felt she had been doing everything she could to keep her children safe.

Cecelia's foster parent knew that she would need to work with Paula and keep the sisters in touch with each other. But it was difficult. When the foster mother called to arrange visits, Paula hung up on her, and they had to communicate through the caseworker. Furthermore, every time Cecelia saw her mother for a visit, she would have tantrums upon returning to the foster home. Paula called frequently to argue with the foster parent about how she was dressing and caring for Cecelia. The foster mother began to wonder if it was worth the effort to keep the family connected.

As these brief vignettes illustrate, the child welfare system usually becomes involved with families when there are child safety concerns as a result of child abuse or neglect, serious parent–child conflict, physical or behavioral health conditions, or family violence. As part of their practice, child welfare workers must make every reasonable effort to safely maintain children within their families, including providing supports and services. However, for some families these preservation services are insufficient, and when this is the case, children are placed in out-of-home care.

Removing children from their homes is difficult for everyone involved. Even when there is serious maltreatment of children, and removal is necessary for their safety, the children's lives are still being disrupted. They are being moved into a new home or shelter, and they may not know the people who will be caring for them. Siblings may be separated while in out-of-home care if it is not possible to find a placement that will accommodate them together. Older children may end up in group homes where they share space with other older youth and may have to go to a different school. Family connections and friendships are disrupted, and everything that is familiar to the child or older youth is taken away. In addition to the trauma that children may have experienced while in the care of their parents, the separation from parents, siblings, and grandparents may generate feelings of helplessness, anger, and fear (Grigsby 1993).

The Needs of Parents

Many parents have co-occurring disorders or behaviors and experience conditions that contribute to the neglect or abuse of their children. Many mothers involved in child welfare are themselves more likely to have substance abuse issues and co-occurring mental health and substance abuse disorders and to have experienced domestic violence (Marcenko et al. 2011). Substance abuse, as well as serious and persistent mental illness, can be chronic and have a high probability of relapse (Kroll 2004), requiring ongoing monitoring and frequent intervention. A multisite national study of women engaged in treatment for co-occurring disorders with a history of interpersonal violence found that almost 70 % of them had been separated from their children and 26 % had had their rights to one or more children terminated (Becker et al. 2005). As Marcenko et al. (2011) write in their study of the context for these families, "analyses revealed a picture of mostly impoverished mothers, struggling to meet their families' most basic needs and coping with early trauma, mental health problems, substance abuse and domestic violence" (p. 436).

It is not surprising that engaging these parents after their children have been removed from their care can be challenging (Kemp et al. 2009). Even when faced with termination of rights to care for their children, parents may fail to complete mandated services for substance abuse, mental health, or parenting (Atkinson and Butler 1996; Butler et al. 1994) and miss regular visits with their children (Perkins and Ansay 1998). This may initially be puzzling, but research suggests that many factors can contribute to what seems like "noncompliance with services." For example, parents of color generally are offered and receive fewer services through the child welfare system than do their white counterparts (Courtney et al. 1996; Hill 2006; Libby et al. 2006). When parents are not offered services to address the problems that led to child welfare system involvement, they are less likely to make progress towards reunification. The ways in which they are engaged may be stigmatizing

(Hunter-Romanelli et al. 2009), and the services they are offered may not be addressing their needs or culture (Richardson 2008). Given the extent of poverty experienced by these families, the cost of transportation to visit their children when the children are in out-of-home care or of transportation to the parents' own services may be a deterrent (Hunter-Romanelli et al. 2009). Parents may also feel that they have no recourse once their children are removed from their care. In a study of caseworkers in Pennsylvania, Rauktis and McCrae (2010) report that caseworkers felt that parents did not know their rights and responsibilities and, even when initially notified, needed to have this understanding reassessed periodically.

The Needs of Children

When children are placed in out-of-home care, the goal is to keep them safe in the least restrictive setting for their individual needs and at the same time provide care and nurturance while keeping them connected to siblings and extended family. Some children may require a higher level of care for social or emotional problems in addition to their dependency needs. The federal government defines foster care broadly to include "24-h substitute care for children outside their own homes" (Code of Federal Regulations, Title 45 §57, 2009). However, 24-h substitute care can occur within a family home setting (kin, non-kin, and treatment foster care) or within a more institutional setting (residential or group homes). There is no commonly accepted definition of "residential" group treatment in the research literature (Leichtman 2006). However, residential treatment programs typically provide mental health services such as therapy and medication. They usually are dormitory-type settings that have on-campus schools, and the size can vary from only a few youth to hundreds (Curtis et al. 2001). Residential treatment is considered to be in the range of most restrictive settings (Rauktis et al. 2009), although wide individual program variations exist. Also included under the "residential" heading is group home care. Group homes are typically smaller facilities which house unrelated youth and which rely on community resources, such as schools and outpatient medical and psychiatric services, for the youth in their care. Although staff members supervise the residents of the homes 24 h a day, they do not live in the home, and the youth may have more freedom to engage in community activities (i.e., going to the local school, working part-time). The degree of restrictiveness between residential and group homes has been found to be similar, although variation exists between programs (Rauktis et al. 2009), with some group homes similar to residential treatment programs in restrictiveness and others similar to foster care.

Treatment foster care (TFC) is another option that is increasingly being used as an out-of-home alternative to residential programs for children and adolescents with significant behavioral, emotional, medical, and/or mental health problems (Chamberlain 1999; Curtis et al. 2001). Children and youth in TFC typically live with nonrelatives in private homes that are licensed and supervised by child welfare agencies. TFC combines a structured therapeutic approach with a family milieu using trained foster parents (Breeland-Noble et al. 2005). Hawkins (1990) identified common model characteristics of TFC: (1) foster parents are considered to be professionals; (2) only one or two children are in the foster home; (3) case-workers have smaller caseloads and provide more supervision to foster parents; (4) foster parents receive skills training in managing behavior and implement the child's treatment plan; and (5) foster parents are provided with support that is available 24 h a day.

Kin can also provide foster care. Historically, families have used kin to infor-mally foster children when parents died or needed support during periods of illness or incapacity (Downs et al. 2009). However, kinship foster care is a form of out-of-home care that involves the legal placement of children who are in the custody of the child protection system with kin. Foster care payments are provided, and the kin foster parents are subject to the same requirements and monitoring as non-kin foster parents. The primary difference between non-kin foster care and kinship foster care is that established relationships already exist among the child/children, parents of the child, and the kinship foster parents (Child Welfare League of America 1994). However, another option is informal foster care that takes place outside the child welfare system, such as when an aunt may care for her niece and nephew while their mother is in treatment. Restrictiveness levels for both kin and non-kin foster care were found to be similar in terms of how restricted youth were in refer-ence to what they could do, where they could go, socialization, and access to family (Rauktis et al. 2009). Likewise, TFC was similar to small group homes in terms of restrictiveness.

Children in Care

The most recent data on children in out-of-home care comes from the 2012 Adoption and Foster Care Analysis and Reporting System (AFCARS) report. As of September 30, 2012 there were 399,546 children in care. The mean age of these children was 9.1 years, and there were slightly more boys (52 %) than girls. These children were in care for an average of 22.7 months, with 18 % of them remaining in care for 3 years or longer (US Department of Health and Human Services 2013).

The majority of children were in non-kin foster homes (47 %), with kinship homes being the next largest category (28 %). Smaller percentages were in group homes (6 %) or institutional settings (9 %). Over half of all children in care had reunification with parents as their case goal. Only 4 % resided in homes that are seen as a prelude to adoption, even though 24 % of children had adoption as their case goal.

A study on racial disparity in foster care admissions (Wulczyn and Lery 2007) examined the percentages of children in foster care relative to their representation in the population. Disproportionate numbers were observed for African-American children, who are 19 % of the population but 47 % of the first-time admissions to foster care, and White children were underrepresented in foster care (38 %) relative to their proportion in the population (61 %). Wulczyn and Lery report that both placement and disparity rates are consistently higher for infants, and this is particularly true for African-American infants. Disparity was also observed to increase for teens over time (Wulczyn and Lery 2007). In fact, the two largest groups in care are infants and very young children and adolescents. Older youth in foster care face some of the same challenges as younger children, but often these challenges are intensified. For example, older children may have experienced more frequent and difficult disruptions in living situations and schools. Achieving the goal of permanency is often more difficult for older children, and only 10 % of all adoptable children who actually get adopted are age 13 or older (the mean age of children finalized for adoption was 6.3 years old in 2012). Older children face different concerns as they get closer to aging out of foster care, which frequently include establishing a viable relationship with their family of origin. Many older children need special services to deal with these challenges while in care, as well as transitional services as they emancipate from foster care without a permanent home. Of the children leaving foster care in 2012, 20 % were age 16 and older (US Department of Health and Human Services 2013).

The stories of Dante, Leah, and their siblings and parents in the beginning of this chapter illustrate that out-of-home placement experiences can vary between siblings, and that there is a great deal of movement between foster care and residential forms of out-of-home care. They also illustrate the roles that parents can play when youth and children are in out-of-home care. However, little research on out-of-home care includes the youth perspective (Barth 2002; Fox and Berrick 2007; Hyde and Kammerer 2009; Kools 1997; Samuels and Pryce 2008; Spencer 2007) or the family perspective of out-of-home care. Qualitative research is a way of gaining a greater understanding of the youth experience (Geenen and Powers 2007; McCoy et al. 2008; McMillen et al. 1997). In the remainder of this chapter, we describe the experiences of youth who have been in out-of-home care using their words and then discuss how caseworkers can effectively support youth's safety and well-being and support healthy development while youth are in out-of-home care. To do so, we use the results of a qualitative study conducted in Pennsylvania, where a recent report revealed that almost half of the youth in out-of-home care (47.3 %) were age 13 and older (Pennsylvania Partnerships for Children 2010). We also provide the perspective of parents who were participating in a support group following the termination of their parental rights. Again, we discuss how workers can help parents to safely play a role in their child's life while the child is in out-of-home care.

Youth Experiences

Youth from different regions were invited to participate in one of six focus groups about out-of-home care held throughout the state, and a total of 40 young adults participated. They were primarily female (64 %) and African American (62 %), and five participants self-identified as being of Hispanic ethnicity. They ranged from 14 to 20 years of age. Almost half (47 %) were living in a foster care home at the time of the interview, 22 % were living in their own home or apartment, 13 % were in a supervised independent living setting, 13 % were living with family (former foster family or birth family), and one person described herself as homeless. More than a third had come into care as young adolescents (39 %), whereas another group (42 %) had been in care for most of their lives. The youth interviewed had spent an average of 5 years cumulatively in out-of-home care. Focus group interviews were recorded, transcribed, and after repeated readings the content specific to out-of-home care was coded. These sections were reviewed and further discussed by the authors in order to determine consistency and agreement of coding as well as reactions and interpretations.

In the groups, the youth discussed what it was like to live in out-of-home care. Not surprisingly, a common theme was their struggles with the instability in their lives. Some didn't mind being in foster care or other forms of out-of-home care as much as they just wanted some form of stability:

"...One thing I wanted as a child, I really wanted to be with my mom or I really wanted to be with my foster parents, the only thing I wanted was consistency and stability and staying with my mom for the whole time or staying with my foster family the whole time. I know it's an issue now, for so many people, like, why kids sign themselves out at 18, because they want to make their own rules and they want to do what they want to do, but it's also because they want to build their stability their own selves." (Jason, 15 years old, 5 years in care)

"We was raised by somebody that we didn't even know and you know, literally, now it only takes me now 45 min to pack all my stuff because I'm used to moving. I got a lot of clothes, a lot of stuff and I'm in an apartment but if you tell me to pack up and move tomorrow, I can do it in less than 45 min. Because I've moved around so much I just used to doing everything, just throwing everything in a bag, come on hurry...." (Ana, 19 years old, 4 years in care)

Another experience was the lack of privacy and the degree of intrusiveness that was typical in all forms of out-of-home care. For example, youth talked about the difficulties of sharing living space with peers they did not know and would not have chosen as roommates:

"I was living at [facility] cause I had the luxury of closing the door on the counselor's face if I wanted to cause it was my own, well, it wasn't my own apartment, it was just me and another roommate—um, she had a baby. But now I'm in a home with two other girls, and it's definitely, that's my downfall, because I'm very neat and I'm very clean. The day that I went there was a Friday. I left it alone. Saturday I was up at seven in the morning cleaning. I mean I cleaned the entire house." (Lola, 17 years old, 6 years in care)

Other youth discussed the intrusiveness of accounting for their money with staff members. The youth often understood why some rules were necessary, but felt like overseeing finances was more about control than about supporting the youth toward the goal of saving money:

"...The fact that you have to save up money, I can understand that so you're able to move on your own. Things like that. But I don't feel the need is to explain what I do with my money. If the money is being taken out and is being put back in there, there shouldn't be no explanation of what I do with my money—it's going back in. Now, unless you want to share information, I mean, we can do that; you tell me what you do with your money, I'll tell you what I do with mine. You know, you show me your receipts, I'll show you mine." (Ricky, 18 years old, 10 years in care)

Others talked even more specifically about the intrusiveness of sharing personal information with workers who were not much older than the youth themselves:

"…Sometimes I feel like they're just too much in your business just to be in your business because they don't have anything else to do. I understand some of the protocols and some of the things that have to be done, but it just comes to a point where you have to like set … put yourself back in the kid's shoes and honestly feel … how would you feel … for instance, your bank information, how would you feel, you know, giving your bank information to a young adult and showing your bank statements to them every month?" (Cole, 17 years old, 3 years in care)

A consequence of this lack of privacy and intrusiveness was that youth often felt depersonalized and felt that they had no control over their lives, as illustrated by this statement:

"… Like do this, do that, do this, like they control you, you feel no privacy, you feel no ease at all. No one gets that. I mean we are people…Go to sleep have a flash light in your face making sure you were in bed. Get up. Can I step out? Yes, go to the bathroom. Can I step in? Go to the bathroom can I step out, can I step back in my room? Yes. There is always constant questioning. You feel like you have nothing. You're just nobody." (Krystal, 15 years old, 1 year in care)

Out-of-home care was also viewed as stigmatizing. Many youth described feeling embarrassed and ashamed and said they hid their life in care from friends, coworkers, and school personnel:

"Everybody labels foster care as bad. I learned a lot. I did. I said earlier I kept myself in a bad situation because I didn't want to go into foster care… At that point of time in my life, I didn't want to go into foster care. It's a bad label." (Aurora, 16 years old, 4 years in care)

The youth were concerned that people would automatically make assumptions that living in out-of-home care was due to something they did wrong. In fact, some felt that the label would follow them even after they aged out of care, as illustrated in this comment by a young woman who hesitated to disclose her time in foster care:

"And it's like, when you get into foster care or group home you get that stereotype that you're a bad kid. I was in foster care because of my parents, not because I did anything wrong. I've never done drugs. I don't drink. I've never been suspended, had detention. But because I was in foster care, I'm a bad kid… like something gets stolen, I did it. I never stole a thing in my life! But it's hard—and even when you grow out of the system, that's still— 'Oh you were in foster care?' Like when I got hired at the job I'm in, I hesitated telling them that I was in foster care because I have not got hired in certain places because of that fact." (Shanese, 17 years old, 3 years in care)

A related theme was that out-of-home care was not only stigmatizing, it also was "not normal" because adolescents were not able to engage in typical experiences. Some of the youth surveyed said the fact that they were not able to date, sleep over with friends, or go to dances made them different from their peers, which also added to their sense of isolation:

"Yeah, I want to spend the night but I need your parent's social security, eye color, weight. I need to know their job, how much they are making, everything about them. It makes you not want to go anymore, and your friends look at you and say you need all this why?" (Daisy, 15 years old, 2 years in care)

They perceived these precautions to be due to agency bureaucracy rather than a real concern about their well-being:

"…Everybody has a right to go to their high school prom. As I found out, some foster youth are not allowed to go to the prom because of liability. You can't go to the prom; you can't leave the house unless it's a very good reason to leave their house. I'm saying to myself, prom of all things, you can't go to prom. It is a rite of passage." (Rochelle, 19 years old, 6 years in care)

While foster care may be a preferred setting because it is in a family home rather than a facility or institution, youth pointed out that the setting does not ensure that they experience normal family life or that they will feel a sense of emotional safety. For example, youth talked about how difficult it was to live in a homelike setting where they felt there were rules that kept them from having normal experiences such as snacking or using the bathroom:

"It makes a place more like a home. Like when you're in foster care, there are some foster parents that make you ask before you can get in the refrigerator. Before you can get into the cupboard. Before you can go to the bathroom. You know what I mean? You have to ask before you go outside. I'm 16 years old and I have to ask you, 'Can I go outside and sit on the porch?' Like, when it's at home you feel like that's your house, you don't always have to ask for stuff." (LaToya, 16 years old, 7 years in care)

"That's one thing I don't understand either. Why do you have to ask to do anything like— when you're at home, you're not going to have to do that. Like you're not asking anyone to go to your own bathroom, to go eat out of your own refrigerator or something. To go to your own room. Why do you have to ask to do stuff like that in placements?" (Rochelle)

In this example, a youth talked about feeling unwanted and "invisible" in her foster home:

"And a lot of foster homes—they don't even talk to you. It's like you're invisible. You're not even there. I was in one foster home where I felt like they wanted me to be there. And I was in like 12, 13 foster homes." (Mara, 19 years old, 12 years in care)

Others talked about being treated like a burden, often in sharp contrast to the caregivers' own biological children:

"That's how my foster mom was. Like her kids would come over and me and my little sister, we'd be sittin' over here and they all over there having fun. First of all we don't go sit there, why you all always upstairs? Because when your kids come over here, you talk to them we be over here and you act like the audience when they get here. But when they not here and you all lonely, you want to be talking to us. So we upstairs in our room when they're not there, and when they are there. Why you always sitting upstairs? Because we don't want to be here no more because you treat us like we're not here like and when they not there, you want to talk to us." (Dwight, 18 years old, 4 years in care)

Sometimes youth reported receiving conflicting messages. In this example a young woman talked about her foster family, who said that she was "family" but did not act as though she was:

"…–like you come in and you bring a child into your home and you tell people that they're part of your family but say you have like a family cookout. You send that kid away to respite care.

And then how does that make that kid feel? Like you're telling me you love me but I can't come to the cookout with you as family 'cause you're embarrassed that I'm there"? (Abby, 16 years old, 2 years in care)

Youth and children who are in out-of-home care struggle with their grief about being removed from their families, particularly their siblings. For some, their lost relationships with siblings were particularly painful:

"…He [my brother] think he was grown. Then he got locked up, then got out, then probably got locked up again. I mean, I see him—I just saw him today and he just does his own thing. I don't even talk to him on a regular basis. I have my life and he has his. I love him to death, but he gotta get his butt together first. I mean, I'm not gonna put myself out there and get my own place, tell him he can come move in, and then have him get me in trouble and I'll lose everything. I'm at the age where it's like, I'm not going to sit there and hold his hand anymore. He's about to turn 20 next week." (Avril, 18 years old, 4 years in care)

Some youth were determined to maintain contact with their family, even when it was not part of their case plan:

"I wasn't supposed to see mine [biological family], I just did. At that time I just felt like if my mom is going to be, you know, down the street, why wouldn't you see your family? It made sense; she's the only family I had in the state. My foster parent, she would get mad at me or yell at me for going … Well, are you going to stop me from going? That's what I told her, I was like, look, my mom lives right down the street … that's my mom. Nobody's gonna … God's the only person who's going to stop me from going to see her." (Tyrone, 17 years old, 5 years in care)

This young man continued to eloquently describe his feelings of grief that his mother was not able to care for him, and he persisted in hoping that she would be there for support, despite repeated disappointments:

"I definitely wanted to be back with my mom and my brother. Growing up, my mom was known as the neighborhood mom. Like, my mom would take a bunch of kids from my neighborhood to the park, to the movies, to a pool, and she would just do that and everybody called her mom and it was one of those things where like, that feeling, felt so strong, when I was younger, that I wanted it back so bad, but I never could get it back. I mean, I still see some of my friends that, you know, would call her mom and everything and they still do when they see them, but, it's like, I thought that once I hit high school, I thought she was gonna be there, you know, all four years, and see me go to college and everything like that … I mean, she sees me go to college, but it's not the same. I mean, she came to my graduation, you know, she saw me graduate, great, she missed my senior night, that was alright, but I mean, it's just little things like that, … comin' out of middle school you picture yourself … I'm gonna be this big star athlete or whatever … but then, like, when it actually happens, and like, your real family is not really there for you, it hurts. But you just continue to dream, like, she's gonna be there anyway, or, we're gonna get back together, but that was mine. I wanted definitely to be back with my family." (Tyrone)

Finally, youth wanted adults to not give up on them. Yes, they said, they would make mistakes, but this was to be expected, and workers and parents needed to persist to find out why they were having problems and explore possible solutions rather than simply remove them from a placement:

"I used to run away a lot. Being a foster parent you've got to understand you're getting a child that have all this stuff going on with him or her and it's not going to be easy to raise them. I had an anger problem. I was mad at the world, I was mad at DHS… today if you say you work for DHS it already means I don't like you." (David, 15 years old, 2 years in care)

"They don't tell you the rules. You go in and they don't tell you what you're not and what you are allowed to do. And then when you mess up they just kick you out. And you didn't even know like you weren't supposed to do that." (Lexie, 17 years old, 1 year in care)

One of the foster care alumni who co-facilitated the focus groups referred to the dreaded acronym "FTA—Failure to Adjust" that workers would use prior to a removal. As he wryly noted, "when you heard FTA, you knew it was time to pack your bags" (C. Nobles, personal communication, March 4, 2011).

It would be incorrect to assume that all out-of-home care experiences were negative ones. Although the youth discussed the challenges of out-of-home placement, many of them talked about the positive aspects of care. The youth spoke strongly about the ways their caregivers made them feel cared for, and several felt that they had positive and loving support from workers and caregivers. Positive and loving support was demonstrated by behavior of equity, fairness, and "claiming" the youth as their own, as illustrated in these passages:

"What tells me when a foster parent loves you is when you do something and they reprimand you and their actual kid does it and they reprimand their kid too. They don't just get on you. You get the same consequences as they do their own kid. They raise you like their own child." (Jared, 19 years old, 3 years in care)

"My foster mom didn't buy her own kids stuff. She bought me stuff. They would honestly put me before they put their own kids. That I can honestly say. My foster parents do more for me then they do for their own kids. They don't throw it up in your face. I did this, this and this…" (Fatima, 17 years old, 4 years in care)

Public claiming of the youth, particularly by the foster parent, was viewed as a powerful indicator of belonging:

"You know that you belong when they call you son in public, not foster child…" (Marc, 16, 1 year in care)
    "Yep, my foster parents do that. They will say about me, 'That's my daughter,' and they are White! [Youth is African-American]. My dad went back and forth with a customer. He said that's my daughter!" (Fatima)

Many of the youth in the focus group acknowledged that they were in care for their own benefit, to maintain their safety and well-being. A few even discussed difficult times they had within their family of origin and said they might have been better off if they had been removed into out-of-home care:

"I was in placement when I was really, really little, I think at 4 or 5 years old… My grandma always abused me physically and mentally, so if anybody says because your family raised you, it's not always good. My grandma would take her anger out on me because my mom left me there with her. Every time my mom would come to get me she would go to programs and leave me at the program or come get me and leave me at a crack house or something so I was always with my family but it was always abusive. I never had the chance to actually be in a foster home. I wished I was in foster care or a group home because then I wouldn't have to be around my grandma and mom." (Janice, 16 years old, 5 years in care)

One participant, who experienced periods of homelessness, talked about the benefits of care as an alternative to being on the streets:

"You're sitting here complaining 'cause you got to go to group at 8 o'clock. I bet there's one kid in this placement that is grateful as hell to have a room right now. I can guarantee you there's one kid that was sleeping outside at one point that don't mind these damn rules at all. Or there's one kid that didn't even have a parent to give them a [expletive] roof. You know what I mean? And… they probably taking these rules and loving them. So while you complaining about the restrictions you need to find something else to complain about." (Avril)

Another important issue for older youth is thinking about their emerging adulthood and their imminent independence from the child welfare system. Although the youth were eager to live independently, they discussed concerns about their level of preparedness and talked about the ways that their out-of-home caregivers provided them with moral guidance:

"My first foster mom, she taught me the values I have … She basically laid the foundation. Since she passed away, it was for other people to build on. So my second foster family taught me how to become more of a man I guess you could say, and helped me to realize that life isn't just a game. It's serious also. So they helped me to see things from a man's perspective, and stop being such a kid. My third foster parent let me see what freedom is, not to abuse it and how it basically is to be on my own. So now I think I'm ready to be on my own." (Jared)

They also described the importance of caregivers coaching and teaching real-life skills, as somewhat humorously described by one young woman:

"She [foster parent] taught me how to learn a snaky landlord when you see one. She taught me how to read in between the lines. You know the landlord's like… when I was supposed to get my apartment and the landlord said to me, 'It's only a little bit of water damage in the basement. So uh I could just knock off a couple dollars for her.' She was like, 'Oh hold up!' She was like, 'That means when it rains it's gonna flood.' That's how she taught me to read people's facial expressions. She taught me uh, how to present myself. Like they teach you how to present yourself in a job interview… She taught me, yeah, she taught me the little things that people really catch on to. … She's teaching me everything. She taught me how to iron. And she told me don't ever touch starch again cause when I was done ironing my pants could stand by themself. [*Laughter*] But she taught me stuff that… she didn't just give me everything I wanted. I mean they had a lot. She didn't do it like that. She didn't do her own kids like that either." (Tiara, 18 years old, 4 years in care)

The subtle skills that this young woman describes—presenting oneself, reading cues, and intuiting a dishonest person—are things that parents either consciously or unconsciously teach their children. Because these skills are critical for a transition to successful independence, they are even more vital for youth in out-of-home care who have limited social support.

In addition to talking about their experiences in out-of-home care, the youth discussed the relationships they had with the child welfare system and its workers. They talked about the behaviors and qualities that they felt were important in a caseworker. A few mentioned the importance of their workers being honest with them, even if the youth was going to be unhappy with the truth:

"I hesitate in, like, saying that I would do this, because everything that your case worker tells you is basically—they lie to you to make you happy. They say whatever they think you need to say so that you don't complain." (Mara)

The youth also talked about how important it was to feel like their worker listened to them. Several discussed how they felt that their worker ignored or minimized problems or sided with the family or residential staff. This left the youth feeling unsupported and alone:

"This room was like a nice-size room for like one person. And she had, um, two beds in it, so ... me and another girl. ...she ended up putting this room that was a nice size for one person, ok for two people, put two bunk beds in it, so we ended up having three girls, and with three girls in, like, one room, all of our stuff, like, it was just ridiculous and stuff like that... I ended up getting moved because, like, I just started, like, acting out. I'm like, you're not going to listen to me, I'm doing what I'm supposed to be doing, but I'm wrong on either end. I'm wrong when I'm in the house with her. I'm wrong when I try to tell you what's happening and stuff like that. So, that's when I got moved to the group home, because, you know, it wasn't working out there. But I found out six months, I think it was 6 or 7 months later, they terminated her as like, a foster parent, because of like, drinking and all this other stuff, which I told them that before and nobody, like, listened to me, because when they come, you sit down and you tell them everything's fine, everything's OK." (Daisy)

Some of the older youth are moving towards independence, and they highlighted the absolute importance of learning life skills while in the child welfare system. Many of the youth spoke favorably about their independent living program and praised their workers' efforts:

"They signed me up with like they help me sign up for college. They didn't just do it for me. They took me there to do it. Um... my first—when I got—when I needed money to get my apartment they didn't just give me it. You know they could have. They didn't just give me it. They helped me find a job to get it... You know what I mean? So it...it helped me out." (Roy, 19 years old, 4 years in care)

Finally, many of the youth did report having positive relationships with their caseworkers and described the negative effect that workers leaving had on them. Several talked about how difficult it was to form a relationship when they didn't know how long the worker would be around:

"Yeah, cause sometimes, they just be there for like, 3 months and they just happen to get you, and then pass you on to somebody else, or they'll be pregnant and they have to leave, which you can't really get mad at, it's life, but ... I had a thing, for 3 or 4 months I had three different caseworkers and they all said like the same thing. They all said they just wanted to meet me and like, I was at practice and I had to leave practice early to come meet her and she didn't even stay, she stayed for like 10 min, and then like, I was mad about it ... I don't even have like one caseworker who was there for a while ...... but she's probably the only person that I could have a relationship with ... she was pregnant and then she came back, she told me ... she said 'don't worry, I'll be back, but you'll have a couple replacements...'" (Brittney, 18 years old, 4 years in care)

"I had the same thing, so many caseworkers and stuff like that, and like, women, not all of them, but like when they were there they were like "I'm here to help you," and they showed that they did care, but they didn't stay long enough. My ... most of them I got were goin' back to school and they were leavin' to go back to school.... But yeah, like, um, she, oh my gosh, she was great. She was probably like the longest person besides the foster parents that, um, helped me out, cause the caseworkers and the other therapists like you can't, you just can't count on them, they're here … some of them are going to be here 100 % when they are here, but they're not gonna be here long enough…" (Tyrone)

Parent Experiences

Like the youth who are placed in out-of-home care, parents also experience a range of feelings in the process of having their children removed from their care. Interviews with parents receiving counseling services after having their parental rights terminated revealed the parents' expressions of sadness, anger, and frustration:

"When I was using [drugs] Evie was only two years old. I was having a hard time, trying to keep us off the streets and trying to get money for meth. My boyfriend was abusive but I thought he was good for Evie; he was always nice to her and brought her gifts, and her own dad was long gone. When CPS got involved I was upset but I thought maybe it could help us. They put her in foster care and I was a little glad at first 'cause I thought I would just have a break to get myself right. I missed her, though, and I tried to make all the visits but it was tough because of transportation and my boyfriend and trying to get clean. I kept making mistakes and using again but I wanted her back. I never really thought I could lose her, you know. I mean, I am her mother, I gave birth to her, I love her even if I wasn't giving her the best life then. And then the state took her away for good and now what do I say if people ask do I got any kids? 'Cause I'm not allowed to care for her no more and it eats my heart out. I have to live with knowing that someone else is being her mother." (Lorie, 28 years old)

Initially this young mother believed that she could use the time while her child was in out-of-home care to get clean and to find healthy relationships. However, similar to what Marcenko et al. (2011) have reported in their research, she lacked the individual and social capital to get to her visits, and frequent relapses contributed to her loss of rights. She also poignantly described a form of unresolved grief that isn't easily addressed when a parent's rights are terminated.

Parents with children in out-of-home care are often very angry about the removal and feel hopeless about the resolution:

"It ain't right the state can take your kids away. I have made mistakes but I know I am a good mother. They didn't give me any chance. As soon as they got involved I felt like they were gonna take them from me all along, and what could I do about it? I had to take classes, and make my house nice, and it was a lot to do. I ain't ever going to be able to live in no fancy mansion but I did my best. And I love my kids, you know? They tell me I cannot get them back but I will get them back somehow." (Ella, 32 years old)

"My kids shouldn't have been taken in the first place. I never hit them or beat them or anything. But DHS came and they ended up in foster care. I was so angry I didn't want to do what the worker told me. Why should I trust her after she takes my kids from me? So I refused to go to their parenting classes and meetings because I did not want to deal with those people. And they said I did not comply with their plan and it ended up a big mess. I lost custody of my two youngest for all time. Those babies are out there thinking I didn't care enough about them to keep them, and that isn't true. I was angry and felt like no one listened to me, and then it only got worse. I don't know if I am more mad at [the county child welfare agency] or at myself." (Queen, 36 years old)

These two women did not feel that either the home conditions or their behaviors created an unsafe environment for the children. In both cases the parents felt that they didn't have much of a chance with the child welfare system, and in the second case, this lack of trust contributed to not doing the work needed to in order to regain custody. The mother had a belated realization of how unwise this approach was in the end. Engaging parents who are angry can be challenging, but the parents need caseworkers to be kind but direct and encourage them to not give up, because their children are depending upon them (Downs et al. 2009). Clark (2007) states that in order to be effective when working with parents, workers must create the conditions of desire, ability, reason, and need. Workers cannot take parental anger personally, but should instead listen respectfully and try to channel the energy into a sense of shared goals for bringing the children/youths home. Caseworkers should also try to come to an agreement with parents on the tasks that must be accomplished in order for this to occur. Workers also need to acknowledge the age, gender, and race barriers that may be interfering with creating shared goals and a sense of motivation. An accomplished caseworker illustrates this approach in the following excerpt from an interview:

> "The other one was an African-American male that, I guess he had been treated poorly throughout his involvement with the agency and then it ends up on my desk and I'm like, sir, my goal is to get your son home with you. He asked me a bunch of questions about who I was and what my ethnicity was and I was open with him because you can't really hide that, and I said, it has nothing to do with, as far as I'm concerned, with what my race is and what your race is, my goal here is to get your son home. And this is how I want to do it, and this is how I want to help you. And he had prostate cancer and I know more about prostate cancer than I ever wanted to know in my entire life because he felt the need to share all of this with me after we worked through our racial differences and the barrier that was there... I understand that you love your son very much; I understand that you've had some poor experiences with some previous caseworkers and I want you to understand that my goal is to get your son home with you. And this is how I want to do it. And I said, are you agreeable? And he said, yeah absolutely, I want my son to come home. And I said, well it sounds like we're talking about the same thing. And you know, the next court hearing is here, and that's when he started talking about his medical things and why he's missed some court hearings in the past was because he had to go to his doctors' appointments and he had this procedure done. So then I got the whole education about prostate cancer and prostate treatment and I ultimately got the kid home and put in a great in-home provider who was a male, even though we didn't have an African American male available at the time, it was a Caucasian male, and he made a great relationship with dad and the son. And it's actually funny because I'll see dad, he's getting more elderly now, and he'll be walking around the [street] and he'll come up to my car with his cane and wave and I'll be like, what's up! And he'll ask, having a good day? And I'll say, yeah." (Sharon, 43 years old, child welfare caseworker for 16 years)

Caseworkers can also promote more productive interaction with parents by encouraging parent–child visitation. Visitation not only helps to maintain the parent–child relationship, but also gives parents the motivation to work on their goals. In a seminal study, Fanshel and Shinn (1978) concluded that parental visitation, particularly frequency of visits, was associated with discharge from out-of-home care regardless of parental ethnic and religious status. Later research by White et al. (1996) supported this early finding that increased social worker contact with parents of children in care was associated with more frequent parental visitation and ultimately with a shorter length of stay. Research also supports the value of involving parents in the services that their children receive while in out-of-home care. When children return home to live with their parents, behavior may escalate (Bellamy 2008; Lau et al. 2003; Taussig et al. 2001). Therefore, having parents involved in mental health and other services while their children are in out-of-home care may provide some benefits for the children, such as a parent's greater understanding of developmental needs and how this is impacted by trauma (Runyon et al. 2004). Parents, to the degree that is safe and possible, should also be encouraged to participate in typical parenting tasks such as attending medical appointments, school conferences, sporting events, and other events that are important to the child or youth. This reinforces the parents' continuing roles and parenting tasks, and it helps the child to feel "normal," the importance of which was a consistent theme in the interviews with youth. Finally, the youth interviewed talked about the problems and emotional distress associated with losing touch with their extended family while in care. Often, it is the parent who maintains information about where extended family is located. Building a relationship with the parents may be the best way to keep children and youth connected to their extended families.

Summary

The youth who participated in the research were eloquent about the difficulties as well as the positive aspects of living in out-of-home care. They were also quite articulate about the behaviors and the qualities that are needed in child welfare caseworkers, youth care workers, and foster parents. These findings are consistent with other youth alliance research (Manso and Rauktis 2011). Youth have identified that workers, parents, or caseworkers who listen, are fair, are transparent, stay engaged, and don't give up are the people that they want to have a relationship with (Manso and Rauktis 2011). Some of the youth observations about privacy and autonomy are consistent with those of "typical" youth (Rauktis et al. 2011); however, other complaints about the lack of relationships, being treated differently, stigma, and emotional neglect are not normative experiences. Foster parents and youth care workers have the potential to make an enormous difference in the lives of children and youth, and child welfare caseworkers are the critical players in ensuring a safe and permanent home as well as normal development. Some of the important roles that caseworkers play for youth in out-of-home care are:

• Establishing multiple relationships with the child/youth, birth parents, foster parents (who may be kin), and staff and managing these relationships without being triangulated or torn between different sides
• Family finding and trying to keep children in touch with family
• Engaging with "burned out" or disconnected family members
• Supporting, coaching, and supervising foster care parents in their work with the child/youth and parents

- Ongoing monitoring of the safety of the placement
- Ensuring youth well-being (physical, emotional, and social)
- Assessing youth for signs of trauma, depression, and other potential consequences of maltreatment
- Supporting healthy development into young adulthood
- Working towards permanency

Caseworkers also play a critical role in working with parents whose children are in out-of-home care. While most of the same roles as in working with children and youth apply, some additional roles for the caseworker when children are in out-of-home care are:

- Building a positive relationship with the parents based on shared goals and honesty
- Providing a bridge between foster parents and parents
- Accurately assessing and providing assistance with finding and accessing services and supports for parents
- Encouraging, motivating, and supporting visitation while children are in out-of-home care
- Ensuring that the parents' perspective is known to others working with the family, including the perspective of birth parents who may have lost their parental rights
- Finding services that are consistent with parents' cultural beliefs and practices
- Providing parents referrals to substance abuse and mental health treatment, therapy, and income supports
- When possible and safe, encouraging and assisting parents to be involved in the services being provided to their children

Conclusion

This chapter started with two case studies of children placed in out-of-home care—Dante, and the sisters Leah and Cecelia. Both were in out-of-home care due to problems within their families. Dante was witnessing interpersonal violence and drug and alcohol use by his parents and was at risk for being hurt or hurting someone in the home. Leah and Cecelia were removed from their mother's care due to her untreated mental illness, which was negatively impacting their safety and well-being. In both cases, being removed from the family home was in their best interests, but as you now know, out-of-home care may not always be developmentally sound, stable, or humane. So what can a social worker do to make sure that while in out-of-home care, children and youth remain connected to their families, and that their healthy developmental needs are addressed and their strengths supported? Let's go back to Dante and Leah and Cecelia to see what happened after they were removed from their homes.

Dante's caseworker, Iris, persevered in building a relationship with him, even when he told her that he "hated her guts" after she made the recommendation that he goes to a thera-peutic wilderness camp. Iris's supervisor told her that a child could still be connected to her even when he/she was acting in ways that suggested otherwise. The supervisor helped Iris see that Dante's comments weren't personal, but were instead a symptom of Dante's anger, experienced trauma, and anxiety about the placement—though the supervisor also said that Iris should not tolerate disrespect. So Iris continued to visit Dante in his placements, driv-ing 2 h to see him at the wilderness camp and often making more than the mandated monthly visit. She followed through on her promise to help him remain in contact with his older sister through his multiple moves. While Dante missed his mother, he reiterated his wish not to be in contact with his parents, and Iris respected this decision. She visited him at all of his placements and tried to respond to and advocate for his requests, such as when he wanted to see his sister and the wilderness camp wouldn't allow the visit. Iris suspected that Dante was experiencing trauma symptoms from witnessing family violence, but Dante did not want counseling, so she made herself available to listen when he brought up things from his past. They laughed over his unfounded fear of bears out in the woods and celebrated when he mastered algebra and log splitting at the camp. When she had to take a 12-week medical leave, she let him know that she would be back and that another worker would be covering for her. She contacted him when she returned. Little by little, they built a trusting relationship. When it became clear that Dante's permanency goal was going to be long-term out-of-home care until age 18, Iris advocated for Dante to attend skills-based indepen-dent living groups and to go into independent supervised living so that he would have some preparation for life on his own. When he moved into his apartment, she, along with his independent living worker, helped Dante find a microwave and some furniture. Iris hoped that when he was ready, Dante would reconnect with his mother, and she also hoped that when he came to this decision, he would ask her, his caseworker, for guidance.

Christine, the caseworker assigned to Paula and her daughters, already knew Leah and Cecelia, since they had been active in her agency in the past. When she had to place the girls in separate homes, she recognized that a big part of her job would be to keep them in touch with each other, as well as their mother, and to support the girls' normal develop-ment. She also knew that as a caseworker, she needed to manage the relationships between Paula and the girls' foster parent, between the girls and their mother, and also to work with the group home staff. Christine didn't allow herself to get triangulated when Paula was upset about how Cecelia's hair was braided and demanded that Cecelia be immediately removed from the foster home. She didn't give in when the foster parent asked that Cecelia not visit her mother anymore because she was "wild" when she returned home. She knew that these were expressions of guilt (Paula), loss and grief (Cecelia), and frustration (foster parent) and instead tried to get each of them to talk about their feelings. Christine arranged for supportive therapy for Cecelia and 24/7 in-home crisis coverage for the foster parents. They created "transition space" so that when Cecelia came back to the foster home after visiting her mother, she could have a quiet but happy activity to ease her transition back into her foster home. Christine monitored the relationship between Cecelia and the foster parents, who became very fond of the little girl. She spoke with both Cecelia and Leah about their options for permanency in order to ensure that their voices were heard in what looked to be a protracted process; she decided that a referral to a guardian ad litem (GAL) was needed. Christine visited Leah in the group home after school, so that she could ensure that Leah was getting adequate care there and also making the adjustment from a fairly independent lifestyle in which she had assumed parenting roles to a structured situation. She also advocated for Leah to continue to play varsity high school volleyball, even though the group home normally wanted all youth home immediately after school. An assessment inventory of life skills and an interview with Leah's counselor revealed that Leah aspired to go to college. Christine referred Leah to an Independent Living skills coordinator so that she could begin preparation. When Leah refused a referral for counseling, Christine made herself available to listen and gently encouraged her to journal her thoughts and emotions and talk to one of the group home staff that she felt a connection with. Finally, she worked with Paula. This wasn't easy, since Paula was angry and grief-stricken about losing her daughters, but Christine knew that she had to build a relationship because Leah and Cecelia were bonded to their mother, as was she to them.

In fact, the primary motivation for Paula to improve her own mental health was the welfare of her daughters. Knowing this, Christine referred Paula to an Assertive Case Management Team (ACT) and communicated frequently with the ACT case manager so that they were working together, rather than at cross purposes. The ACT manager worked tirelessly to create an alliance with Paula, and while she wasn't able to convince her to take her medication regularly, she was able to help her with obtaining services and financial support, thereby creating a more stable living situation. Paula also began attending some of the behavioral health sessions that Cecelia was attending with her foster mother, and attended school events. Christine sometimes felt discouraged, particularly at the 12-month hearing when it was recommended that the permanency goals remain the same, but she continued to work on the goals of maintaining family connections, supporting development, supporting the foster parent, and preparing Leah for young adulthood. Finally, with the help of the GAL and the ACT worker, she was able to identify and engage some extended family members who, while wary, were willing to be part of the girls' network of support. A Family Group Decision Making meeting was held to provide support for the family. With everyone communicating and working together—professionals, extended family members, foster parents, and birth parent—both girls were able to be safe and also maintain family connections. Equally important, Leah and Cecelia were both able, with some restrictions, to have as normal a "home" experience as was possible, given their circumstances.

It is never easy when children are removed from the care of their parents and placed into an out-of-home setting such as a foster care or group home. The parents and the children who were interviewed in this study describe what it is like to live in someone else's home, lose contact with your family, or try but not succeed in keeping your family together. Their voices are powerful, and they remind social workers and other helping professionals that home and family are critical to our identity. When being placed out of the home is unavoidable, social workers and other helping professionals must ensure that the youth in their care are being nurtured, supported, and connected to their families.

Questions for Discussion

1. In what ways are the restrictions that the youth in this chapter describe similar to "typical" youth complaints about restrictions imposed by parents? In what ways are they different? Why do you think the differences exist?
2. Imagine you are the administrator of a group home for older youth. Draft three policies that put youth suggestions from this chapter into action.
3. Imagine you are the social worker assigned to one of the two cases described. Do a role play in which you are in charge of visitation for one of the children.
4. Draft a plan for one of the youth from the case studies that focuses on the goal of keeping him or her connected to his or her family. Present the plan to another student.

References

Atkinson, L., & Butler, S. (1996). Court-ordered assessment: Impact of maternal non-compliance in child maltreatment cases. *Child Abuse and Neglect, 20*, 185–190.

Barth, R. P. (2002). *Institutions vs. foster homes: The empirical base for the second century of debate*. Chapel Hill, NC: University of North Carolina, School of Social Work, Jordan Institute for Families.

Becker, M. A., Noerther, C. D., Larson, M. J., Garz, M., Brown, V., Heckman, J. P., & Giard, J. (2005). Characteristics of women engaged in treatment for trauma and co-occurring disorders: Findings from a national multi-site study. *Journal of Community Psychology, 33*, 429–433.

Bellamy, J. L. (2008). Behavioral problems following reunification of children in long term foster care. *Children and Youth Services Review, 30*, 216–228.

Breeland-Noble, A. M., Farmer, E. M., Dubs, M., Potter, B. A., & Burns, B. J. (2005). Mental health and other service use by youth in treatment foster care and group homes. *Journal of Child and Family Studies, 14*, 167–180.

Butler, S. M., Radia, N., & Magnatta, M. (1994). Maternal compliance to court-ordered assessment in cases of child maltreatment. *Child Abuse and Neglect, 18*, 203–211.

Chamberlain, P. (1999). What works in treatment foster care. In M. Kluger, G. Alexander, & P. Curtis (Eds.), *What works in child welfare* (pp. 157–162). Washington, DC: Child Welfare League of America.

Child Welfare League of America. (1994). *Kinship care: A natural bridge*. Washington, DC: Child Welfare League of America.

Clark, M.D. (2007). *The research on motivation and human behavior change: The critical conditions of desire, ability, reason and need*. Paper presented at Substance Abuse: The Road to Recovery and Reunification Conference, Lansing, MI.

Code of Federal Regulations, Title 45§ 57 (2009).

Courtney, M. E., Barth, R. P., Berrick, J. D., Brooks, D., Needell, B., & Parks, L. (1996). Race and child welfare services: Past research and future directions. *Child Welfare Journal of Policy and Practice, 75*, 99–137.

Curtis, P. A., Alexander, G., & Lunghofer, L. A. (2001). A literature review comparing the outcomes of residential group care and therapeutic foster care. *Child and Adolescent Social Work Journal, 18*, 377–392.

Downs, S. L., Moore, E., & McFadden, E. J. (2009). *Child welfare and family services: Policies and Practice* (8th ed.). Boston: Pearson Education, Inc.

Fanshel, D., & Shinn, E. (1978). *Children in foster care: A longitudinal investigation*. New York: Columbia University Press.

Fox, A., & Berrick, J. D. (2007). A response to No One Ever Asked Us: A review of children's experiences in out-of-home care. *Child and Adolescent Social Work Journal, 24*(1), 23–51.

Geenen, S., & Powers, L. E. (2007). "Tomorrow is another problem": The experiences of youth in foster care during their transition into adulthood. *Children and Youth Services Review, 29*, 1085–1101.

Grigsby, R. K. (1993). Theories that guide intensive family preservation services: A second look. In E. S. Morton & R. K. Grigsby (Eds.), *Advancing family preservation practice* (pp. 16–18). Newbury Park, CA: Sage.

Hawkins, R. P. (1990). The nature and potential of treatment foster care programs. In R. Hawkins & J. Brieling (Eds.), *Treatment Foster Care: Critical issues* (pp. 5–36). Washington, DC: Child Welfare League of America.

Hill, R. (2006). *Synthesis of research on disproportionality in child welfare: An update*. Seattle, WA: Casey Family Programs.

Hunter-Romanelli, L., Landsverk, J., Levitt, J. M., Leslie, L. K., M. M, H., Bellonci, C., & The Child Welfare Mental Health Best Practices Group. (2009). Best practices for mental health in child welfare: Parent support and youth empowerment guidelines. *Child Welfare, 88*, 189–219.

Hyde, J., & Kammerer, N. (2009). Adolescents' perspectives on placement moves and congregate settings: Couples and cumulative instabilities in out-of-home care. *Children and Youth Services Review, 31*, 265–273.

Kemp, S., Marcenko, M. O., Hoagwood, K., & Vesneski, W. (2009). Engaging parents in child welfare services: Challenges, promising practices and policy opportunities. *Child Welfare, 88*, 101–126.

Kools, S. M. (1997). Adolescent development in foster care. *Family Relations, 46*(3), 263–271.

Kroll, B. (2004). Living with an elephant: Growing up with parental substance misuse. *Child and Family Social Work, 9*, 129–140.

Lau, A. S., Litrowik, A. J., Neuton, R. G., & Landsverk, J. (2003). Going home: The complex effects of reunification on internalizing problems among children in foster care. *Journal of Abnormal Child Psychology, 31*, 345–358.

Leichtman, M. (2006). Residential treatment of children and adolescents: Past, present, and future. *American Journal of Orthopsychiatry, 76*, 285–294.

Libby, A. M., Orton, H. D., Barth, R. P., Webb, M. B., Burns, B. J., Wood, P., & Spicer, P. (2006). Alcohol, drug and mental health specialty treatment services and race/ethnicity: A national study of children and families involved with child welfare. *American Journal of Public Health, 96*, 628–631.

Manso, A., & Rauktis, M. E. (2011). What is therapeutic alliance and why does it matter? *Reclaiming Children and Youth, 19*, 45–50.

Marcenko, M. O., Lyons, S. J., & Courtney, M. (2011). Mothers' experiences, resources and needs: The context for reunification. *Children and Youth Services Review, 33*, 431–438.

McCoy, H., McMillen, J. C., & Spitznagel, E. L. (2008). Older youth leaving the foster care system: Who, what, when, where and why? *Children and Youth Services Review, 30*, 735–745.

McMillen, J. C., Rideout, G. B., Fisher, R. H., & Tucker, J. (1997). Independent-living services: The views of former foster youth. *Families in Society, 78*(5), 471–479.

Pennsylvania Partnerships for Children. (2010). *The State of Child Welfare, 2010*. The Porch Light Project. Retrieved from: http://www.porchlightproject.org/reports_and_media_socw10.shtml/

Perkins, D. F., & Ansay, S. J. (1998). The effectiveness of a visitation program in fostering visits with noncustodial parents. *Family Relations, 47*, 253–259.

Rauktis, M. E., Fusco, R. A., Cahalane, H., Bennett, I. K., & Reinhart, S. M. (2011). "Try to make it seem like we're regular kids": Youth perceptions of restrictiveness in out-of-home care. *Children and Youth Services Review, 33*, 1224–1233.

Rauktis, M. E., Huefner, J., O'Brien, K., Pecora, P., Doucette, A., & Thompson, R. (2009). Measuring restriction of living environments for children and youth. *Journal of Emotional and Behavioral Disorders, 17*, 145–163.

Rauktis, M. E., & McCrae, J. S. (2010). *The role of race in child welfare system involvement in Allegheny County*. Pittsburgh, PA: University of Pittsburgh, Center on Race and Social Problems. Retrieved from: http://www.alleghenycounty.us/dhs/research-cyf.aspx.

Richardson, B. (2008). Comparative analysis of two community-based efforts designed to impact disproportionality. *Child Welfare, 87*, 297–37.

Runyon, M. K., Deblinger, E., Ryan, E. E., & Thakkan-Kolar, R. (2004). An overview of child physical abuse. *Trauma, Violence & Abuse, 5*, 65–85.

Samuels, G. M., & Pryce, J. M. (2008). What doesn't kill you makes you stronger: Survivalist self-reliance as resilience and risk among young adults aging out of foster care. *Children and Youth Services Review, 30*, 1198–1210.

Spencer, R. (2007). [Review of the book *On their own: What happens to kids when they age out of the foster care system*, by M. Shirk & G. Stangler]. *Qualitative Social Work, 6* (2), 245–250

Taussig, H. N., Oyman, R. B., & Landsverk, J. (2001). Children who return home from foster care: A six year prospective study of behavioral health outcomes on adolescence. *Pediatrics, 108*, e10–13.

U.S. Department of Health and Human Services, Administration for Children and Families, Administration on Children, Youth and Families, Children's Bureau. (2013). *The AFCARS Report. Preliminary FY 2012 estimates as of July 2013(20)*. Retrieved from: http://www.acf.hhs.gov/programs/cb/resource/afcars-report-20

White, M., Albers, E., & Bitonti, C. (1996). Factors in length of foster care: Worker activities and parent–child interaction. *Journal of Sociology and Social Welfare, 23*, 75–84.

Wulczyn, F., & Lery, B. (2007). *Racial disparity in foster care admissions*. Chapin Hall Center for Children at the University of Chicago. Chicago, IL. Retrieved from www.chapinhall.org

Chapter 3
Family Engagement Strategies in Child Welfare Practice

Helen Cahalane and Carol M. Anderson

Abstract Engagement with families involved in the child welfare system is challenging for even the most seasoned professionals. Effective engagement can become compromised by the complexity of legal mandates, the crisis nature of the work, the economic and social challenges faced by children and families, an often critical public, and less than optimal agency staffing patterns. Opportunities to impact the lives of children and families in crisis, to improve a family's capacity to care for their children, and to enhance a young person's options for permanency rest upon the ability to engage clients in a meaningful partnership. Workers who operate from a strengths-based, solution-focused perspective are able to see opportunities for change in even the most complicated family situations and understand that establishing a meaningful connection is the first step in addressing difficult life issues.

To effectively engage families as partners, child welfare workers must be prepared to share power, ask for and use feedback, and see themselves as coaches or mentors who stand beside families and not in front of them. The skills that are required include the ability to suspend quick judgments, recognize one's own frame of reference, respect differences, and anticipate challenges. Family engagement practices such as Family Group Decision Making and Family Finding can help to transform the child welfare system of care from one of legal authority over families to one of partnership with families. As these practices mature and become more widely disseminated, one measure of success will be the adoption of the core principles into a community philosophy. Integration of family engagement practices

H. Cahalane (✉)
Child Welfare Education and Research Programs, School of Social Work,
University of Pittsburgh, Pittsburgh, PA, USA
e-mail: hcupgh@pitt.edu

C.M. Anderson
Western Psychiatric Institute and Clinic, School of Medicine, University of Pittsburgh
Medical Center, Pittsburgh, PA, USA

H. Cahalane (ed.), *Contemporary Issues in Child Welfare Practice*,
Contemporary Social Work Practice, DOI 10.1007/978-1-4614-8627-5_3,
© Springer Science+Business Media New York 2013

into traditional child welfare services can provide families with opportunities to assume control of their lives, as well as more options for child welfare professionals to engage in supportive interventions that are likely to increase job satisfaction.

Keywords Family engagement • Strengths-based • Solution-focused • Family Group Decision Making • Family Finding

Introduction

The child welfare field has become increasingly focused on the importance of strengths-based, family-centered practices that engage families as partners in determining what is best for themselves, their children, and their communities (Altman 2005; Antle et al. 2012; Berg and Kelly 2000; Dawson and Berry 2002; Yatchmenoff 2005). After decades of operating from the patriarchal, deficit-based perspective that once permeated human service systems, child welfare practice has become more inclusive of models grounded in ecological systems theory, family support and empowerment principles, respect for cultural differences, and solution-oriented approaches to care. While practice based upon collaboration, mutual decision making, and social justice is in keeping with core social work values, operationalizing these principles has not always been an easy task within the child protection system. Effective engagement with families can become compromised by the complexity of legal mandates, the crisis nature of the work, the economic and social challenges faced by children and families, an often critical public, and less than optimal agency staffing patterns.

Child welfare professionals must keep in mind that families typically enter into the child welfare system with a sense of apprehension, inequality, and mistrust. Findings from studies exploring engagement with child protective services highlight an intimidating, difficult, and stressful experience for both youth and families based upon personal as well as systemic factors (Altman 2005, 2008; Dale 2004; Diorio 1992; Dumbrill 2006; Haight et al. 2002; Spratt and Callan 2004). Despite shifts in philosophy and operational procedures, perceptions and attitudes related to involvement with the child welfare system are difficult to change. Influenced in part by past experiences, stereotypes rooted in negative portrayals of child protection in the media, stigma, or perceptions of social control, families are often less than positive about their interactions with child welfare organizations. Additionally, families and child welfare professionals often have different views of their work together.

In a study of service users' views of child protective services, Buckley et al. (2011) found that youth and families experienced child welfare involvement as coercive, despite management reforms and efforts to assure family and youth participation in meetings and service planning. Previous studies examining the congruence between professional and client perceptions of therapeutic interventions have found that professionals believed there was a greater therapeutic alliance than did the client and that the professionals did not question their assumptions

(Bickman et al. 2004). Differences in perception between professionals and family members have also been noted in studies examining specific family engagement practices in child welfare (Rauktis et al. 2011), suggesting that practitioners may need to check in periodically rather than assuming that families feel empowered and that their needs are being met.

Mallon (2011) observes that meaningful family engagement in child welfare services is "...still relatively new compared to other well-established modes of practice" (p. 5). While involvement with the child welfare system occurs as a result of many factors related to child safety, child and family well-being, and permanency, there exists a unique opportunity for engaging with families in a partnership focused on solutions and change. The following section describes the basic elements of family engagement and reviews some of the challenges specific to engagement within child welfare services. Practical advice is provided to frontline child welfare professionals who must balance the mission of child protection with a commitment to promote family empowerment and self-reliance. A description of two family engagement practices follows, concluding with recommendations for shifting service delivery within the child welfare system in order to better support families in making decisions about their lives and those of their children.

Engaging Families in the Context of Involuntary Child Welfare Services

Engaging families in any type of service is challenging, since each individual member has a unique perspective about the family's problems and what should be done about them. Engagement in child welfare services is particularly difficult because most families have not asked for help and the process is frequently involuntary and adversarial. In most cases contact between child welfare and families begins during a crisis that involves judgment of the parents' behaviors and potential changes in child custody. Parents may feel that their own struggles with poverty, trauma, substance abuse, and mental health disorders are unappreciated as the child welfare system works to rescue their children from their inadequate or even destructive care. Yet many of these parents have their own history of serious trauma and loss, in addition to a history of negative encounters with social service systems that have left them feeling defensive, intimidated, and disrespected (Buckley et al. 2011). When they are approached by someone who has a mandate to evaluate their competence and focus primarily on their child's needs, it isn't surprising that their response is often one of anger and fear. It also isn't surprising that they become defensive and noncompliant, reactions that further contribute to the risk of their child being removed and their parental rights terminated (Dawson and Berry 2002).

It is in this threatening context that child welfare workers are faced with the complex task of forming a therapeutic relationship that will help families make difficult changes. Not only must workers confront the universal tendencies of all families to resist change and resist being influenced (Anderson and Stewart 1982), but they must do so while they are representing a powerful system that has a mandate to evaluate family behaviors and impose changes on the way family members live their lives. It is difficult to even imagine how threatening early encounters with child welfare must be to parents who fear they could lose their children. Any defensive or resistant response they have should be seen as completely reasonable. Effectively engaging them requires time and sensitivity, not an easy task for workers with little time and a conflicting investigative mandate.

To begin the process of engaging a family, it is important to understand all of the likely emotional reactions that will make engagement difficult. Attributing the problems of engaging family members in services solely to their fears, anger, or lack of motivation is an oversimplification of the problem. The procedures of child welfare programs, as well as the characteristics, biases, and assumptions of workers, will also make it more difficult to develop a helping relationship between a worker and a family. In addition to understanding the families' reactions and defensiveness, to effectively engage families, workers should learn to appreciate the barriers generated by the child welfare system and their own personal biases. This broader systems perspective will help to reduce the adversarial nature of the process and decrease tendencies to simply blame families (Dawson and Berry 2002). It will also help workers prove that they are not the enemy. The following section will review the barriers to engagement produced by the characteristics of each of these three system components and suggest strategies for minimizing their impact.

The Characteristics of Families

Most of the families seen by child welfare professionals will be a challenge to engage. They are likely to have had past negative experiences with social service agencies that will make it difficult for them to accept help from the average worker whose values, belief systems, experiences, and own family history will most likely differ from their own. They will see workers as representatives of society's power structure, there to judge them and hold them responsible for the problems of their children. In short, they will be resistant because they have a lot to lose. As child welfare workers become involved in their lives, they will be resentful because their parenting has been questioned and almost certainly will deny that a child welfare investigation is necessary. To be prepared to intervene effectively, it is important not to dwell on the fact that families resist investigation, but to think about *how* and *why* they are resisting.

Families often already have a history of having been disenfranchised by poverty, immigration, race, culture, or other factors. The stress of poverty itself accounts for many of the problems in parental functioning and poor child outcomes (Berger 2007; Crosier et al. 2007; Edin and Kissane 2010; Zahn and Pandy 2004). Families who enter the child welfare system usually live in troubled communities, are disproportionally exposed to stressful life events, and possess fewer resources to manage these life events. A high percentage will be single parents trying to manage children alone, and many of these parents come with their own history of trauma, neglect, and loss that makes parenting difficult (Haight et al. 2005). Many households will be unstructured, unpredictable, and even chaotic, factors that appear to contribute to engagement difficulties (Perrino et al. 2001).

A disproportionally high number of families will be racial and ethnic minorities and, given that there are fewer minority child welfare workers, more workers will need to find ways to engage across the cultural divide that breeds distrust and misunderstanding. In addition, many parents of all races and cultures will have a history of negative interactions with public agencies. They will have had experiences of being disrespected by schools, landlords, and a range of other external authorities. Some will be "known to child welfare" with generations of involvement with child welfare systems and intergenerational patterns of abuse/neglect/poverty. These interactions will have left them acutely sensitive to threats to their autonomy and signals of disrespect. For many parents, their ability to provide good child care under these strains will be further compromised by depression (DeGarmo and Forgatch 2005; Feder et al. 2009), a condition for which they are reluctant to seek help for fear that receiving mental health services will be seen as evidence of their inadequacy. They believe the system will not appreciate their ability to survive while managing the daily hassles of poverty and the stresses of living in dangerous neighborhoods (Ceballo and McLoyd 2002).

Characteristics of the Child Welfare System

Child welfare systems have a legal mandate to protect children by investigating reports of potential abuse and neglect, making decisions about custody, and developing a safety plan within a specified time frame. This mandate indirectly places the needs and concerns of parents in second place, making it difficult for workers to simultaneously engage parents, allow them to be part of the decision-making process, and demonstrate that there is something about the process that will also help them (Olson 2009). Child welfare workers often start with the disadvantage of having the reputation of being "baby snatchers," making their attempts to engage families in services a difficult task. The engagement difficulties exacerbated by the system's reputation and mandate are further compounded by agency rules and procedures that drive the system, making it less responsive to the cultural and community perspectives of families in crisis.

Low salaries and high caseloads often leave child welfare professionals discouraged, overwhelmed, and having to react to crises rather than thoughtfully responding to client needs. The Child Welfare League of America (CWLA) places the national caseload standard at 15 cases, but staff shortages and turnover often leave workers with at least twice as many cases, allowing them to accomplish little more than superficial work. Their enthusiasm for engaging difficult clients can diminish when they feel they are providing minimal services, yet are required to document these attempts to help with endless paperwork (Magennis and Smith 2005; Smith 2009). Some workers describe themselves as having to place band-aids on problems rather than being able to provide serious help. The supervisors assigned to support workers in managing their multiproblem caseloads can often do so only after they have ensured the completion of legal forms and administrative paperwork. Following all the rules leaves even the most dedicated workers with little time to individualize care and create unique and relevant intervention plans for the families they see. All of this means that despite theoretical support for child welfare agencies to maintain a strengths-based and systemically focused approach, it is a challenge for workers to hold on to these concepts when the system itself is part of the problem.

Characteristics of Caseworkers

Most workers begin their careers in child welfare with good intentions, earnestly wanting to be helpful to the children and families they see. However, many also enter the field with no training in social services or related fields. This means they may begin with little preparation for understanding the impact that different cultures and communities can have on their clients and the difficult lives of the impoverished families they will see. Those without a social work degree are unlikely to have much training in the professional value of confidentiality nor in the nuanced skills of "starting where the client is" (Perlman 1957) and engaging the client. Even workers with a background in the social sciences often come with a full range of biases and assumptions developed in their particular culture and family of origin, which can get in the way of engaging families in services. How much workers understand the impact of their own family of origin in terms of what they are likely to perceive as "normal," and what they are likely to miss, will determine in part how helpful they can be. Biases are inevitable; the only questions are whether workers are conscious of them and how much those biases are imposed on clients.

In child welfare, workers often find themselves primarily exposed to the values, traditions, and experiences of clients from races, cultures, and classes that differ from their own. Their personal characteristics will, in part, determine how their clients perceive them, with such things as age, gender, and race influencing how acceptable they will be to any given family. For instance, when workers are young clients may not see them as having sufficient life experience to appreciate their problems. Workers who are male may have the challenge of being seen as unlikely to understand the problems of a single mother raising children on her own. Workers of another race, class, or culture may be seen by clients as not able to understand their differing social and cultural experiences and worldviews. Whatever the specifics, workers often struggle with maintaining and communicating a respect for differences and appreciating their impact. Without the skill to bridge differences, they will always be seen as outsiders representing a system that does not understand the complicated lives of the clients they serve.

Many of the mistakes beginning and even experienced workers make with clients fall into the category of "microaggressions," largely unconscious insults or demeaning messages sent by well-intentioned workers who do not even notice their impact (Sue 2010). While the term originally referred to the negative, demeaning behaviors and messages of whites addressing minorities, such messages can be sent by child welfare workers of any race to any of their disenfranchised clients. Even well-meaning attempts to be empathic can be perceived by clients as evidence of insincerity, criticism, and condescension. Personal views of desirable or normal behaviors imposed on disadvantaged clients unwittingly demonstrate a lack of respect for the clients' approach to their problems. What makes these small negative communications so powerful and damaging, particularly to the process of engaging, is that they are rarely discussed or acknowledged. Workers may continue to believe they are doing everything they can to engage families, yet continue to behave in ways that clients find disrespectful and that signal to clients that their differences are evidence of class, cultural, or racial inferiority.

There are a range of other attitudes and behaviors that act as barriers to engagement. Underlying negative beliefs regarding single parenthood, public assistance, or working mothers can influence a worker's perception of disadvantaged parents trying to manage on their own. Those who assume a child rescue approach that emphasizes family deficits are more likely to alienate parents who may have themselves been raised in neglectful and abusive homes and who have a full range of other presenting problems (e.g., substance abuse, parental mental health issues, poverty, single parenthood). And while removing a child from his or her family home may sometimes be necessary, workers who assume this as their primary role have difficulty establishing the kind of relationship that makes parents receptive to working to improve their lives and their parenting. Views like these are not helpful in engaging parents and helping them more effectively manage their children.

Barriers to engagement are also generated when workers approach parents with conceptual frameworks that emphasize "pathology." These views limit the workers' ability to be empathic and cloud workers' appreciation of the difficulties parents face. Labeling parents "dysfunctional," "manipulative," "resistant," or "noncompliant" leaves workers less likely to appreciate concurrent parental strengths. Even if parents have serious limitations, they rarely want to be bad parents. Rather, they are overwhelmed or simply lack the necessary skills for good parenting. Emphasizing pathology decreases the chance of engaging them and impairs their motivation to work on necessary changes.

Finally, all of these barriers are likely to be exacerbated over time when child welfare professionals have developed fatigue or burnout. If they are exhausted by the difficulty of the cases they see, if they have lost the necessary enthusiasm to engage clients, and if they are frustrated with the administrative tasks of the job, workers end up jaded and "running on empty." They can become more critical, less aware of how they are imposing their biases, and more hopeless about their own abilities. Their lack of the energy and compassion for clients makes it difficult for these workers to reach out to families and provide the help they need.

Strategies for Engaging Families

Gallagher et al. (2011) describe features of family engagement in child welfare services, such as initiating dialogue with family members about how they view their problems and what they see as solutions, supporting family members to participate in meetings, giving due regard to the views of both parents and children, and taking different communication styles into account. All of the specific strategies of engaging families that follow are based on these principles and the fundamental goal of creating a respectful climate. Despite the adversarial nature of the child welfare worker's role, this basic respect will allow families to begin to feel that the worker has some understanding of them and their issues, cares about their needs, and can be trusted.

1. *Weave attempts to engage into initial investigations.* As noted earlier, families are inevitably anxious and defensive in their first contacts with the child welfare system. Whether or not you are the person who must do the initial investigation, in your first contacts it is important to adopt the classic social work principle of starting where the client is (Hepworth et al. 2010). This means your first goal is to decrease their anxiety, even while you work to gain the needed information about the child who is the subject of the referral. If you begin with a bit of neutral conversation, you may decrease the formality of the encounter, making the family feel just a little less upset.

   Next, turn to efforts to build trust. It is important to acknowledge what all parents know: that the worker's first imperative is assessing for child safety. Moving on to find ways to express concern about the needs and problems of the parents helps to build a level of trust. Honesty builds trust, even when it involves things parents don't want to hear. Relationship building also involves expressing empathy about how difficult it must be for parents to be involved in the child welfare process. None of these efforts will automatically eliminate a family's distrust, but gradually you can work to balance the necessary tasks of child protection with care and concern (Buckley et al. 2011; Jack et al. 2005).

   If by the end of the first meeting you are able to communicate at least some understanding of what has contributed to the family's contact with child welfare, what caused someone to refer them to services, and how they feel about this, you will have the beginnings of a connection. Your humanity will have begun to soften what would otherwise be a thoroughly coercive and hierarchical process.

2. *Orient families to the process and the power differential.* Providing information increases predictability and decreases anxiety, so it is important to tell a family about the child protection process and to put in context exactly what is going to

happen, even when parts of the process may be threatening (Altman 2008). No matter how well-meaning you are, no matter how much you want to help, you are also an agent of social control with the power to remove children from their parents' care. Families have a right to be suspicious of you and of the process. To establish trust, it helps to be honest about this fact and be prepared to address it openly. It is the elephant in the room. An honest relationship is complicated, but it will be the most important factor in engaging child welfare clients.

Provide information about the processes of child protective services and why they exist, the interventions you must make, and the reports that must be filed. This is also a good time to empathize about the family's feelings of being judged and coerced. You can say such things as, "They can tell you we have to work together, but they can't tell you everything you have to work on. How can we best use the time we have to help your family?" This gives you the chance to let clients know that there is something in it for them. If they or their friends have had experiences with the child welfare system in the past, asking about those experiences will provide you with opportunities to clarify how you hope this experience will be different or at least to commiserate with them for having to go through it another time.

Without giving up your authority, you can begin to share some power with the family. Begin to collaborate by offering parents the chance to ask questions and ensure that those questions are answered respectfully. The more you can share power, the less the family will resist and fear your influence; emphasize the fact that they still have some control and autonomy. While you must acknowledge the involuntary aspects of the relationship, you can work to collaboratively establish an explicit agreement to work together on specific, realistic, and mutual goals. For instance, as you discuss the possible goals of working together, make it clear to families that you are interested in making sure there is something in it for them (Altman 2008; Rooney 2009). As you help families choose their goals, it is important to remember that your mandate to help does not include the right to critique everything about how they live their lives. Not everything can and should be fixed, so keep your goals realistic.

3. *Expect challenges to your ability to help without taking them personally.* In addition to decreasing a family's defensiveness, it is important to decrease our own tendencies to be defensive. It's easier to tolerate challenges to your competence if you see them as normal and inevitable. Clients beginning to engage in any sort of services tend to question the personal and professional credentials of those offering them, and encountering suspicions about the potential helpfulness of child welfare services is almost a given. Involuntary clients feel intimidated and stressed and need reassurance. They will have concerns about you whether or not they express them overtly. Expecting skepticism from your clients will help you to respond to ambivalent or angry clients without becoming defensive. Instead, you can focus your efforts on listening to their concerns and demonstrating your understanding.

Most parents will be less concerned about your degrees and training and more concerned about your life experience and ability to empathize with their situation. So, in advance, think about which of your characteristics might provoke questions. For instance, young workers are likely to be faced with personal questions about their age and whether they are parents. Older workers may be more likely to be asked about whether they have encountered similar kinds of challenges and perhaps what keeps them doing child welfare work. In either case, what parents really want to know from any worker is whether he/she understands how hard it is to raise children and has enough empathy for the parent's situation to help. Refusing to become reactive or put off by client challenges will allow you to establish a beginning relationship that can be a helpful foundation for working with parents over time. The point is that if you decrease your own anxiety, you will have greater freedom to focus on client needs.

4. *Adopt a strengths-based, collaborative family perspective.* Engaging families in child welfare services involves coping with and minimizing the tremendous pressure to focus on family deficits, making it particularly important to add a focus on strengths as soon as possible (Child Welfare Information Gateway 2010; Ferguson 2001). Strengths exist even in the most troubled families, and including a focus on them will help to avoid exacerbating family resistance and defensiveness. It will also promote hope in parents that they have the power to be better parents to their children. A focus on strengths begins by accepting that there are many ways to live and raise children successfully and many varied family structures that manage to do so. Whether a family structure involves a young single mother, gay parents, or a grandparent raising a child, that family can provide the love, limits, and values a child needs. A focus on family strengths will allow you to mitigate the impact of system challenges (i.e., bureaucracy, legal mandates) by using the relationship as a bridge between the child protection system and the needs of the family.

5. *Work to be culturally proficient.* We all like to think we are good human beings devoid of racism, sexism, and judgmental attitudes, but the truth is that we all have a tendency to distrust people who are different from us in any way. We could all spend the rest of our lives increasing our ability to be culturally proficient and there would still be work to do. The families that workers encounter in child welfare are particularly sensitive to signals of what you don't know and understand and what you don't respect. They will have been through it all before. The key first step in learning to understand and accept family structures, ethnicities, and racial groups that are not your own is to consistently work at noticing the differences between you and your clients. You can't learn to accept differences if you pretend they don't exist. You also can't learn everything about every specific way families differ, but you can learn that there are worldviews and lifestyles that are not like yours that you should respect. There are many realities and, as Watzlawick (1993) noted, believing there is one reality is the most dangerous of all delusions.

The second step in increasing cultural sensitivity is to learn to avoid assuming that you understand what differences mean to your clients, including their views of their problems, their children, and what they see as appropriate solutions. The third step is to set up a routine of asking questions that will allow your clients to teach you what you need to know. This means carefully listening to how clients respond to your questions, but also listening to what their responses tell you about their concerns, priorities, values, and life views (Altman 2008). As you practice these approaches, you will engage families in more culturally sensitive ways.

6. *Ask for and accept feedback about the agency and you.* You should ask clients about their experiences with the child welfare process and with you personally, consistently soliciting feedback that will correct inevitable misunderstandings and assumptions. Regular requests for honest feedback require listening to negative perceptions rather than implicitly sending the message that they need to reassure you how caring you are. If you ask for feedback and listen to what your clients have to say, they will educate you. Listening to their feedback will allow you to demonstrate receptivity and respect for their views and let them know what collaborating in the process could do for them. You should work to be honest and straightforward, but never make promises that you can't keep.

7. *Strive for a broader view of family systems.* Adopt and maintain a perspective that looks at the behaviors of families in the larger context of their extended network. Widening the lens will allow you to see both sources of stress and hidden resources that can be recruited to help families cope more effectively. Even if you are available to provide immediate help, there is a limit to how much you can do if you see only the problems of a distressed nuclear family or the limited resources of a single parent and child. A broader perspective of the family's network will help you discover others who may be important resources and those who may be currently missing but who are possibly available to be helpful.

    You can't mobilize a network you don't know is there, so it is important to ask families who they rely on, who they turn to for support, and who is missing or has become disconnected. You can nurture a parent's long-term support system in ways that will help them to keep their children and raise them effectively. Extended family, particularly grandparents and other kin, can provide webs of supportive connections that will allow respites from stress and improve parenting. Particular attention should be given to finding ways to include uninvolved fathers in the family when at all possible. Many fathers, including those who are incarcerated, desire involvement with their children but simply don't know what to do (Dyer 2005). Helping mothers to explore the possibility of reinforcing the father–child bond offers hope for better relationships (Johnson 2001).

8. *Maintain your morale.* Despite the nationwide movement to empower child protective service workers and families (Hewitt et al. 2010; Mosley and Smith 2004),

over time it is easy to become jaded and drained by the difficulty of the job. In some cases your own emotional reactions to clients can cause fatigue. Workers who want to help may tend to fear or react negatively to families with multiple problems and needs, because they feel incompetent or unable to do all that is necessary to help them. It is also exhausting to keep reaching out to clients in trouble if you believe the trouble they have is their own doing. Morale is also at risk for relatively inexperienced child welfare workers when supervision is administrative or task focused and doesn't address the complicated clinical issues they face in the field (See Chap. 10).

It is crucial to find ways to nurture your own well-being and to manage the secondary traumatic stress that often occurs with child protection work (See Chap. 9). Secondary traumatic stress refers to symptoms of increased arousal and/or avoidance following exposure to traumatic material (Figley 1995). Child welfare work, in particular, has been found to be a strong predictor of secondary trauma as a result of the frequent, ongoing contact with the consequences of multiple forms of violence against children (Sprang et al. 2011). It helps to learn the skills that will provide increased confidence in your ability to do your job, to learn to set boundaries with clients, and to find ways to get social support from colleagues and supervisors. It is also important to spend time with your own network and family to maintain a balance that will help to combat burnout (Smith et al. 2007).

Summary

Working in child welfare is challenging, involving large caseloads with daily exposure to families in upsetting situations and overwhelming crises. Not surprisingly, many workers experience trauma secondary to these experiences. Furthermore, most families engaged in the child welfare system distrust and resent the system and may project similar emotions toward their worker. However, despite the barriers introduced by the involuntary nature of the system, the biases of workers, and the characteristics of the families needing services, it is possible to successfully engage families in a helping relationship. By focusing on family strengths, seeing resistances as normal, developing open channels of feedback and communication, and working to develop an overall respect of differences of all kinds, child welfare practitioners can engage families in a collaborative process.

Avoiding coercive and adversarial encounters will make it possible to create relationships that are acceptable to even very resistant families who come into contact with child welfare services. Forming a working relationship with parents under stress requires an awareness of the potential barriers that are likely to arise from all parts of the system, including behaviors and attitudes of workers and the policies and procedures of the child welfare organization. It is absolutely crucial to account for and address these barriers that contribute to family reactivity. Recognizing that you and the system in which you work will also provoke resistance or barriers to engagement will allow you to be more sensitive to the impact of your biases and the obstacles to trust often produced within bureaucratic organizations.

Promising Family Engagement Practices in Child Welfare

This section describes Family Group Decision Making and Family Finding, two models of child welfare intervention that contribute to effectively engaging child welfare populations while facilitating connections between children and their family network. Both models have common goals: supporting families to meet their needs, helping families to maintain a connection among themselves and their communities, and empowering families to provide the best possible care for their children. The origin, theoretical base, key elements, method of delivery, and evidence base for each practice are discussed, along with the essential elements of change. It is important to keep in mind that these practices involve specific processes as well as an overarching orientation to working with families in the child welfare system. The following core characteristics are common to both practices:

- Systemic focus
- Strengths-based, solution-oriented perspective
- Empowerment
- Collaboration and partnership
- Sharing of power by families and professionals
- Cultural relevance and respect for differences
- Emphasis upon the perspectives of youth and family members
- Skill development and enhancement
- Strengthening of social networks
- Interagency cooperation
- Concrete, written plans of action

Family Group Decision Making

Family Group Decision Making (FGDM) is a process by which families, members of the family's informal network, relevant community members, and representatives of the child welfare agency join in collaborative planning for children and youth who require protection or care. FGDM can be initiated at any point in the service pathway and at any time when critical decisions about a child's safety, permanency, or well-being are needed. While FGDM is targeted toward children and adolescents ages 0–17, local policies and practices vary regarding the inclusion of children younger than age 12 in FGDM meetings. The child's developmental stage, level of maturity, and wish for inclusion, as well as parental concerns, all contribute to decisions about the extent of the child's inclusion (California Evidence-Based Clearing House for Child Welfare 2012b; Merkel-Holguin 2003; Pennell 2005a, b). Although the focus here is on the use of FGDM in child welfare, FGDM is utilized in other child-serving systems as well. Juvenile justice, schools, programs focusing on self-sufficiency, and the mental retardation and mental health systems also implement the practice. FGDM has also begun to be used to address concerns in the aging and adult probation systems.

Origin and Theoretical Base

Family Group Conferencing (later known as Family Group Decision Making) was first legislated in New Zealand after protests of the indigenous Maori tribe against the European-based child welfare system (Hudson et al. 1996). The *Children, Young Persons and Their Families Act of 1989*, a progressive child welfare and juvenile justice policy, created the "family group conference" as a formalized mechanism for bringing family members and government officials together to work toward common goals of child protection and community cohesiveness. The intent of the legislation was "to promote family group responsibility, child safety, cultural respect, and community–government partnerships in place of expert-driven intervention" (Hassall 1996 as cited in Pennell 2005a, b, p. 3). Central to this social and political movement was the recognition that institutionalized racism and paternalism affected the child welfare system in ways that were destructive to the children and families it was designed to serve (American Humane Association 2008). Since this time, FGDM has spread to other parts of the world and is now practiced in Europe, Canada, Australia, and the United States.

Family Group Decision Making began in the United States in the mid-1990s. Although some local practices vary from the New Zealand model, derivatives of family group conferencing all have central core elements of bringing family members and their supports together with child welfare professionals to plan for children. Unlike in New Zealand, FGDM in the United States is not mandated by law. However, statutory and policy support for FGDM and other family engagement approaches has been identified in at least 15 states and the District of Columbia (American Humane Association 2009), and recent federal child welfare legislation has bolstered support for the practice. The passage of the Fostering Connections to Success and Increasing Adoptions Act (H.R. 6893/P.L. 110–351) in 2008 increased resources for FGDM through the provision of special grant funding for services that promote family connection, community involvement, and family decision making in children's lives. Family Group

Decision Making and Family Finding (discussed later in this section) are two key child welfare practices supported in the Fostering Connections legislation.

Empowerment theory (Maluccio and Daly 2000; Pennell 2005a, b; Rapport 1987) provides a theoretical framework for FGDM. Empowerment is both a value orientation and a process. The essential elements include exerting influence and control over decisions that impact three areas: one's life, the functioning of organizations, and the quality of life within a community (Zimmerman 2000). Also central to FGDM are the strengths-based (Saleebey 1997) and person-in-environment perspectives (e.g., Appleby et al. 2007; Hartman 1988) that guide social work practice. The construct of empowerment and the strengths-based perspective share the basic assumption that all individuals have inherent strengths, competencies, and capabilities. Burford (2000) and Pennell (2005a, b) expand the theoretical framework for FGDM to include restorative justice, cultural inclusiveness, and participatory democracy. Restorative justice approaches assume a democratic process of non-domination, democratic deliberation, mutual caring and respect, and fairness in conflict resolution (Burford 2000, p. 16). Cultural inclusiveness involves the awareness of one's own preconceptions and the openness to learning from those who are culturally different. Participatory democracy denotes the process by which family participants build a consensus through collaborative planning (Pennell 2005a, p. 7). All of these elements contribute to the process that occurs in the family group conference.

Key Elements

Family Group Decision Making is a collaborative process between family members and child welfare professionals for addressing concerns for child safety, identifying what may be contributing to the presenting issues, and developing a plan of action. It can also be used to address well-being and permanency issues and is used frequently for the purpose of transition planning. This deceptively simple process is not only a practice of bringing professionals together with important individuals in a child's life in order to develop plans; it also represents a philosophical shift in how to work collaboratively with youth and families in the child protection system. The practice of FGDM requires the relinquishment of control by professionals who have typically assumed a directive stance in working with clients receiving child welfare services and the sharing of power (Rauktis et al. 2011).

Family Group Decision Making is based upon five central values: safeguarding, family voice, worker accountability, community involvement, and consensus building (Pennell 2005a, b). A guiding metaphor of FGDM is "widening the circle" (Pennell and Anderson 2005), which refers to developing family leadership, cultural safety, and community partnerships in order to provide safety and protection to children, youth, and families. Widening the circle frames FGDM as a

Table 3.1 Key principles and practices of family group conferencing

---

1. Build broad-based support and cultural competence
    (a) Wide range of community and public organizations
    (b) Partners retain roles and responsibilities
2. Enable coordinators to work with families to organize their conferences
    (a) Coordinators respect families and communities
    (b) Primary role of the coordinator is conference organizing
    (c) Culture and practice considerations
    (d) More family members than professionals
3. Have the conference belong to the family group
    (a) Hold conferences in a place that fits the family's culture
    (b) Give clear reasons for holding the conference that professionals and families understand
4. Foster understanding of the family and creativity in planning
    (a) Invite different sides of the family
    (b) Broadly define who is "family"
5. Help participants take part safely and effectively
    (a) Prepare family group and service providers
    (b) Build in supports and protections
    (c) Arrange transportation and childcare as needed
    (d) Ask providers to share concerns, knowledge, and resources, but not dictate solutions
6. Tap into family strengths in making a plan
    (a) Ensure that the family group has private time to develop a plan
7. Promote carrying out the plan and fulfilling the mission
    (a) Approve plans regarding safety and resourcing in a timely manner
    (b) Integrate supports and resources of the family group organizations and public agencies
8. Fulfill the purpose of the plan
    (a) Support efforts of the family group and service providers
9. Change policies, procedures, and resources to sustain partnerships among family groups, community organizations, and public agencies
    (a) Use program evaluation as a means of change
    (b) Develop and use integrative and culturally competent approaches

---

Adapted from Pennell (1999). Used with permission

practice and as a "way of doing business" that levels the playing field between families and professionals by creating partnership, mutual respect, shared responsibility, and collective accountability. Key principles and practices of FGDM are described in Table 3.1.

Method of Delivery

FGDM consists of a five-phase process with the specific end task of developing a plan to assure the care and protection of children. Figure 3.1 illustrates the sequential stages of family engagement, exploration, decision making, and follow-up that represent an approach to practice as well as a series of concrete actions.

Fig. 3.1 FGDM process.
Adapted from Pennell &
Anderson, 2005. Used with
permission

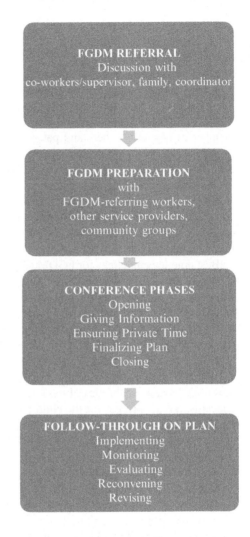

FGDM conferences are arranged and guided by an independent coordinator who typically works in a public or private child welfare agency. It is preferable for the FGDM coordinator not to carry the family on his or her caseload so that the coordinator is truly independent and able to facilitate an unbiased discussion and planning process. Whenever possible, the family group is asked whether they would prefer a coordinator from their cultural group and/or one who speaks their language. Arrangements can also be made for an interpreter to be present to support communication in instances in which a coordinator cannot be found to match the family's language or culture (American Humane Association 2010). Co-coordinators can be used when there is a high level of conflict or antagonism within the family group or if the meeting is expected to have a large number of participants.

The FGDM coordinator's role involves preconference preparation during which the purpose of the group meeting is clearly defined; the participants are identified and prepared; and the meeting place, time, and structure are determined (Pennell and Anderson 2005). Efforts are made to ensure a safe environment where all participants feel comfortable and understand what to expect. FGDM participants may include maternal and paternal relatives, friends, neighbors, community members, religious leaders, step or half siblings, mentors, and others who have a significant relationship with the child or family members. The coordinator also negotiates with the family to broaden participation as much as possible by asking about other family members, especially fathers and paternal relatives who are frequently left out or overlooked in child welfare case planning and services (Bellamy 2009; O'Donnell et al. 2005). The FGDM process requires skillful work on the part of the coordinator, who must respect the worldview and preferences of family members, while also challenging the exclusion of particular relationships or connections important to the child. Planning for the FGDM conference also involves arranging for concrete resources such as transportation, child care, travel funds, and/or arrangements with family members' employers.

Best practice guidelines for FGDM (American Humane Association 2010) specify that the coordinator should also fulfill the function of facilitating the FGDM conference. This provides greater consistency for family members, increases the level of comfort in the process, and limits the number of professionals involved with the family. While the primary role of the child welfare worker in the family group conference remains that of child protection, the group context provides an opportunity for the worker to join in problem solving with the family. The information sharing that occurs at the beginning of the FGDM conference includes a focus on the strengths and capabilities of the family; these strengths are used to address the concerns that are present for the child and the potential solutions that exist within the family. As a participant in the FGDM conference, the child welfare worker is able to assist the family in solution building and identifying steps toward change that are practical and meaningful.

A central element of the FGDM conference is private family time. This phase of the conference provides an opportunity for the family to meet alone, without nonfamily members and statutory authorities present, to process information, discuss options, and formulate a culturally consistent plan (American Humane Association 2008). The plan must be sound, reasonable, and clear and must specify what is to be done, by whom, and in what time frame (Merkel-Holguin 2003). Plans include concrete action steps and reasonable and attainable goals and must be accepted by the family and the child welfare agency. Family ownership of the plan is central to its success and is consistent with FGDM's focus on family empowerment and participatory decision making.

Following the FGDM conference, the family group and the child welfare agency representatives are responsible for implementing, monitoring, and evaluating the plan. Agency backing and the provision of services ordered by the court help to assure that plans are followed and that the family is supported in the timeliest manner possible. Plans are reviewed and revised as needed, sometimes through the reconvening of subsequent FGDM conferences.

Evidence Base

There is a growing evidence base for FGDM, most of which focuses on the process and strategies of the practice. Studies consistently find that youth and families are satisfied with FGDM meetings and the opportunity to participate in planning (Bell and Wilson 2006; Crampton and Jackson 2007; Crea and Berzin 2009; Darlington et al. 2012; Rauktis 2008; Sheets et al. 2009). Evidence has also been found for the effectiveness of FGDM as an early intervention strategy (Brady 2006), in reducing child protective services events (Crampton and Jackson 2007; Pennell and Burford 2000), and in facilitating kinship care (Edwards et al. 2007; Pennell et al. 2010; Wang et al. 2012; Weisz et al. 2006).

Crampton (2007) notes that some significant challenges for FGDM outcome studies are finding appropriate comparison groups and the lack of randomized trials. While there are few FGDM outcome studies, there is evidence suggesting that use of the practice increases rates of reunification and has a demonstrable impact on family-focused permanency goals (Edwards et al. 2007; Pennell et al. 2010; Shore et al. 2002). Outcome findings have also provided evidence for FGDM's impact on expedited exits from care and increased rates of reunification for Hispanic and African American children (Sheets et al. 2009). These findings are echoed in the work of Barn et al. (2009), who note the benefit of embedding family group conferencing in community-based organizations serving minority families.

Other studies have found no difference between outcomes of maltreatment, placement stability, and permanence among children who received FGDM and those who received traditional child welfare services (Berzin 2006; Center for Social Services Research 2004; Weigensburg et al. 2009). These mixed results suggest that further research is needed to evaluate the short- and long-term outcomes of FGDM. FGDM is a developing child welfare practice with a growing body of knowledge. An ongoing, international review of family engagement research and evaluation studies in child welfare by Burford et al. (2010) is the first collection of its kind to provide an annotated bibliography of the wide range of studies devoted to family decision making.

As with any innovation, adoption of a new practice is often complicated by both personal and institutional barriers. Challenges with implementing FGDM have been identified in a number of studies (e.g., Brodie 2008; Connolly 2006; Crampton et al. 2008; McBeath et al. 2009; Rauktis et al. 2010) and point to issues such as lack of resources, shifts in the power balance between professionals and families, lack of support from leadership, and the risk-adverse environment of child welfare agencies. Model fidelity is also a challenge for FGDM, as it is typically a grassroots effort driven by champions who believe in its principles and their practices, but who may have different methods for delivering it. FGDM is not a manualized intervention in which specific procedures are used to measure whether it is delivered as intended (adherence) and how well it is delivered (competence) (Ollendick and King 2012). Rather, the benefit of the model lies in its adaptability and flexibility to local contexts and cultures, and this variability makes FGDM outcomes difficult to study. Pennell (2005a, b) notes that weak outcome findings may be the result of failure to carry out the model consistently.

> **FGDM: A Case Example** *Justin, a 16-year-old Caucasian male, entered foster care at the age of 14 due to truancy, running away from his parents' home, and experimenting with drugs and alcohol. Both of his parents worked long h to make ends meet and Justin was often left unsupervised late into the evening. When Justin entered care, his parents refused to consider placement with any relatives or friends and feared that Justin was involved in criminal activity.*
>
> *Justin's worker, Cindy, met with Justin and his parents weekly. Cindy was trained in youth and family engagement practices and used her skills to engage the family in the assessment, planning, and decision-making process. With the family's permission and Justin's agreement, Cindy made a referral to the FGDM agency responsible for coordinating and facilitating the family conference. Chris, the FGDM coordinator, located Justin's maternal grandparents, two maternal uncles, a 21-year-old sister, two paternal aunts, and numerous younger cousins. Chris also identified a football coach from Justin's elementary school. Chris met with each person during the preparation phase of the FGDM process and everyone agreed to attend a family meeting. Chris worked with the family to identify a time, location, and purpose for their conference.*
>
> *Chris had everyone introduce themselves and their relationship to Justin during the introductory phase of the conference. He also reintroduced the purpose of the conference and facilitated a group discussion of strengths and concerns so that the family could use all of the information to plan solutions to help Justin get back on the right track. The family met alone for 2 h in private family time, while Cindy and Chris waited in an adjoining room. Cindy and Chris rejoined the family as they discussed their plan for Justin to live with his uncle Mike for at least 6 months. Mike was single, employed as a teacher, and lived in the same school district as Justin's parents. Justin and his parents set up visits every Sunday with the hopes of longer visits and eventual reunification. At the suggestion of the football coach, everyone agreed that getting Justin re-involved with football would assist with school attendance, grades, friends, structured free time, and physical activity. The diagnostic assessments revealed that Justin did not have a drug or alcohol abuse issue or the propensity for criminal activity.*
>
> *The family agreed to have Cindy present their plan to the court. They also agreed to have Cindy stay involved to assist them and to reconvene a follow-up conference in 3 months to share their progress. The conference ended with the signing of the plan by all attendees and the scheduling of the follow-up conference.*

Family Finding

Like Family Group Decision Making, Family Finding is a practice that recognizes family involvement as a key component of establishing a successful service plan for a child. Family Finding is a philosophical orientation and set of discrete practices designed to locate, engage, and connect children in the child welfare system with lost biological relatives and kin. Through careful exploration, outreach, and engagement, family members who have lost contact with young persons in foster care can be identified and potentially involved in a carefully designed process of reconnection. Internet-based search technologies can be used as a tool for identifying relatives and kin after other engagement strategies have been employed. Pioneered by Catholic Community Services of Western Washington, Family Finding was first implemented in 2000. The strategy began attracting national attention in 2003 and was quickly embraced as a promising practice for promoting permanency by the Children's Bureau of the US Administration for Children and Families (Children's Defense Fund 2010; Malm and Allen 2011).

The Family Finding model was designed for children and youth ages 0–25 who have been exposed to chronic trauma and who are disconnected or at risk of disconnection from their families through placement outside of their home and community (California Evidence-Based Clearing House for Child Welfare 2012a). The majority of Family Finding programs target older youth who have been in care for a number of years and have experienced multiple placements. However, the practice is also used with youth who are new to out-of-home care, as well as with youth who are living at home. Family Finding can result in permanent connections for youth who have experienced a series of placements and those who have lost contact with extended family members over the years. Among children who are new to care, Family Finding practices are used to strengthen family supports and promote reunification.

Origin and Theoretical Base

Family Finding is modeled after the diligent search strategies developed by the International Committee of the Red Cross, the United Nations, and the reintegration of children in post-conflict Rwanda (Bissell and Miller n.d.; International Rescue Committee 2003). The roots of Family Finding can be found in Article 32 of the Geneva Convention of 1949, which codified a family's "right to know" what has happened to their relatives as the result of war, political upheaval, or natural disasters (International Committee of the Red Cross 2009). A child's right to know his or her identity and family is also underscored in the provisions of the United Nations Convention on the Rights of the Child (UN General Assembly 1989). These efforts directed toward family reunification for those separated by international conflicts and natural catastrophes have a direct application to children in the foster care system who have lost contact with parents, extended family, and kin as a result of abuse, neglect, and various forms of abandonment.

A basis for Family Finding is found in attachment theory (Ainsworth and Bowlby 1991). Bowlby (1977) described the origin of many forms of emotional distress, such as anxiety, anger, depression, and emotional detachment, as resulting from unwilling separation and loss. Ainsworth (1973) added the concept of the attachment figure as a "secure base" and described varied patterns of attachment (secure, avoidant, anxious, and disorganized) based upon naturalistic observations of mothers and children. Insecure, anxious attachment is typically associated with child maltreatment by the parent or primary caregiver. The parallels between Bowlby's work, the family-tracing strategies embraced by international organizations, and efforts to assure permanent connections for children and families in the foster care system are striking. In 2012, for example, 399,546 children were living in foster care in the United States. The average length of stay in foster care was 22.7 months, and reunification with parent(s), principal caretaker(s), or other relative(s) was the case goal for over half (53 %) of these children (U.S. Department of Health and Human Services 2013). Evidence suggests that the more time children spend in

Table 3.2 Guiding principles for Family Finding

• Finding a family is a youth-driven process
• Every youth deserves, and can have, a permanent family
• Youth have the right to know about their family members; family members have a right to know about their youth
• Youth should have connections with the biological family, regardless of whether they will live with them, unless there is a compelling reason not to
• With support, most youth can live in a home rather than in foster care or institutions
• Family and fictive kin (individuals unrelated by either birth or marriage who have an emotionally significant relationship with another individual) help develop, plan, and bring about the youth's permanence
• The goal of Family Finding is permanency through reunification, guardianship, adoption, or another form of permanent commitment—long-term placement in foster care is not a permanent plan

Adapted from the National Resource Center for Family Centered Practice and Permanency Planning and the California Permanency for Youth Project n.d. Used with permission

foster care, the greater the chance they will change placements, change schools, and lose contact with friends and family (Casey Family Programs 2011).

Studies of former foster youth indicate that many youth end up living with members of their family of origin when they leave out-of-home care, while others grapple with a lack of connection and the absence of potential sources of support as they enter adulthood (Courtney et al. 2004). Empirical evidence (e.g., Rutter et al. 2001) suggests that even later opportunities for attachment can be a positive mediating factor against earlier adversity. Family Finding methodology offers a viable tool for reuniting children with lost and unknown relatives, engaging families in decision making and case planning, and building a sense of belonging among children and families who have been displaced through out-of-home care.

Key Elements

Family Finding is built upon the foundation of achieving permanency and permanent lifelong connections for youth in care. Permanency is both a process and an outcome that includes involvement of the youth as a participant or leader in finding a permanent connection with at least one committed adult who can provide safety, stability, and a secure parenting relationship. The commitment may be in the context of reunification, legal adoption, or guardianship in which the youth has the opportunity to maintain contact with extended family, siblings, and other important persons (California Permanency for Youth Project 2007). Lifelong connections can be established with biological relatives as well as individuals unrelated by birth or marriage who have emotional or personal ties to the youth. The key elements are that the adult enters into an unconditional and enduring parental relationship with the youth and the youth agrees that the adult will assume this role in his or her life.

Guiding principles for Family Finding are shown in Table 3.2 above. It should be noted that Family Finding is an engagement practice and a philosophy of care, not simply a process of locating or identifying family members. The actual finding of

Table 3.3 Goals of Family Finding

• Creation of more options for support and planning
• Engagement of those who know the child best and have a historic and/or inherent connection in helping the child by sharing information and adding support for the child
• Participation of parents, family members, and others important to the child in planning for the successful future of the child or young person
• Enactment of timely decisions to provide the young person with appropriate levels of affection and belonging that are expected to be enduring
• Development of an inclusive, individualized, unconditional, and timely plan to achieve legal and emotional permanency
• Provision of support to the child or young person and their family in planning for and accessing formal and informal support

Adapted from Campbell (2005a). Used with permission

family members is an essential but insufficient component of a broader practice strategy of family connection and support that requires highly developed skills and supervision. Implicit to the model is the team approach, involvement of the youth, and active communication with the child welfare worker. The youth's guardian ad litem or CASA volunteer is often involved as well.

On the surface, the goals of Family Finding appear simple and straightforward. Yet they are complex and difficult to accomplish without aggressive efforts to identify and engage both maternal and paternal relatives, as well as kin. This has particular implication for fathers, who have typically been overlooked in child welfare services and tend to be absent from both investigations and interventions (Coohey and Zang 2006; Risley-Curtiss and Heffernan 2003; Strega et al. 2008). The overarching goals of Family Finding are identified in Table 3.3. Further discussion of the activities leading to each goal is provided in the following section.

Method of Delivery

The descriptions of the Family Finding model that follow are drawn from the emerging base of literature devoted to family finding programs (Allen et al. 2011; Campbell 2005a, b, 2010, 2011; Catholic Community Services of Western Washington and EMQ Children and Family Services 2008; Malm and Allen 2011; National Resource Center for Family Centered Practice and Permanency Planning and the California Permanency for Youth Project n.d.; Williams et al. 2011). Family Finding involves a six-step process that is preceded by a planning phase known as "Setting the Stage." After an extensive case review, a team is formed that consists of professionals and others who know and care about the youth. Team members can include current and former resource parents, teachers, probation officers, behavioral health therapists, tribal contacts, CASA volunteers, guardians ad litem, Independent Living specialists, and youth peers. The youth is a central member of the team, but also has the option of not participating in meetings.

An important component of planning is establishing the parameters for communication and collaboration. Permissions and protocols for contacting family members are discussed, and approval (caregiver consent or judicial order) must be given to the child welfare agency for contacting family members. Safety considerations are paramount, and premature release of the child's whereabouts is avoided. Youth are prepared for the family search and engagement process through developmentally appropriate discussions that include establishing realistic expectations. Unresolved loss and grief issues are often activated as youth begin to work toward permanency, and attention must be paid to the clinical issues that arise related to self-identity, trauma, trust, and security. Henry (2005) has developed a practice model known as "3-5-7" that provides a useful framework for assisting young persons in this process. Using a structured intervention, children are helped to reconcile unresolved losses as they move toward permanency in a family. This involves helping a child to understand life events and to explore the answers to critical questions regarding loss, identity formation, attachment, relationships, and safety (pp. 201, 210).

In summary, the primary goals of the planning phase are to gather as much information about as many family members as possible, orient the team to the process, and assure safety, support, and a voice for the child. This introductory component to the Family Finding model provides a necessary foundation for preparing a child for permanency. The subsequent steps in the Family Finding process are briefly described below. While states and jurisdictions may operationalize the model differently, the descriptions that follow illustrate the key components of Family Finding and the essential elements of the practice.

Step One: Discovery

The intent of discovery is to identify as many family members and significant adults as possible. These individuals can include parents, fictive kin, siblings, step and adoptive siblings, and foster family members. The child is often a source of information and sometimes has information unknown to professionals. Campbell (personal communication 2012) maintains that a minimum of 62 family members should be identified through record reviews, conversations, and the use of free and fee-based websites. Non-Internet sources can also be used to gather information, including birth registries, child support records, coroner records, and records from the Department of Motor Vehicles. A comprehensive list of Family Finding search tools is available on the Seneca Center website (http://www.senecacenter.org).

Parameters for involvement, legalities (including background checks), safety, the youth's specific needs, privacy issues, and logistics are considered as the list of connections to the child is compiled. Agreement is reached regarding next steps in locating and engaging new family members, and decisions are made regarding what information is shared prior to any contacts. Preparation for the first calls or visits with new connections is critical to the success of the engagement efforts.

Step Two: Engagement

At this stage of Family Finding, the support of as many family members and others important to the child as possible is enlisted. The goal at this point is finding information and connections for a youth, not a placement. In-person interviews, phone conversations, and e-mails are used in identifying the child's extended family network. Family members are provided with general information about the youth, and various levels of involvement are explored, such as letters, e-mails, telephone calls, or visits. The adult team members must understand the importance of following through with promises and agreements made to the youth. Campbell (personal communication 2012) recommends that 12 or more family or kin who are willing to take part in a "Blended Perspective Meeting"[1] should be identified at this point.

A strengths-based, solution-focused perspective is helpful both in focusing on the importance of connection and support for the youth and in enlisting the family member as part of the team. Essential engagement skills of empathy, warmth, openness, curiosity, and the ability to communicate respectfully are needed to move the process forward. In practice, the steps of discovery and engagement are not truly independent of one another; they occur simultaneously and represent an overall effort to identify and connect as many family members and kin as possible who may serve as sources of information, support, and lifelong connection for the youth.

Step Three: Planning

At this point, the team moves toward bringing newly identified family members and the youth together. During Blended Perspectives Meetings, individuals join together to form the youth's "Network for Life," a group of individuals constituting the young person's lifelong planning and support team. The youth is prepared for interaction with family members by sharing information, exploring how contact might occur (e.g., phone calls, e-mails, letters, pictures, internet, or in-person visits), and discussing the youth's expectations and concerns. Psychoeducation is provided to family members to enhance an understanding of the social and emotional needs of youth in foster care and how to interpret behavioral expressions of grief, loss, trauma, and disrupted attachment they may see in the youth.

The contact ends with a plan for a follow-up visit or next steps. A contingency arrangement is made in the event that a family member doesn't attend, and debriefing following the visit is arranged. This is the beginning of the process to develop a permanent plan for the youth.

Step Four: Decision Making

The team now enters a process of making timely decisions and developing a plan to provide the youth with lifelong connections and belonging. Often considered the

---

[1] Blended Perspectives Meetings are used to allow family/kin to see how isolated the child/youth/caregiver is, to identify strengths and needs of the child/youth/caregiver, to identify the overarching need in a young person's or family's life, and to identify the individuals who will be active members of the child's lifelong support network. They are not forums for decision making.

most difficult part of the Family Finding process, decision making occurs as the relationship between the youth and the family is developing. The role of professionals on the team is to coach and support the emerging relationship, while also pursuing a larger network of connections for the youth. Concurrent planning is an important aspect of the work as the youth and/or family may have second thoughts, unanticipated life events may occur, and other family connections for the youth may emerge through the ongoing search process.

Plans involving reunification, adoption, guardianship, kinship care, and other formal commitments must all be developed in collaboration with the courts and the child welfare system. The team identifies timelines, resources, needs, and backup plans in order to evaluate permanent possibilities for the youth. Placements without legal permanency are not considered a successful decision. A support plan is put in place to assist in the transition and manage relationships with biological parents, siblings, and others who may interact with the youth. Backup plans involving family members and other adults are created so that at least three additional options are available if the primary plan is unsuccessful. A commitment is made to reconvene the team in the event that challenges arise.

Step Five: Evaluation

The individualized plan is reviewed by the team and evaluated for its ability to achieve legal and emotional permanency. The support and backup plans put in place during the Decision Making stage are monitored, and the team's commitment to reconvene in the event of challenges is assessed. Success for this stage of Family Finding is defined as how well formal supports can decrease their presence in the family's life. Through assuring that proper natural and community supports are in place, the professional staff become less central and provide less assistance as the family moves forward.

Step Six: Follow-Up on Supports

As this point, the youth is either living with family, on the verge of living with family, in another permanent situation, or has established new family or long-term connections. Efforts are directed toward preparing the new family team to be self-sustaining by equipping them with plans for resolving legal, financial, safety, and future challenges. Sustaining access to services, supports, and key relationships is needed to ensure stability.

Success in this stage is measured by the family's ability to take the primary role in sustaining a permanent relationship with the youth. Measures of achievement are different for every child. For some youth, the introduction to previously unknown family members and/or reconnection with lost relatives can help to establish a realistic picture of the family. For others, increasing the number of months the youth can live successfully with family is a positive result. A return to foster care is not considered an optimal outcome. Youth are supported in developing an understanding of the capabilities, and the limitations, of family members.

Evidence Base

Family Finding is a promising child welfare practice that is supported by studies of placement stability, which demonstrate that care in relative placement is almost twice as stable as care with nonrelatives (see Chamberlain et al. 2006; Farmer 2009; James et al. 2004; National Resource Center for Family Centered Practice and Permanency Planning and the California Permanency for Youth Project n.d.; Proctor et al. 2011; Rubin et al. 2008). Preliminary results from an experimental study by Landsman and Boel-Studt (2011) indicate that youth receiving Family Finding had greater involvement of family, kin, and informal supports in their lives and a higher likelihood of reunification or relative placement compared with those receiving standard child welfare services. These findings are echoed in the evaluation results of a 3-year, federally funded Family Connection Demonstration Project conducted in the state of Washington (Applied Research Center for Strong Communities and Schools 2012; TriWest Group 2012). Intensive Family Finding services were found to be effective in establishing familial connections for over three-quarters of youth and helped to improve permanency and stability for these young persons.

Efforts to build the evidence base for Family Finding are underway. Because it is a relatively new practice, few effectiveness studies have been completed, although a significant amount of practice evidence shows that Family Finding has a positive impact on securing connections for youth and decreasing the number of children in foster care. Several states have incorporated Family Finding into best practice models for judges and child welfare professionals as a result of an increased focus on permanency and safe reduction of placements in the courts (e.g., Pennsylvania's Permanency Practice Initiative: http://www.ocfcpacourts.us).

Qualitative findings from a multisite study of focus groups held with youth, parents, and relatives participating in Family Finding indicate that participants perceive benefits as well as challenges with the intervention. Positive outcomes noted by both youth and adults include the discovery of new family members, the expansion of a support network, and a decrease in feelings of isolation and abandonment. Concerns include anxiety, trusting unknown family members, the pace and timing of the engagement efforts, and sustaining connections over time (Bringewatt et al. 2013).

A controlled process and outcome study involving random assignment to Family Finding or services as usual is currently in progress in five states. Qualitative evaluation findings from two of these sites indicate that Family Finding interventions may be best initiated early in the investigation process and that the strengthening of family bonds may be a better measure of successful outcome than legal permanence (Malm and Allen 2011). Recent discretionary grants requiring an effectiveness study of the practice will add to the evidence base (see http://www.childtrends.org). Campbell (2011) has released a Family Finding Quality and Fidelity Index to measure adherence to the model.

Family Finding: The Case of Carla *Carla is an 18-year-old African American female about to graduate from high school and soon to enter a world of unknowns. Now a senior in high school, Carla lives in a group home and is contemplating her options: enroll in college while continuing to live in the group home, move out of the group home, and/or leave the child welfare system. No option seems easy and Carla doesn't feel prepared for any of them.*

Carla was just 2 years old when she entered the child welfare system. She was placed with Mavis, a resource parent, with whom she stayed for the next 4 years. Carla's younger sister and brother also came to live with Mavis. At the age of six, Carla was adopted and left Mavis' care. She has vague memories of leaving Mavis and her siblings. Carla's adoptive family changed her name and moved her across the state. Mavis tried to stay in touch with Carla, but their contact discontinued over time. There were difficulties within Carla's adoptive family and Carla left home at age 15. After moving in with a friend, Carla experienced problems that led to several brief hospitalizations and an admission to a youth correctional center. Placement in the group home followed.

Several months ago, Carla's child welfare worker, JoAnne, initiated a Family Finding process with Carla to identify relatives or other close adults who might be sources of support and connection for her. They began by doing a "mobility mapping" exercise that involved sketching a tree on poster board and writing down on the tree's branches the names of kin within three degrees of consanguinity, friends, resource parents, and adults who had significance to Carla. Mavis was one of the people who Carla identified. Over the next several months, Carla reached out to family and friends with JoAnne's assistance.

Now, JoAnne plans and prepares for Carla to meet with Mavis at her home. When Carla arrives back at her first foster home, she finds handprints in the sidewalk that she had made in wet cement as a child. Next to those handprints is Carla's previous name. Mavis shares pictures of Carla as a baby and tells her stories of her childhood. Mavis also reveals that Carla's birth mother recently had another child and that Mavis' adult daughter, Barbara, has adopted the baby.

Carla and Mavis reconnect after almost a dozen years of separation, reestablishing a relationship that had weakened due to complicated circumstances. Carla reconnects with her former foster sister and discovers a new sibling. She also tracks down her mother and finds her to be in the same unstable condition as she had been almost 16 years earlier when Carla went into care. However, Carla has the skill to manage this aspect of her family life. She is able to view her mother's difficulties more realistically and with a sense of compassion. She is able to acknowledge what her mother couldn't provide. Most importantly, Carla validates her early history and rekindles a relationship with Mavis that will serve as a permanent connection.[2]

Conclusions

Engagement with families involved in the child welfare system is challenging for even the most seasoned professionals. Opportunities to impact the lives of children and families in crisis, to improve a family's capacity to care for their children, and to enhance a young person's options for permanency rest upon the ability to engage clients in a meaningful partnership. Workers who operate from a strengths-based, solution-focused perspective are able to see opportunities for change in even the most complicated family situations and understand that establishing a meaningful connection is the first step in addressing difficult life issues. The ability to suspend

---

[2] Adapted from (Gibson 2011).

quick judgments, recognize one's own frame of reference, respect differences, and anticipate challenges are key engagement skills when using any model of intervention. To effectively engage families as partners, child welfare workers must be prepared to share power, ask for and use feedback, and see themselves as coaches or mentors who stand beside families and not in front of them. "Engagement" in the manner described here reflects a guiding principle of practice and a philosophy of service, rather than a discrete set of tools or a specific process.

Family engagement practices such as Family Group Decision Making and Family Finding can help to transform the child welfare system of care from one of legal authority over families to one of partnership with families. As these practices mature and become more widely disseminated, one measure of success will be the adoption of the individual practice principles into a community philosophy. Integration of the practices into traditional child welfare services will provide families with opportunities to assume control of their lives, as well as more options for child welfare professionals to engage in supportive interventions that are likely to increase job satisfaction.

Questions for Discussion

1. What are some small but meaningful steps that workers can take to help children and families view the child welfare system as having something positive to offer them?
2. Think carefully about your own family history. What kind of family structure did you grow up in? Who raised you and who played an important role in your life? Who was missing? What kind of exposure did you have to issues such as poverty, substance abuse, mental illness, interpersonal or community violence, and traumatic loss? Did you grow up in a diverse social context or one that was largely comprised of individuals from your own racial, ethnic, and/or religious background? Consider how these issues in your own life may impact your work with clients receiving child welfare services.
3. How might the cases of Justin and Carla have turned out differently if Family Group Decision Making and Family Finding had not been used as interventions?
4. How might the widespread implementation of family engagement principles and practices within child welfare impact the job satisfaction of workers? How would the child welfare agency environment be impacted if the principles of family engagement were integrated into the everyday life of the organization?

Acknowledgements The authors thank Gene Detter, Wendy Unger, and Rob Winesickle of the Pennsylvania Child Welfare Resource Center for their contributions to this chapter.

The case of Carla was adapted from the story of Jasmine Winters, written by Elizabeth Gibson of *The Patriot-News*, Mechanicsburg, PA. The authors thank Eva Domalski of Dauphin County Children and Youth Services for her work with Jasmine.

References

Ainsworth, M. D. S. (1973). The development of infant–mother attachment. *Review of Child Development Research, 3,* 1–94.

Ainsworth, M. D. S., & Bowlby, J. (1991). An ethological approach to personality development. *American Psychologist, 46,* 331–341.

Allen, T., Malm, K., Williams, S. C., & Ellis, R. (2011). *Putting together the puzzle: Tips and techniques for effective discovery in family finding (Publication No. 2011–31).* Washington, DC: Child Trends. Retrieved from http://familyfinding.org/resourcesandpublications.html.

Altman, J. C. (2005). Engagement in children, youth, and family services: Current research and best practices. In G. Mallon & P. Hess (Eds.), *Child welfare for the twenty-first century: A handbook of practices, policies and programs* (pp. 72–86). New York: Columbia University Press.

Altman, J. C. (2008). A study of engagement in neighborhood-based child welfare services. *Research on Social Work Practice, 18*(6), 555–564.

American Humane Association. (2008). *Family Group Decision Making in child welfare: Purpose, values and processes.* Retrieved from http://www.americanhumane.org/fgdm.

American Humane Association. (2009). *A compilation of state and provincial laws, policies, rules and regulations on Family Group Decision Making and other family engagement approaches in child welfare decision making.* Retrieved from http://www.americanhumane.org/fgdm.

American Humane Association. (2010). *Guidelines for Family Group Decision Making in child welfare.* Englewood, CO: Author.

Anderson, C. M., & Stewart, S. (1982). *Mastering resistance.* New York: Guilford.

Antle, B. F., Christensen, D. N., van Zyl, M. A., & Barbee, A. P. (2012). The impact of the Solution Based Casework practice model on federal outcomes in public child welfare. *Child Abuse and Neglect, 36*(4), 342–353.

Appleby, G. A., Colon, E., & Hamilton, J. (2007). *Diversity, oppression, and social functioning: A person-in-environment assessment and intervention.* Boston: Pearson/Allyn and Bacon.

Applied Research Center for Strong Communities and Schools (2012). *Family connection demonstration project: Supplemental evaluation report.* Prepared by Michelle M. Maike, Gregory J. Benner and D. Scarsella. Tacoma, WA: University of Washington Tacoma. Retrieved from http://familyfinding.org/resourcesandpublications.html

Barn, R., Das, C., & Sawyerr, A. (2009). *Family group conferences and black and minority ethnic families: An evaluation study of two community-based organisations in London.* London: Family Rights Group.

Bell, M., & Wilson, K. (2006). Children's views of family group conferences. *British Journal of Social Work, 36,* 671–681.

Bellamy, J. L. (2009). A national study of male involvement among families in contact with the child welfare system. *Child Maltreatment, 14*(3), 255–262.

Berg, I. K., & Kelly, S. (2000). *Building solutions in child protective services.* New York: Norton.

Berger, L. M. (2007). Socioeconomic factors and substandard parenting. *Social Service Review, 81*(3), 485–522.

Berzin, S. C. (2006). Using sibling data to understand the impact of family group decision making on child welfare outcomes. *Children and Youth Services Review, 28,* 1449–1458.

Bickman, L., Vides de Andrade, A. R., Lambert, E. W., Doucette, A., Sapyta, J., Boyd, A. S., & Rauktis, M. E. (2004). Youth therapeutic alliance in intensive treatment settings. *Journal of Behavioral Health and Services Research, 31*(2), 134–148.

Bissell, M. & Miller, J. (n.d.). *Background on family finding.* Retrieved from http://www.childfocuspartners.com

Bowlby, J. (1977). The making and breaking of affectional bonds. I. Aetiology and psychopathology in the light of attachment theory. An expanded version of the Fiftieth Maudsley Lecture, delivered before the Royal College of Psychiatrists, 19 November 1976. *British Journal of Psychiatry, 130*(3), 201–210.

Brady, B. (2006). *Facilitating family decision making: A study of the family welfare conference service in the HSE Western Area*. Galway, Ireland: National University of Ireland, Department of Political Science and Health Service Executive, Child & Family Research and Policy Unit. Retrieved from http://www.childandfamilyresearch.ie/documents/fwcfinal report.pdf.

Bringewatt, E., Allen, T., & Williams, S. C. (2013). *Client voices: Youth, parent and relative perspectives on Family Finding (Publication No. 2013–23)*. Bethesda, MD: Child Trends. Retrieved from http://familyfinding.org/resourcesandpublications.html.

Brodie, K. (2008). *Family group conference: An exploratory study describing the relationship between an internal agency environment and the process*. Unpublished doctoral dissertation, Howard University, Washington, D.C.

Buckley, H., Carr, N., & Whelan, S. (2011). "Like walking on eggshells": Service user views and expectations of the child protection system. *Child and Family Social Work, 16*(1), 101–110.

Burford, G. (2000). Advancing innovations: Family Group Decision Making as community-centered child and family work. *Protecting Children, 16*(3), 4–20.

Burford, G., Connolly, M., Morris, K., & Pennell, J. (2010). *Family engagement strategies in child welfare international review: Annotated bibliography*. American Humane Association. Retrieved from http://www.americanhumane.org/protecting-children/programs/family-group-decision-making.

California Evidence-Based Clearing House for Child Welfare (2012a). *Family Finding*. Retrieved from http://www.cebc4cw.org/program/family-finding/detailed

California Evidence-Based Clearing House for Child Welfare (2012b.). *Family Group Decision Making (FGDM)*. Retrieved from http://www.cebc4cw.org/program/family-group-decision-making/

California Permanency for Youth Project. (2007). *Definition of permanency/permanent lifelong connection*. Retrieved from http://www.senecacenter.org/perm_permanency_def

Campbell, K. (2005a). *Goals of Family Finding*. Used with permission by the Pennsylvania Child Welfare Training Program.

Campbell, K. (2005b). *Six steps for family finding*. Center for Family Finding and Youth Connectedness. Retrieved from http://www.senecacenter.org/familyfinding/resources

Campbell, K. (2010). *Basic family finding practice scaffold*. National Institute for Permanent Family Connectedness, Seneca Center. Retrieved from http://www.senecacenter.org/familyfinding/resources

Campbell, K. D. (2011). *Family Finding Quality/Fidelity Index*, Version 4. Retrieved from http://www.iowacourtsonline.org/wfdata/frame11866-2115/File3.pdf

Casey Family Programs. (2011). *Ensuring safe, nurturing and permanent families for children: Foster care reductions and child safety*. Seattle, WA: Author. Retrieved from http://www.casey.org.

Catholic Community Services of Western Washington and EMQ Children and Family Services. (2008). *Family search and engagement: A comprehensive practice guide*. Retrieved from http://www.ccsww.org/site/DocServer/Family_Search_and_Engagement_Guide_CCS-EMQ.pdf?docID=641

Ceballo, R., & McLoyd, V. C. (2002). Social support and parenting in poor, dangerous neighborhoods. *Child Development, 73*(4), 1310–1321.

Center for Social Services Research. (2004). *The California Title IV-E child welfare waiver demonstration study evaluation: Final report May 31, 2004*. Retrieved from http://cssr.berkeley.edu/childwelfare/projectdetails.asp?name=waiver

Chamberlain, P., Price, J. M., Reid, J. B., Landsverk, J., Fisher, P. A., & Stoolmiller, M. (2006). Who disrupts from placement in foster and kinship care? *Child Abuse & Neglect, 30*(4), 409–424.

Child Welfare Information Gateway. (2010). *Family engagement*. Retrieved from http://www.childwelfare.gov/pubs/f_fam_engagement/

Children's Defense Fund. (2010). *Promising approaches in child welfare: Helping connect children and youth in foster care to permanent family and relationships through Family Finding and engagement*. Retrieved from http://www.childrensdefense.org/child-research-data-publications/data/promising-approaches.pdf

Connolly, M. (2006). Up front and personal: Confronting dynamics in the family group conference. *Family Process, 45*(3), 345–357.

Coohey, C., & Zang, Y. (2006). The role of men in chronic supervisory neglect. *Child Maltreatment, 11*(1), 27–33.

Courtney, M. E., Terao, S., & Bost, N. (2004). *Midwest evaluation of the adult functioning of former foster youth: Conditions of youth preparing to leave state care.* Chicago: University of Chicago, Chapin Hall Center for Children. Retrieved from http://www.chapinhall.uchicago.edu.

Crampton, D. (2007). Research review: Family group decision-making: A Promising practice in need of more programme theory and research. *Child and Family Social Work, 12*(2), 202–209.

Crampton, D. S., Crea, T. M., Abramson-Madden, A., & Usher, C. L. (2008). Challenges of street-level child welfare reform and technology transfer: The case of team decision making. *Families in Society, 89*(4), 512–520.

Crampton, D., & Jackson, W. (2007). Family group decision making and disproportionality in foster care: A case study. *Child Welfare, 86*(3), 52–69.

Crea, T. M., & Berzin, S. C. (2009). Family involvement in child welfare decision-making: Strategies and research on inclusive practices. *Journal of Public Child Welfare, 3*, 305–327.

Crosier, T., Butterworth, P., & Rodgers, B. (2007). Mental health problems among single and partnered mothers: The role of financial hardship and social support. *Social Psychiatry and Psychiatric Epidemiology, 42*(1), 6–13.

Dale, P. (2004). "Like in a fish bowl": Parents' perceptions of child protection services. *Child Abuse Review, 13*(2), 137–157.

Darlington, Y., Healy, K., Yellowlees, J., & Bosly, F. (2012). Parents' perceptions of their participation in mandated family group meetings. *Children and Youth Services Review, 34*(2), 331–337.

Dawson, K., & Berry, M. (2002). Engaging families in child welfare services: An evidence-based approach to best practice. *Child Welfare, 81*(2), 293–317.

DeGarmo, D. S., & Forgatch, M. S. (2005). Early development of delinquency within divorced families: Evaluating a randomized preventive intervention trial. *Developmental Science, 3*, 229–239.

Diorio, W. (1992). Parental perceptions of the authority of public child welfare caseworkers. *Families in Society: The Journal of Contemporary Human Services, 4*, 222–235.

Dumbrill, G. (2006). Parental experience of child protection intervention: A qualitative study. *Child Abuse and Neglect, 30*(1), 27–37.

Dyer, W. J. (2005). Prison, fathers, and identity: A theory of how incarceration affects men's paternal identity. *Fathering, 3*(3), 201–219.

Edin, K., & Kissane, R. J. (2010). Poverty and the American family: A decade in review. *Journal of Marriage and Family, 72*(3), 460–479.

Edwards, M., Tinworth, K., Burford, G., & Pennell, J. (2007). *Family team meeting (FTM) process, outcome and impact evaluation phase II report.* Englewood, CO: American Humane Association.

Farmer, E. (2009). How do placements in kinship care compare with those in non-kin foster care: Placement patterns, progress and outcomes? *Child & Family Social Work, 14*(3), 331–342.

Feder, A., Alonso, A., Tang, M., Liriano, W., Warner, V., Pilowsky, D., & Weissman, M. M. (2009). Children of low-income depressed mothers: Psychiatric disorders and social adjustment. *Depression and Anxiety, 26*(6), 513–520.

Ferguson, H. H. (2001). Promoting child protection, welfare and healing: The case for developing best practice. *Child & Family Social Work, 6*(1), 1–12.

Figley, C. R. (Ed.). (1995). *Compassion fatigue: Coping with secondary traumatic stress disorder in those who treat the traumatized.* New York: Brunner/Mazel.

Gallagher, M., Smith, M., Wosu, H., Stewart, J., Hunter, S., Cree, V. E., & Wilkinson, H. (2011). Engaging with families in child protection: Lessons from practitioner research in Scotland. *Child Welfare, 90*(4), 117–134.

Gibson, E. (2011). Jasmine Winters, 18, is outgrowing foster are, but is leaving with family-like support network. *The Patriot News*, July 7. Retrieved from http://www.pennlive.com/midstate/index.ssf/2011/07/jasmine_winters_18_is_outgrowi.html

Haight, W., Black, J., Mangelsdorf, S., Giorgio, G., Tata, L., Schoppe, S., & Szewczyk, M. (2002). Making visits better: The perspectives of parents, foster parents, and child welfare workers. *Child Welfare, 81*(2), 173–202.

Haight, W. L., Mangelsdorf, S., Black, J., Szewczyk, M., Schoppe, S., Giorgio, G., & Tata, L. (2005). Enhancing parent–child interaction during foster care visits: Experimental assessment of an intervention. *Child Welfare, 84*(4), 459–482.

Hartman, A. (1988). Foreword. In R.A. Dorfman (Ed.), (pp. vii–ix). New York: Bruner/Mazel

Hassall, I. (1996). Origin and development of family group conferences. In J. Hudson, A. Morris, G. Maxwell, & B. Galaway (Eds.), *Family group conferences: Perspectives on policy and practice* (pp. 17–36). Monsey, NY: Willow Tree Press.

Henry, D. (2005). The 3-5-7 model: Preparing children for permanency. *Children and Youth Services Review, 27*, 197–212.

Hepworth, D. H., Rooney, R. H., Rooney, G. D., Strom-Gottfried, K., & Larsen, J. (2010). *Direct social work practice: Theory and skills* (8th ed.). Belmont, CA: Brooks/Cole.

Hewitt, N. M., Crane, B., & Mooney, B. (2010). The Family Development Credential Program: A synthesis of outcome research on an empowerment-based human service training program. *Families in Society, 91*(1), 76–84.

Hudson, J., Morris, A., Maxwell, G., & Galaway, N. (Eds.). (1996). *Family group conferences: Perspectives on policy and practice*. Monsey, NY: Willow Tree Press.

International Committee of the Red Cross. (2009). *Restoring family links strategy including legal references*. Geneva, Switzerland: Author.

International Rescue Committee. (2003). *Family reunification, alternative care and community reintegration of separated children in post-conflict Rwanda*. New York: Author.

Jack, S. M., DiCenso, A., & Lohfeld, L. (2005). A theory of maternal engagement with public health users and family visitors. *Journal of Advanced Nursing, 49*(2), 182–190.

James, S., Landsverk, J., & Slymen, D. J. (2004). Placement movement in out-of-home care: Patterns and predictors. *Children and Youth Services Review, 26*(2), 185–206.

Johnson, W. E. (2001). Paternal involvement among unwed fathers. *Children and Youth Services Review, 23*(6–7), 513–536.

Landsman, M. D., & Boel-Studt, S. (2011). Fostering families' and children's rights to family connections. *Child Welfare, 90*(4), 19–40.

Magennis, R., & Smith, D. B. (2005). All used up: Factors associated with burnout among Missouri social service workers. *Missouri Electronic Journal of Sociology, 5*, 1–33. Retrieved from http://www.mosoc.org/MEJS/mejs.htm.

Mallon, G. P. (2011). Meaningful family engagement. *Child Welfare, 90*(4), 5–7.

Malm, K., & Allen, T. (2011). *Family Finding: Does implementation differ when serving different child welfare populations? (Publication No. 2011–27)*. Washington, DC: Child Trends.

Maluccio, A. N., & Daly, J. (2000). Family group conferences as "good" child welfare practice. In G. Burford & J. Hudson (Eds.), *Family group conferencing: New directions in community-centered child and family practice* (pp. 65–71). New York: Aldine de Gruyter.

McBeath, B., Briggs, H. E., & Aisenberg, E. (2009). The role of child welfare managers in promoting agency performance through experimentation. *Children and Youth Services Review, 31*, 112–118.

Merkel-Holguin, L. (2003). Promising results, potential new directions: International FGDM research and evaluation in child welfare [Special issue]. *Protecting Children, 18*(1–2), 2–11.

Mosley, J. & Smith, D. B. (2004). *A preliminary evaluation of the Missouri Family Development Training and Credentialing Program*. Retrieved from http://ipp.missouri.edu/files/ipp/attachments/a_preliminary_evaluation_of_the_missouri_family_development_training_and_credentialing_program.pdf

National Resource Center for Family Centered Practice and Permanency Planning and the California Permanency for Youth Project (n.d.). *Six steps to find a family: A practical guide to family search and engagement*. Written by Mardith J. Louisell. Retrieved from http://www.nrcpfc.org/downloads/SixSteps.pdf

O'Donnell, J. M., Johnson, W. E., D'Aunno, L. E., & Thornton, H. L. (2005). Fathers in child welfare: Caseworkers' perspectives. *Child Welfare, 84*(3), 387–414.

Ollendick, T. H., & King, N. J. (2012). Evidence-based treatments for children and adolescents: Issues and commentary. In P. C. Kendall (Ed.), *Child and adolescent therapy: Cognitive-behavioral approaches* (4th ed., pp. 499–519). New York: Guilford.

Olson, K. B. (2009). Family group conferencing and child protection mediation: Essential tools for prioritizing family engagement in child welfare cases. *Family Court Review, 47*(1), 53–68.

Pennell, J. (2005a). Widening the circle. In J. Pennell & G. Anderson (Eds.), *Widening the circle: The practice and evolution of family group conferencing with children, youths, and their families* (pp. 1–8). Washington, DC: NASW Press.

Pennell, J. (2005b). Before the conference-promoting family leadership. In J. Pennell & G. Anderson (Eds.), *Widening the circle: The practice and evolution of family group conferencing with children, youths, and their families* (pp. 13–32). Washington, DC: NASW Press.

Pennell, J., & Anderson, G. (2005). Preface. In J. Pennell & G. Anderson (Eds.), *Widening the circle: The practice and evolution of family group conferencing with children, youths, and their families* (p. xi). Washington, DC: NASW Press.

Pennell, J., & Burford, G. (2000). Family group decision making and family violence. In G. Burford & J. Hudson (Eds.), *Family group conferencing: New directions in community-centered child and family practice* (pp. 171–185). New York: Aldine de Gruyter.

Pennell, J., Edwards, M., & Burford, G. (2010). Expedited family group engagement and child permanency. *Children and Youth Services Review, 32*(7), 1012–1019.

Pennell, J. (with the assistance of Hardison, J., & Yerkes, E.). (1999). North Carolina Family Group Conferencing Project: Building partnerships with and around families: Report to the North Carolina Division of Social Services, Fiscal year 1998–1999. Raleigh: North Carolina State University, Social Work Program, North Carolina Family Group Conferencing Project.

Perlman, H. H. (1957). *Social casework*. Chicago: The University of Chicago Press.

Perrino, T., Coatsworth, J. D., Briones, E., Pantin, H., & Szapocznik, J. (2001). Initial engagement in parent-centered preventive interventions: A family systems perspective. *Journal of Primary Prevention, 22*(1), 21–44.

Proctor, L. J., Van Dusen Randazzo, K., Litrownik, A. J., Newton, R. R., Davis, I. P., & Villodas, M. (2011). Factors associated with caregiver stability in permanent placements: A classification tree approach. *Child Abuse & Neglect, 35*(6), 425–436.

Rapport, J. (1987). Terms of empowerment/exemplars of prevention: Toward a theory for community psychology. *American Journal of Community Psychology, 15*, 121–148.

Rauktis, M. E. (2008). *Family Group Decision Making: A profile of practices in Pennsylvania 2008*. University of Pittsburgh, Child Welfare Training Program. Retrieved from http://www.pacwcbt.pitt.edu/FGDM_EvaluationPage.htm

Rauktis, M. E., Huefner, J., & Cahalane, H. (2011). Perceptions of fidelity to family group decision making principles: Examining the impact of race, gender and relationship. *Child Welfare, 90*(4), 41–59.

Rauktis, M. E., McCarthy, S., Krackhardt, D., & Cahalane, H. G. (2010). Innovation in child welfare: The adoption and implementation of Family Group Decision Making in Pennsylvania. *Children and Youth Services Review, 32*(5), 732–739.

Risley-Curtiss, C., & Heffernan, K. (2003). Gender biases in child welfare. *Affilia, 18*(4), 395–410.

Rooney, R. H. (2009). *Strategies for work with involuntary clients* (2nd ed.). New York: Columbia University Press.

Rubin, D., Downes, K. J., O'Reilly, A. L. R., Mekonnen, R., Luan, X., & Localio, R. (2008). Impact of kinship care on behavioral well-being for children in out-of-home care. *Archives of Pediatrics & Adolescent Medicine, 162*(6), 550–556.

Rutter, M., Kreppner, J., & O'Conner, T. G. (2001). Specificity and heterogeneity in children's responses to profound institutional privation. *British Journal of Psychiatry, 179*, 97–103.

Saleebey, D. (Ed.). (1997). *The strengths perspective in social work practice* (2nd ed.). New York: Longman.

Sheets, J., Wittenstrom, K., Fong, R., James, J., Tecci, M., Baumann, D. J., & Rodriguez, C. (2009). Evidence-based practice in family group decision-making for Anglo, African American and Hispanic families. *Children and Youth Services Review, 31*(11), 1187–1191.

Shore, N., Wirth, J., Cahn, K., Yancey, B., & Gunderson, K. (2002). Long term and immediate outcomes of family group conferencing in Washington state (June 2001). Retrieved from http://www.iirp.edu/iirpWebsites/web/uploads/article_pdfs/fgcwash.pdf

Smith, D. B. (2009). Change in frontline family workers' burnout and job satisfaction: Evaluating the Missouri Family Development Credential Program. *Professional Development: The International Journal of Continuing Social Work Education, 12*(1), 51–60.

Smith, D. B., McCarthy, M., Hill, J. N., & Mosley, J. (2007). *Changes in frontline family workers: Results from the Missouri Family Development Credential program evaluation.* University of Missouri-Kansas City Family Studies Program Research Report 2007–01. Retrieved from http://www.fdc-pa.org/resources/MO_research_article.pdf

Sprang, G., Craig, C., & Clark, J. (2011). Secondary traumatic stress and burnout in child welfare workers: A comparative analysis of occupational distress across professional groups. *Child Welfare, 90*(6), 149–168.

Spratt, T., & Callan, J. (2004). Parents' views on social work interventions in child welfare cases. *British Journal of Social Work, 34*(2), 199–244.

Strega, S., Fleet, C., Brown, L., Dominelli, L., Callahan, M., & Walmsley, C. (2008). Connecting father absence and mother blame in child welfare policies and practice. *Children and Youth Services Review, 30*(7), 705–716.

Sue, D. W. (2010). *Microaggressions in everyday life: Race, gender, and sexual orientation.* Hoboken, NJ: Wiley.

TriWest Group (2012). *Family connections demonstration project final progress report.* Submitted to Catholic Family and Child Service by Tonya Aultman-Bettridge and Peter Selby. Boulder, CO: author. Retrieved from http://familyfinding.org/resourcesandpublications.html

UN General Assembly, *Convention on the Rights of the Child*, 20 November 1989, United Nations, Treaty Series, vol. 1577, p.3, available at: http://www.unhcr.org.refworld/docid/3ae6b38f0.html

U.S. Department of Health and Human Services, Administration for Children and Families, Administration on Children, Youth and Families, Children's Bureau. (2013). *The AFCARS Report. Preliminary FY 2012 estimates as of July 2013(20).* Retrieved from: http://www.acf.hhs.gov/sites/default/files/cb/afcarsreport20.pdf

Wang, E. W., Lambert, M. C., Johnson, L. E., Boudreau, B., Breidenbach, R., & Baumann, D. (2012). Expediting permanent placement from foster care systems: The role of family group decision making. *Children and Youth Services Review, 34*(4), 845–850.

Watzlawick, P. (1993). *The language of change: Elements of therapeutic communication.* New York: W.W. Norton.

Weigensburg, E. C., Barth, R. P., & Guo, S. (2009). Family group decision making: A propensity score analysis to evaluate child and family services at baseline and after 36-months. *Children and Youth Services Review, 31*(3), 383–390.

Weisz, V., Korpas, A., & Wingrove, T. (2006). *Nebraska family group conferencing: Evaluation report.* Lincoln, NE: University of Nebraska, UN-L Center on Children, Families, and the Law, Nebraska Court Improvement Project.

Williams, S. C., Malm, K., Allen, T., & Ellis, R. (2011). *Bringing family to the table: Tips and techniques for effective family engagement (Publication No. 2011–32).* Washington, DC: Child Trends. Retrieved from http://familyfinding.org/resourcesandpublications.html.

Yatchmenoff, D. (2005). Measuring client engagement from the client's perspective in nonvoluntary child protective services. *Research on Social Work Practice, 15*(2), 84–96.

Zahn, M., & Pandy, S. (2004). Economic well-being of single mothers: Work first or postsecondary education? *Journal of Sociology and Social Welfare, 31*(3), 87–112.

Zimmerman, M. A. (2000). Empowerment theory: Psychological, organizational and community levels of analysis. In J. Rappaport & E. Seidman (Eds.), *Handbook of community psychology* (pp. 43–63). Dordrecht, Netherlands: Kluwer Academic Publishers.

Chapter 4
Permanency

Caroline Donohue, Cynthia Bradley-King, and Helen Cahalane

Abstract Permanency for children and youth in the child welfare system can take many forms, involving biological family members, relatives, fictive kin, adoptive families, or long-term foster families. When the decision is made to remove a child from parents who are unable to provide essentials of life or safety, it is important to keep in mind what many parents offer to their children. The strong affection that many parents feel for their children is a positive emotion that can form the basis for parental behavior changes necessary in order to maintain or create a safe environment for the child. These changes may sustain family preservation or enable family reunification.

Reunification, legal guardianship (with and without subsidy), and adoption all provide permanency options for young people that can promote a long-term sense of connectedness. Post-placement services and aftercare can provide concrete support and assurance to youth and families by increasing opportunities for stability. Community-wide interventions can address the larger systemic support necessary for all families and children to grow and thrive. However, it is clear that none of these placements, services, or efforts at larger scale community building can flourish in the absence of a committed federal effort to reorganize child welfare financing. Only with adequate federal funding can child welfare agencies direct resources toward early intervention, offer services to maintain the bonds of connection between children and families when possible, and provide both concrete and instrumental resources that ensure the well-being of youth and their caregivers.

Keywords Permanence • Family preservation • Reunification • Legal guardianship • Adoption • Kinship • Foster care • Concurrent planning

C. Donohue (✉) • C. Bradley-King • H. Cahalane
Child Welfare Education and Research Programs, School of Social Work,
University of Pittsburgh, Pittsburgh, PA, USA
e-mail: carolinedonohue6@gmail.com

H. Cahalane (ed.), *Contemporary Issues in Child Welfare Practice*,
Contemporary Social Work Practice, DOI 10.1007/978-1-4614-8627-5_4,
© Springer Science+Business Media New York 2013

Introduction

According to the Child Welfare Information Gateway:

The concept of permanency is based on certain values, including the primacy of family, significance of biological families, and the importance of parent–child attachment. Research has shown us that children grow up best in nurturing, stable families. These families:

- Offer commitment and continuity—they survive life's challenges intact.
- Have legal status—parents have the legal right and responsibility to protect their children's interests and welfare.
- Have members who share a common future—their fates are intertwined (n.d.).

Without question, establishing permanency in living situations for children is a guiding ideal for child welfare practice (Mather et al. 2007). Establishing a permanent home for a child in foster care who lacks one is central to the child's life and must be treated with the same urgency as providing food, clothing, education, and health care. We understand that permanence in a child's living situation and the opportunity for the child to form and maintain deep attachment to caretaker(s) must be present to ensure the child's optimal physical and emotional growth and health (Szalavitz and Perry 2010). The absence of a permanent home and the lack of a consistent caretaker appear to result in deficits in development which may not be fully recoverable (Szalavitz and Perry 2010).

Attachment and Relationships

Animal research showing the damage to infants deprived of a familiar, comforting caregiver was popularized by Harry Harlow in the late 1950s and early 1960s, and similar effects on human infants have been hypothesized. The most extreme examples of lack of care in Harlow's experiments were baby rhesus monkeys who received no physical contact and were fed via bottles attached to monkey-shaped wire frames. These infants were photographed huddled helpless and alone in their cages and were deeply damaged in almost all aspects of life, especially in their fear of any unfamiliar stimulus and their lack of ability to interact socially (Harlow and Mears 1979). Other rhesus infants were given terrycloth-covered effigies in addition to the milk-giving "wire mothers." These babies clung persistently to their "terrycloth mothers," although these surrogates provided no food. The babies only briefly visited the wire effigies in order to feed. Harlow's experiments have had a lasting impact on the field of developmental psychology at least in part because we cannot help but compare the plight of these baby primates to that of neglected human babies.

The clear preference of the baby monkeys for the cloth-covered but milkless figure over the wire milk-giving figure reveals what Harlow called the need for contact comfort, an important aspect of nurture for the monkey infants (Harlow and Mears 1979). The idea that these babies clung devotedly to the motionless, changeless cloth figure, leaving for only very brief periods to nurse, might imply that a constant parent who offers familiar contact comfort but little else is as important to a baby's survival as food is. Harlow remarks, "We were not surprised to discover that contact comfort was an important basic affectional … variable, but we did not expect it to overshadow so completely the variable of nursing…" (Harlow 1958, p. 680)

Children in Care

When the decision is made to remove a child from parents who are unable to pro-vide essentials of life or safety, it is important to keep in mind what many parents (no matter their challenges) do offer to their children. The strong affection that many parents feel for their children is a positive emotion that can form the basis for parental behavior changes necessary in order to maintain or create a safe environ-ment for the child. These changes may sustain family preservation or enable family reunification. Placement of a child away from a loving parent, no matter how neces-sary or well-planned and regardless of the excellence of the substitute caretakers, always represents for the child the loss of the familiar caretaker (Berrick et al. 1998).

Where affectionate attachment between parent and child does not exist or is weak, the prospect of modifying serious parental behavior problems in order to cre-ate a safe, nurturing environment is more challenging. A brief consideration of some of the difficult, tiring, and repetitive aspects of child care begins to make clear why, without the rewarding pleasure for the caretaking adult of loving interaction with a responsive child, a parent may find much-needed care so onerous that he or she simply omits that care or leaves it to others. This often results in neglect which, if severe or continued, may be sufficient reason to remove a child from parental care (Bundy-Fazioli et al. 2009).

Once removal from the home has occurred, stability for children in protective care may become difficult to achieve. A grieving child may not be able to form a strong attachment to a foster parent (and vice versa), leading the foster parent to request that the child be removed from his/her care, thus again reducing stability. In many child welfare agencies, services may be offered to help preserve a foster home placement, and with some additional time, there is the hope that the child and care-taker will begin to relate in a more positive, satisfying manner. However, the value of these services is open to question. For example, in a study of children who had multiple moves in care, children who received services from the Children and Youth Investment Team aimed at preserving their current placement did not move less than children who did not receive the service. Interestingly, in this study services for the foster parent were rarely recommended (Rolock et al. 2009).

If a fostering relationship does not improve, frustrated foster parents may press for the child's removal, sometimes expressing the hope that someone else might be better able to "help" the child. If the child welfare agency is unable to intervene in a way that creates a caring, pleasurable relationship between the child and caretaker, the agency must reluctantly carry out the foster parent's request and move the child to another placement. Foster children are almost always upset and frightened by these moves in foster care, just as they were when they were removed from their biological parents. Behavioral manifestations of these feelings may differ depending on the child's age and developmental level, but are nearly always present. Most people, especially agency staff and foster parents, will recognize behavior that reflects feelings of loss, sadness, and anger early in a new placement. Within a few days or weeks, however, adults may expect the child's behavior to become more "normal" and for expressions of loss or unhappiness to diminish or disappear. When, in a relatively brief period, the child seems unresponsive to a foster parent's efforts to soothe, comfort, or distract, another request for removal can occur. The same study mentioned above (Rolock et al. 2009) also found that 49% of foster children who moved frequently in care were moved at a foster parent's request. With each move, children of any age are confused and frightened by the loss of familiar people and surroundings, respond with upset and upsetting behavior, and so arrive at a new placement with less ability to begin the long process of mutual attachment with a new caretaker and adjustment to a new foster home environment. In general, the foster child who has a history of many placement changes usually has had foster parents and even sometimes residential treatment providers request removal.

Agencies must do a thorough job in preparing and supporting foster parents, in order to hopefully extend the time period during which foster parents expect a child to "settle in" and "warm up." However, agency staff are faced with the reality that foster parents are, for the most part, unpaid volunteer caretakers (payment to foster parents is usually considered only reimbursement for a foster child's expenses) who expect some emotional satisfaction from caring for the children they foster. Without that expected gratification, some foster parents may find the caretaking tasks too difficult and unrewarding and ask that the child be moved. Despite the challenges, many children in foster care find placement with loving foster parents and establish a reciprocal exchange of affection. Casework staff are usually attentive to the relationships between foster children and foster parents, and caseworkers' statements about a child doing well in placement are often a shorthand description of a beginning, growing, or secure mutual attachment between foster parent and child.

The dimensions of the problem of permanency for children in care are large by any standards, with 254,162 children entering care in FY 2012 (U.S. Department of Health and Human Services 2013). Of this number, 60,223 were under age 2. This is how lack of permanency begins, and while fully 47 % of all children entering care exit care in less than a year, another 15 % are still in foster care 3–5 (or more) years later. While these are staggeringly high numbers to those in the child welfare field, the children are not so numerous as to catch and hold the attention of policymakers and funders, especially in a negative economic climate. Scarce state and federal funds often mean service and program cuts at the child welfare agency level for everything other than the most basic services (services which by mandate address abuse investigation and child safety issues). Such program cuts make improving foster care and its outcomes far more challenging.

Financing Foster Care

The provision that links receipt of current federal Title IV-E funding by agencies for providing foster care to children eligible for the now defunct Aid to Families with Dependent Children (AFDC) is usually referred to as "look back." The question is whether the child would have been eligible, based on the family's current economic need, for AFDC on July 16, 1996, just as AFDC was being replaced by Temporary Aid to Needy Families (TANF). As a result of the "look back" provision, only 44 % of children who now enter care are eligible. Nevertheless, the fiscal incentive of IV-E reimbursement and the attendant regulations remain a powerful driver of much casework and court activity for children in foster care (The Children's Monitor, July 15 2011).

What Is Permanency?

The definition offered by Barth and Chintapalli (2009, p. 88) is useful as a starting point as we seek to define permanency: "Permanency is a state of security and attachment involving a parenting relationship that is mutually understood to be a lasting relationship." Legally assured ties, like those in adoption or legal guardianship, are important in permanency planning, as is the ability of the agency to close out its protective and foster care services to the child, but these considerations often mean more to agency staff than to the child or young person and the adult caregiver involved in creating permanency. Positive outcomes for foster children and youth involve an exit from foster care into a lasting relationship with a caring adult that is intended to be permanent. The positive foster care outcomes usually identified as those intended to be permanent are return to birth parent(s), adoption, and legal guardianship. The latter may involve the creation of a subsidized legal guardianship arising from a kinship foster care placement.

While it is sometimes possible for a child to find a permanent home within the foster care system or with a kin caregiver without guardianship, our look at permanence will focus on the three most often recognized permanent placement options for children in care, all of which involve leaving the foster care system.

Why do we emphasize permanency for children? Courtney et al. (2001) found the attainment of permanency for youth exiting foster care to be correlated with positive findings in their development, education, health, and mental health. Despite such positive results for those attaining permanency, a member of the public might wonder what all this emphasis on leaving foster care is about. Isn't the idea to get kids away from seriously harmful home situations that involve physical abuse or neglect, or even sexual or psychological abuse? Don't kids just need to be safe from these horrors, live in a clean house, and have decent clothes to wear, good food, schooling, other kids to play with, and watchful adult supervision? Does it really matter so much who meets these basic needs, or even how often kids have to move from house to house, family to family, as long as they are safe? Of course, it does matter, and a brief way to express what else children need beyond the food, clothing, and shelter basics is that they need permanency or stability and security in a mutually attached ongoing relationship with an adult caregiver.

Attaching to a responsive caretaking adult is an early and critical survival task for young mammals, including humans. Infants do not thrive when early attachments do not form or are flawed or interrupted. Babies, with their long period of dependence on others to meet their needs, suffer when those needs are not met in familiar patterns by familiar caretakers who are attuned to the baby's unique individual cues and responses. Even the most willing and attentive caretaker must spend time learning about a new baby. The learning process is not always smooth and may not proceed well if the caregiver is unable to learn about the baby.

For example, Sapolsky (2005) describes the horrific death rates in early twentieth-century America for infants placed in orphanages or other institutions. The negative responses noted in infants in orphanages were also seen among babies hospitalized for longer than a week or two. The children became listless, lost weight despite adequate food intake, and had an extremely high rate of infections. In 1942, Harry Bakwin discovered that this failure to thrive was caused by "emotional deprivation" (Sapolsky 2005, p. 153). The babies suffered from attachment disruption because they were separated from their familiar caretakers as parental visits in the hospitals were extremely limited, and indeed all human contact was limited because of the belief that such sterile measures would reduce infection.

Some of the most compelling accounts of disrupted attachment come from Szalavitz and Perry. The case histories they describe provide a memorable human dimension to the question of permanence, and the clear message is that if babies do not receive individualized loving attention and care, important neural structures and functions may not develop properly (Szalavitz and Perry 2010). It appears that what is missing or damaged in the baby who lacks such care is the critical ability to self-regulate stress. When the infant does not learn that basic needs will be met in a predictable way by a familiar caretaker, the perceived threat that survival needs will not be met hinders the developing ability to internally regulate stress. Under better conditions, proper maturation of this same stress-regulation system enables the infant to develop awareness of and responsiveness to the emotional states of others—in other words, empathy. Thus, appropriate internal stress regulation promotes health and well-being and forms the foundation of vital social behavior. The particular neurochemical involved in this type of development is oxytocin. According to Szalavitz and Perry, "Oxytocin is the substance that connects stress relief, relaxation and calm with a baby's specific caregivers" (2010, p. 66). Only with repeated, satisfying contacts with the same people over time will the optimal oxytocin connection be made.

Fortunately, the importance of attachment to development and functioning is now widely recognized. It underlies policies which promote permanence and must become even more central to practice for child welfare agency staff and other professionals who deal with children who are at risk of separation from their families or who are already in foster care. When children must leave their homes or move from one caretaker to another, the losses include the familiar people, places, and things that create their daily environment. Even in a home where care is disorganized, neglectful, or abusive, all conditions of care are usually not negative. There may be some comfort and nurture provided. Fragmented parental attention and affection still have meaning and value to most children.

In addition, the home may hold other possible sources of care, including siblings or other relatives. Neighbors, friends, or even family pets may be important sources of affection. As children mature, resources in the larger environment beyond the family home increase in importance, and when a child must move, these losses assume increasing importance. Even loss of familiar objects, like a favorite toy or game or a valued item of clothing, can be another source of pain and bewilderment to a child who is moved. For preschoolers, a familiar day care program or caretaker may be lost, while for older children, critically important ties to peers and school are usually severed by a move (Stone 2007).

Evidence of educational delay associated with school changes is compelling, and the levels of stress, anxiety, and personal hardship encountered by youth who must deal with school changes are likely to be a significant contributing factor in lowered school performance. Indeed, in writing about chronic stress in children, Thorson and Eagleston (1983) group changing schools with other destructive events like parents' divorce or the death of a family member. In the minds of many school-age children who must move, the biggest educational issues have to do with loss of existing peer connections and attempts to establish relations with new peers at school: Who will they sit with on the school bus? Who will they eat lunch with? Will they be picked for a team in gym class? Additionally, it appears that at least three different systems of hierarchies must be negotiated by any school newcomer. West et al. (2010, p. 1,246) describe "scholastic, peer, and sports hierarchies."

Outside school, a major source of anxiety for the child who moves is the need to establish a place in a neighborhood peer hierarchy. Strong peer alliances can buffer the impact of other losses and stresses and may offer protection against depression and bullying (Goldbaum et al. 2003, p. 142). Loss of these potential protections is a serious matter for the child who changes placements, neighborhoods, and schools. Here, again, evidence from experiments in primate psychology can be instructive. The uncertainty involved in negotiating (or failing to negotiate) necessary peer alliances was a major source of stress to the baboons studied for more than 30 years in Kenya by Robert Sapolsky (2001). It is likely that children asked to navigate a changing array of peers (as well as other unfamiliar environmental demands) may suffer the same internal state of prolonged and intense anxiety as the young baboons.

Consider for a moment that among the very young baboons Sapolsky studied, baboons who lacked any social connections at all were even more stressed than low-ranking individuals trying for a better spot in the social hierarchy. Isolation appears to be a much more potent predictor of stress-related disease than even low social rank. Low-ranking baboons are more likely to be ill than high-ranking ones, but isolated baboons are far more likely to suffer illnesses connected with stress than even their low-ranking groupmates. The parallels between Sapolsky's young low-ranking or isolated baboons and young humans faced with establishing and reestablishing themselves within a new environment and with a new peer group are painfully clear (Swartz 2007). Moving to a new neighborhood or entering a new school may be a challenging but manageable situation for a well-supported child but can become a source of "toxic stress" (Middlebrooks and Audage 2008, p. 4) if the child lacks warm, caring adult support.

Challenges to Permanence

While a child welfare worker's first priority is to help a child in his or her care achieve permanence, for all of the reasons discussed above, it is important to acknowledge the larger circumstances that contribute to abuse and neglect in some families. It is generally acknowledged that families known to public child welfare agencies due to allegations of abuse or neglect are often poor. While most poor families do not abuse or neglect their children, there are many ways in which poverty may hamper the formation of caretaker/child attachment. The formulation provided by Bolton (1983) called "Family Resource Theory" is both concise and compelling. When incomplete or failed attachment coincides with scarce environmental resources, a baby or child can be viewed by a parent (or other caretaker) as a competitor for those scarce resources. The demands of the infant or child for care and attention create negative emotional responses in the adult, and neglect or abuse may result. This summary of a damaging parent–child dynamic provides a clear illustration of a case in which the child's removal may be necessary. Unless the poverty and scarcity of resources in the family environment can be remedied and the parent's view of the child as competitor is changed quickly, it is difficult to establish the child's ongoing safety from abuse or neglect in the home (Bolton 1983). And once a child is removed from a family situation in which inadequate resources and flawed attachment have caused a parent to view the child as a competitor with resulting neglect and abuse, the stage is set for potential ongoing problems in establishing stability and permanence.

To address these critical issues, major social reforms to reduce poverty must be a high priority for advocacy. At the same time, intense research efforts must be undertaken to improve our knowledge of how to construct or repair fragmentary parent–child bonds. This population of children and parents needs specific, evidence-based treatment protocols immediately. As Berrick puts it, "We know very little about how to help troubled parents love and protect their children or, in short, how to help maltreating parents make their children a priority" (2009, p. 8). This describes the barriers to family preservation that also become the barriers to family reunification. While there are a few programs that seek to repair disordered attachments, these programs often presume the willingness and ability of the adult to attach and nurture and frequently do not account for severe environmental stressors (e.g., poverty) in the home. As a result, such programs may be more relevant to helping an adoptive parent bond with a newly placed child than to repairing families torn by abuse or neglect. See, for example, the Attachment and Biobehavioral Catch-Up Program (Dozier et al. 2002) which is aimed at foster parents trying to meet the needs of young children who have experienced seriously disrupted attachments. The program teaches foster parents to provide nurturing responses to children whose behavior does not invite or elicit nurture. The goal is to help young children learn to self-regulate in response to predictable, warm adult caregiving.

A related concern when considering prospects for permanence, or even stability in out-of-home care, is that possible placement providers may also be resource poor. This situation is more frequently seen in kinship care placements. Not only does the kinship caregiver often share the general financial status of the child's often poor parent, but kin caregivers are frequently older, less often married, and have less income, less education, and a lower rate of homeownership than nonrelative caretakers (Scannapieco 1999).

The early stages of a child's placement, even with a known relative, may be characterized by the absence of a strong mutual attachment between child and caregiver. If that early lack of attachment is coupled with scarce resources, the child may again be perceived as a competitor for, or a drain upon, those resources. Instances of abuse or neglect in foster homes, while fortunately rare, are not unknown (DePanfilis and Girvin 2005). More frequently, a stressed, resource-poor foster parent requests removal of the child. The child is then faced with an increasingly difficult struggle to again adjust to new surroundings, attach to new caregivers, and perhaps find a place in school and peer groups.

A child's typical response to such continual moving and the accumulated losses it precipitates is distress. Usually there are no explicitly targeted service responses for re-placed children, and indeed these services are usually prompted only when a child's unhappiness results in extreme and negative behavior. In such cases, the treatment provided may itself require another move, for example, to a hospital or a residential treatment setting (James 2004). What has, in fact, occurred when most youngsters are placed in restrictive levels of care is that the agency does not have a foster home or kinship caretaker who will agree to accept the child. Thus, the move is made to a residential facility where staff working in shifts may have a somewhat higher tolerance for a child's upset behavior than do kin or foster parents. However, for most youth, these placements offer little opportunity to form the strong personal attachment between child and caring adult that might prove therapeutic.

To summarize, placement instability and exit from care are closely related, as frequent moves in placement increase the risk that there will be no permanent exit from care to a family (Barth and Chintapalli 2009). As we consider risks posed by lack of a stable home and familiar, nurturing caregiver, it is important to note that attachment seems to be a basic physiological requirement for healthy growth and development. The absence of such stability increases risks for a variety of pathological conditions. It is possible that some of the effects of lack of permanent attachment are not reversible even with later care and nurture (Szalavitz and Perry 2010).

Disrupted Attachment Case Example: Corey

Corey, an African-American child, first entered care at 6 months of age. After three failed foster home placements, he was returned to the home of his mother, Lisa, at age 4. Three years later, he returned to agency care, after being found home alone late at night. For both Corey's entries into care, his mother's long-standing drug addiction appears to have contributed to her serious neglect and abandonment of Corey.

Corey's biological father, James, left Corey and Lisa when the child was only a few months old. He was not involved with Corey after that point and was serving a long prison sentence in another state for the past 3 years. Efforts made by the child welfare agency to engage him in at least corresponding with Corey were unproductive.

Reentering care at age 7, Corey was highly active, usually appeared distressed, and had outbursts of aggression directed at caregivers and at other children. Upon his reentry into foster care, he was evaluated and began taking medication for his activity level and was placed in a special classroom for part of the school day. Despite some ongoing problems with self-control, difficulty in forming relationships with adults, and occasional aggression toward classmates, his behavior became much more manageable. He began living with his maternal grandmother, a widow, who asked that he be placed with her following his second removal from his mother. On a day-to-day basis, Corey and his grandmother, Ida Knox, seemed to get along well. She managed his rather complicated medication and therapy schedules and was in close touch with Corey's school and his caseworker. In fact, her contact with the caseworker was quite frequent and often consisted of a litany of fairly minor complaints about Corey's behavior. When discussion of permanency planning for Corey began, Mrs. Knox quickly ruled out the option that she adopt Corey herself. She told the caseworker she was worn out by Corey's behavior, wasn't well herself, and saw ongoing efforts to explore these factors with her as pressuring her to adopt. Four months later, Mrs. Knox told the caseworker to place Corey somewhere else if he "needed to be adopted."

Corey continues to live in his grandmother's home, though she has expressed her desire that he stay for only a few more months. Concurrent planning for Corey now includes visits with both his mother, Lisa, and a paternal aunt, Rose. Family Finding efforts located Rose, who lives about 200 miles away. Rose didn't know Corey well before visits began, but has recently agreed to become his foster parent and consider adoption at a later point, if, in fact, Corey is not returned to his mother's care. Corey has also had a few overnight stays with his mother, and a weekend-long visit has been planned. Corey's grandmother is concerned that the two set of visits (from Rose and from Lisa) are an added burden for her, but has agreed that Corey can stay with her for a few months more. She agrees that this time is necessary for Corey's caseworker to determine the extent of Lisa's progress in her present drug treatment program and to see how she copes with Corey during weekend visits.

The options being considered for Corey are reunification with his mother, adoption, or legal guardianship. If his mother appears to continue to do well in her recovery and treatment and is able to deal with Corey's behavior with patience, it is likely he will be returned to her care. If Lisa begins to miss visits, leaves Corey alone at any point, or does not adhere to the requirements of her drug treatment program, it is likely that the agency and the court will opt to move to establish an adoptive home for Corey. So far, placement with his Aunt Rose appears to be the best prospect for adoption for him. Visits with Aunt Rose, although not frequent, have gone well, and Corey likes the special things they do when his aunt visits. Because she does not live locally, Rose usually plans visits with Corey around a trip to the zoo or an amusement park. Although it is a bit difficult to separate how Corey feels about his aunt from his enthusiasm for the special places she takes him, she and Corey seem to like one another and look forward to the time they spend together. Potential challenges involved in a placement for Corey with his aunt include the fact that it would (at least initially) be another foster care placement for him and would take Corey away from close contact with many family members he knows.

Another possible permanency option for Corey has been discussed very recently by the child welfare agency staff. Corey and his grandmother have been part of these preliminary discussions, and the caseworker has noticed that the relationship between Corey and his grandmother has been less strained in the past several months. He has been more responsive to her, less resistant to her supervision, and has had fewer aggressive outbursts. The improvement may be due, at least in part, to Corey's positive response to medication, which his grandmother monitors closely; she also appears to be more accepting and affectionate with him than she was before. It is possible that Mrs. Knox could be a permanent placement resource for Corey after all, if neither a return to his mother nor an adoption by his aunt materializes. Mrs. Knox, despite her concerns about Corey's visiting schedule, appears to thrive on the additional support from agency staff that she and Corey have received as part of the concurrent planning process. Mrs. Knox is always glad to have one of the caseworkers or case aides talk with her and acknowledge the care she provides to Corey, as well as the sacrifices she has made in her own life in order to provide for her grandson.

With a plan for ongoing support and encouragement, could Mrs. Knox become a permanent legal guardian for Corey? The placement could be subsidized, so that the financial support she now receives as an agency foster parent would continue. Mrs. Knox clearly enjoys the recognition and respect she hears voiced by her family, the child welfare agency, and others in Corey's life for the excellent job she has done in managing his special needs. Often times, however, sources of support are minimal after subsidized legal guardianship is finalized. Quarterly Family Group Decision Making meetings and ongoing weekly casework visits could be of significant help to Corey and Mrs. Knox, but limited agency resources do not allow for this level of support post-permanency. Difficult choices face Mrs. Knox, the agency staff, and the court, with outcomes both serious and unknown. Permanence for Corey is the desired goal, but the pathway to that goal is unclear. Which of the adults in Corey's life is best able to provide him with a safe and nurturing relationship that is lifelong?

Let us look more closely at each of the three permanency options being considered for Corey.

Reunification

In a large ($N=3,351$) cohort of children studied for type of exit from foster care, 2,522 (75.3 %) did exit, and of those who exited, 51 % were reunified (Akin 2011). This is a typical finding and is confirmed by the AFCARS Report FY 2012 estimates, which note that of the children who exited foster care, 51 % of children (122,401) were reunified with parent(s) and another 8 % were placed with relative caregivers (U.S. Department of Health and Human Services 2013).

Whether Corey's care exit will be to his mother depends in large part upon his needs and characteristics and the likelihood that Lisa can meet those needs. For example, can his mother monitor and facilitate the ongoing behavioral treatment and psychotropic medication which appear to have provided Corey with some relief from symptoms of restlessness and aggression? No doubt his needs and any caretaker's projected ability to meet them in an ongoing way will be central to a placement decision. This concern for Corey's needs leads directly to a close examination of his mother's strengths and challenges as a caretaker. Without question, Lisa's history of drug abuse is a primary consideration. Corey has entered foster care twice in his life due to his mother's addiction. She will have to demonstrate by maintaining sobriety and continuing her treatment program that she can prioritize Corey's needs and address her substance dependence.

While few would disagree that parents who struggle with substance abuse should be treated for their addictions as a prerequisite to the return of a child from foster care, there is less uniformity on what defines a successful treatment outcome. The general understanding of addiction is that it is a lifelong illness, with relapses, an expected part of both treatment and recovery (Marsh et al. 2011). It is difficult for the staff involved with Corey's case to specify with precision what phase of her treatment or recovery Lisa must complete before Corey can be returned to her, but they are clear that ongoing noncompliance with her treatment will cause them to move toward the other permanency alternatives for Corey rather than continue to work toward reunification. Indeed, scrutiny of Lisa's treatment is more intense because both Corey's current and previous episodes in foster care resulted from her drug abuse and because Lisa has withdrawn from several previous treatment programs.

Lisa's history of addiction is not the only factor caseworkers must weigh as they consider returning Corey to his mother. The fragmented attachment between Corey and Lisa also looms large. The strong ties and warm memories that provide pleasure and comfort in many families are not part of Corey and Lisa's past life. Corey's sadness, anger, and fear occasionally surface as he thinks of or interacts with his mother, sending clear signals of concern to those who know Corey and see the two together. Corey's feelings are not often expressed verbally but reveal themselves in sullen stubbornness as he fails to respond to Lisa's attempts to engage him during visits. She, in turn, feels hurt when her overtures are rebuffed and tends to withdraw from him while she focuses on all the work she's doing to move toward reunification. Corey's upset feelings about his mother tend to spill over into his other relationships with adults, and when he returns from his mother's home, he is also sometimes detached or angry with his grandmother who is, by far, his most stable adult caregiver.

Again, even if therapeutic intervention continues to modify or control some of Corey's most troublesome behavior, his mother still could face strong challenges in caring for him. Beyond treatment for her addiction, there are psychological and environmental problems that cause Lisa to struggle to function as an adult even when she abstains from substances. Even abstinent, she may struggle to be a reliable parent and caretaker. It is possible that Lisa's drug use serves to mask the pain of her own rootless childhood. She manifested clear symptoms of depression following her father's death when she was eight. Her mother remarried within a year, and Lisa never had an easy relationship with her stepfather. Longer and longer periods of time away from home marked her late latency and adolescence. She moved around among maternal relatives in three states, sometimes returning home only to quarrel bitterly with her stepfather and leave again. The impact of these years remains, and if Lisa is drug free, she will have to find other ways to manage her ambivalence toward her mother, whom she believes always took the stepfather's side against Lisa, and who now has custody of Corey.

Another source of concern is Lisa's tendency to view the world primarily in terms of satisfaction of her own needs. If her substance abuse could be managed and if she were able to find and use help for her recurrent depression, Lisa would still have to learn to become less self-centered. In the past, she has repeatedly lacked the desire or ability to act responsibly in caring for her child's needs. While Lisa did not abuse Corey, she repeatedly neglected his care while she sought and used drugs. Limited financial resources were frequently diverted from items needed for his health and well-being to the satisfaction of Lisa's addiction. Lisa believes that her attitudes and behavior around Corey's care have changed as a result of her drug treatment. Agency staff hope to find signs that this is the case. They have noticed a somewhat sibling-like quality to Lisa's behavior toward Corey and a permissiveness regarding his behavior during their visits. Might this be a consequence of their separation? An indication of weak mutual attachment? Lisa's lack of practice in assuming some of the more difficult but routine aspects of parenting? Most likely, it is a combination of all these factors.

A recent study by Akin (2011) points to other risks that seem to reduce the likelihood of reunification. For example, children with serious mental health problems, children who entered care due to neglect, and children who have a history of prior removals all seem to have a lower likelihood of successful reunification. At least two of these three factors apply in Corey's case. The reasons for the lower likelihood of reunification for children with some or all of these issues resonate as we think about Corey's needs, his mother's needs, and the questions that must be resolved by agency staff if he is to be returned to his mother's care.

Considering the number and nature of the problems Corey and his mother have had in their history together, some might wonder why efforts toward reunification are being made. The answer is threefold. First, federal regulations for children in care require that the child welfare agency make reasonable efforts to prevent placement and facilitate a child's return to his or her parent. Second, Lisa has indicated her desire to resume care of Corey and has made steps toward her recovery. Third, Corey and Lisa's caseworker has a strengths-based orientation to her work and believes that Lisa should have a final opportunity to improve her life and regain custody of Corey before he is permanently placed elsewhere. In addition, the caseworker knows that the court would be unlikely to grant a termination of Lisa's parental rights as a necessary step toward adoption or grant a contested petition for legal guardianship of Corey if all appropriate opportunities for Lisa to regain custody were not first provided.

Some of the strengths noted by the caseworker in her work with Corey's mother include Lisa's close compliance with her current treatment program and her almost perfect adherence to her visiting plan with Corey. Lisa has also made gains in her ability to moderate her angry responses to her mother. Despite the often volatile history of this relationship, Lisa has been able and willing to cooperate with Mrs. Knox around some aspects of Corey's care. Lisa sometimes takes Corey to his after-school therapy appointments when Mrs. Knox has scheduling conflicts. Lisa relishes the somewhat cautious praise she gets from her mother at such times, and Mrs. Knox recognizes the efforts her daughter is making toward being a more consistent parent to Corey. Other signs of Lisa's increasing maturity are more subtle, but perhaps more significant. Lisa acknowledges the harm she has done to Corey in the past and seems to be beginning to understand his occasional lack of response to her during visits. She knows he does not trust her and tries to think of ways she can make their interaction more positive. She is able to discuss these issues with the caseworker and has shown both some insight and a determination to improve.

Finally, as another strength that Lisa brings to the decision-making process, the caseworker believes there is one other family issue that deserves consideration. If Corey is placed with his mother, his grandmother, Mrs. Knox, will continue to be a big part of his life and will no doubt be a strong support to Corey throughout his childhood. The willingness of Lisa and her mother to build a new connection with each other and join together in parenting Corey is an asset to build upon and a strong factor to consider when making a final recommendation for Corey's placement.

Adoption

The security and permanence of adoption make it the best outcome for children who must be placed away from their birth parents. Since a hierarchy of foster care outcomes was enunciated in the Adoption Assistance and Child Welfare Act of 1980 (ACCWA, or P.L. 96–272), federal policy has supported adoption above other options. ACCWA authorized federal funds to be used for adoption subsidies and to reimburse families for "costs incident to adoption" (nonrecurring costs such as filing fees or attorney fees). The Family and Medical Leave Act (FMLA) provides for "12 work weeks of unpaid leave during any 12 month period for...placement of a son or daughter with the employee for adoption..." Adoption income tax credits cover qualifying expenses for adoptive parents (U.S. Office of Personnel

Management, n. d.). Explicit permission for concurrent planning as part of the Adoption and Safe Families Act (ASFA) is another policy assist for adoption of children in foster care (Child Welfare Information Gateway 2005). Adoption is clearly favored by federal policy over other forms of non-reunification permanency. The legal creation of a new family unit not only promises permanence to a foster child but also provides the agency a way to maximize service time and resources.

Ensuring safe, permanent homes for foster children and reducing the size of the foster care caseload are both highly desirable outcomes for agencies involved with child placement. This has been the case at least since the passage of ACCWA, which prioritized adoption as the second most desirable placement exit or outcome (after return home), provided for federal subsidy for those who adopted special needs children, and spelled out a detailed sequence of tasks (required case plans, court reviews, notice to parents) to be accomplished regularly and repeatedly as long as a child remained in foster care. The federal financial incentive, Title IV-E foster home care reimbursement, was an infusion of funds that few jurisdictions could afford to forego, so serious efforts at compliance were virtually assured. This continues to be the case for most agencies today, despite the decline in the number of children in care who qualify for these federal funds.

In local practice, adoption-friendly policies in agencies may include a specific provision that adoption is to be considered first when reunification is not possible, and that adoption must be explicitly "ruled out" before another permanency plan is finalized. Thus, in many jurisdictions, it is not possible to decide against return to a parent and then move directly to permanence via subsidized legal guardianship, for example. Adoption must be considered and ruled out as a prior step. Indeed, at least one state has a policy which precludes guardianship as a care exit for a child younger than 14 years old (Akin 2011). At this age, a child's refusal of adoption will be a serious, if not insurmountable, barrier to permanency. The implication is that younger children would not or could not reject adoption as the preferred permanency plan, while for older children, the less preferred plan of permanent legal guardianship is acceptable.

Adoptions of children active with public child welfare agencies are currently the second most common type of adoption (Evan and Donaldson Adoption Institute 2010), while the most common is adoption by a stepparent. In FY 2009, for example, 57,466 children from the child welfare system found permanence through adoption. They represented 68 % of non-stepparent adoptions in that year. Thirty-two percent of these adoptions were by relatives, while 54 % were by unrelated foster parents. This is a dramatic increase in child welfare exits to permanence via adoption compared to only about 15,000 such adoptions in 1988 (Akin 2011, pp. 8–9). The policy preference and related adoption incentives appear to be working, and these are impressive permanency outcomes, especially when considering the potential array of risks present in the histories of these children as they enter placement. Most of these risks are present in Corey's history, including "malnutrition before and after birth, inadequate nurture, exposure to drugs or alcohol… and multiple placements as well as potential genetic vulnerability" (Akin 2011, p. 9). To our knowledge, Corey was not physically or sexually abused, but the array of other adverse life experiences has made a deep impact on him, and in this he is not alone. In FY 2012, for example, fully 92 % of children adopted while in child welfare agency care were designated as "special needs" and thus qualified their adoptive parents to receive an Adoption Assistance Subsidy (U.S. Department of Health and Human Services 2013), another adoption incentive policy.

When we think of adoption for Corey or any child for whom return to a parent is not possible, we think of a viable, favored, legally assured path to permanence. This is why, in Corey's case, visits with his paternal aunt were begun and continue while Corey continues to visit his mother. Placement with Aunt Rose is the concurrent contingency plan for a permanent placement for Corey if he does not return to his mother. While it is true that the agency would like his aunt's interest in adoption to be a bit stronger, she is more comfortable at this stage with just getting to know Corey better and planning that if he came to live with her, it would initially be as a foster child. Since most public child welfare adoptions begin as foster care placements, this would not be at all an unusual plan, nor would it be unlikely to lead to adoption. According to the FY 2012 AFCARS, 56 % of children adopted from foster care were adopted by their foster parents (U.S. Department of Health and Human Services 2013). However, the central thrust of permanency planning for Corey is that his next move, if he must make one, should be his last. It may be that his aunt would like to determine whether she and Corey are able to make a deep and lasting attachment to one another before she commits to adopting him. This may require a period of time for the two to live together as parent and child. But this pre-adoption "test period" could be extremely disruptive to Corey if it did not result in adoption and turned into just more foster care. Additionally, because of Corey's history of neglect and impermanence, he may not be able to form the deep attachment his aunt (and many other adoptive parents) may hope for.

Any outcome beyond a lasting adoption for Corey could not justify the risks posed by a move, and so the agency staff planning for Corey must appraise the chances both for adoption and for adoption disruption. They might consider, for example, to what extent Corey would be able to develop and display attachment to an adoptive parent. Dance and Rushton (2005) found that adopted children who, after a year of placement, failed to display attachment to the adoptive mother faced a greater risk of disruption. Specifically, they determined there was "…an eight-fold increase [in disruption] where the adoptive mother perceives a lack of attachment by the child" (Dance and Rushton 2005, p. 276). Unless Corey's aunt soon begins to view the reality of adoption as a clear, close, and desirable plan for her and Corey, his current placement with his grandmother might be the one most likely to result in permanence for Corey.

Subsidized Guardianship

A growing number of children in foster care are living with relatives or adults with whom they have a kinship bond. The number of children in care placed with relatives, for example, has increased to 28 % of all children in care (U. S. Department of Health and Human Services 2013). The Child Welfare League of America defines kinship care as "… the full time care, nurturing and protection of children by relatives, members of their tribes or clans, godparents, stepparents, or any adult who has a kinship bond with a child" (Child Welfare League of American, n.d.). Presently, 38 states and the District of Columbia have instituted some form of legal guardianship with subsidy (American Bar Association Center on Children and the Law 2011, p. 7). In legal guardianship, legal responsibility for a child is transferred by the court from the court or agency to an individual who becomes the guardian. In the United States, the adult involved is often related to the child and has been acting as the child's foster parent prior to the establishment of guardianship. Subsidized guardianship provides financial support to both relative and nonrelative caregivers who assume legal responsibility of a child in out-of-home care (Child Welfare Information Gateway, n.d.).

Running directly counter to the desire of agencies to ensure permanency for children in foster care via adoptions, and to close cases and thus maximize staff time for other critical services, is the desire of many kinship foster caretakers to avoid the family disruption that would arise from the necessary prelude to adoption, termination of parental rights (Rockhill et al. 2009, p. 9). Relative foster parents are too numerous and far too important a placement resource to have their concerns about adoption ignored, and since many legal actions to terminate parental rights are "involuntary" (i.e., undertaken without the parent's consent and requiring a finding of abandonment or lack of fitness by the parent), these actions clearly have a potentially disruptive impact.

In involuntary termination, not only is the parent–child bond legally severed, but the parent may see the relative who is the child's caretaker (often the child's grandmother) as complicit in the painful legal process. Other family members may become allied with either the parent or the kin caretaker, and major family discord and estrangement are possible. Relatives who resist agency efforts to persuade them to adopt their related foster child often fear this exact outcome. In addition, relative caretakers often believe that they, rather than agency staff, know what is in the best interest of the child placed in their home. As a result, discussion by caseworkers of adoption as a means to promote permanency and the security of the child is often perceived by kin caretakers to be a lack of belief in their ability to care for the child to adulthood without adoption. Repeated urging to consider adoption by citing practice wisdom or research data may, indeed, have a negative impact, and the caretaker's relationship with the caseworker and the agency may become strained. Children's own feelings of loyalty and affection for an absent parent may be overlooked as the adults involved struggle to agree on a permanency plan. While age-appropriate discussion with children is needed, care must be taken to avoid compounding any existing fear or guilt for the child.

Finally, agencies that are determined to bring about permanency through adoption may decide to attempt to remove the child from kinship care and place the child elsewhere for adoption. Whether the kin caretaker relents and decides to adopt or the child is moved to be adopted by another person, lasting bitterness about what the agency sees as good permanency planning and the kin caretaker sees as additional

Table 4.1 Determination of Subsidized Legal Guardianship

Identification of cases eligible for subsidized guardianship in the Oregon Title IV-E Waiver II Evaluation proceeded with caseworkers responding positively to [child] criteria which included the following:
1. 12 months or longer in custody
2. 6 months or more with current caregiver
3. Placement with an approved certified foster parent
4. IV-E eligibility
5. Reunification with birth parent(s) has been ruled out
6. Adoption has been ruled out
7. Youth has a strong and stable relationship with caregiver
8. Continued placement with this caregiver would be in the best interests of the youth
9. Child and caretaker can function effectively without casework support/supervision

In the Oregon study, an additional criterion was applicable to non-Native American youth only, but probably echoes similar points in other jurisdictions
10. Placement with a relative or guardian over the age of 12

(Rockhill et al. 2009, p. 14)

harm to the birth family may result. To resolve both concerns—that of the agency for a legally sanctioned permanency outcome for the foster child and that of the kin caregiver for the child and extended family to remain undisturbed by legal action for termination—Subsidized Legal Guardianship was developed as a permanency option that seems to be a compromise acceptable to most stakeholders.

Subsidized Legal Guardianship is currently considered a viable permanency option, thanks at least in part to several Title IV-E Waiver Demonstration Projects (Freundlich 2009). The children and youth studied were usually those who had both reunification and adoption ruled out as permanency options. Interest was strong in comparing guardianship to other outcomes, as well as in understanding and describing those cases in which guardianship became the preferred option (Rockhill et al. 2009). As an example, in the Oregon study (Rockhill et al. 2009, p. 34), 64 % of the 18,876 children and youth exiting care between February 2002 and December 2008 were reunified. Of the 6,714 children *not* reunified, 10 % achieved guardianship (70 % with a relative), while 55 % were adopted.

The criteria for the Oregon study are shown in Table 4.1.

Another question about permanency outcomes investigated by the Oregon study is the question of whether they *are* in fact permanent, at least during the child's minority. A partial answer emerges from the Oregon data, which compares guardianship and reunification 24 months post-permanency. Removals within 24 months post-permanency were significantly lower among youth in subsidized legal guardianship compared to youth who had been reunified (4.3 % and 14.7 %, respectively). Differential outcomes were also observed between the groups in regard to founded abuse, with 2.1 % of founded cases occurring among those youth in subsidized legal guardianship compared to 16.3 % among youth who had been reunified (Rockhill et al. 2009, p. 13).

Nationally, the FY 2012 AFCARS Report shows that only 4 % (14,829) of the 399,546 children in foster care have a case plan goal of guardianship (U. S. Department of Health and Human Services 2013, p. 1). However, it may be that these goal numbers do not reflect the actual interest in exploring guardianship as a route to permanency, because concurrent planning goals of reunification or adoption may not be changed to guardianship until these other options have been ruled out and guardianship is close to being accomplished.

Subsidized guardianship can offer substantial benefits, not the least of which is usually the chance for the caretaker to continue to receive some level of financial support for the placement without involuntary agency processes and services such as caseworker visits, court hearings, or case planning meetings, which may be seen as intrusive (Rockhill et al. 2009, p. 23). Because legal guardians are able to provide consent, ordinary aspects of living for youth, like attending a school trip or participating in a team sport, are normalized and freed from the delay arising from the agency's need for parental or judicial permission. Even in unusual circumstances, for example, when legal permission is required for surgery or for joining the military, most parties acknowledge the legal integrity of the family unit created by the court's decree of guardianship. While parents do not lose the right to visit the child, guardians are vested with the important rights they need to provide day-to-day care without having to appeal to the child's parent(s), the court, or the agency. When agency staff or court personnel think about legal permanency, they may not consider that normalizing a child's daily life may be both the most compelling sign of permanency and its greatest benefit to that youngster. Legal guardianship provides a mechanism for this normalization just as adoption or reunification would.

In the case discussed above, permanent legal guardianship may be the best route to permanency for Corey. Corey would prefer to remain permanently in his grandmother's home and under her care. Unlike many children in foster care who yearn to return to a parent's care despite previous abuse or neglect (Block et al. 2010, p. 665), Corey prefers to remain with his grandmother. When he discusses this at all, which is rarely, he says he likes visiting with his mother but likes their visits best when they both eat dinner with his grandmother and watch TV at his grandmother's house. He rarely expresses his feelings for his grandmother verbally, but after visits with either his aunt or mother, he relaxes visibly in his grandmother's presence and in her home.

To maintain Corey's placement with Mrs. Knox, permanent placement with his mother would have to be ruled out, and Mrs. Knox herself would need to be open to becoming Corey's legal guardian. If she decides to take that legal step, it is less likely that the caseworker would recommend moving Corey to his aunt's home for another foster care placement, even if adoption could result at some point in the future. Plans to support Mrs. Knox in caring for Corey would have to be in place prior to agency case closure, for several reasons. Corey's mental health needs will continue to require professional intervention, and Mrs. Knox herself needs encouragement, recognition, and validation as she works hard to care for Corey. Membership in a voluntary support group in the community for seniors caring for grandchildren could help to sustain Mrs. Knox, as will access to concrete resources such as health care, adequate housing, and an appropriate educational placement for Corey. She and Corey will also need support from the agency staff who know the two well. The ability to receive services from the agency on a voluntary, as-needed basis may be a critical key to making subsidized legal guardianship a true permanency plan for Corey. Family Team Conferencing and Family Group Decision Making meetings can help in accomplishing these goals.

One needed source of ongoing post-permanency support for Corey and Mrs. Knox (if she becomes his guardian) is collaboration and joint case management within the county human services system, as they are using several of these services. For example, Corey and Mrs. Knox are active with child protective services; Corey's mental health care is managed by the local branch of the behavioral health system; and because Mrs. Knox is a senior citizen with a limited income and is caring for her grandson, she is eligible for a range of services provided by the county's agency on aging.

Service providers in Mrs. Knox's county have formed a children's coalition around the needs of vulnerable children and families who are joint consumers of services. All three county agencies, as well as Corey's school and the hospital clinic where he gets medical care, are members of the coalition and attend the monthly meetings regularly. While the coalition is only in its third year, some very positive results have been possible via the collaborative efforts of the agencies and individuals involved. Corey's caseworker operates from a systems of care framework (see Chap. 1) and attends interagency coalition meetings on a regular basis to coordinate services for the children and families on her caseload. At the monthly coalition meeting, any of the attending agencies may present a case situation calling for collaborative work toward a goal or goals for a child and family. Input from the other agencies is then offered and recorded by the presenting agency. The meeting notes are prepared and distributed to the member agencies. After a short period of time for additions or amendments, the notes become a plan for joint services to the child and family. The presenting agency serves as the monitor to ensure service use/delivery across the multiple systems (Technical Assistance Partnership, n.d.). Using this structure, Corey's caseworker hopes to offer Mrs. Knox ongoing support if she becomes Corey's guardian and the child welfare case is closed. The same structure could also provide ongoing mental health services to Corey and monitor his mother's recovery if he is returned to her.

The other two permanency options for Corey would also require post-placement agency services. Obviously, if Corey is returned to his mother or if he is placed with his Aunt Rose, the early months of his placement in either home would require agency services and supervision. However, if he is permanently placed with his mother, it could become difficult to provide ongoing services after a final court hearing and closure of Corey's foster care case. Limited resources and budgets often force the child welfare agency to use its limited staff to handle incoming crises and abuse cases rather than providing the preventive long-term services that would be needed to monitor and manage Lisa's drug treatment and Corey's mental health care.

If Corey is placed with his Aunt Rose, it could be months before she decides if she wants to proceed to adopt him and, at least while he remains in foster care, agency services must continue. An area of concern here for Corey's caseworker is that Aunt Rose lives in another service jurisdiction, so that child welfare services from that area must be involved both in Corey's placement and in the follow-up services needed pre- and post-permanency. Again, prioritization of such long-term post-permanency services is sometimes not a feasible option for many child welfare agencies. Although prompt permanency planning and placement for young-sters is required, funding for comprehensive post-permanency support services does not follow. Such services will be essential to support true permanency for Corey and thousands of children like him beyond their exit from foster care to a permanent home.

Community-Wide Interventions for Children in Foster Care

Beyond the present and future efforts to find safe and secure relationships and homes for foster children who exit the child welfare system, additional supports and services are badly needed for children who remain in agency care without a real home and family. Solutions for children who wait too long to find permanent homes or never find them must improve, or the annual cohort of youth aging out of foster care will continue to be often homeless, unemployed, and undereducated (Courtney 2009). Fully 30 % of the 1.66 million youth exiting foster care nationally between federal fiscal years 2002 and 2005 had no permanence as they left care. Twenty-five percent aged out or were emancipated, and 5 % simply ran away (Maza 2009, p. 33). Few resources are dedicated to this population as they exit care, and the need for housing and medical care is especially acute (Courtney 2009, p. 55). For a group caught between urgent needs and scant resources, choices are limited. National attention is urgently required to prevent additional risk to these youth, to meet their real needs and support their future aspirations.

Finally, while we must ponder the best individual plans for children like Corey, perhaps we usually think too narrowly about what it takes to strengthen families, reduce foster care entry, create stable foster home care when it is needed, and estab-lish lasting permanency for children exiting foster care. Most prevention efforts and therapeutic interventions target individuals or families, when it may be that neighborhood-wide interventions represent the most effective method of helping families facing a variety of problems. There is room for confusion here, so it is well to clarify that the brief discussion that follows will focus not on the more common community-based interventions but on two model community-wide interventions.

Hope Meadows

Recognizing the power of neighborhoods to assist struggling families, the Casey Foundation in 1999 recommended that New York City's public child welfare ser-vices should be decentralized and that "the neighborhood strategy will prevent far more children from entering the system, reunite far more families, recruit a large, additional number of quality foster and adoptive parents..." (Epstein 2003, p. 686). The scathing critique leveled by Epstein (2003) against the Casey recommendations notes that these "(n)eighborhood-based services presume socialized, nurturing, amiable communities of people with shared interests, histories, and goals." Epstein contends such neighborhoods are not to be found in New York City or elsewhere in our country and our time and asserts that the politically appealing, modestly priced agency reorganization will fail, as have similar previous attempts. Epstein's arguments are persuasive, but what if "socialized, nurturing, amiable communities" could be created? Would these be able to support and maintain children and families? We are fortunate to be able to view at least a partial answer to the question.

In 1993, Hope Meadows, a community in Illinois, was created as a "geographically contained, intergenerational, planned community where foster and adoptive families, children, and senior citizens live together and care for one another" (Eheart et al. 2003, p. 19). While biological parents are not part of the community at Hope Meadows, the difficult work of sustaining troubled children and the foster families who adopt them appears to have moved away from a model of an agency treating the child and family to one in which the agency becomes only a part of the array of human resources available for problem solving in the community. "Many children with troubled pasts who would ordinarily be raised in group homes and orphanages can be sustained in adoptive families, if these families are enveloped within an appropriately designed intergenerational community with the capacity to buffer the inherent difficulties" (Eheart et al. 2003, p. 24). Central to the support of children and foster parents are the seniors (age 55 and up) in the community who befriend the children and spend time with them, acting as surrogate grandparents. Poverty is not a concern since the foster parents receive salaries and free housing and the seniors receive housing at much-reduced cost. The idea of planned supportive communities is being expanded by the Generations of Hope Development Corporation, formed in 2006, with populations served to include:

- "…youth exiting foster care or juvenile justice systems
- Parents reentering society from drug treatment or prison."

(Generations of Hope, n.d.)

Harlem Children's Zone

Another approach is to alter existing neighborhoods so that families and their children are supported. Parents are helped to do well in caretaking, and children get support within the neighborhood and at school to perform well academically. All of this is already taking place in New York City, in Harlem. Beginning in 2000, Geoffrey Canada created the Harlem Children's Zone, a 97-block area of Harlem, with a child population estimated to be between 8,000 and 10,000 (Tough 2008). This large, urban, antipoverty program aims to educate children in the neighborhood so they can escape poverty. Because Canada recognized that schools alone cannot accomplish this goal, he decided to focus on building supportive structures that create a network of family and neighborhood enrichment agencies, classes, and programs. The concepts behind this program are being replicated in urban areas throughout the United States (Otterman 2010), using combinations of federal, state, and philanthropic funding. While it may be decades before there is any conclusive proof as to whether large-scale projects like the Harlem Children's Zone can halt or even reduce the ravages of poverty on the lives of families, the possibility that large-scale neighborhood-level support can alter for the better the lives of resident children and families offers a compelling vision of future possibilities.

Conclusion

Permanency for children and youth in the child welfare system can take many forms, involving biological family members, relatives, fictive kin, adoptive families, or long-term foster families. Reunification, legal guardianship (with and without subsidy), and adoption all provide permanency options for young people that can promote a long-term sense of connectedness. Post-placement services and aftercare can provide concrete support and assurance to youth and families by increasing opportunities for stability. Community-wide interventions can address the larger systemic support necessary for all families and children to grow and thrive. However, it is clear that none of these placements, services, or efforts at larger scale community building can flourish in the absence of a committed federal effort to reorganize child welfare financing. Only with adequate federal funding can child welfare agencies direct resources toward early intervention, offer services to maintain the bonds of connection between children and families when possible, and provide both concrete and instrumental resources that assure the well-being of youth and their caregivers.

Questions for Discussion

1. What issues of loyalty might be present for Corey as he negotiates his relationship with his mother, his grandmother, and his aunt?
2. How might you use family engagement and teaming practices (Family Group Decision Making, Family Team Conferencing) to plan with Corey and his family?
3. What perspective might Corey's grandmother, Mrs. Knox, have on what is best for her grandson, her daughter, and herself?
4. How can Corey's treatment and educational needs be best managed and coordinated?

References

Akin, B. A. (2011). Predictors of foster care exits to permanency: A completing risks analysis of reunification, guardianship, and adoption. *Children and Youth Services Review, 33,* 999.
American Bar Association Center on Children and the Law. (2011). *Judicial guide to implementing the Fostering Connections to Success and Increasing Adoptions Act of 2008 (PL. 110–351).* Washington, D.C.: Author.

Barth, R. P., & Chintapalli, L. K. (2009). Permanence and impermanence for youth in out-of-home care. In B. Kerman, M. Freundlich, & A. N. Maluccio (Eds.), *Achieving permanence for older youth in foster care*. New York: Columbia University Press.

Berrick, J. D. (2009). *Take me home: Protecting America's vulnerable children and families*. Oxford: Oxford University Press.

Berrick, J. D., Needell, B., Barth, R. P., & Jonson-Reid, M. (1998). *The tender years: Toward developmentally sensitive child welfare services for very young children*. Oxford: Oxford University Press.

Block, S., Oran, H., Oran, D., Baumrind, N., & Goodman, G. S. (2010). Abused and neglected children in court: Knowledge and attitudes. *Child Abuse and Neglect, 34*, 659–670.

Bolton, F. G. (1983). *When bonding fails: clinical assessment of high-risk families*. Beverly Hills: Sage.

Bundy-Fazioli, K., Winokur, M., & Delong-Hamilton, T. (2009). Placement outcomes for children removed for neglect. *Child Welfare, 88*(3), 85–102.

Child Welfare Information Gateway. (2005). *Concurrent planning: What the evidence shows*. Washington, DC: Children's Bureau/ACYF.

Child Welfare Information Gateway. (n.d.). Concept and history of Permanency in U. S. child welfare. Retrieved from http://www.childwelfare.gov/permanency/overview/history.cfm.

Child Welfare League of America. (n.d.). Kinship care: Fact sheet. Retrieved from http://www.cwla.org/printable/printpage.asp.

Courtney, M. E. (2009). Outcomes for older youth exiting the foster care system in the United States. In B. Kerman, M. Freundlich, & A. N. Maluccio (Eds.), *Acheiving permanence for older children and youth in foster care* (pp. 40–74). New York: Columbia University Press.

Courtney, M. E., Piliavin, I., Grogan-Kaylor, A., & Nesmith, A. (2001). Foster youth transitions to childhood: A longitudinal analysis of youth leaving care. *Child Welfare, 80*, 685–717.

Dance, C., & Rushton, A. (2005). Predictions of outcome for unrelated adoptive placements made during middle childhood. *Child & Family Social Work, 10*(4), 269–280.

DePanfilis, D., & Girvin, H. (2005). Investigating child maltreatment in out-of-home care: Barriers to effective decision-making. *Children and Youth Services Review, 27*, 353–374.

Dozier, M., Dozier, D., & Manni, M. (2002). Attachment and biobehavioral catch-up: The ABC's of helping infants in foster care cope with early adversity. *Zero to Three, 22*, 7–13.

Eheart, B. K., Power, M. B., & Hopping, D. E. (2003). Intergenerational programming for foster-adoptive families: Creating community at Hope Meadows. *Journal of Intergenerational Relationships, 1*(1), 17–28.

Epstein, W. M. (2003). The futility of pragmatic reform: The Casey Foundation in New York City. *Children and Youth Services Review, 25*(9), 683–701.

Evan, B., & Donaldson Adoption Institute. (2010). *Keeping the Promise: The critical need for post-adoption services to enable children and families to succeed*. New York: Author.

Freundlich, M. (2009). Permanence for older children and youth: Law, policy, and research. In B. Kerman, M. Freundlich, & A. M. Maluccio (Eds.), *Achieving permanence for older children and youth in foster care* (pp. 127–146). New York: Columbia University Press.

Generations of Hope (n.d.). Retrieved August 31, 2011, from http://www.generationsofhope.org/about-us/.

Goldbaum, S., Craig, W. M., Pepler, D., & Connolly, J. (2003). Developmental trajectories of victimization: Identifying risk and protective factors. In M. J. Elias & J. E. Zins (Eds.), *Bullying, peer harassment, and victimization in the schools: The next generation of prevention* (pp. 139–156). Philadelphia, PA: Haworth Press.

Harlow, J. F. (1958). The nature of love. *American Psychologist, 13*, 673–685.

Harlow, H. F., & Mears, C. (1979). *The human model: Primate perspectives*. New York: Wiley.

James, S. (2004). Why do foster care placements disrupt? An investigation of the reasons for placement change in foster care. *Social Service Review, 78*, 601–627.

Marsh, J. C., Smith, B. D., & Bruni, M. (2011). Integrated substance abuse and child welfare services for women: A progress review. *Children and Youth Services Review, 33*(3), 466–472.

Mather, J., Langer, P. B., & Harris, N. J. (2007). *Child welfare: Policies and best practices.* Belmont, CA: Thompson Brooks/Cole.

Maza, P. L. (2009). A comparative examination of foster youth who did and did not achieve permanency. In B. Kerman, M. Freundlich, & A. N. Maluccio (Eds.), *Achieving permanence for older children and youth in foster care.* New York: Columbia Press.

Middlebrooks, J. S., & Audage, N. C. (2008). *The effects of childhood stress across the lifespan.* Atlanta, GA: Centers for Disease Control and Prevention, National Center for Injury Prevention and Control.

Otterman, S. (2010, October 12). Lauded Harlem schools have their own problems. *The New York Times*

Rockhill, A., Centeno, J., Cooper, C., Duong, T., Kothari, B., Mitchell, L., Newton-Curtis, L., Poirier, C., Rodges, A., & White, J. (2009). *Final report: Oregon's Title IV-E waiver demonstration project evaluation 2004–2009: Subsidized guardianship component.* Portland: Child Welfare Partnership.

Rolock, N., Koh, E., Cross, T. & Eblen-Manning, J. (2009). Multiple move study: Understanding reasons for foster care instability. Children and Family Research Center, School of Social Work, University of Chicago at Urbana-Champaign. Retrieved August 9, 2011, from http://www.cfrc.illinois.edu/publications/rp_20091101_MultipleMoveStudyUnderstandingReasonsFor FosterCareInstability.pdf.

Sapolsky, R. M. (2001). *A primate's memoir.* New York: Scribner.

Sapolsky, R. M. (2005). *Monkeyluv: and other essays on our lives as animals.* New York: Scribner.

Scannapieco, M. (1999). Kinship care in the public child welfare system: A systemic review of the research. In R. L. Hegar & M. Scannapieco (Eds.), *Kinship foster care: Policy, practice and research* (pp. 141–154). Oxford: Oxford University Press.

Stone, S. (2007). Child maltreatment, out-of-home placement and academic vulnerability. A fifteen-year review of evidence and future directions. *Children and Youth Services Review, 29*(2), 139–161.

Swartz, R. (2007, March 7). Robert Sapolsky discusses physiological effects of stress. *Stanford Report.* Retrieved July 7, 2011, from http://news.stanford.edu/news/2007/march7/sapolsky-030707.html.

Szalavitz, M. S., & Perry, B. D. (2010). *Born for love.* New York: Harper Collins.

Technical Assistance Partnership (n.d.). *Benefits of systems of care for child welfare.* Retrieved August 18, 2011 from www.tapartnership.org/docs/benefitsOFSOCChildWelfare.pdf.

The Children's Monitor (July 15, 2011). *Children in care continue to be left behind.* Retrieved 8/31/2011, from http://childrensmonitor.worldpress.com/2011/07/15children-in-care-continue-to-be-left-behind/

Thorson, C. E., & Eagleston, J. R. (1983). Chronic stress in children and adolescents. *Theory into Practice, 22*(1), 48–56. Retrieved August 12, 2011 from http://www.jstor.org/stable/1476240.

Tough, P. (2008). *Whatever it takes: Geoffrey Canada's quest to change Harlem and America.* Boston: Houghton Mifflin Company.

U. S. Office of Personnel Management (n.d.). Adoption benefits guide. Retrieved August 8, 2011 from U. S. Office of Personnel Management: http: www.opm.gov/employment_and_benefits/worklife/officialdocuments/handbooksguides/adoption/index.dsp.

U.S. Department of Health and Human Services, Administration for Children and Families, Administration on Children, Youth and Families, Children's Bureau (2013). *The AFCARS Report. Preliminary FY 2012 estimates as of July 2013(20).* Retrieved from: http://www.acf.hhs.gov/sites/default/files/cb/afcarsreport20.pdf.

West, P., Sweeting, H., Young, R., & Kelly, S. (2010). The relative importance of family socioeconomic status and school-based peer hierarchies for morning cortisol in youth: An exploratory study. *Social Science & Medicine, 70*(8), 1246–1253.

Chapter 5
Transitioning into Adulthood: Promoting Youth Engagement, Empowerment, and Interdependence Through Teaming Practices

Mary Elizabeth Rauktis, Ben Kerman, and Chereese M. Phillips

Abstract The conventional models used for preparing youth for emancipation from child welfare emphasize independent living services in which youths learn how to find an apartment, apply for jobs or college, and manage money and budget for household expenses. Yet the focus on "independence" for youth leaving the child welfare system does not fit with the developmental tasks of adolescence. A more fitting goal for youth would be "interdependence," as most young people do not achieve instant independence, but gradually take on the roles of an adult as they navigate through their twenties. During this period they require considerable emotional and practical support from families. Youth become independent and exercise autonomy within these supportive and empowering relationships.

Youth who come into care when they are older may return home, whereas those who enter at younger ages and experience multiple placements may lose contact with extended family and not form a consistent relationship with helping caregiver(s). Youth who are supported into young adulthood by birth or adoptive families or an extended period of assistance from foster parents fare better than youth who do not have these supports. Interventions that engage youth in progressively deepening responsibility for their own destiny, while simultaneously strengthening the support network so critical to successful interdependence beyond foster care, recognize that these youth are not all the same and that "one size does not fit all." Teaming practices that respect youth voices, promote emerging autonomy, and engage a broad support system represent a needed step beyond life skills curricula that focus on the youth in isolation. They offer a variety of options to agencies working with complex

M.E. Rauktis (✉)
Child Welfare Education and Research Programs, School of Social Work,
University of Pittsburgh, Pittsburgh, PA, USA
e-mail: mar104@pitt.edu

B. Kerman
Strategic Learning and Evaluation, The Atlantic Philanthropies, New York, NY, USA

C.M. Phillips
School of Social Work, University of Pittsburgh, Pittsburgh, PA, USA

H. Cahalane (ed.), *Contemporary Issues in Child Welfare Practice*,
Contemporary Social Work Practice, DOI 10.1007/978-1-4614-8627-5_5,
© Springer Science+Business Media New York 2013

families by building secure interdependence for the youth in their care and can be used as a time-limited decision-making intervention as well as a more comprehensive framework for providing ongoing services.

Keywords Transition • Teaming and Conferencing • Interdependence • Youth Engagement and Empowerment

Introduction: Jasmine's Story

Eighteen-year-old Jasmine arrives for an intake interview at the homeless shelter where you are employed as a social worker. You observe that she is an attractive, mixed-race young woman who is carefully dressed and well groomed. She tells you that her mother, Sharon, abruptly moved out of their modest apartment and that her own part-time job did not cover the full rent. She wrote on her application for assistance that she is without a home and that "sometimes your family can be there for you and sometimes they can't."

In the course of your interview, it becomes apparent that Jasmine's needs have overwhelmed her closest friends from high school, two particularly supportive and encouraging teachers who saw in her a world of potential and encouraged her to prepare for college, and a former group home counselor who was always there for her crisis calls. Each of these caring individuals tried to follow her through placement moves, mood swings, emotional exhaustion and uncertainty, and finally Jasmine's apparent rejection. Having run out of friends open to indefinite couch surfing, Jasmine wants to work something else out, and that is why she is sitting across from you.

How did Jasmine get here? Jasmine was "lucky," enjoying a string of stable foster families since her placement at age eight. Jasmine enjoyed a good relationship with her most recent foster family and her last three caseworkers. She was "lucky": As an older teen in foster care in her state, she was entitled to ongoing support through age 21 as long as she remained in school and fulfilled her service plan. In school, Jasmine was a well-rounded, hard-working, insightful, and hopeful student, having overcome early learning challenges and occasional problems with anxiety, depression, and disruptive behavior. Jasmine was "lucky," even though placement moves, caseworker turnover, terminations of parental rights, restricted internet and phone access, and inconvenient supervised visits contributed to her losing touch with her brothers, father, and her extended family. In addition to her continuing foster placement, her plan included a weekly life skills development group, job readiness and search assistance, and aid with transition to an apartment. She also received counseling with a clinical social worker, medication support, and monthly visits from her individual caseworker.

As a result, Jasmine's caseworker and foster family were surprised when, shortly after turning 18, she rejected her education and life skills plan and suddenly exited her foster home to go to live with her mother. Jasmine decided that she wanted to try to put aside her disappointment and anger with her birth family for having failed to care for her (impaired by drug addiction, Jasmine's mother, Sharon, had abandoned her and her twin brothers and moved to another state; Jasmine knew little about her father). Jasmine avoided her caseworker and negotiated her own reunification with her mother. Jasmine's relationship with her mother had been inconsistent and conflictual even before the state discontinued reunification efforts. Since 12-year-old Jasmine insisted that she would not allow an adoption, none of her workers revisited the permanency plan of long-term foster care, as the placements were stable and everyone was satisfied. In fact, there had been little outreach to Jasmine's family, since it was determined at that time that there were no kin placement options. Her caseworker may not have even known that Sharon was living in the same county as Jasmine, having returned to the state several years before.

Jasmine found her mother through her brother, who contacted her through a friend on Facebook. Jasmine was overjoyed to finally reconnect with her mother, as well as her two brothers, who had been adopted. Jasmine started to put words to a simmering longing to be part of a family, and this seemed to be the happy ending of which she had dreamed. When she signed herself out of care, she felt her real life as an adult and her relationship with her family was about to begin.

While Jasmine's friends and mentors usually supported her choices and efforts to be independent, few celebrated when Jasmine decided to leave care. Jasmine said she had "had enough of people telling me what to do, jerking me around and being in my business"— she wanted out. Her caseworker warned her that if she left, she couldn't return. Jasmine thought that was pretty funny—why would she ever want to return to the child welfare system?

Jasmine's new life started off well—she was happy to be with her mother, and Sharon truly wanted to make up for her earlier failings. However, a lot had changed. As a young adult, Jasmine was trying to figure out who she was and what she wanted to become. She wasn't always reliable or responsible or even pleasant. Despite a conscious effort to forgive, Jasmine felt resentful because her mother had "disappeared." She also felt alone and confused as she tried to reconcile contradictions in the history she remembered with the explanations Sharon provided. She got angry when Sharon tried to parent her or give advice.

Her mother was trying, but it was hard. Jasmine was no longer the sweet eight-year-old she remembered. In fact, Sharon reflected that she really didn't know her daughter and was troubled by feelings of guilt when she admitted that she did not even like Jasmine much of the time. Sharon felt that Jasmine was judging her for her past, and she resented it. The two lacked a supply of good memories to sustain them when things got tense, and it didn't take long to awaken both women's feelings of being attacked, deprived, and abandoned. Finances also became a source of contention. Jasmine had a part-time job with inconsistent hours and Sharon's salary wasn't sufficient for two adults to live on. She didn't feel that Jasmine was trying hard enough to find a better-paying job. They argued over who was the "boss," curfews, money, and space in the small apartment. Sharon began to feel there was room for only "one woman in this house."

Complicating matters was the fact that Jasmine didn't like Sharon's boyfriend and didn't hide this fact. Sharon even worried that her sobriety was at risk because she was feeling stressed. Consequently, when Sharon's boyfriend asked her to join him in moving to New Orleans, she couldn't come up with a good reason to say no and bringing Jasmine along wasn't part of the deal.

So now Jasmine finds herself in a difficult situation. Sharon's relocation was not part of Jasmine's plan, and she has no backup plan. In addition to most of the household's monthly income, Sharon took with her information concerning the whereabouts of Jasmine's father and links to extended family members. Among these was Aunt Gwen, who Jasmine fondly remembered visiting as a young child. Sharon also took with her Jasmine's hope that "all they needed was some time together and they could make it all work out."

Now that Sharon is gone, Jasmine doesn't know where to turn. She doesn't want to ask her younger brothers for help, since they are still living with their adoptive parents and she feels that she wouldn't be welcome in their home. She believes she has exhausted the goodwill of her friends, and she remembers her caseworker's warning that she could not reenter care. When she arrives for her intake appointment with you, Jasmine brings all of her possessions: $100 in cash, a social security card, a suitcase with some clothes, and a cell phone.

Jasmine's story is not unusual. Of the 254,162 children who entered foster care in 2012, 32 % (83,495) were between 11 and 18 years of age (U.S. DHHS 2013). Achieving permanency for youth in the foster care system is difficult. Challenges abound, particularly for adolescents, reflected by the 30 % (30,709) of youth awaiting adoption compared to the 17 % (8,634) actually adopted (U.S. DHHS 2013). Reunifications with family, many unplanned and without the full guidance and support of the system, represent a common exit path for older youth (Maza 2009;

McMillen and Tucker 1999; McCoy et al. 2008; Wulczyn 2009; U.S. DHHS 2007). Aging out, perhaps with self-reunifications like Jasmine's, and without formal reunification, adoption, or guardianship, was the path for 23,439 young adults who exited care in 2012 (U.S. DHHS 2013).

Jasmine's story illustrates what can happen when youth leave care without having established family relationships and other sources of support and concrete resources (Casey Family Programs 2010). Although the typical transition to adulthood is characterized by periods of moving back home with parents and continued reliance on parental financial support (Arnett 2000), these young adults are expected to be immediately independent at a young age. Youth describe feeling unprepared, insecure, and unsure of how to make the abrupt transition to being self-sufficient (Garcia et al. 2003; McCoy et al. 2008; McMillen et al. 1997). Moreover, the focus on "independent living" for youth negates their need for connections, fosters isolation, and creates unrealistic expectations. In fact, developmental scholars are suggesting that a more appropriate concept is "interdependent living" rather than "independent living," since most young adults do not achieve total independence from their families until later in adulthood (Arnett 2000). Interdependence is a concept which promotes connectedness and collaboration (Collins 2001; Propp et al. 2003), two factors that are particularly important for young adults who have been in the child welfare system and lack familial supports.

Although all youth who leave care for "independent" rather than "interdependent" living are a serious concern, individuals with impairments, long histories of adversarial relationships, chronic stress, and multiple placement moves pose significant challenges to successful family engagement. Only recently has the field begun to overcome the dearth of research-supported guidance on how to engage and involve families and extended kinship and friend networks so that they can be a source of support for youth transitioning into adulthood.

New approaches to family engagement recognize that youth who came into care as adolescents may have longer-standing relationships with friends and extended kin despite more ambivalent relationships with their immediate family (Wulczyn 2004). They may also have close relationships with adults such as former foster parents and group home or residential staff. Young adults like Jasmine, who entered care at a young age, often lose connections with family though placement changes and caseworker turnover. However, as they grow older, they may use the internet and social networking to find or be found by family members who then enter their lives again. They are likely to have also formed relationships with foster families or other adults who may not have been recognized by the service providers, yet who nonetheless provide important relationships and sources of emotional and practical support.

Three practice approaches that help youth in care to successfully transition to interdependent adulthood provide a focus for this chapter: Family Group Decision Making (FGDM), Team Decision Making (TDM), and Lifelong Family Connections (LFC). These three approaches differ in purpose and format, but each (1) actively engages and empowers youth to make decisions, (2) identifies and facilitates connections with systems and individuals who can support the youth, and (3) uses a team approach to make decisions and identify additional resources. Each approach recognizes that young people in the child welfare system have little input into decisions that impact their lives, as well as a lack of consistent adult relationships that can inform them, guide them, and help them cope with the often imperfect decisions they make along the path to greater autonomy and interdependence (Hyde and Kammerer 2009; McMillen et al. 1997; Samuels and Pryce 2008). Creating a team of individuals focused on the youth who are invested and willing to work together to provide different types of support helps to give youth the necessary "emotional investments to take into their adulthoods" (Samuels and Pryce 2008, p.1208). By providing long-term mentorship and guidance, team members recognize emerging autonomy, empower the youth, encourage growth, and support efforts to make sound life decisions. Finally, utilizing a team approach may create a lasting support network which the youth can draw on in future times of need (Courtney 2009).

In this chapter we first provide information about the developmental phases of adolescence and young adulthood, placing the idea of interdependence into a developmental context. We then summarize the principles of each model and the evaluation research to date. Lastly, each approach is applied to Jasmine's transition experience.

Adolescence, Youth Development, and Foster Care

Adolescence is a period of great physical, cognitive, and social-emotional growth. There is great activity in regions of the brain responsible for regulating behavior, emotion, and perception of risk. However, many of these changes precede the full development of self-regulation, so that emotions and motivation may not be in sync with reason. Consequently, adolescents may engage in behaviors such as drinking or using drugs, or unsafe sexual activity or driving, putting themselves at risk (Steinberg 2005a). However, establishing autonomy, self-governance, and self-regulation amidst increasingly complex and stressful environments are critical developmental tasks of adolescence (Steinberg 2005b). During adolescence, youth develop the cognitive capacities to monitor, reflect, and see the perspective of others, all of which are essential to becoming an autonomous individual. These biological, cognitive, and developmental changes typically occur within the context of family and community. The degree to which youth are positively connected to others while being exposed to regulating forces and are encouraged in developing psychological autonomy will impact their healthy development as adults (Barber 1997).

The conventional models used for preparing youth for emancipation from child welfare emphasize independent living services in which youths learn how to find an apartment, apply for jobs or college, and manage money and budget for household expenses. Yet the focus on "independence" for youth leaving the child welfare system does not fit with the developmental tasks of adolescence. Given that independence may in fact be unattainable and developmentally inappropriate (Avery 2010; Collins 2004; Propp et al. 2003; Shin 2009), a more fitting goal for youth would be interdependence. Support from family is an important predictor of a successful transition to adulthood (Mortimer and Larson 2002). Studies of young adult development suggest that a period of "emerging adulthood" exists for 18-25-year-olds and is characterized by residential and occupational mobility and an extended period of family support (Arnett 2000). This is a period of exploration in tandem with exploring romantic relationships, work, and education. Moving back home, changes in jobs and a need for financial support are typical during this period, until young people make lasting choices about work and relationships, often in their late twenties. Interestingly, Arnett (2000) also identifies this as a time in which young adults are more likely to engage in risky behavior as they explore a wide range of experiences before assuming the roles and responsibilities of an adult. In studies of family relationships, autonomy and relatedness with family were found to be complementary in that the young adults may have a great deal of family support and live within the parental household yet simultaneously have a great deal of autonomy (O'Connor et al. 1996). During this period of emerging adulthood, youths explore, experiment, and take risks, knowing there is a supportive family to assist them if they should fail. The current models of independent living for youth in care presume that young adults rapidly assume the roles and tasks of young adulthood without having a safety net of family and friends to turn to if they are in need of help. In reality, transitioning into adulthood and the development of independent living skills (ILS) is a lifelong process that requires the assistance of caring individuals (Arnett 2000; Shin 2009).

Independent living services (ILS) have also been criticized for being atheoretical, (Collins 2001; GAO 1999; Mares 2010). Propp et al. (2003), Montgomery et al. (2006), Pecora et al. (2008), Courtney (2009), and Avery (2010) all suggest that ILS needs to be more rigorously evaluated, given the limited evidence to support the effectiveness of services preparing youth to live independently. One example of a program that engages youth in their own planning is the Transition to Independence Process (TIP). Evaluation suggests that participation in TIP improves educational attainment, wages, and financial self-reliance while demonstrating substantial savings in costs (Clark and Crosland 2009).

The struggles many youth encounter after leaving foster care point to an urgent need for improvement. The outcomes of former foster youth transitioning into adulthood have been well documented, particularly in the Midwest Evaluation of the Adult Functioning of Former Foster Youth (Courtney et al. 2007) and the Northwest Alumni Study (Pecora et al. 2005). Both longitudinal studies found foster care alumni do not fare as well as their peers in the general population. The alumni functioned less successfully than their peers in most aspects necessary for successful adulthood, such as securing employment or going on to secondary education and establishing stable housing. They also had higher rates of teen pregnancy, mental illness, and criminal justice involvement.

Using data from the Midwest Study, Courtney et al. (2007) describe distinct subgroups of youth with differing profiles which help to explain the range of outcomes that are observed after youth leave care (Courtney et al. 2007). The largest subgroup, the "accelerated adults," successfully transitioned into adulthood.

However, they experienced brief periods of homelessness and unemployment as they managed this process. The second subgroup, the "struggling parents," had the lowest rate of finishing high school and were the least likely to be employed. As a group, their experiences were greatly shaped by being parents at a young age, and they had the least amount of social capital to support them in this role. A small subgroup was classified as "emerging adults," and this group most closely resembles the profile of emerging adults as described by Arnett (2000). The final subgroup was the smallest and characterized as the "troubled and troubling" subgroup. These youth were the least likely to be employed and more likely to be incarcerated or homeless, and needed considerable assistance to become independent. Understanding that youth are not all the same and that "one size does not fit all" provides an opportunity to create interventions that meet the needs and build on the strengths of these differing subgroups of youth.

When evaluating how well youth make the transition to adulthood, it is also important to consider how foster youth exit care. Youth can leave care in a variety of ways. Some achieve permanence through reunification, adoption, or through a permanent guardianship arrangement. Others do not achieve permanence, but age out of care or run away. Using national data, Maza (2009) found most youth who exit foster care achieve permanence through reunification with parents. Her findings suggest that when youth entered care at an older age and had fewer placements, they were able to maintain ties to family. Youth who entered care at a young age were at the highest risk for not achieving permanence and exiting by aging out of care (Maza 2009).

Once youth transition from care, one of the defining factors in their success or failure in building independent lives for themselves is their level of empowerment. For youth this would mean they would gain personal power, identify their own strengths, and build upon those strengths to achieve their goals. Both empowerment and engagement theories are intertwined and are a part of the interdependence process.

Kerman et al. (2002) looked specifically at the outcomes for self-sufficiency, well-being, and adult functioning among youth in long-term foster care who did not reunify and were assessed to be poor candidates for any other permanency path. The outcomes of youth who were adopted and those who remained in foster care until young adulthood were better than those of the youth who left the agency at age 18 or younger. In addition, those who remained for extended support in foster care were doing as well as those youth who were adopted (Kerman et al. 2002). Having additional support, provided through a foster family, adoptive family, or through a carefully considered supportive program, may provide youth with the emotional and practical support needed to navigate into adulthood. Yet many youth choose to leave care prematurely, even when they have the option of remaining longer. Those who emancipate early do so because they are frustrated with their inability to make choices (McMillen et al. 1997) and have a desire for autonomy, independence, and control over their lives (Goodkind et al. 2011). Youth in out-of-home care have limited opportunities to practice making choices (Rauktis et al. 2011). It is not the norm for older youth in out-of-home care to feel empowered; quite the opposite is true. Youth describe feeling powerless and controlled by the adults who are making decisions for them about important factors in their life (Rauktis et al. 2011).

This review highlights several important points. First, most young people do not achieve "instant independence," but gradually take on adult roles as they navigate through their twenties. Secondly, during this period they require considerable emotional and practical support from families. Thirdly, youth become independent and exercise autonomy, an important developmental task, within these supportive and empowering relationships. Those who come into care as older youth may return home, whereas those who enter at younger ages and experience multiple placements may lose contact with extended family and not form a consistent relationship with helping caregivers. Finally, youth who are supported into young adulthood by birth or adoptive families or an extended period of assistance from foster parents fare better than youth who do not have these supports. The following brief review points towards practices that engage youth in progressively deepening responsibility for their own destiny while simultaneously strengthening the support network so critical to successful interdependence beyond foster care.

Engagement, Empowerment, and Interdependence Through Family and Youth Teaming Practices

Increasingly, family and youth teaming practices are being used as communities and systems look for ways of keeping children safe while preserving family and community relationships. Family and youth teaming practices broadly refer to a collection of group processes in which service providers and public agencies come together with family, friends, community members, and other persons important to the youth for the purpose of solidifying relationships, building supports, and creating plans for youths and young adults. These practices recognize the important leadership role of the youth and the essential need for a supporting cast, the family. Youth teaming practices are built on the premise that achieving a sense of autonomy within the context of family and social connections is a critical developmental task for adolescence and an antecedent to successful adulthood. While the teaming practices described in this section are focused largely on planning and implementation tasks, each also affords opportunities to realize therapeutic benefits within the teaming interaction (Crampton and Natarajan 2005). Although detailed, rigorous, model-specific studies are limited, the accumulating evidence suggests that family and youth teaming practices help keep youth connected to their families without endangering their safety, and that they can enhance permanence by increasing kin caregiving, stabilizing placements, and cementing family connections (Pennell and Crampton 2009).

Table 5.1 outlines the characteristics of the three family and youth teaming practices that are the focus of this chapter. Each has demonstrated the potential for engaging youth and tapping network strengths for youth involved in foster care.

Table 5.1 Family teaming for youth permanence: comparison of approaches

	Family Group Decision Making (FGDM)	Team Decision Making (TDM)	Lifelong Family Connections (LFC)
Purpose	Engage youth in a group process that rebuilds their family and social network and serves as a platform to elevate youth and family voices in decision making (Merkel-Holguin et al. 2007, p. 38)	Engage youth and their communities in making an immediate decision about placement based on safety, well-being, and permanency (Annie E. Casey, Matrix of Family Teaming: Comparison of Approaches, 2011)	Develop a plan for youth to exit foster care with enduring family and other adult relationships and with family-based preparation for adulthood (Annie E. Casey, Matrix of Family Teaming: Comparison of Approaches 2011)
Goal of the teaming meeting	Prepare and empower the family group to create a plan to achieve the purpose of the FGDM	Obtain a consensus decision regarding the placement of the youth	Over time, engage youth and partners in a team process with the youth voice as a central element, so as to make a plan that addresses youths' needs for safety, permanency, and well-being
Core practices	Attendance of youth; youth-focused and youth actively engaged; independent coordinators; skillful facilitation of the group; diligent search; conference preparation; family meeting	Teamwork; consensus; active involvement; skillful facilitation; safety planning; strengths-based assessment; needs-driven services; feedback loops; formation of community into long-term support networks (Annie E. Casey 2002)	Fully involving youth; family focused; birth, siblings, birth and foster families involved; agency involved; use of direct practice tools; four types of meetings; collaborative, concurrent planning; shared decision making (Greenblatt et al. 2010; Kerman et al. 2009)
Specific professional roles	Coordinator and facilitator, who may be the same person. Both roles require training. The coordinator/facilitator is someone with no case-specific responsibilities to the youth	Trained facilitator who is a caseworker for the agency and who, as a team member, shares responsibility for making decisions	Permanency social worker who is a trained and assigned case manager
Team members	All members of the youth's birth and extended family network. A coordinator works with the youth in preparation to identify and invite family, professionals, and community network members	Emphasis is on inclusion of all individuals who can contribute to the decision about placement change	Team members are drawn from natural network including birth and extended family, caregivers, and adults with informal relationships

(continued)

Table 5.1 (continued)

	Family Group Decision Making (FGDM)	Team Decision Making (TDM)	Lifelong Family Connections (LFC)
Number of meetings and length	One or more meetings can be held with variable length of 1–3 h	One meeting; on average 1–2 h	Four types of meetings: safety, individual, joint, and large-team meetings that are held every 4–6 weeks until permanency is achieved
Teaming activities	(1) Referral (2) Active and diligent search (3) Preparing youth and participants (4) Family meeting (5) Follow up	(1) Referral (2) Individual meetings to prepare youth (3) Creating a group (4) TDM meeting	(1) Referral and safety parameters meeting (2) Individual meetings with youth, preparing and creating team (3) Individual and joint group meetings with team members to complete assessment and prepare (4) Formulation and implementation of plan to address youth's developmental needs (5) Large group meetings to explore different care options concurrently
Preparation	The youth and all of the family members and professionals are contacted by youth and coordinator and invited to the meeting. The purpose of the meeting is explained. The coordinator has the responsibility for preparing all team members	Caseworker and youth invite family members and friends and professionals and explain the purpose of the TDM meeting	Individual and small group meetings are held to explain the LFC, prepare members to contribute, build relationships between and among group members, and explore different care options concurrently
Plan responsibility	Family/Youth crafts plan and agency representatives collaborate to finalize the plan. Agency has responsibility for oversight and for ensuring plan achieves safety, permanency, and well-being	Family/Youth social worker makes the decision if consensus regarding the placement issues cannot be achieved. Agency has ultimate responsibility for decisions made	Decision making is shared by team; public child welfare agency ensures that the plan achieves safety, permanency, and well-being. Responsibility shifted from agency to team to permanent parent

Evaluation of effectiveness	Two studies: Gunderson (2005), Velen and Devine (2005). Positive findings for decreasing restrictiveness of living environment and increasing permanency	Children who had a TDM within 1 day of the substantiated referral significantly less likely to experience recurrence than those who had a TDM more than 1 day later. http://www.unc.edu/~lynnu/anchoreval.pdf and also see Wildfire et al. (2009)	According to Greenblatt et al. (2010), 44 % of youth in the pilot group exited care within 18 months, and 24–31 % achieved legal permanence within 18 months
Distinctive elements of each approach	Comprehensive preparation of the youth, family, and other members by a coordinator; private family time during meeting; independent coordinator and facilitator; when agency's concerns are met, youth's preferences are followed	Held for every placement decision for child/youth involved with a public child welfare agency	"Permanency social worker" assigned to each youth; youth is active in the process and the intervention is customized for youth's age and developmental readiness; emphasis on relationship building between and among youth and team members; continuous process until permanency achieved
Usage	Implemented in more than 35 states and 22 countries	TDM has been used as a core strategy in more than 70 Annie E. Casey Family to Family sites	All divisions of Casey Family Services use this approach

Adapted from the following matrices

"Family to Family: Key Characteristics of Family Meetings" available at http://www.aecf.org/initiatives/familytofamilytools/tdm/3_7_key_characteristics_of_family_meetingspdf

Center for the Study of Social Policy. (2002) "Bringing Families to the Table: A Comparative Guide to Family Meetings in Child Welfare." Retrieved from: http://www.cssp.org/publications/child-welfare/child-welfare-misc/bringing-families-to-the-table-a-comparative-guide-to-family-meetings-in-child-welfare.pdf

Salem-Woodburn CSD family meeting study group, Fall (1993), comparative study of models adapted for PA use

While there are other worthy varieties, these three practice models were selected because they represent a continuum. They range from a family-driven, typically single-event model in which the professional plays a secondary role (i.e., Family Group Decision Making), to a systems-based outreach to engage family members at critical decision points during their involvement in the life of a family (i.e., Team Decision Making), to a reorientation of all foster care services to optimize opportunities to strengthen permanent family connections, increase interdependence, and reduce nonnormative intrusion (i.e., Lifelong Family Connections).

A 2002 survey from the Center for the Study of Social Policy described some of the commonalities across family team applications. This survey emphasized several common values and practices embraced within the models examined that characterize family engagement practice:

- Mutual respect among families, community partners, and providers
- Power shift from system authorities to shared decision making and control of resources
- Inclusive definition of family and team composition
- Welcoming and safe meeting place
- Commitment to balance individual participant and family needs while focusing on safety, permanency, and well-being

Family Group Decision Making

Chapter 3 includes a full description of Family Group Decision Making (FGDM). In the current chapter, a brief overview of the term as it is used to cover a variety of team practices that shift decision making from a professionally-driven to a family-driven approach is given. FGDM, sometimes known as family group conferencing, was first legislated in New Zealand after protests by indigenous people against the European-based child welfare system (Hudson et al. 1996). FGDM has spread to other parts of the world, and child welfare systems in Europe and the USA are increasingly integrating FGDM into their child protection practices. The model is based on the beliefs that (a) children do better when they are connected to their families, including extended kin; and (b) child welfare interventions that assume primary responsibility for the care of children can be disempowering to a family, depriving them of support from extended family and partners in the community (Merkel-Holguin 2001). For transitioning youth, FGDM is intended to engage them in a group process that rebuilds their family and social networks and serves as a platform to elevate youth and family voices in decision making (Merkel-Holguin et al. 2007).

The research on the effectiveness of FGDM with older youth has yielded mixed results. A study of placement and relationship outcomes for youth ages 11–18 after using FGDM found that 34 % of the youth returned home or were placed with kin, and most moved to less restrictive settings (Gunderson 2005). Another study which used FGDM to help with the permanency of older youth who were in care for a prolonged period of time found that plans were created for all of the children and that a small percent of these unlikely candidates for permanency still achieved permanent family relationships (Velen and Devine 2005). A rigorous random assignment control trial of FGDM in California showed no benefits related to substantiated maltreatment placement stability or case closure (Berzin et al. 2008). These authors noted that the benefits of FGDM may lie more in family engagement and improved relationships, even if they are not detected as impacts on safety, permanency, and well-being outcomes. Similarly, Weigenberg et al. (2009) used propensity score analysis to create a comparison group and found that families with FGDM were better connected to counseling and parenting services, even though there were no significant differences at a 36-month follow-up. Although evidence of the effectiveness of FGDM with older youth is limited, the positive findings on engagement and outcomes with no deterioration of safety reflect considerable promise.

Jasmine's Family Group Decision Making Conference

Referral and Preparation

Approximately 6 months prior to Jasmine being eligible to decline services and leave care, Cynthia, her social worker, talks to her about having a family group conference. She anticipates that Jasmine may be planning to leave care and wants her to have a supportive and committed group of family, friends, and professionals to turn to for help after she leaves. Jasmine cautiously agrees; she is concerned that the adults will gang up on her. Cynthia contacts the independent living (IL) coordinator, who sends a referral to the private nonprofit agency that will coordinate and facilitate the FGDM. The conference will be coordinated and facilitated by Mike, an experienced FGDM professional. Mike first meets with Jasmine to talk about the purpose of FGDM and to engage her in the process. They talk about her goals for permanency and how a FGDM conference could be helpful to her in achieving her goals. They also discuss her concerns about the conference and how these will be addressed. Jasmine agrees to FGDM and they begin to make a list of persons to invite to the meeting. Jasmine wants her mother and brothers to be there but would prefer if Sharon's boyfriend didn't attend. She wants to invite her current and former foster parents and several friends. After some probing, she identifies her teachers, the IL worker, a nurse, a former group home counselor, her former therapist, and Cynthia as these friends.

Mike also meets with Sharon to explain the purpose of the meeting and to enlist her help in finding other family members. He stresses that the meeting is focused on and directed by Jasmine, but he knows that in order to be part of the process, Sharon needs support as well. Sharon identifies her NA sponsor and a neighbor as supportive persons, and Jasmine agrees to invite them to the meeting. Mike facilitates a discussion with Sharon and Jasmine about ways that Sharon's boyfriend can attend but says that Jasmine has the final word on whether he is invited to the meeting. Sharon, Mike, and Jasmine use the internet and phone book to search for paternal relatives and Sharon's relatives in Kentucky. Jasmine's father is in jail, but her paternal grandmother and paternal Aunt Gwen both live in the area and agree to attend. Sharon also reconnects with her older sister, who is invited. Jasmine invites her brothers and their family to the conference. Over 20 people have been invited, and Sharon and Jasmine agree to hold the conference on a Sunday afternoon at a church where Sharon's NA group meets. Jasmine decides on the food for the meeting.

FGDM Meeting

Welcome/Introduction: *Mike gives a short welcome and Aunt Gwen offers a prayer. Mike asks each person to say who they are and their relationship to Jasmine. Mike reiterates that the purpose of the family group meeting is to help Jasmine identify where she is going to live and how she will function independently. He also reminds everyone of the process steps, mandated reporting policies/procedures, and the roles of the attendees.*

Information Sharing: *Cynthia and the independent living coordinator share Jasmine's current situation and her goal of leaving care and talk about what that means in terms of housing, insurance, employment, and school. Jasmine's teacher and nurse practitioner provide an update on her grades, health, and graduation status and whether she is eligible to receive financial aid for college. The IL coordinator describes potential housing options and services, such as supported independent living and aftercare. All of this is shared so that the family and Jasmine know what resources are available in developing a plan.*

As they share information, the group participants highlight the strengths that Jasmine has—how far she has come and the good choices she has made. The caseworker emphasizes that the plan created by the family needs to address the following: providing a safe and stable place for Jasmine to live and ensuring that she attends school or has full-time employment. Jasmine says that her goals are to have a safe place to live and an income and to attend college and have relationships with her family. For Jasmine, one of the most positive aspects of information sharing is hearing her strengths talked about by everyone in the meeting. She recognizes that she has a lot of positives on which to build.

Private Family Time: *Mike introduces private family time, during which the family meets alone to share a meal and decide how to help Jasmine. All of the professionals remain in a separate room so they can be part of the process when the family returns with a plan.*

Plan Finalization: *After 2 h the professionals rejoin the meeting and the family presents their plan. Jasmine is going to live with her mother for the first 6 months, and during this time, she will find a part-time job and save her money. Her IL worker will help her to identify part-time jobs close to her mother's apartment. With Cynthia's help, Jasmine is going to prepare to take the SAT and apply to a state college in the town where her Aunt Gwen lives. She will live at school and then stay with her Aunt during the summer and semester breaks.*

Resources included in the plan are assistance with financial aid forms, college applications, and health insurance. Jasmine's grandmother, her brother's family, and her former foster parents invite her to come to their homes for Sunday and holiday dinners. However, the IL worker and caseworker express their concerns that the housing could collapse. Jasmine and her mother have not lived together in 10 years and there is already some evidence of conflict. If the housing becomes insecure, the rest of the plan would be in jeopardy. They request that the family comes up with a contingency plan as a way to prevent future housing disruption. The family reconvenes and 30 min later returns with additions to the plan. Sharon's NA sponsor will meet with her three times a week for coffee and support, and Sharon's neighbor offers her apartment as "cool off" space for Jasmine. These are included in the plan. Jasmine and her mother do not want to attend family therapy, but they agree to contact the caseworker if they change their mind.

Close the Meeting: *To close the meeting, everyone signs the plan and, after a discussion, they all agree to meet in 3 months in order to evaluate how the plan is working. Jasmine offers to post status updates on her Facebook page as a way of keeping in touch until the next meeting. The meeting adjourns.*

Follow-Up

The caseworker follows up on the meeting by ensuring that written copies of the plan are distributed and that the plan is adequately resourced and implemented. She stays in touch with Jasmine, monitoring the implementation of the plan. A month after the meeting, Jasmine contacts her to be referred to family therapy. The caseworker assists Jasmine and Sharon in making the connection to a therapist.

Team Decision Making

For youth who are transitioning, the primary goal of Team Decision Making (TDM) is to engage them and their communities in decision-making processes regarding permanence. Achieving permanence involves creating a network of resources and supports to assist youth in transitioning out of foster care into adulthood and beyond. TDM meetings capitalize on the critical opportunities present at decision-making points, such as when a child is at risk of removal, when a placement change is being contemplated, and during decisions about moving to permanency. Team Decision Making utilizes a family- and community-centered process to create a collaborative decision-making team. Meetings occur with consistency and regularity, and a hallmark of these meetings is an emphasis on engagement through good communication. This involves inclusivity, feedback loops, and reaching consensus. The TDM process may be repeated at subsequent choice points when a placement change is being considered. In a permanency TDM meeting, the intention is to facilitate the development of long-term, community-based safety nets for families at risk by linking families with natural supports within their neighborhoods (Annie E. Casey Foundation 2002). With older youth, a TDM meeting may be convened to consider upcoming decisions about independent living or emancipation (Crampton and Pennell 2009) or as the first step towards a permanent living arrangement with a family for youth living in long-term care.

The eight essential elements intrinsic to the TDM process include teamwork (mutual knowledge sharing), consensus, active family involvement, skillful facilitation, safety planning, strength-based assessment, needs-driven services, and, perhaps most importantly for youth in transition, formation of long-term support networks that include community members (Annie E. Casey Foundation 2002).

TDM meetings are facilitated by a trained senior child welfare staff person who has considerable clinical knowledge and a thorough understanding of how complex systems function. As with FGDM, a referral is made and the facilitator meets with the youth to describe the purpose of a TDM meeting and to identify individuals who should be invited to the meeting.

The flow of a TDM meeting is as follows: First, the facilitator introduces him or herself and asks the participants to introduce themselves and explain their relationship to the youth/family. The facilitator also explains the purpose of the TDM meeting and goes over the ground rules for the meeting, which are that everyone involved must be honest and respectful during discussions as they seek to reach their shared objective of developing the best plan for the youth. The caseworker explains why he/she called the meeting, reconfirms its purpose, and presents any relevant history including strengths, resources, current needs, and risk and safety concerns. The participants are encouraged to give their perspectives, and then the caseworker recommends a plan of action based on the discussion up to that point. The next stage of the meeting occurs when the facilitator leads the group in a brainstorming session in which the recommendation is discussed and alternate plans are considered. When all of the possible solutions have been identified and discussed, the facilitator assesses the group's movement towards a consensus decision and states the decision. Action steps for implementing the decision are then outlined, and, once again, the facilitator moves the group to consensus about the action steps. If consensus cannot be reached by the group on either the decisions or the actions, then the caseworker will make a decision on behalf of the agency. At the conclusion of the meeting, the facilitator verbally summarizes the team's decision, what contingency plans have been made, what the resources are, and who will be providing those resources. All of the members receive a copy of the written summary of the meeting.

Team Decision Making, like FGDM, has been shown to promote high satisfaction among family participants and workers (Crea and Berzin 2009). It has been shown to be particularly effective in cases involving older youth (Annie E. Casey Foundation 2002). However, research also suggests that TDM is most successful when the essential elements mentioned above are included in the practice. For instance, recommendations for preserving the family were made in 70 % of the decisions when 7–8 of the essential elements were present, but only 22 % when only one element was present (Wildfire et al. 2009). Other studies conducted by Crea et al. (2008) examined how TDM translates across different communities and settings. Because complying with the essential elements is an important component of the TDM approach, variation in implementation was found to lead to differences in outcomes (Crea et al. 2008).

Jasmine's Team Decision Making Meeting

Referral and Preparation

Jasmine's caseworker, Cynthia, makes the referral to TDM as Jasmine approaches the age of emancipation. Since Jasmine is intent on leaving the child welfare system but has not made any preparations, Cynthia wants her to make the best possible choice for independence by helping to find supportive adults and family members before leaving care. Cynthia meets with Jasmine to explain the purpose of a TDM meeting and to ask if Jasmine agrees to participate. She also helps Jasmine identify people to invite to be on her team. After some initial reluctance, Jasmine agrees and wants her mother, brothers, and friends from school to be at the meeting. Cynthia also suggests that Jasmine considers some other supportive adults who have been involved in her life now and in the past, and Jasmine identifies her teachers, nurse, current and former foster parents, and some of the group home staff from an earlier placement. These individuals are informed about the purpose of Jasmine's TDM meeting and invited to participate. In the process of talking with her mother, Jasmine reconnects with her Aunt Gwen and paternal grandmother, and they are invited as well. The caseworker arranges for Jasmine's meeting to be led by Mike, an experienced facilitator of TDM.

Team Decision Making Meeting

Introductions and Opening: *Mike introduces himself and asks the participants to introduce themselves and share their relationship to Jasmine. He explains the purpose of the meeting and the basic ground rules, clarifying that the agency maintains responsibility for the plan if consensus cannot be reached in the group. He reminds everyone that information is private, but it may be used for case planning or in court if necessary. He encourages everyone to be open and honest and to work towards developing the best plan for Jasmine's transition. Cynthia explains why she called the meeting and reiterates that the purpose of the group is to come to a decision about where Jasmine should live after she leaves care and to help her to create a network of supportive individuals who will be there for her.*

Cynthia describes the situation at hand: Jasmine wishes to leave care and live with her mother, but this placement may be problematic given that Jasmine and her mother have just recently reconnected. Without additional resources, Jasmine could end up homeless or living in a shelter if the current plan does not work out. Cynthia also outlines concerns about Jasmine being able to receive ongoing medical care and continue her education. Cynthia concludes by talking about Jasmine's strengths, such as her resourcefulness, the good choices she has made about school and relationships, and how she has connected with supportive adults. Mike asks the other participants to give their perspectives on the current situation. At the end of the discussion, the caseworker recommends that Jasmine emancipate and live with her mother.

Brainstorming: Mike now leads the group in a brainstorming session, inviting the group to help determine whether this is the best plan through discussing additional ideas and solutions. Should Jasmine live with her mother? Could Jasmine live alone or move into an independent living program? What about living with her Aunt Gwen or her grandmother? What other solutions do the participants have that the agency has not considered? As ideas are put forth, Mike leads the group in logically working through each option, asking about the potential problems as well as the benefits of each possibility and how each idea could meet the objectives of providing a safe place for Jasmine to live and a circle of supportive friends and family.

Since Mike is experienced at TDM facilitation, he is able to perceive fairly early in the discussion that people are avoiding talking about Sharon's history of relapse and their concerns about her remaining drug-free while coping with the stress of living with another person. He asks the group to talk honestly but respectfully about their concerns, and this also gives Sharon permission to express her own fears and worries. Jasmine admits that she doesn't like Sharon's boyfriend and says she feels her mother would side with him rather than her when they inevitably have disagreements.

Although she is disappointed, Jasmine concedes that living with her mother probably isn't a good idea, and the group quickly comes to consensus that this isn't the best placement decision. They are then able to consider each of the other options identified in the brainstorming part of the meeting. In the course of this discussion, it becomes clear that consensus is being reached on a decision for Jasmine to live with her Aunt Gwen after Jasmine graduates from high school and to remain with her foster parents until that time. Mike states this and the group agrees that this is the decision.

Implementation: *Mike leads the group into the final phase of the meeting, which is to identify the action steps for implementing this placement decision. Arranging for professional, community, and familial supports will be critical to ensuring that this placement decision is successful. While she is eager to live with her Aunt, Jasmine wants to live on campus when she attends college and stay with her Aunt during the semester breaks and summer. Mike leads the group in identifying who will provide assistance to Jasmine and Gwen in helping Jasmine to successfully apply for admission and financial aid. Offers of assistance in areas of need are made, and Mike documents this. At the conclusion of the meeting, he verbally summarizes the team's decision, what contingency plans have been made, what the resources are, and who will be providing those resources. All of the participants receive a copy of Mike's written summary of the meeting.*

Lifelong Family Connections

In contrast to the FGDM focus on maximizing family empowerment in a discrete event or TDM's use of critical decision-making points to engage additional perspectives and resources, the third model examined in this chapter, Lifelong Family Connections (LFC), represents an ambitious attempt to apply teaming principles across an array of ongoing service activities (Casey Family Services 2005). The hallmarks of LFC include consistent elevation of the youth's developmental needs; a balanced, persistent focus on permanency and family strengthening through ongoing team meetings; and assembly of team members in various configurations over time (i.e., both the full group as well as subsets of team members contribute to the team effort). Underlying values of LFC include the importance of family connections, facilitating the youth's exit from the child welfare system to a permanent legal parent, the unique advantages of collaboration, and attention to the ever-present backdrop of trauma.

Building on existing models such as FGDM, the LFC model emphasizes shared planning and decision making to guide timely permanency planning while strengthening relationships for children in out-of-home care (Greenblatt et al. 2010). Proponents of LFC believe that better plans and resources lead to better outcomes and that the best plans are informed by sound decisions based on accurate information and made with the youth's best interests at the forefront. However, good information can only be obtained by building collaborations, creating shared ownership, and engaging fully with youth. Core practices (Table 5.1) include fully involving youth in the team process; preparing for permanence using a variety of practice tools, with the child welfare agency, birth and foster parents, siblings, and extended family members being involved in the process; diligently searching to find and involve family members in the LFC process; and using four different types of meetings to ensure that permanency is achieved. Since the youth-voiced need for permanent connections is foremost, this requires looking anew at present and past connections, as well as anticipating what will be needed to help the youth transition into young adulthood. Similarly, youth who have previously declined a permanence path are respectfully encouraged to reassess. This also necessitates promoting understanding of the past, how it has shaped the present situation, and how it can provide keys to solving current challenges.

Though the process begins much like conventional services provision (e.g., the professional caseworker is responsible for case management), the course of work is marked by transferring parental responsibilities from worker to team to permanent lifelong parent and family. The permanency social worker facilitates the team process for each youth using a series of individual, joint, and large team meetings. The meetings have different purposes. For example, a safety parameters meeting must be held when the youth is first referred, when there is a social worker or supervisor change, or if there are changes in case circumstances that have safety implications. Extensive preparatory meetings occur before the first meeting of the whole team in order to explain the process and expectations for each individual, to identify areas that pose likely points of conflict, and to help each participant be ready to assume a well-informed and constructive role in the process. Youth engage in a number of permanency preparation practices. For example, one practice is intended to help them identify who should be on the team and another is intended to assist them in mastering the skills that can support family life and avoiding the pitfalls that can undermine it. When the full-team meetings begin, information and resources are pooled to increase the number and quality of supports and options, while the team is ever mindful to tap individual and family strengths without ignoring the impact that trauma plays in youth development. Joint meetings are held to build relationships, resolve conflicts, and prepare for large meetings. Large team meetings are held once essential members are on board and adequately prepared through individual and joint meetings, and may begin with a small core team, with additional members added as they are identified and prepared.

These meetings are continually scheduled for every 4–6 weeks until legal permanency is achieved and the youth exits the system to family care. Additional meetings are added as necessary. By meeting regularly but not focusing on particular decisions, this team model is designed to foster ongoing relationship building between and among members and with the youth. The team facilitator helps team members keep the youth's needs central and share information and concerns while suspending their individual agendas in order to meet the best interests of the youth. Individual team members are helped to tolerate feelings of frustration and uncertainty, should they arise. As a group, the team also works to anticipate obstacles to success and to create response plans and a concurrent plan should the primary plan for a permanent parent and lifelong family connections become unattainable.

Research is limited, but early findings from pilot evaluations are promising. In an early application of the approach to groups of older youth with permanency challenges (e.g., older youth with terminated parental rights residing in residential treatment centers), Greenblatt et al. (2010) found that 46 % of the youth served achieved adoption, guardianship, or a lifelong connection. Results from a 5-year implementation and outcome evaluation indicate that the practice model can be implemented effectively and established as standard practice within 18–24 months, in part facilitated by the use of case assessment and planning practice tools (Frey et al. 2008). Perhaps more importantly, permanency and timeliness have been improved without sacrificing safety. For instance, early results from an FLC implementation study involving public child welfare agencies in New England show that the percentage of entry cohorts achieving exit with legal permanence within 18 months has increased over 200 % since using the LFC program (Greenblatt et al. 2010). With more rigorous evaluation underway, this practice-based model continues to be honed for manualization and integrated alongside several promising child welfare practices (e.g., Family Finding, Permanency Preparation using Henry's 3-5-7 model (2005), and evidence-based interventions [e.g., Trauma-Focused Cognitive Behavioral Treatments] to help ready youth for successful living with family members).

Jasmine and Her Family Participate in Lifelong Family Connections

Referral, Team Building, and Planning: *Whether Jasmine is in her first or 51st placement, the goal of LFC is to create a team committed to ensuring that her needs for safety, permanency, and well-being are met while also making her current foster placement her last one. Her primary worker, Cynthia, uses individual preparatory meetings to orient Jasmine, her current caregivers, easily identified and available parents or family members, and any other professionals or providers to the model. Each of them is helped to understand that the ultimate goal of the teaming process is for Jasmine to exit the system to a primary legal parent willing and able to provide for her safety and well-being permanently, and that teaming is intended to build a wider circle of supportive family and adult relationships that will be there for her into the future. They are asked about their hopes and dreams for Jasmine and their willingness to play a role in helping her plan for her future. Parents, family members, and other supportive adults are encouraged to also see themselves as essential role models and links to the community as Jasmine expands her access to resources and strengthens or builds skills associated with successful adult living.*

After the orientation of key team members and some initial discussion of her own goals, Jasmine is encouraged to identify and invite other potential team members. To help identify potential supports and permanent family connections, Cynthia asks questions such as the following: "Who do you care about?" "Who cares about you?" "Who would you turn to if you wanted to share good news?" "What if you had just received bad news?" "Who would take a collect call from you no matter what?" "Who wants you to succeed?" "Who knows you best?" "Who thinks you're a special kid?" "Who gives you good advice about life?" "Who is the kind of adult or parent you would like to become?" "If you could pick your parent, who would it be?" and "Who could help you achieve your goals for the future?"

Jasmine includes her mother, her brothers, her father, and some extended family members she only vaguely remembers in her list. Jasmine's list of team members also includes her closest friends and teachers, her former counselor, her current foster parents as well as some former foster parents, and her Aunt Gwen, plus her current treatment providers. Cynthia helps Jasmine research the whereabouts of family, friends, and community members with whom Jasmine has lost contact, and Cynthia and Jasmine make an initial approach to these people. Even if Jasmine does not identify some of these as potential supports, Cynthia will likely approach them after a careful record review. She also helps Jasmine consider people she may not readily identify on her own or who Jasmine may feel would not want to join in her LFC group. For example, Cynthia encourages Jasmine to contact her former foster parents, even though Jasmine believes that some of them are mad at her or "done with" her because of how the placements ended. Cynthia also suggests that they contact Jasmine's imprisoned father to see if he is willing to participate in the fullest way possible—via telephone or even written correspondence. Although he is not able to participate in large team meetings, he does decide to join key joint meetings with Jasmine and Cynthia by phone and provides meaningful family history and information. He also gives a stamp of approval on Jasmine's future plans and permission for her to fully embrace another parent figure into her life if that is what she wants.

As Cynthia orients new members to the process, she invites them to consider what they would wish for Jasmine and how they can help. When Cynthia reviews the expectations for each member, she particularly emphasizes that the members should concentrate on Jasmine's best interests and stay focused on a plan for her permanency, safety, and well-being. Preparatory meetings also include joint work to identify team member relationships that present risky combinations and potentially unproductive or toxic areas that Cynthia should consider when she facilitates the full group. Because first challenges often revolve around group composition and direction, such as whether and how to include both Sharon and Jasmine's father as well as Sharon's boyfriend, each challenge provides opportunities for Cynthia to help the team keep a realistic but balanced view of reasonable concerns, the urgency of permanency, and the importance of respecting Jasmine's voice.

Cynthia and Jasmine work together to set an agenda for the early meetings that addresses Jasmine's permanency as well as her safety and well-being needs. Jasmine expresses an interest in working on her relationship with her mother and perhaps going to live with her. Sharon also shares her hopes as well as her misgivings about this. Other team members, perhaps concerned that this placement would be unlikely to succeed, use the meetings to express their concerns. Without invalidating Jasmine, Sharon, or other members' concerns, Cynthia acknowledges the concerns and turns to the group membership for the recommendations, supportive activities, and backup plan suggestions needed to make Jasmine's placement with Sharon successful. At the same time, Cynthia works with the group to develop consensus on a concurrent plan, one that identifies where Jasmine would live and who would become the primary parent figure(s) in her life should her placement with Sharon fail.

Implementation and Monitoring: *Cynthia encourages several permanency preparation activities to pave the way for Jasmine and Sharon's reunification. For example, she helps Jasmine construct a timeline of her life, including past moves, placements, events, and endings and beginnings of important relationships. This exercise is designed both to help Jasmine feel rooted in the past and to make her feel grounded in the present as she plans for the future. Cynthia involves Sharon, Jasmine's father, Jasmine's Aunt Gwen, and previous foster parents in this project to assist Jasmine in building a sense of continuity in her life. In the process the group can also correct misinformation about past life events and incorporate positive family identifications, which are often limited for youth with child welfare system involvement. Cynthia also keeps an eye on relationships that require healing or need further strengthening through joint meetings, so that these relationships will not short-circuit the teaming process or, more importantly, put Jasmine's future or healthy family connections at risk.*

Cynthia, Sharon, Jasmine, and the other team members continue to convene individual, joint, and full-team meetings in order to monitor plan implementation, progress on goals, problem solve and manage crises, and continue shifting the responsibility for leadership and direction to Sharon and Jasmine. When Jasmine and Sharon's relationship starts to derail, Cynthia draws on their permanency preparation work together to rebuild a sense of connection. Team members also offer material or emotional support and backup arrangements during this time. If the team is unable to prevent stressors or life circumstances from derailing the primary plan for Jasmine to be parented and have a safe and stable living arrangement, then Cynthia will help the team implement the concurrent plan. (Early in the planning, Cynthia will have prompted the team to identify a "Plan B" if "Plan A" does not work out in Jasmine's best interests.) For example, if living with Sharon is "Plan A" for Jasmine, then options such as having Jasmine live with her Aunt Gwen, her most recent foster parents, or one of her former foster parents would be explored for potential as "Plan B."

Then Cynthia would prioritize joint meetings between Sharon and the other parent figure(s) identified as "Plan B," so these adults could see themselves in a role of shared parenting, rather than seeing themselves as competitors for Jasmine's love and loyalty. Understanding full well that the plan will only be as successful as the strength of the relationships it represents, Cynthia does her best to help the important parent figures and significant adults in Jasmine's life set aside any tendencies towards competition or exclusion and recognize the unique and essential roles they each play in Jasmine's family tapestry.

Conclusion

Teaming practices that respect youth voices, promote emerging autonomy, and engage a broad support system represent a needed step beyond life skills curricula that focus on the youth in isolation. Though still far short of conclusive, preliminary research, intuitive appeal, and emphasis on both youth empowerment and family engagement identify these as promising practices. These teaming practices offer a variety of options to agencies working with complex families building secure interdependence for the youth in their care, even as they utilize many overlapping features. The vignettes about Jasmine in this chapter illustrate the choice points through which these principles can be integrated into different phases of work, whether a time-limited decision-making intervention or a more comprehensive framework for providing ongoing services is required.

Questions for Discussion

1. Apply each of the three approaches of FGDM, TDM, and LFC to Jasmine when she was eight and her mother abandoned the family. Follow the structure outlined in the case presentation for each model. Hypothesize which approach may have led to a more permanent place for Jasmine and her brothers. Would these approaches have better engaged Jasmine's mother and extended family?
2. Think of three questions that you would ask of the team in order to assure that the teaming process is being followed (as outlined in the table).
3. What do you think are the most important behaviors and personality characteristics for a facilitator of FGDM, TDM, and LFC, and why?
4. As the caseworker, what steps would you take to assure that you are promoting Jasmine's interdependence while also helping her to manage the frustrations and disappointments that are likely to occur within the context of her family relationships?

Acknowledgements Special thanks to the following individuals: The Pennsylvania Child Welfare Resource Center team of Wendy Unger, Christina Fatzinger, Cynthia Gore, and Justin Lee, who assisted with the FGDM section; Suzanne Barnard of the Annie E. Casey Foundation, who provided assistance with the TDM portion of this chapter; and Lauren Frey, who assisted with the LFC sections.

References

Annie E. Casey. (2011). *Matrix of Family Teaming: Comparison of Approaches, 2011.* "Family to Family: Key Characteristics of Family Meetings." Retrieved from http://www.f2f.ca.gov/res/revision_matrix.pdf.

Annie E. Casey Foundation. (September, 2002). *Family to family: Tools for rebuilding foster care. Team decision making. Involving the family and community in child welfare decisions,* part Two. Baltimore, MD. Retrieved from http://www.aecf.org.

Arnett, J. J. (2000). Emerging adulthood: A theory of development from the late teens through the twenties. *American Psychologist, 55,* 469–480.

Avery, R. J. (2010). An examination of theory and promising practices for achieving permanency for teens before they age out of foster care. *Children and Youth Services Review, 32,* 399–408.

Barber, B. K. (1997). Introduction: Adolescent socialization in context—connection, regulation and autonomy in multiple contexts. *Journal of Adolescent Research, 12*(2), 173–177.

Berzin, S. C., Cohen, E., Thomas, K., & Dawson, W. C. (2008). Does family group decision making affect child welfare outcomes? Findings form a randomized control study. *Child Welfare, 87,* 35–54.

Casey Family Programs. (2010). *Ensuring safe, nurturing and permanent families for children: the need for federal finance reform.* Seattle, WA: Author. Retrieved from http://www.casey.org/Resources/Publications/pdf/NeedForFinanceReform.pdf.

Casey Family Services. (2005). A call to action: An integrated approach to youth permanency and preparation for adulthood. Retrieved from http://www.aecf.org/upload/publicationfiles/casey_permanency_0505.pdf.

Center for the Study of Social Policy. (2002). *Bringing families to the table: A Comparative Guide to Family Meetings in Child Welfare.* Washington, DC: Author.

Clark, H. B., & Crosland, K. A. (2009). Social and life skills development : Preparing and facilitating youth for transition into young adults. In B. Kerman, M. Freundlich, & A. Maluccio (Eds.), *Achieving permanence for older children and youth in foster care.* New York: Columbia Press.

Collins, M. (2001). Foster youth transition to adulthood: a longitudinal view of leaving care. *Child Welfare League of America, 86,* 6.

Collins, M. E. (2004). Enhancing services to youths leaving foster care: Analysis of recent legislation, its potential and impact. *Children and Youth Services Review, 26,* 1051–1065.

Courtney, M. E. (2009). The difficult transition to adulthood for foster youth in the US: implications for the State as corporate parent. *Society for Research in Child Development, 23*(1).

Courtney, M. E., Dworsky, A., Cusick, G., Havlicek, J., Perez, A., & Keller, T. (2007). *Midwest evaluation of the adult functioning of former foster youth: outcomes of youth at age 21.* Chicago: Chapin Hall Center for Children at the University of Chicago.

Crampton, D., & Natarajan, A. (2005). Connections between group work and family meetings in child welfare practice: What can we learn from each other? *Social Work with Groups, 28*(1), 65–79.

Crampton, D., & Pennell, J. (2009). Family involvement meetings with older children in foster care: Promising practices and the challenge of child welfare reform. In B. Kerman, M. Freundlich, & A. Maluccio (Eds.), *Achieving permanence for older children and youth in foster care.* New York: Columbia Press.

Crea, T. M., Crampton, D. S., Abramson-Madden, A., & Usher, C. (2008). Variability in the implementation of Team Decisionmaking (TDM): Scope and compliance with the family to family practice model. *Children and Youth Services Review, 30,* 1221–1232.

Crea, T. M., & Berzin, S. C. (2009). Family involvement in child welfare decision making: Strategies and research on inclusive practices. *Journal of Public Child Welfare, 3,* 305–327.

Frey, L., Cushing, G., Freunlich, M., & Brenner, E. (2008). Achieving permanency for youth in foster care: Assessing and strengthening emotional security. *Child & Family Social Work, 13,* 218–226.

Garcia, J. A., Sivak, P., & Tibrewal, S. (2003). Transforming relationships in practice and research: What is the Stanislaus model? *Protecting Children, 18*(1&2), 22–29.

Goodkind, S., Schelbe, L. A., & Shook, J. J. (2011). Why youth leave care: Understandings of adulthood and transition successes and challenges among youth aging out of child welfare. *Children and Youth Services Review, 3*(6), 1039–1048.

Greenblatt, S., Kerman, B., Freundlich, M., & Frey, L. (2010). Permanency teams and other permanency practices: Ongoing strategies to strengthen family relationships in child welfare. *Protecting Children, 25*, 52–63.

Gunderson, K. (2005). *Family group conferences for youth in care.* Seattle, WA: Northwest Institute for Children and Families and Washington State Children's Administration.

Henry, D. L. (2005). The 3-5-7 model: Preparing children for permanency. *Children and Youth Services Review, 27*, 197–212.

Hudson, J., Morris, A., Maxwell, G., & Galaway, B. (Eds.). (1996). *Family group conferences: Perspectives on policy and practice.* Annandale, New South Wales, Australia/New York: The Federation Press/Criminal Justice Press.

Hyde, J., & Kammerer, N. (2009). Adolescents' perspectives on placement moves and congregate settings: Couples and cumulative instabilities in out-of-home care. *Children and Youth Services Review, 31*, 265–273.

Kerman, B., Lahti, M., & Lee, J. (2009). *Intensive ongoing permanency teams in child welfare: getting inside the black box of teaming.* Presented at the American Humane FGDM & other engagement approaches conference, June 4, 2009. Pittsburgh, PA.

Kerman, B., Wildfire, J., & Barth, R. (2002). Outcomes for young adults who experienced foster care. *Children and Youth Services Review, 24*(5), 319–344.

Mares, A. (2010). An assessment of independent living needs among emancipating foster youth. *Child Adolescence Social Work Journal, 27*, 79–96.

Maza, P. J. (2009). A comparative examination of foster youth who did and did not achieve permanency. In B. Kerman, M. Freundlich, & A. Maluccio (Eds.), *Achieving permanence for older children and youth in foster care* (pp. 32–39). New York: Columbia Press.

McCoy, H., McMillen, J. C., & Spitznagel, E. L. (2008). Older youth leaving the foster care system: Who, what, when, where and why? *Children and Youth Services Review, 30*, 735–745.

McMillen, J. C., Rideout, G. B., Fisher, R. H., & Tucker, J. (1997). Independent-living services: The views of former foster youth. *Families in Society, 78*(5), 471–479.

McMillen, J. C., & Tucker, J. (1999). The status of older adolescents at exit from out-of-home care. *Child Welfare, 78*, 339–360.

Merkel-Holguin, L. (2001). Family Group Conferencing: An "Extended Family" process to safeguard children and strengthen family-well being. In: E. Walton, P. Sandau-Beckler, M. Mannes (Eds.), *Balancing family-centered services and child well-being: exploring issues in policy, practice, theory and research.* Columbia University Press: New York

Merkel-Holguin, L., Tinworth, K., & Horner, A. (2007). Using family group conferencing to achieve permanency for youth. *Protecting Children, 22*(1), 38–49.

Montgomery, P., Donkoh, C., & Underhill, K. (2006). Independent living programs for young people leaving the care system: The state of the evidence. *Children and Youth Services Review, 28*(12), 1435–1448.

Mortimer, J. T., & Larson, R. W. (Eds.). (2002). *The changing adolescent experience: societal trends and the transition to adulthood.* New York: Cambridge University Press.

O'Connor, T. G., Allen, J. P., Bell, K. L., & Hauser, S. T. (1996). Adolescent-parent relationships and leaving home in young adulthood. *New Directions in Child Development, 71*, 39–52.

Pecora, P. J., Kessler, R. C., Williams, J., O'Brien, K., Downs, A. C., English, D., White, J., Hiripi, E., White, C. R., Wiggins, T., & Holmes, K. E. (2005). *Improving family foster care: Findings from the Northwest Foster Care Alumni Study.* Seattle, WA: Casey Family Programs.

Pecora, P., Whittaker, J., Maluccio, A., Barth, R., DePanfilis, D., & Plotnick, R. (2008). *The child welfare challenge policy, practice, research* (3rd ed.). New Jersey: Aldine.

Pennell, J., & Crampton, D. S. (2009). Family-involvement meetings with older children in foster care: Promising practices and the challenge of child welfare reform. In B. Kerman, M. Freundlich, & A. Maluccio (Eds.), *Achieving Permanence for Older Children and Youth in Foster Care.* New York, NY: Columbia University Press.

Propp, J., Ortega, D. M., & NewHeart, F. (2003). Independence or interdependence: Rethinking the transition from "ward of the court" to adulthood. *Families in Society, 84*(2), 259–266.

Rauktis, M. E., Fusco, R. A., Cahalane, H. G., Bennett, I., & Reinhart, S. (2011). "Try to Make It Seem Like We're Regular Kids": Youth perceptions of restrictiveness in out-of-home care. *Children and Youth Services Review, 33*(7), 1224–1233.

Samuels, G. M. & Pryce, J. M. (2008). What doesn't kill you makes you stronger: Survivalist self-reliance and risk among young adults aging out of foster care. *Children and Youth Services Review, 10*, 1198–1210.

Shin, S. (2009). Improving social work practice with foster care adolescents: examining readiness for independence. *Journal of Public Child Welfare, 3*, 354–371.

Steinberg, L. (2005a). Cognitive and affective development in adolescence. *TRENDS in Cognitive Sciences, 9*(2), 69–74.

Steinberg, L. (2005b). *Adolescence* (7th ed.). New York: McGraw-Hill. Retrieved from http://www.acf.hhs.gov/programs/cb/stats_research/afcars/tar/report17.htm.

US Department of Health and Human Services, Administration for Children and Families, Administration on Children, Youth and Families, Children's Bureau. (2007). *Child welfare Outcomes (2004–2007). Report to Congress*. Washington, DC: Author. Retrieved from an http://www.acf.hhs.gov/programs/cb/pubs/cwo04-07/cwo04-07.pdf.

US Department of Health and Human Services, Administration for Children and Families, Administration on Children, Youth and Families, Children's Bureau (2013). *The AFCARS Report. Preliminary FY 2012 estimates as of July 2013(20)*. Retrieved from http://www.acf.hhs.gov/programs/cb/resource/afcars-report-20.

US General Accounting Office (GAO). (1999). *Foster care: Effectiveness of independent living services unknown*. Washington, DC: General Accounting Office, GAO/HEHS-00-03.

Velen, M., & Devine, L. (2005). Use of FGDM with children in care the longest: It's about time. *Protecting Children, 19*(4), 25–35.

Weigenberg, E. C., Barth, R. P., & Guo, S. (2009). Family group decision making: A propensity score analysis to evaluate child and family services at baseline and after 36 months. *Children and Youth Services Review, 31*, 383–390.

Wildfire, J., Rideout, P., & Crampton, D. (2009). Transforming child welfare one team decision making meeting at a time. *Protecting Children, 25*(2), 40–50.

Wulczyn, F. (2004). Family reunification. *Future of Children, 14*(1), 95–113.

Wulczyn, F. (2009). In B. Kerman, M. Freundlich & A. Maluccio (Eds.), Foster youth in context. *Achieving permanence for older children and youth in foster care*. (pp. 13–31). New York: Columbia Press

Chapter 6
Lesbian, Gay, Bisexual, Transgendered, Questioning, and Queer Youth: The Challenge for Child Welfare

Elizabeth A. Winter

Abstract Lesbian, gay, bisexual, transgendered, questioning, and queer youth (LGBTQ or sexual minority youth) experience elevated risks to their safety, well-being, and permanency compared to heterosexual youth. Current evidence paints a picture of sexual minority youth as being disproportionately overrepresented in the child welfare system and as frequently receiving disparate, inappropriate, and unsafe treatment. In order to adequately provide services to LGBTQ youth in the child welfare system, policy makers, administrators, supervisors, and workers need to understand not only the higher risks experienced by these youth but also their particular developmental needs and how to deliver and access culturally competent services and supports for them.

LGBTQ youth require competent child welfare professionals who understand their particular concerns and can address their needs without either deliberately or inadvertently being discriminatory. Caseworkers need to be able to make sure that the needs of LGBTQ youth are competently assessed and then find appropriate services and community supports. While child welfare services have not yet achieved cultural competence, model policies and training curricula are readily available to guide the provision of competent services for LGBTQ youth. A sustained commitment by state and local agency leaders is required to make the cultural and practice changes that are needed. The adaptation of existing promising child welfare practices, such as family finding and family group conferencing models, is one way to leverage existing resources to meet the permanency and stability needs of sexual minority youth.

The most urgent need is for child welfare agencies to be equipped to recognize and address issues of physical and emotional safety among LGBTQ youth. The next priority is the competent management of issues related to sexual orientation and

E.A. Winter (✉)
Child Welfare Education and Research Programs, School of Social Work,
University of Pittsburgh, Pittsburgh, PA, USA
e-mail: eaw44@pitt.edu

H. Cahalane (ed.), *Contemporary Issues in Child Welfare Practice*,
Contemporary Social Work Practice, DOI 10.1007/978-1-4614-8627-5_6,
© Springer Science+Business Media New York 2013

gender identity in the area of placement and placement stability. The third imperative is to support and facilitate the well-being of these highly vulnerable and often invisible children and youth. Although cultural change is challenging, the combination of growing interest and support for LGBTQ youth and the availability of the tools to help them can lead to improvements in service for sexual minority children and youth coming into contact with the child welfare system.

Keywords Lesbian • Gay • Bisexual • Transgender • Queer • Questioning • Child welfare • LGBT • LGBTQ • Children and youth • Homophobia • Transphobia • Heterosexism • Sexual minority • Gender-nonconforming

Carlie is a 7-year-old white transgendered child born with a biologically male body (her legal name is Charles). Carlie identified herself as female as a preschooler, despite her male body. When she went to kindergarten, she lined up with the girls to go to the bathroom and didn't understand why she had to go with the boys. Carlie has experienced prejudice and victimization both at school and at home; she has become quiet and withdrawn and hangs back from other children. The school called child protective services after finding the marks of what looked like a severe beating with a belt. Carlie's father admits having beaten her with a belt twice for not behaving as a boy should; having "a boy who wants to be a girl" is inconceivable and shameful to him. Carlie's mother wants to be supportive but is confused and does not know whether to "encourage" Carlie to express herself as female, or to force her to "be Charles." Both parents feel humiliated and wonder what they have done wrong.

Carlie's primary safety needs include physical and emotional safety at home and at school. Her well-being needs include access to medical and behavioral healthcare providers who are competent in the assessment and treatment of transgendered children and youth. She needs support at school from staff, preferably including access to a unisex bathroom. As Carlie grows up, assuming that she is indeed a transgendered child, she will need access to hormonal treatment to suppress the effects of male hormones that would deepen her voice and lead to the development of other male secondary sexual characteristics. She and her family will need social and other supports (such as psychoeducation and connections to other families with transgendered children) to help them in managing the transitions and risks that Carlie faces as an individual and that they face as a family. Carlie's permanency needs include a supportive, permanent living situation, preferably with her family of origin. Her developmental needs include access to supportive adults (including, if possible, maintaining/developing a positive relationship with her parents) and appropriate and safe social interactions with other children and youth, including age-appropriate access to dating and sexual education particular to her needs.

Jamaica is a 16-year-old African-American female youth who is living with her parents; she is the youngest of three girls, who all live at home. Her older sister, brother-in-law, and their young children also live in the home. Jamaica is experiencing conflict with her family about her sexual orientation, risky sexual behavior, and marijuana use. Jamaica is forbidden to be in the same room with her nieces, whom she adores, because her family thinks she will "turn them." She is no longer welcome at her church—a traditional, predominantly African-American, Southern Baptist church—unless she is willing to renounce her homosexuality and name it a sin. Since much of the family's social life is connected to family and church, Jamaica is now socially isolated from her primary community. Jamaica's parents feel ashamed and believe that they have failed in some ways in raising her. Jamaica reveals that she is only attracted emotionally, romantically, and sexually to other girls, which suggests that she is a lesbian. However, she has been sexually active with multiple male partners and her family has just found out that she is about 3 months pregnant; she has not yet had any prenatal care. Due to the level of conflict at home, Jamaica wants to leave and her parents have told her to "get over this gay thing" or move out. She has come to the attention of child welfare because she has been repeatedly truant from school. Her permanency is threatened since she is at risk of either leaving or being put out of her home. Her well-being needs are high. Jamaica needs access to prenatal medical care and education; she and her family need access to social and other supports in relation to her sexual orientation, her drug use, and the conflict in the family. As part of her healthy relationship development, Jamaica needs to meet other youth like her and to date girls in an age-appropriate manner.

Eduardo is a Latino, homosexual male youth, aged 15. Eduardo is currently in a juvenile justice placement following adjudication as delinquent for aggravated assault. Since he is also adjudicated dependent, his child protective services caseworker is looking for a suitable placement for him when he returns to the community.

Eduardo lived with his biological parents until the age of 13, when he was ejected from the home because they found out that he was sexually involved with another male youth. His parents are Catholic and viewed Eduardo's homosexual orientation as unacceptable according to their religious beliefs. They believe Eduardo's homosexuality is a choice he has made and can change, if he wishes, rather than an identity, which is not voluntary. When Eduardo was thrown out of their home, he stayed with the family of the boy he had been sexually involved with for a few weeks but was then told to leave. A neighbor called child protective services and Eduardo was placed in a foster home, where he remained for 2 months. At that point the foster parents requested that Eduardo be removed because of his sexual orientation, which the foster parents had not known about when Eduardo was initially placed with them. He was then placed in a group home, from which he ran away after several weeks.

Eduardo was homeless for about 6 months, during which time he started drinking and using drugs daily. He engaged in survival sex (prostitution) until he was picked up by the police and placed in a residential rehabilitation program. Eduardo says that people "… treat you like an animal once they know you're gay and on the street"; he was sexually assaulted more than once during his period of homelessness. Eduardo was arrested for aggravated assault when he wounded a youth at school with a knife; Eduardo says that prior to the attack, the other youth had bullied him relentlessly.

Eduardo says that even being homeless is safer than being at home or "in the system"; he describes being raped and otherwise sexually victimized in his previous placement, where he says staff refused to help him. He reports one staff member saying, "You're a faggot, you must want it." Eduardo has difficulty getting to sleep and often has violent nightmares; he also has dissociative symptoms, saying he can "go away when things get really bad." Eduardo has been diagnosed with posttraumatic stress disorder and polysubstance dependence. He frequently reports suicidal ideation and has attempted suicide (using moderately lethal means) on two occasions. His well-being needs include mental health treatment. His developmental needs include validation and acceptance, as well as the opportunity for social support and interaction with other gay youth. His permanency needs include a safe, gay-supportive placement; he is too young for an independent living program. His child welfare caseworker has not been successful in finding a kinship placement for him for when he is discharged. A coworker has told her about a local contracted provider agency which has been recruiting and training gay-friendly resource families. The caseworker is hopeful that she will be able to find an appropriate placement for Eduardo, although his mental health needs are challenging.

Jackson is a 13-year-old white male youth who has been in foster care for several years and has had six placements in the last 2 years. He has been in a pre-adoptive placement for several months, which has been going well. While Jackson has been interested in and attracted to girls for some time, he has recently become aware of being attracted to boys, although he has not yet been sexually active with another male youth. However, he did confide his sexual and romantic attraction to a boy in school. This boy rejected him and has told everyone in school about Jackson's interest in him. As a result, Jackson has been bullied and is now reluctant to go to school. He has started being truant from school and his grades are suffering badly. He has been feeling confused, but when he talked to his prospective adoptive parents, they were shocked. They did not talk with him about his confusion and told him they were not sure they wanted to proceed with the adoption. Jackson has been receiving counseling for oppositional defiant disorder and attention deficit disorder (hyperactive type). He spoke with his counselor about his recent attraction to the boy at school; she told him that it was probably just "a phase" that he will and should grow out of and that people are often confused about their sexual orientation at his age. The counselor also told him that she would be willing to continue working with him "even if you do turn out to be gay or bi."

Introduction and Background

Lesbian, gay, bisexual, transgendered, questioning, and queer youth (LGBTQ or sexual minority youth) experience elevated risks to their safety, well-being, and permanency compared to heterosexual youth. Current evidence paints a picture of sexual minority youth as being disproportionately overrepresented in the child welfare system and as frequently receiving disparate, inappropriate, and unsafe treatment. How can this be, despite calls from all leading professional associations in social work, psychology, counseling, medicine, and law for the validation and equal and appropriate treatment of LGBTQ youth? Child welfare scholars such as Mallon (1998) have called for recognition of the problems faced by sexual minority youth in child welfare and for the development of solutions. Several national organizations have responded with the development of guidelines and resources for addressing the needs of this population, and child welfare systems in some locations have begun to address the problem. In order to adequately provide services to LGBTQ youth in the child welfare system, policy makers, administrators, supervisors, and workers need to understand not only the higher risks experienced by LGBTQ youth but also the particular developmental needs of these youth and how to deliver and access culturally competent services and supports for them.

In this chapter we will start by giving some definitions, followed by an overview of relevant literature that highlights the particular challenges experienced by LGBTQ youth both generally and in the child welfare system. The second part of the chapter will focus on initiatives designed to provide sufficient and appropriate services to LGBTQ youth, including national guidelines for working with LGBTQ youth in the child welfare system and the need for system requirements (such as policies and procedures). The next section of the chapter will focus on practice skills necessary for competent work with LGBTQ youth, including how to assess the need for and then access appropriate supports and referrals for LGBTQ youth, as well as the need to work from a whole family perspective. Resource lists for practitioners and youth and families will be provided.

Table 6.1 Sexual orientations and gender identities

What does "LGBTQ" mean?
In recent years it has become common to use the string of letters "LGBTQ" to be inclusive of all individuals and communities who identify as lesbian, gay, bisexual, or transgender or who are questioning their sexual orientation and/or gender identity. There is no right or wrong way to order the letters (e.g., GLBTQ), and some people add additional letters, including "I" for intersex (or what used to be called hermaphrodism), "Q" for queer, and "A" for non-LGBTQ allies (e.g., LGBTQQIA)
Lesbian: A woman who is emotionally, romantically, and sexually attracted to other women
Gay: A man or woman who is emotionally, romantically, and sexually attracted to the same gender. Some use the term only to identify gay men. The word *gay* is preferred over the word *homosexual*, which has clinical overtones that some people find offensive
Bisexual: A man or woman who is emotionally, romantically, and sexually attracted to both genders. Sometimes the attraction to each gender is equal, while for others there may be a preference for one gender over the other
Transgender: An umbrella term used to describe a person whose gender identity—their inner sense of being male or female—differs from the sex assigned to them at birth. The term is also used to describe a gender-nonconforming person—one whose behaviors, mannerisms, or clothing differs from expectations associated with the sex assigned to them at birth. Transgender people may identify as heterosexual, lesbian, gay, bisexual, or questioning
Questioning: A person, often an adolescent, who has questions about his or her sexual orientation or gender identity. Some questioning people eventually come out as lesbian, gay, bisexual, or transgender; some do not
Reproduced from Fostering Transitions, *Getting down to basics: Tools to support LGBTQ youth in care* (CWLA and Lambda Legal 2012)
Other important terms
Heterosexual: A man or woman who is emotionally, romantically, and sexually attracted to people of a different sex. Sometimes known "straight"
Gender identity: A person's internal, deeply felt sense of being male or female, or something other or in between. Everyone has a gender identity. The expectation that a person's gender identity perfectly matches their biological sex is so culturally normalized that there is no specific term for it. It is only when the two do not match that the term transgender is used
Reproduced from "National Recommended Best Practices for Serving LGBT Homeless Youth" (Lambda Legal, National Alliance to End Homelessness, National Network for Youth, and National Center for Lesbian Rights 2009, p. 15)

Definitions

The starting point for building cultural competence with LGBTQ youth is to understand what these terms mean. Table 6.1 reproduces definitions given in the Getting Down to Basics Toolkit, developed by the Child Welfare League of America (CWLA) and Lambda Legal Defense Fund (CWLA and Lambda Legal 2012) and in the National Recommended Best Practices for Serving LGBT Homeless Youth (Lambda Legal, National Alliance to End Homelessness, National Network for Youth, and National Center for Lesbian Rights 2009).

These groups are also referred to collectively as "sexual minority" children and youth. From the definitions and individual stories above, it can be seen that

Table 6.2 Definitions

Heteronormativity: A belief system that assumes heterosexuality is normal and that all people are
  heterosexual

Heterosexism: A belief system that assumes that heterosexuality is inherently preferable and
  superior to other forms of sexual orientation

Homophobia: Fear, hatred of, aversion to, or discrimination against: homosexuality, LGBT
  people, individuals perceived as LGBT, and people associated with LGBT people

Transphobia: Fear, hatred of, aversion to, or discrimination against transgender people or people
  who are gender-nonconforming

Reproduced from "National Recommended Best Practices for Serving LGBT Homeless Youth"
(Lambda Legal, National Alliance to End Homelessness, National Network for Youth, and
National Center for Lesbian Rights 2009, pp. 15–16)

members of each of the LGBTQ groups (lesbians, gay males, bisexual males and
females, transgendered males and females, and youth who are questioning their
sexual orientation or gender identity) have distinct characteristics, distinct developmental needs, and distinct service needs. The experiences and needs of Carlie
as a transgendered female child (who is biologically male) cannot be compared to
the experiences of a lesbian youth like Jamaica. Both youths may have experienced discrimination, bullying, and physical abuse, and, if they are fortunate,
acceptance in their families of origin. However, their service needs are very
different.

Need for Cultural Competence with LGBTQ Youth

All the children and youth described above are fictional, but the problems described
are all actual examples. All of these youths require competent professionals who
understand their particular concerns and can address their needs using appropriate
language, without either deliberately or inadvertently being discriminatory. Their
caseworkers need to be able to make sure that their needs are competently assessed
and then find appropriate services and community supports, which may not be readily available in many areas. In many cases, the primary need is for emotional and
physical safety. Discriminatory behavior and attitudes in relation to LGBTQ youth
may be based in heteronormativity, heterosexism, homophobia, or transphobia.
These terms are defined above in Table 6.2.

For example, Carlie needs accepting professionals and others who have expertise
in assessment, treatment, and support of transgender children. A culturally competent caseworker will know that making Carlie "act male" is based in transphobic
attitudes and is not in accordance with the current standard of care. The caseworker
will be able to find supports and information for the family through the Internet if
such supports are not readily available locally.

Jamaica certainly needs prenatal care for her and her unborn child. She also
needs professionals and others who understand that her sexual behavior does not

determine her sexual orientation. In other words, based on what she has said, a knowledgeable caseworker will recognize that Jamaica's sexual orientation is probably lesbian and not bisexual. This is because the determining factor in sexual orientation is how she feels about herself and her partners and not simply her behavior in having had sex with both males and females. A well-informed counselor will also explore the reasons for Jamaica's sexual activity with males and will address the cultural issues related to her family's struggles concerning Jamaica's likely sexual orientation. As will be further described below, there are a number of possible reasons for lesbian youth to be sexually active with male youth.

Eduardo needs professionals and others who understand that what has happened to him is due to the reactions of others to his sexual orientation, and not because there is something wrong with being gay. Eduardo needs a supportive counselor who can help him to manage emotionally and physically healthy same-sex sexual relationships and develop appropriate personal boundaries, which may be very difficult for him given his history of survival sex and victimization. He also needs a lawyer who understands and performs his or her role in advocating for Eduardo's current safety and for an appropriate future placement.

Jackson needs a culturally competent counselor who can help him explore his feelings without trying to label them for him and who will be supportive to him as a person. His current counselor may feel she is being supportive of him by saying she will continue to work with him despite his sexual orientation. She may not even hear the homophobia and heterosexism embedded in her use of the phrase "even if" he is gay or bisexual, which clearly implies that being gay or bisexual is undesirable or "less than" in her view. Jackson's prospective adoptive family also needs skillful and sensitive support to help them understand Jackson's struggles with his sexual orientation, and part of this support must be an attempt to make them realize that he is still the same young man they initially welcomed into their home. The support program for Jackson and his potential adoptive parents would address their hopes and fears in addition to Jackson's and, in the best possible outcome, would help them to reach a point where they could be supportive of him. This would save Jackson from yet another disrupted placement and allow him to finally have a family again.

All sexual minority youth face higher risks for experiencing certain problems than do heterosexual youth. The next section will first address the major areas in which risk is elevated for all LGBTQ youth and will then look at the risks that affect LGBTQ youth who have entered the public child welfare system. It is important to note that at this time, there is much less evidence available concerning transgender youth than evidence relating to LGB youth and that the needs of transgender youth are even less frequently met than those of LGB youth. Recent data from the first large survey of over 6,000 transgender and gender-nonconforming people will be included in this review to illustrate some of the risks faced by this population in the United States (Grant et al. 2011). Although all respondents were adults, 19 % of the sample were young adults aged 18–24 years old.

Risks for Lesbian, Gay, Bisexual, Transgender, and Questioning or Queer Youth

Risks Faced by LGBTQ Youth Generally

One of the primary problems faced by LGBTQ youth is discrimination (Woronoff et al. 2006). Research has demonstrated that these youth experience increased risks for suicidality, substance abuse, sexual risk behaviors, and homelessness compared to their non-LGBTQ counterparts (Lock and Steiner 1999).

Suicide and Suicidality

Suicide is the third leading cause of death for all youth aged 15–24 in the USA, and these numbers are significantly higher for LGBTQ youth (Garofalo et al. 1999). A population-based study by Remafedi et al. (1998) found that 28.1 % of gay or bisexual males in grades 7 through 12 had attempted suicide at least once during their lives, while only 4.2 % of heterosexual males in those grades had attempted suicide. The corresponding percentages for females were 20.5 % for lesbian or bisexual females and 14.5 % for heterosexual females. A recent meta-analysis by Marshal et al. (2011) reported significantly higher rates of suicidality and depression symptoms for sexual minority youth compared to heterosexual youth. Ryan et al. (2009) examined the impact of family rejection on health problems in white and Latino young adults. Lesbian, gay, and bisexual young adults who had experienced higher rates of family rejection were 8.4 times more likely to have attempted suicide and almost six times more likely to report high levels of depression than lesbian, gay, and bisexual young adults who had experienced little or no family rejection.

Eduardo's story above provides an example of gay youth suicidality and family rejection. Grant et al. (2011) reported higher lifetime rates of suicidality among transgender and gender-nonconforming respondents, with 41 % reporting attempts overall, rising to 51 % of those who also reported experiencing significant family rejection.

Some researchers have compared the seriousness of suicide attempts by lesbian, gay, and bisexual youth with that of attempts by heterosexual youth by asking people about their intent to end their lives. Safren and Heimberg (1999) found that 58 % of LGB youth who had attempted suicide reported that they really hoped to die. In contrast, only 33 % of heterosexuals attempting suicide reported that they really hoped to die. Another measure of seriousness is the lethality of the means used to attempt suicide. For example, people who use firearms in a suicide attempt have a higher rate of suicide deaths than people who use other means, simply because firearms are more lethal (Shenassa et al. 2003). Remafedi et al. (1991) found in interviews with gay and bisexual males, aged 14 through 21 years, that 54 % of suicide attempts in this group could be classified as moderately to highly lethal.

The study also reported that one-fifth of lesbian, gay, and bisexual youth who attempted suicide needed hospitalization, and the majority of these youth were rated as being at the highest risk for completing suicide.

Substance Abuse

Research indicates that sexual minority youth have significantly higher rates of drug and alcohol abuse than their non-LGBTQ peers. In one study, lesbian, gay, and bisexual youth were five times more likely to use cocaine, ten times more likely to use crack, and ten times more likely to use injection drugs (Garofalo et al. 1998). A rigorous meta-analysis of 18 published studies on sexual orientation and substance abuse was conducted by Marshal et al. (2008). The reviewed studies concluded that lesbian, gay, and bisexual youth were almost 200 % more likely to abuse drugs and alcohol, and those percentages increased to as much as 400 % for some subpopulations, such as females. Among all youth, substance abuse is associated with other high-risk behavior, such as more lethal suicide attempts and inconsistent condom use (Garofalo and Katz 2001). Grant et al. (2011), in their study of the experiences of transgender and gender-nonconforming adults, reported that 32 % of those who had been rejected by their families because of their gender identity and expression status had used alcohol and other drugs to cope with mistreatment. Once again, Eduardo's story demonstrates the elevated risk for substance abuse for LGBTQ youth.

Health, Sexual Health, and Sexual Risk Behaviors

LGBTQ youth are at risk for poorer health outcomes when compared to their non-LGBTQ peers, due to several contributing factors. LGBTQ youth often feel less comfortable with medical professionals, especially regarding sexual health issues (Saewyc et al. 1999). They are less likely to disclose their sexual orientation, and providers may not ask about it. Fully half of the transgender and gender-nonconforming respondents in the Grant et al. (2011) study reported that they had to educate their medical providers about transgender care. Almost one-fifth of respondents (19 %) reported being refused healthcare by a provider altogether. The numbers were even higher for people of color; 32 % of Latino and Latina respondents were refused treatment by a physician or hospital.

LGBTQ youth are at high risk of sexually transmitted infections (STIs) such as hepatitis B, chlamydia, gonorrhea, and HIV (Garofalo and Katz 2001). Approximately 80,000 new HIV infections occur in the USA every year, and one-half of these newly infected people are youth under the age of 25. Although gay men are known to be at high risk, there is evidence that lesbian youth who experiment with opposite-sex partners are also at high risk for HIV infection (Perrin 1996). Although STIs and HIV infections occur due to health behaviors, not sexual orientation, LGBTQ youth are at higher risk because they often receive healthcare information with an exclusively heterosexual orientation (Saewyc et al. 2006).

Kann et al. (2011), reporting results from the Youth Risk Behavior Surveillance System, which monitors priority health risk behaviors, found that between 2001 and 2009 the prevalence of all the risk behaviors measured was higher for gay and lesbian students than for heterosexual students. The prevalence of all health risk behaviors was also higher for bisexual students than for heterosexual students.

Lesbian and bisexual girls are also at elevated risk of teen pregnancy compared to their heterosexual peers. A series of population-based research studies found that bisexual or lesbian girls were more likely to have multiple partners, more frequent sexual intercourse, and to use no or ineffective birth control (Forrest and Saewyc 2004; Saewyc et al. 1999, 2006). Pregnancies among these youth were attributed to several factors. First, many young women may have heterosexual behavior before identifying themselves as bisexual or lesbian and may even try to deny their emerging sexual orientation by engaging in heterosexual sex (Rotheram-Borus and Fernandez 1995). Due to the stigma LGBTQ adolescents face, a girl may know clearly that she is lesbian or bisexual but may intentionally become pregnant as a way to stop people from asking questions about her sexual orientation. Second, lesbian and bisexual girls are at higher risk of forced sexual contact than their heterosexual counterparts (Saewyc et al. 1999). One or more of these factors is likely to apply to Jamaica in the case study above.

Homelessness

Sexual minority youth appear to be disproportionally at risk for becoming homeless. Of the estimated 1.6 million homeless American youth, up to 42 % identify as lesbian or gay, grossly out of proportion to their representation in the general population (Ray 2006). LGBTQ youth often leave home due to physical, sexual, and/or emotional abuse (Mallon 1998; Woronoff et al. 2006). One study found that 26 % of gay teens who came out to their parents or guardians were told to leave home (Mallon et al. 2002).

Also, many lesbian and bisexual girls become homeless at some point and may be forced to turn to prostitution for survival (Saewyc et al. 1999). A recent study of over 6,000 high school students in Massachusetts (Corliss et al. 2011) indicated that sexual minority youth were up to 13 times more likely to be homeless than heterosexual youth. While 3 % of exclusively heterosexual youth were homeless, 25 % of lesbian or gay students and 15 % of bisexual students were homeless. In the stories above, Eduardo has been homeless and Jamaica is at risk for homelessness. Additionally, Jackson may lose the opportunity for an adoption, as adoptions occur more rarely for youth in the child welfare system as they get older (Children's Bureau 2011a).

Adult transgender and gender-nonconforming respondents reported severe problems with homelessness also (Grant et al. 2011). One-fifth reported homelessness as a result of their gender status, while 29 % were refused access to homeless shelters and more than half (55 %) of those who were successful in accessing a shelter reported harassment by staff or residents.

Risks Faced by LGBTQ Youth in the Child Welfare System

One of the primary problems for LGBTQ youth in child welfare is discrimination, closely followed by lack of knowledge, lack of appropriate services, and victimization while in care (Woronoff et al. 2006). Sadly, these factors make the goals of the child welfare system—namely safety, permanency, and well-being—much harder to reach for LGBTQ youth.

Based on estimates of the proportion of LGBTQ people in the USA overall, at least 10 % of youth in the child welfare system are believed to be LGBTQ (Sullivan et al. 2001). In actuality, the number of LGBTQ youth in foster care is likely to be much higher, following higher rates of abuse and neglect in their families of origin because of their sexual minority status (Courtney et al. 2009; Friedman et al. 2011; Mallon 1998).

Out-of-Home Placement: Physical and Emotional Safety

Far from being safer in the foster care system, LGBTQ youth often continue to be victimized as a result of their sexual orientation or gender identity while in out-of-home placements (Woronoff et al. 2006). One gay youth placed in a community-based group home reported, "I had at least two fights a day. The boys used to do stupid things like throw rocks at me or put bleach in my food because I was gay. Once I was thrown down stairs and I've had my nose broken twice. They even ripped up the only picture of my mother that I had" (Desetta 2003, p. 46–47).

Many LGBTQ youth placed in foster care run away due to victimization. A study in New York City found that 78 % of LGBTQ youth were removed from or ran away from foster care placement as a result of hostility and violence due to their sexual orientation or gender identity (Feinstein et al. 2001). Every youth interviewed (100 %) in New York City group homes reported verbal harassment and 70 % reported physical violence due to their sexual orientation or gender identity. Like Eduardo, more than half of the youth said they spent time living on the streets because it seemed "safer" than living in their group or foster homes, where they were harassed and sometimes brutalized by peers and caregivers.

One focus group study with foster care families in Pennsylvania demonstrated negative attitudes toward and misconceptions about lesbian, gay, and bisexual foster youth (though not specifically transgender or questioning youth) (Clements and Rosenwald 2007). When these families were asked how they felt about sexual minority children placed in their homes, several themes emerged. This group of foster parents was dismayed that lesbian, gay, and bisexual children existed in the foster care system, as they believed that these children should have received help to "counsel them out" of their sexual orientation. Parents' greatest concerns were focused on gay boys, who they feared would molest the foster parents' own children. They also expected that gay boys would cross-dress. These parents believed that lesbians were passive and therefore less of a threat to others and that bisexual youth were primarily confused due to histories of sexual abuse. Finally, many participants described religious beliefs that being LGB was morally wrong. These parents tended to have two attitudes toward lesbian, gay, and bisexual youth in foster care: one group felt it would be wrong for them to help sexual minority youth, and the other group felt that it would be their responsibility to pray with these youth to "help them find the right path" (p. 64). While these foster parents may not be representative of foster parents in general, there is little existing research in this area, so it is not known how widespread these views may be.

In the "Out of the Margins" focus group study with LGBTQ youth (Woronoff et al. 2006), respondents described being emotionally, sexually, and physically abused in group care, sometimes with staff knowledge and inaction. Others reported being taunted by staff or foster parents. One spoke of being put in a room alone because of being gay and not being allowed to be with other youth. Another youth reported that when he complained to the group home director about being assaulted, the director responded, "Well, if you weren't a faggot, they wouldn't beat you up." Youth rarely reported being treated well.

Since youth in the child welfare system may also have juvenile justice involvement, some of the major findings of a study of professionals and sexual minority youth in the juvenile justice system are mentioned here (Majd et al. 2009). The major themes in the report "Hidden Injustice" were that the few jurisdictions and professionals working to improve their work with LGBT youth were the exceptions. More frequently found were denials of due process, unduly punitive and harmful responses, and unsafe conditions of confinement. This report also listed a number of myths about sexual minority youth which affect their treatment in the juvenile justice system; these misconceptions apply equally to sexual minority youth involved in child welfare.

Service Disparities

There appears to be some disparity in how LGBTQ youth receive services once they have entered the child welfare system. While there are few studies on the outcomes of LGBTQ youth in the foster care system, alarmingly, lesbian and gay youth in out-of-home care receive fewer mental health, substance abuse, and health services than nongay youth, despite evidence that their needs are much greater (Mallon 1998). The child welfare system has been described as slow to address the particular needs of LGBTQ youth (Freundlich and Avery 2004).

Lambda Legal and CWLA conducted a comprehensive assessment of the current policies and practices for LGBTQ youth in the foster care system in 14 US states that were selected to represent the geographic and ethnic diversity of the country (Sullivan et al. 2001). State child welfare agencies were asked to respond to detailed questionnaires about policies and practices concerning nondiscrimination provisions, training of foster care staff and parents on sexual orientation issues, and programs and services for LGBTQ youth. Results showed that LGBTQ youth are not being adequately served within these systems and are frequently invisible.

One state child welfare official reported that there were no sexual minority youth in that state's child welfare system, so their state needed neither policies nor services for them. However, some states and municipalities have taken important first steps to address the issues LGBTQ adolescents face in the child welfare system. For example, Connecticut offers optional training for supervisors, caseworkers, and direct care workers. The New York City Administration for Children's Services also provides training to its child welfare workforce on sexual diversity and requires the same of all its contracted providers.

Lesbian, gay, and bisexual youth also face the risk of being sent for therapy to try to change their sexual orientation. These therapies may be termed "reparative therapy" or "conversion therapy" and are regarded as unethical by all well-established national professional organizations, including CWLA, the National Association of Social Workers, the American Psychological Association, the American Psychiatric Association, and the American Academy of Pediatrics. These organizations have all unequivocally supported the view that gay, lesbian, bisexual, or heterosexual orientations are all healthy sexual orientations (Woronoff et al. 2006).

Developmental Needs of LGBTQ Youth

LGBTQ youth have the same developmental needs shared by all youth (Ragg et al. 2006). However, LGBTQ youth face additional challenges in getting these needs met, since they also face discrimination and lack of knowledge and skills among parents and service providers (Woronoff et al. 2006).

Identity formation and integration are part of the developmental pathway for all adolescents. For sexual minority youth, healthy identity formation includes recognition and coming to terms with a sexual or gender identity that is highly stigmatized, in settings where they are likely to experience victimization (Sullivan 1994). The Best Practice Guidelines for serving sexual minority youth in out-of-home care describe appropriate services for sexual minority youth (as for all youth) as including opportunities to safely disclose and discuss feelings of attraction and sexual and gender orientation (CWLA, American Bar Association Center on Children and the Law, Elze, Family Acceptance Project, Lambda Legal Defense, Legal Defense Services for Children et al. 2012; Wilber et al. 2006). Services should provide for connection to safe and healthy socialization opportunities for sexual minority youth as for other youth, such as age-appropriate dating opportunities.

Since all sexual orientations are healthy orientations, all youth should be able to choose clothing, hairstyles, and jewelry expressing their sexual orientation, whatever it may be. This presents a challenge to caseworkers who need to advocate on behalf of the youth, while at the same time working to address issues of safety and culture. Perhaps most fundamentally, a caseworker needs to seek a safe placement where a youth does not have to pretend either to be heterosexual or to have a stereotypical gender presentation. By definition, a placement in which it is not safe to be openly gay or transgendered is not a safe placement. For example, it may not be safe for a female transgender youth (born biologically male) to be placed in a male congregate care setting. Or a caseworker may negotiate with foster parents to permit hairstyles and makeup for a female transgender youth that they would permit for a youth born biologically female. Alternatively, a caseworker may advocate with a foster care agency to recruit resource families who are comfortable with freedom of personal dress and grooming (within developmentally appropriate limits) for sexual minority youth, such as a gay male youth wearing makeup on a date. This is comparable to supporting an African-American youth in skin care or hair care and styling. At the same time, it is important to work with the youth themselves to address cultural norms of all kinds (including religious, ethnic, and racial norms) and to help youth negotiate the threats, challenges, and barriers they are likely to face. For example, a gay Latino youth from a strict Catholic family is likely to face significant conflict with his or her family and to face exclusion from his or her church. These issues are examined further in the sections that follow.

Developing LGBTQ Cultural Competence

Achieving cultural competence in any area of social work practice is an ambitious goal. It requires extensive commitment from child-serving systems and individual organizations to make available the necessary resources to develop policies and programs, train and supervise staff, obtain technical assistance, and monitor processes and outcomes. One starting point in thinking about cultural competence for sexual minority children and youth in child welfare is to look at some of the myths and misconceptions about these youth that still persist and to examine what the possible consequences are for a child or youth. Some of the more prevalent myths and misconceptions and the distressing and often unjust service problems they can lead to for an individual are shown in Table 6.3.

Additionally, payment for child welfare services does not include money for developing culturally competent services, although grant funding for developing culturally competent programs may be available from time to time. For example, in 2003, the US Children's Bureau funded demonstration grants to develop and test the efficacy of a systems of care approach to child welfare in order to foster collaboration across child-serving systems (National Technical Assistance and Evaluation Center for Systems of Care 2009). This initiative involved six guiding principles, of which cultural and linguistic competence was one. (For further details of the Systems of Care approach, see Chap. 1.) In addition to resources, the development of cultural competence in service provision for a particular population also takes time and a commitment to that population. CWLA (2002) uses the following definition of cultural competence:

> The ability of individuals and systems to respond respectfully and effectively to people of all cultures, races, ethnic backgrounds, sexual orientations, and faiths or religions, in a manner that recognizes, affirms, and values the worth of the individuals, families, tribes, and communities and protects the dignity of each (p. viii).

Table 6.3 Facts, misconceptions, and possible consequences for LGBTQ youth

Misperception	Fact	Possible consequences
There are no LGBTQ youth in juvenile justice/child welfare	LGBTQ youth are either overlooked or hiding in an attempt to maximize their safety	Since they are invisible, competent and appropriate services for these youth are not developed LGBTQ youth safety is not addressed LGBTQ youth are more likely to be charged with disorderly conduct/assault when defending themselves against bullying
LGBTQ youth are too young to know their sexual orientation or gender identity	Youth often know their sexual orientation and gender identity in elementary school, although they lack the vocabulary to express it	Competent and appropriate services for these youth are not developed LGBTQ youth safety is not addressed
Minority sexual orientations and gender identities are choices ("sexual preferences")	Sexual orientation and gender identity are typically experienced as core aspects of personal identity	Competent and appropriate services for these youth are not developed because expression of identity is mistakenly seen as chosen "behavior" Unethical "conversion" therapies ordered in an attempt to change sexual orientation, gender identity, or expression
LGBTQ orientation/identity is a form of mental illness or sexual deviance	All sexual orientations and gender identities are healthy expressions of core aspects of personal identity	Unethical "conversion" therapies ordered Unnecessarily restrictive placements occur Inappropriate sexual offender evaluations/treatment ordered Youth contact with girlfriends/boyfriends prohibited
LGBTQ youth are sexual predators	LGBTQ people are no more or less likely to be sexual predators than are others	Unnecessarily restrictive placements occur Inappropriate sexual offender evaluations/treatment ordered Separation from young family members occurs
Gender nonconformity (through hairstyle, clothing, name, or mannerisms) is an expression of rebellion	Gender nonconformity is a reflection of core identity and important to the youth's well-being	Punitive attempts are made to impose gender-stereotypical behavior and appearance based on the youth's physical sex

While this definition is broad and explicitly includes sexual orientations, it does not include gender or gender expression. Immediately, this raises a difficulty typical of work with gender-nonconforming populations. When policies and definitions do not explicitly include a group of people, then policy makers and administrators are less likely to address the needs of a population which, in addition to being highly stigmatized, is not mentioned. This omission compounds the problems of populations that are not only marginalized but also frequently unrecognized (Sullivan et al. 2001). Added to this is the issue of isolation for most LGBTQ youth. Unlike minority racial or ethnic groups, sexual minority children are frequently raised by parents whose sexual orientation and gender identity is different from theirs. Therefore, sexual minority children are relatively unlikely to see people like themselves in their families of origin and can feel very alone.

The provision of culturally competent services in child-serving settings has been conceptualized along a continuum. This continuum has six stages, namely, (a) cultural destructiveness, (b) cultural incapacity, (c) cultural blindness, (d) cultural precompetence, (e) basic cultural competence, and (f) advanced cultural competence (Cross et al. 1989).

Cultural destructiveness is characterized by policies, attitudes, and practices that are intentionally destructive to cultures and the individuals within them. Examples of cultural destructiveness for sexual minority youth are sadly not hard to find. Youth in foster care report having sexual and physical assaults ignored (Woronoff et al. 2006). Youth in juvenile justice settings report being unsafe, being denied due process, or having dangerous or developmentally inappropriate judicial orders imposed by the court (Majd et al. 2009). In one case, the attorney for a transgender female youth who was being sexually and physically abused in a boys' facility argued that she should remain in the facility because of her nonconforming gender identity, instead of seeking safety on her behalf. In Eduardo's story above, his attorney failed to advocate for his safety. Majd et al. (2009) also reported the case of a gay male youth who was ordered to receive a sexual offender assessment solely because he was gay, which is an example of homophobic bias whereby a homosexual orientation is confused with sexual offending.

Cultural incapacity is characterized not by deliberate discrimination or destructiveness, but by not having the capacity to serve the minority client group in question (Cross et al. 1989). The organization or system is still biased and may reflect the view that members of the dominant group are superior. An example of this would be an assumption that being gay is a phase that a youth will "grow out of." Hiring practices are likely to be discriminatory, and other indications that members of the minority group are not valued are also likely. An example of this would be an agency in which anti-gay slurs are tolerated, and sexual minority staff are likely to remain deeply closeted. An agency in this stage might put sexual minority youth in solitary confinement to "ensure their safety," rather than develop appropriate services to ensure minority youths' safety. It should be noted that the court in the case of R.G. v. Kollar (2006) held that the use of isolation to "protect" sexual minority youth was unconstitutional. Cross and colleagues (1989) also note that an organization in this stage may have an unreasonable fear of the minority group. This could manifest as a fear that a minority sexual orientation is "catching" and that a youth or an employee could therefore make others gay or lesbian. Jackson's story provides an example of cultural incapacity in the statement by Jackson's therapist that she will work with him "even if" he is gay or bisexual. This is a clear indication that, in her mind, being gay or bisexual is undesirable.

The next step on this continuum is cultural blindness (Cross et al. 1989). In this case the organization's goal is to be unbiased, often by treating everyone the same, in the belief that approaches used by the dominant culture are applicable to everyone. The organization is unaware of specialized knowledge or competence related to a particular group. The assertion by staff members or an agency that "everyone is treated the same, so we don't discriminate" is also an example of cultural blindness. An example of this would be leaving a transgender female youth in a boys' congregate care facility because her biological sex is male, without consideration of the particular safety threats this youth is likely to face. Another example would be failing to take into account a child or youth's sexual minority status in the course of permanency planning.

An agency in the cultural pre-competence stage indicates that the organization is committed to civil rights, has realized that it needs to improve its services to the minority group, and is attempting to make improvements (Cross et al. 1989). This may include initiatives to hire sexual minority staff and train staff on sexual minority issues. The agency has started to move toward cultural competence, but while emerging competence may be found among particular staff, it is not yet institutionalized.

An agency with basic cultural competence shows acceptance of and respect for differences and is committed to learning and to improving services (Cross et al. 1989). This organization pays attention to power differentials and makes changes to its services to better serve minority populations. An agency with basic cultural competence takes pains to hire unbiased employees and seeks advice and consultation from minority communities.

Advanced cultural competence is characterized by a commitment to develop programming, add to the knowledge base concerning culturally competent practice, and disseminate results of demonstration projects. Advanced cultural competence is seen as a goal toward which agencies can strive.

It can be seen that organizational commitment is key to developing cultural competence at the institutional level. Where this commitment is lacking, LGBTQ youth may be fortunate to find a competent and unbiased caseworker, but this will be by happenstance, and if this person leaves the agency, their cultural competence leaves with them. Creating an LGBTQ-inclusive organizational culture is an intentional process requiring organizational introspection (CWLA 2002).

Best Practice Guidelines and Promising Initiatives in Child Welfare

Over the last decade, several national initiatives have emerged to support LGBTQ youth in both child welfare and juvenile justice and to develop the tools to facilitate the development of culturally competent services. A training curriculum called "Moving the Margins" was developed by Elze and McHaelen (2009) specifically for child welfare workers. The Model Standards Project (Wilber et al. 2006) and

Table 6.4 Major resources for practitioners

Source	Resource type
National Resource Center for Youth in Care (http://www.nrcyd.ou.edu/lgbtq-youth)	LGBTQ Youth in Care: Information and Resources
CWLA (http://www.cwla.org)	Reports: Youth in the Margins
Lambda Legal (http://www.lambdalegal.org)	Out of the Margins
CWLA (http://www.cwla.org) NCLR (http://www.nclrights.org)	Recommended Practices to Promote the Safety and Well-being of LGBTQ Youth and Youth at Risk of or Living with HIV in Child Welfare Settings
CWLA (http://www.cwla.org) Lambda Legal (http://www.lambdalegal.org)	Getting Down to Basics Toolkit: Tools to Support LGBTQ Youth in Care
American Bar Association (http://www.americanbar.org/groups/child_law/what_we_do/projects/openingdoors.html)	Opening Doors for LGBTQ Youth in Foster Care Representing Transgender Youth
Equity Project for LGBT Youth in the Juvenile Justice System (http://www.equityproject.org)	Reports: Hidden Injustice
National Association of Social Workers (http://www.socialworkers.org) Lambda Legal (http://www.lambdalegal.org)	Moving the Margins: Training curriculum for child welfare services with lesbian, gay, bisexual, transgender, and questioning youth
National Alliance to End Homelessness (http://www.endhomelessness.org/content/article/detail/2239)	National Recommended Best Practices for Serving Homeless Youth
Gay and Lesbian Medical Association (http://www.glma.org)	Resources for Patients: Provider Directory

Fostering Transitions (Woronoff and Estrada 2006) are aimed at improving child welfare services themselves. From the legal perspective, the Opening Doors initiative (Laver and Khoury 2008) is aimed at improving legal services for LGBTQ youth in child welfare, while the Equity Project addresses LBGTQ youth in the juvenile justice system (Marksamer 2008). Since youth may be dually adjudicated and LGBTQ youth are at increased risk for juvenile justice involvement, a working knowledge of all these resources is important for all child welfare workers, as well as for attorneys working with these populations. Table 6.4 shows resources which will be primarily relevant for practitioners. Many of the resources shown in Table 6.4 include materials to be shared with children, youth, and their families. Some of these resources will be discussed in greater detail in the next section of this chapter.

As an indication of federal-level recognition of the need for culturally competent services, the Administration for Children and Families recently issued an Information Memorandum (IM) calling attention to the overrepresentation and disparate treatment of LGBTQ children in the child welfare system and encouraging child welfare agencies and all those who work with young people in foster care to ensure that all children are protected and supported (Children's Bureau 2011b). The memorandum calls for workforce development to address bias and to ensure that caseworkers have the skills and knowledge they need to serve these youth effectively. The memorandum also highlights the need to recruit and train foster and adoptive parents to provide safe homes for LGBTQ youth, and closes by providing links to resources.

Best Practice Guidelines

In 2002, several organizations collaborated to start the Model Standards Project to produce best practice guidelines, training materials, resource toolkits, and information to share with LGBTQ youth and their caregivers (Wilber et al. 2006). The primary resource to emerge from the Model Standards Project is the "CWLA Best Practice Guidelines: Serving LGBT Youth in Out-of-Home Care" (Best Practice Guidelines), which provides step-by-step directions for helping assure the safety, permanency, and well-being of LGBTQ youth (Wilber et al. 2006). An updated edition of the Best Practice Guidelines is now available (CWLA, ABA Center on Children and the Law, Elze, Family Acceptance Project, Lambda Legal Defense, Legal Defense Services for Children, et al. 2012). The Best Practice Guidelines note that where services have been available to LGBTQ youth, there has historically been a tendency to serve these youth as individuals and not from a family-centered approach. Information is provided on how to increase family communication and understanding while working toward preserving family connections whenever possible.

Fostering Transitions

CWLA and Lambda Legal partnered with the goal of improving how LGBTQ youth are treated throughout the United States child welfare system (Woronoff and Estrada 2006). Named "Fostering Transitions: CWLA/Lambda Legal Joint Initiative to Support LGBTQ Youth and Adults Involved with the Child Welfare System" ("Fostering Transitions"), this initiative has produced "Getting Down to Basics: Tools for Working with LGBTQ Youth in Care" (CWLA and Lambda Legal 2012). Getting Down to Basics is an online tool kit, downloadable at no cost, including information sheets in a number of different areas, such as basic facts about being LGBTQ, information for families and foster parents with LGBTQ children and youth, and information about legal rights for LGBTQ youth (and those who may be targeted because someone thinks they are LGBTQ). The toolkit also provides information for child welfare agencies, such as basic policies for working with LGBTQ youth and recommendations for training. The following are examples of content from two of the items in the toolkit; one is addressed to foster parents, the other is addressed directly to LGBTQ youth.

Excerpt from "Foster Parents Caring for LGBTQ Youth":

Apply the same standards to LGBTQ youth that you apply to others for age-appropriate adolescent romantic behavior. It's important for LGBTQ youth to be able to engage in developmentally-appropriate romantic behavior and to feel as validated and respected in this area as other young people.

Excerpt from "Information for LGBTQ Youth in Care":

Report mistreatment to your attorney or guardian ad litem. Your attorney may be able to take legal action on your behalf to protect you from discrimination and mistreatment. Your conversations with your attorney are confidential, and you do not need to come out to receive protection and legal advocacy.

The Opening Doors Project

This project was developed, starting in 2005, through the American Bar Association's Center on Children and the Law, with the goal of improving the legal system's approach to LGBTQ youth in foster care (Laver and Khoury 2008). The Opening Doors Project provides tools to enable attorneys to advocate more effectively on behalf of LBGTQ youth in the child welfare system. Materials for attorneys include a manual for lawyers and judges (Laver and Khoury 2008) and information for effective advocacy for transgender children (Bevel 2011). The Opening Doors Project has published "It's Your Life," a legal guide for LGBTQ foster care youth, which explains LGBTQ youths' legal rights, what to expect from the child welfare system, and who to turn to if their rights are violated (Desai 2010).

National Resource Center for Youth Development

The National Resource Center for Youth Development (NRCYD) lies within the Children's Bureau of the Administration for Children and Families, a component of the Department of Health and Human Services. The NRCYD's website, titled "LGBTQ Youth in Care: Information and Resources," provides links to publications and other resources of help to professionals working with LGBTQ youth in child welfare.

The Equity Project

The goal of the Equity Project is to ensure that sexual minority youth are treated with dignity, respect, and fairness in the juvenile justice system (Marksamer 2008). The project partners are Legal Services for Children (located in San Francisco), the National Center for Lesbian Rights, and the National Juvenile Defender Center. The Equity Project provides information and resources on legal issues and has produced a report on the experiences of juvenile-justice-involved youth, "Hidden Injustice" (Majd et al. 2009).

The Family Acceptance Project ™

The Family Acceptance Project™, although not a national program, is included as a community research, intervention, education, and policy initiative that studies the impact of family acceptance and rejection on the health, mental health, and well-being of LGBTQ youth (Ryan et al. 2010). The Family Acceptance Project™ is the first family-centered approach to working with LGBTQ youth and their families to improve outcomes for youth and prevent family dissolution. The goal of the project is to develop and disseminate an evidence-based intervention model that strengthens families and promotes healthy development and positive outcomes. The project has adopted a culturally grounded approach working with ethnically, socially, and religiously diverse families to decrease rejection and increase support for LGBTQ children.

Further Resources

Table 6.5 shows resources with which practitioners should be familiar and which are particularly important to share with sexual minority children and youth and their families. Some of these resources are described in more detail below.

The Trevor Project

The Trevor Project was founded in 1998 with goal of ending suicide among LGBTQ youth. The Trevor Project originally provided a nationwide crisis hotline and has since developed a digital community along with advocacy and educational programs and resources.

Table 6.5 Major resources for youth and families

Source	Resource type
The Trevor Project (thetrevorproject.org) TREVOR Lifeline: 866-488-7386	Crisis intervention and suicide prevention; 24/7 national crisis hotline
It Gets Better Project™ (itgetsbetter.org)	Online media to prevent suicide and support youth being bullied
Parents & Friends of Lesbians & Gays (pflag.org)	Support, information, and meetings. More than 250 local chapters in 50 states
American Bar Association (americanbar.org/groups/child_law/what_we_do/ projects/itsyourlife.html)	Guide to legal rights for LGBTQ youth in child welfare: It's Your Life
Gay, Lesbian, and Straight Education Network (glsen.org)	Materials related to safety in schools
Family Acceptance Project™ (familyproject.sfsu.edu)	Information for families: Supportive Families, Healthy Children

The It Gets Better Project™

The It Gets Better Project™ was started in 2010 by nationally syndicated sexuality columnist Dan Savage on YouTube, with the goal of reducing the number of LGBTQ youth suicides occurring due to bullying and victimization (Savage and Miller 2011). Videos of adults with the message that life will improve after high school are intended to provide hope and inspiration to LGBTQ youth. The project grew rapidly and is now housed on its own website, where thousands of videos are available, including one from President Obama.

Gay, Lesbian, and Straight Education Network

GLSEN, the Gay, Lesbian, and Straight Education Network, is the leading national education organization focused on ensuring safe schools for all students. This website includes tools and tips for educators, students, and supporters to create safe educational environments for all young people.

Practice Skills

We know that LGBTQ youth are diverse in many ways. They differ by age, gender identity, gender expression, sexual orientation, level and type of sexual activity, likes and dislikes, families of origin, and other personal characteristics. The ability to find accurate and detailed information about these youth is critical for child welfare workers. Since these youth are so heterogeneous, determining their service needs is also critical and, having done so, the ability to advocate effectively and to find appropriate and safe referrals for them is essential. This requires specialized knowledge and skills, particularly when needed resources are scarce or not available locally.

The following scenarios show the diversity of competencies (both knowledge and skills) needed to provide effective services and to give a taste of practice situations. Please reread the story of each child or youth at the beginning of the chapter and see the section on "Further Resources" at the end of the chapter for links to some of the more frequently needed resources in each case. Note that the following approaches are not exhaustive; more or different resources may be appropriate or available, and caseworkers should always be sensitive to cultural, spiritual, and local traditions and mores in addressing the needs of a particular youth and family.

Carlie

Assessment: A complete physical child abuse investigation needs to be conducted, and in addition Carlie's family needs to be linked to resources which would include a medical evaluation (e.g.,, to check whether Carlie is biologically male or intersex and whether she has any immediate medical needs), an evaluation to explore Carlie's gender identity, and family support services to help her family understand and hopefully come to terms with her gender-nonconforming behavior.

Information Needed: In order to understand the family's current level of knowledge and access to services, the following questions can be posed:

- Can you tell me what you have been able to find out about children like Carlie who don't act the way you would expect for their sex?
- Has Carlie seen anyone, maybe a pediatrician or a therapist, who is trained in care for transgendered children?
- Have you been able to talk with other parents who have children like Carlie?

Identifying Referrals and Resources: If the family has not received any services and is isolated, then several referrals should be considered:

- A physician with appropriate training. If there is no local LGBTQ organization which maintains listings of professionals, search the Gay and Lesbian Medical Association's Provider Directory by zip code or state. If there is no one locally, calling a listed provider for a local referral may be successful.
- A social worker or other human services professional with appropriate training. If there is no local LGBTQ organization that maintains listings of professionals, a search of the websites of the National Association of Social Workers or other national organizations, such as the American Psychological Association, will give provider listings in the area by specialty.

Family Supports

- The nearest chapter of Parents and Friends of Lesbians and Gays (PFLAG) should be located, using the PFLAG website (http://www.pflag.org). PFLAG has a section (TNET) devoted to the needs of the parents of transgendered children, and local chapters are widely distributed. PFLAG provides parents with the opportunity to find support from parents who have had similar experiences and who have found ways to support their children and themselves, and the organization can pass on details of resources that may be helpful.

Exploring Spiritual Supports May Be Helpful

- A web search using "gay-affirming churches" or similar search terms and the location (or nearest large town or city) of the family in question is likely to produce resources that can be discussed with the family.

Jamaica

Assessment: Jamaica is pregnant and needs access to prenatal care. It is known that she has had multiple male sexual partners, but little is known about her relationship status and dating behavior. In order to support her development as a teenager, she needs to be able to have socialization opportunities comparable to those of heterosexual youth, including dating. The family is not connected to any supports that will help them in supporting a sexual minority youth, and their church is not LGBTQ affirming or welcoming.

Information Needed: Whether Jamaica is currently romantically connected to a male or female youth, or neither, in order to help her family address her situation. (Note the use of open-ended questions.)

* Is there someone special to you or that you feel particularly close to?
* Would you tell me something about your feelings for them?

Additional Information Needed: Whether the family has social support and access to information.

* Have you been able to talk with other parents who have children like Jamaica?

Identifying Referrals and Resources: Jamaica tells her caseworker that she is romantically connected to another female teen, so she and her family will need support in finding a way to come to terms with her sexual orientation and appropriate dating. Her family says that they do not want to discuss this with their friends and extended family and have no one to turn to. Since the family does not have an LBGTQ-supportive network and does not wish to "out" themselves to friends and family, the caseworker will look for community-based supports.

Family Supports

* The nearest chapter of PFLAG can be located to provide support for Jamaica's parents, her siblings, and their families, as well as Jamaica herself. PFLAG welcomes LGBTQ individuals as well as their families and friends.
* Family Acceptance Project™ materials can be provided to the family, such as *Supportive Families, Healthy Children: Helping Families with Gay, Lesbian, Bisexual, and Transgender Children* (Ryan 2009).
* An exploration of spiritual supports is needed. Since Jamaica's family attends a predominantly Black, Southern Baptist church, finding an affirming Baptist congregation locally may be of interest to Jamaica's family. The Southern Baptist church has taken the view that homosexuality is a sin to be struggled against, but other Baptist churches have a more welcoming attitude ("Homosexuality," n.d.). The caseworker can also present the information that there is a group supportive of LGBTQ individuals, namely the Association of Welcoming and Affirming Baptists, which provides a listing of member congregations (Welcoming and Affirming Churches n.d.).

Socialization Opportunities

- Find out if there is a local resource which provides adult-organized socialization opportunities for LGBTQ youth, which might be acceptable to Jamaica's parents. A web search using the search terms "lesbian, gay," and the family's location should help in locating local resources.

Eduardo

Assessment: Eduardo needs a safe and supportive resource family, which can support him culturally in terms of his Latino ethnicity and his sexual orientation. Eduardo particularly needs support related to his suicidality and other mental health concerns, through access to LGBTQ-informed and supportive behavioral health services.

Identifying Referrals, Resources, and Advocacy

- Eduardo's caseworker should follow up on the referral for an appropriate resource family at the local agency, which has been recruiting LGBTQ-friendly resource families. The caseworker can advocate for Eduardo (and other LGBTQ youth who are involved with the child welfare agency) by asking for LGBTQ-supportive families to be recruited and for training to be offered to all resource families.
- The caseworker may use the Getting Down to Basics Toolkit both with Eduardo, so that he is aware of his rights and knows how to obtain help, and with prospective foster parents, to help them understand Eduardo's developmental needs.
- Additionally, for the resource family, materials from the Family Acceptance Project™ are available in English, Spanish, and Chinese versions and address cultural issues relevant to the youth and the resource family. The publication "Supportive Families, Healthy Children: Helping Families with Gay, Lesbian, Bisexual, and Transgender Children" is recognized as a best practice resource for suicide prevention for sexual minority youth and young adults by the Best Practices Registry for Suicide Prevention (Ryan 2009). This is particularly important for Eduardo, since these materials will address his suicidality and his culture.
- A social worker or other behavioral healthcare provider with appropriate training will be another essential resource for Eduardo. If there is no local LGBTQ organization which maintains listings of professionals, searching the websites of the National Association of Social Workers or other national organizations, such as the American Psychological Association, may yield provider listings in Eduardo's area.

Jackson

Assessment: Jackson's counselor has made it clear to him that she regards a heterosexual orientation as preferable to a gay or bisexual orientation. Jackson is entitled to receive the same care and affirmation of his sexual orientation as any other youth. Jackson's pre-adoptive family is very uncomfortable with the possibility that he is not heterosexual and needs support and information.

Identifying Referrals, Resources, and Advocacy

- To ensure supportive and appropriate counseling, Jackson's caseworker could contact the counselor to see if she realizes the impact of what she said and is able to offer fully supportive services in the future. The caseworker can offer a copy of the Best Practice Guidelines to the counselor and go over the need for equal treatment both from the developmental perspective and as a legal right. If the counselor is not able to offer fully supportive services, then locating another counselor or therapist is appropriate.
- It is appropriate to use the Getting Down to Basics Toolkit both with Jackson, so that he is aware of his rights and knows how to obtain help, and with Jackson's prospective adoptive parents.

Family Supports

The nearest chapter of PFLAG can be located to provide support for Jackson's prospective adoptive parents, as well as for Jackson.

- Family Acceptance Project™ materials can also be provided to the family, such as *Supportive Families, Healthy Children: Helping Families with Gay, Lesbian, Bisexual, and Transgender Children* (Ryan 2009).

The Importance of Identifying Referrals

Since studies on the outcomes of LGBTQ youth in the foster care system indicate that lesbian and gay youth in out-of-home care receive fewer mental health, substance abuse, and health services than nongay youth (Mallon 1998), it is important to be able to refer sexual minority youth to these services. However, it is equally important to find service providers who are knowledgeable about and friendly to LGBTQ youth. This may be very difficult in some areas; services are more likely to be available in large urban areas than in smaller towns and rural areas.

In many cases, a caseworker will have to be a detective to find LGBTQ-friendly and LGBTQ-knowledgeable services. There may well be services available, but they are more likely to be provided by a particular person at an agency than to be available generally at that agency. However, when that person leaves the agency, the competent service does also. Fortunately, collaborations are emerging between long-established LGBTQ-specialized agencies and child- and family-serving agencies. One example of this is in Pittsburgh, Pennsylvania, where Persad Center, a specialized LGBTQ agency with 30 years of experience, has partnered with Every Child, an agency providing foster care, adoption, and family-centered mental health services for children at risk for out-of-home placement. Their 2-year partnership has successfully targeted agency culture change and the development of LGBTQ-competent services using a combination of training, technical assistance, case consultation, and a train-the-trainer element (B. Hill, personal communication, February 20, 2012). Initiatives of this kind show that developing LGBTQ-competent services can be achieved in existing agencies, when the necessary commitment of expertise and resources is made by agencies and funders.

Conclusion

While child welfare services have not yet achieved cultural competence, Woronoff et al. (2006), in concluding their report "Out of the Margins," note that "No public or private child welfare agency should feel a need to 'reinvent the wheel' with regard to the development of policies, training initiatives, and the provision of competent services for LGBTQ youth" (p. 142). They go on to say that model policies and training curricula are readily available, as noted earlier in this chapter.

This availability of resources is necessary but not, by itself, sufficient to ensure the safety, permanency, and well-being of sexual minority youth. The next step required is sustained commitment by state and local agency leaders to make the cultural and practice changes needed. Commitment of resources, such as fees for trainers and consultants, training time for caseworkers and supervisors, and the time needed to ensure that a true transfer of learning into the day-to-day practice environment occurs, is also required.

One way to leverage existing resources is to adapt existing promising child welfare practices, particularly those that have been developed to meet the needs of racial and ethnic minority youth. For example, family finding practices, for either youth new to care or those who have lingered in foster care (Malm and Allen 2011), and family group conferencing models (American Humane Association 2008) are ripe for adaptation to meet the permanency and stability needs of sexual minority youth. These models are described fully in Chap. 3 of this book. In the course of family finding, explicitly seeking family members who are themselves members of a sexual minority or who are LGBTQ affirming and willing to provide support for the child or youth in relation to their sexual orientation or gender identity or expression may reveal a family resource that would otherwise be overlooked.

Similarly, including a parent from the local PFLAG chapter in family group conferences is a simple way to engage the expertise and support of a parent who has learned from their own child's experiences. In addition, the support and experience of a minister, rabbi, or other cleric from an LGBTQ-welcoming and LGBTQ-affirming congregation can also be brought to bear.

As noted above, the most urgent need is for child welfare agencies to be equipped to recognize and address issues of physical and emotional safety. Beyond safety, the next goal is the competent management of issues related to sexual orientation and gender identity in the area of placement and placement stability. The third goal is to support and facilitate the well-being of these highly vulnerable and often invisible children and youth. Emerging interest from some states and localities is promising. Although cultural change is challenging, the combination of growing interest and support for LGBTQ youth and the availability of the tools to help them will hopefully lead to improvements in service for sexual minority children and youth coming into contact with the child welfare system.

Questions for Discussion

1. From your own cultural perspective, what challenges, if any, would you experience in advocating for LGBTQ children and youth? How do you think your beliefs impact your views of LGBTQ children and their families?
2. In your local area, how many LGBTQ-specific community supports can you name and describe?
3. What steps will you take to improve your skills in providing services to achieve safety, permanency, and well-being for LGBTQ children and youth?
4. What is the difference between sexual orientation and gender identity?

References

American Humane Association. (2008). *Family Group Decision Making in child welfare: Purpose, values and processes.* Retrieved from http://www.americanhumane.org/children/programs/family-group-decision-making/.
Association of Welcoming and Affirming Baptists. (n.d.). *Welcoming and affirming churches.* Retrieved from http://www.wabaptists.org/wachurches.htm
Bevel, G. (2011). Representing transgender youth: Learning from Mae's journey. *ABA Child Law Practice, 29*(11), 169–174.
Child Welfare League of America. (2002). *Cultural competence agency self assessment.* Washington, DC: Author.
Child Welfare League of America & Lambda Legal Defense and Education Fund. (2012). *Getting down to basics: Tools to support LGBTQ youth in care.* New York, NY & Arlington, VA: Authors. Retrieved from http://www.lambdalegal.org/take-action/tool-kits/getting-down-to-basics/.
Child Welfare League of America, American Bar Association Center on Children and the Law, Elze, D., Family Acceptance Project, Lambda Legal Defense, Legal Defense Services for

Children, et al. (2012). *Recommended practices to promote the safety and well-being of lesbian, gay, bisexual, transgender and questioning youth and youth at risk of or living with HIV in child welfare settings*. Washington, D.C.: Child Welfare League of America and Lambda Legal Defense and Education Fund.

Children's Bureau, Administration on Children, Youth and Families; U.S. Department of Health and Human Services. (2011). *The AFCARS report #18: Preliminary FY 2010 estimates as of June 2011*. Washington, DC: Author. Retrieved from http://www.acf.hhs.gov/programs/cb/stats_research/afcars/tar/report18.htm.

Children's Bureau, Administration on Children, Youth and Families; US Department of Health and Human Services. (2011). *Information Memorandum, ACYF-CB-IM-11-03*. Washington, DC: Author. Retrieved from http://www.acf.hhs.gov/programs/cb/stats_research/afcars/tar/report18.htm.

Clements, J. A., & Rosenwald, M. (2007). Foster parents' perspectives on LGB youth in the child welfare system. *Journal of Gay & Lesbian Social Services, 19*(1), 57–69.

Corliss, H. L., Goodenow, C. S., Nichols, B. A., & Austin, S. B. (2011). High burden of homelessness among sexual minority youth: Findings from a representative Massachusetts high school sample. *American Journal of Public Health, 101*(9), 1683–1689.

Courtney, M., Dworsky, A., Lee, J., & Raap, M. (2009). *Midwest evaluation of the adult functioning of former foster youth: Outcomes at age 23 and 24*. Chicago: Chapin Hall at the University of Chicago.

Cross, T. L., Bazron, B. J., Dennis, K. W., & Isaacs, M. R. (1989). *Towards a culturally competent system of care: A monograph on effective services for minority children who are severely emotionally disturbed*. Washington, DC: Child and Adolescent Service System Program.

Desai, K. (2010). *It's your life*. Chicago, IL: American Bar Association.

Desetta, A. (Ed.). (2003). *In the system and in the life: A guide for teens and staff to the gay experience in foster care*. New York, NY: Youth Communication/NY Center, Inc.

Elze, D., & McHaelen, R. (2009). *Moving the margins: Training curriculum for child welfare services with lesbian, gay, bisexual, transgender, and questioning youth*. Washington, DC: National Association of Social Workers and Lambda Legal Defense & Education Fund.

Ethics and Religious Liberty Commission of the Southern Baptist Convention. (n.d.). *Homosexuality*. Retrieved from http://erlc.com/homosexuality/)

Feinstein, R., Greenblatt, A., Hass, L., Kohn, S., & Rana, J. (2001). *Justice for all? A report on lesbian, gay, bisexual and transgendered youth in the New York juvenile justice system*. Report commissioned by the Lesbian and Gay Youth Project of the Urban Justice Center. Retrieved from http://www.urbanjustice.org/pdf/publications/lesbianandgay/justiceforallreport.pdf.

Friedman, M. S., Marshal, M. P., Guadamuz, T. E., Wei, C., Saewyc, E., Wong, C. F., & Stall, R. (2011). A meta-analysis to examine disparities in childhood sexual abuse, parental physical abuse, and peer victimization among sexual minority and non-sexual minority individuals. *American Journal of Public Health, 101*(81), 1481–1494.

Forrest, R., & Saewyc, E. (2004). Sexual minority teen parents: demographics of an unexpected population. *Journal of Adolescent Health, 34*(2), 122.

Freundlich, M., & Avery, R. J. (2004). Gay and lesbian youth in foster care: Meeting their placement and service needs. *Journal of Gay & Social Services, 17*(4), 39–57.

Garofalo, R., & Katz, E. (2001). Health care issues of gay and lesbian youth. *Current Opinion in Pediatrics, 13*(4), 298–302.

Garofalo, R., Wolf, R. C., Kessel, S., Palfry, J., & DuRant, R. H. (1998). The association between health risk behaviors and sexual orientation among a school-based sample of adolescents. *Pediatrics, 101*(5), 895–902.

Garofalo, R., Wolf, R. C., Wissow, L. S., Woods, E. R., & Goodman, E. (1999). Sexual orientation and risk of suicide attempts among a representative sample of youth. *Archives of Pediatrics and Adolescent Medicine, 153*, 487–493.

Grant, J. M., Mottet, L. A., & Tanis, D. (2011). *Injustice at every turn: A report of the National Transgender Discrimination Survey*. Washington, DC: National Center for Transgender Equality and National Gay and Lesbian Task Force.

Kann, L., Olsen, E. O., McManus, T., Kinchen, S., Chyen, D., Harris, W. A., & Wechsler, H. (2011). Sexual identity, sex of sexual contacts, and health risk behaviors among students in grades 9–12: Youth risk behavior surveillance, selected sites, United States, 2001–2009. *Surveillance Summaries, 60*(SS07), 1–133.

Lambda Legal Defense and Education Fund, National Alliance to End Homelessness, National Network for Youth, & National Center for Lesbian Rights. (2009). *National recommended best practices for serving LGBT homeless youth.* New York, NY: Authors.

Laver, M., & Khoury, A. (2008). *Opening doors for LGBTQ youth in foster care: A guide for lawyers and judges.* Chicago IL: American Bar Association.

Lock, J., & Steiner, H. (1999). Gay, lesbian, and bisexual youth risks for emotional, physical, and social problems: Results from a community-based survey. *Journal of the American Academy of Child and Adolescent Psychiatry, 38*(3), 297–304.

Majd, K., Marksamer, J., & Reyes, C. (2009). *Hidden injustice: Lesbian, gay, bisexual, and transgender youth in juvenile courts.* San Francisco, CA: The Equity Project.

Mallon, G. P. (1998). *We don't exactly get the welcome wagon: The experiences of gay and lesbian adolescents in child welfare systems.* New York: Columbia University Press.

Mallon, G. P., Aledort, N., & Ferrera, M. (2002). There's no place like home: Achieving safety, permanency, and well-being for lesbian and gay adolescents in out-of-home care settings. *Child Welfare, 81*(2), 407–439.

Malm, K., & Allen, T. (2011). *Family Finding: Does implementation differ when serving different child welfare populations?* Washington, DC: Child Trends, Inc.

Marksamer, J. (2008). And by the way, do you know he thinks he's a girl? The failures of law, policy, and legal representation for transgender youth in juvenile delinquency courts. *Sexuality Research & Social Policy, 5*(1), 72–92.

Marshal, M. P., Dietz, L. J., Friedman, M. S., Stall, R., Smith, H. A., McGinley, J., et al. (2011). Suicidality and depression disparities between sexual minority and heterosexual youth: A meta-analytic review. *Journal of Adolescent Health, 49*(2), 115–123.

Marshal, M. P., Friedman, M. S., Stall, R., King, K. M., Miles, J., Gold, M. A., Bukstein, O. G., & Morse, J. Q. (2008). Sexual orientation and adolescent substance use: A meta-analysis and methodological review. *Addiction, 103*(4), 546–556.

National Technical Assistance and Evaluation Center for Systems of Care. (2009). *A closer look: Cultural competency.* Fairfax, VA: Author.

Perrin, E. C. (1996). Pediatricians and gay and lesbian youth. *Pediatrics in Review, 17*(9), 311.

Ragg, D. M., Patrick, D., & Ziefert, M. (2006). Slamming the closet door: working with gay and lesbian youth in care. *Child Welfare, 85*(2), 243–265.

Ray, N. (2006). *Lesbian, gay, bisexual and transgender youth: An epidemic of homelessness.* New York, NY: National Gay and Lesbian Task Force Policy institute and the National Coalition for the Homeless.

Remafedi, G., French, S., Story, M., Resnick, M. D., & Blum, R. (1998). The relationship between suicide risk and sexual orientation: results of a population-based study. *American Journal of Public Health, 88*(1), 57–60.

Remafedi, G., Farrow, J., & Deisher, R. (1991). Risk factors for attempted suicide in gay and bisexual youth. *Pediatrics, 87*, 869–875.

Rotheram-Borus, M. J., & Fernandez, M. I. (1995). Sexual orientation and developmental challenges experienced by gay and lesbian youths. *Suicide and Life-threatening Behavior, 25*(Suppl), 26–34.

R.G. v. Koller, 415 F.Supp.2d 1129 (D. Hawai'i, 2006).

Ryan, C. (2009). *Supportive families, healthy children: Helping families with lesbian, gay, bisexual, and transgender children.* San Francisco, CA: Family Acceptance Project, Marian Wright Edelman Institute, San Francisco State University.

Ryan, C., Huebner, D., Diaz, R. M., & Sanchez, J. (2009). Family rejection as a predictor of negative health outcomes in white and Latino lesbian, gay, and bisexual young adults. *Pediatrics, 123*, 346–352.

Ryan, C., Russell, S. T., Huebner, D., Diaz, R., & Sanchez, J. (2010). Family acceptance in adolescence and the health of LGBT young adults. *Journal of Child and Adolescent Psychiatric Nursing, 23*(4), 205–213.

Saewyc, E. M., Bearinger, L. H., Blum, R. W., & Resnick, M. D. (1999). Sexual intercourse, abuse and pregnancy among adolescent women: Does sexual orientation make a difference? *Family Planning Perspectives, 31*, 127–131.

Saewyc, E. M., Pettingell, S., & Skay, C. (2006). Teen pregnancy among sexual minority youth during the 1990s: Countertrends in a population at risk. *Journal of Adolescent Health, 34*(2), 125–126.

Safren, S. A., & Heimberg, R. G. (1999). Depression, hopelessness, suicidality and related factors in sexual minority and heterosexual adolescents. *Journal of Consulting and Clinical Psychology, 67*(6), 859–866.

Savage, D., & Miller, T. (Eds.). (2011). *It gets better: Coming out, overcoming bullying, and creating a life worth living.* New York, NY: Penguin Group.

Shenassa, E. D., Catlin, S. N., & Buka, S. L. (2003). Lethality of firearms relative to other suicide methods: A population based study. *Journal of Epidemiology & Community Health, 57,* 120–124.

Sullivan, T. R. (1994). Obstacles to effective child welfare services with gay and lesbian youth. *Child Welfare, 73,* 291–304.

Sullivan, C., Sommer, C., & Moff, J. (2001). *Youth in the margins: A report on the unmet needs of lesbian, gay, bisexual, and transgendered adolescents in foster care.* New York: Lambda Legal Defense and Education Fund.

Wilber, S., Ryan, C., & Marksamer, J. (2006a). *Best practice guidelines: Serving LGBT youth in out of home care.* Washington, DC: Child Welfare League of America, Inc.

Wilber, S., Reyes, C., & Marksamer, J. (2006b). The Model Standards Project: Creating inclusive systems for LGBT youth in out-of-home-care. *Child Welfare, 85*(2), 133–149.

Woronoff, R., & Estrada, R. (2006). Regional listening forums: An examination of the methodologies used by the Child Welfare League of America and Lambda Legal to highlight the experiences of LGBTQ youth in care. *Child Welfare, 85*(2), 341–360.

Woronoff, R., Estrada, R., & Sommer, S. (2006). *Out of the margins: A report of listening forums highlighting the experiences of lesbian, gay, bisexual, transgender, and questioning youth in care.* Washington, DC: Child Welfare League of America, Inc.

Chapter 7
Race, Racial Disparity, and Culture in Child Welfare

Cynthia Bradley-King, Marlo A. Perry, and Caroline Donohue

Abstract Throughout American history, race, minority issues, and inequity of treatment have affected every area of human life. Child welfare systems and the demographic makeup of the systems' participants are influenced by these issues and much of our current literature focuses on African-American/Black communities and their disproportionate representation in human services and criminal justice systems. Other minority groups have also experienced both disproportionate representation and disparate treatment in child welfare systems, including Native Americans, Latinos/Hispanics, and Asian Americans/Pacific Islanders (AAPI). The scope of child welfare concerns makes a clear case for cooperative efforts between child welfare providers and researchers to provide additional studies of the dynamics that contribute to disproportionality and unequal policy implementation, as well as practices in child welfare service delivery for minority children as a whole and African Americans in particular.

It is incumbent upon child welfare workers to have an understanding of the historical context and the ramifications of racial disproportionality and disparity in child welfare in order to move toward equal treatment and policy implementation. In order to work effectively with families, child welfare workers must thoughtfully consider how race and culture intersect with social and economic risk factors that contribute to poor service outcomes. Combined with a balance of cultural awareness and humility, this knowledge will enable practitioners to successfully engage with the families with whom they work. It is critical for caseworkers to learn from families about their values and traditions, especially when these cultural norms are different from what the caseworker thinks s/he knows. Learning the nuances of the myriad cultures, races, and ethnicities on the American landscape is a lifelong process, and each family will express their own culture in their own way.

C. Bradley-King (✉) • M.A. Perry • C. Donohue
Child Welfare Education and Research Programs, School of Social Work,
University of Pittsburgh, Pittsburgh, PA, USA
e-mail: ckb11@pitt.edu

H. Cahalane (ed.), *Contemporary Issues in Child Welfare Practice*,
Contemporary Social Work Practice, DOI 10.1007/978-1-4614-8627-5_7,
© Springer Science+Business Media New York 2013

Collaborative, trusting relationships can only be built when families are treated with dignity and respect, regardless of the caseworker's cultural lens or any cultural differences between the caseworker and family members.

Keywords Racial disparity • Disproportionality • Cultural competence • Cultural humility

Introduction

Throughout American history, race, minority issues, and inequity of treatment have affected every area of human life. Child welfare systems and the demographic makeup of the systems' participants are influenced by these issues, and much of our current literature focuses on African-American/Black communities and their disproportionate representation in human services and criminal justice systems. Other minority groups have also experienced both disproportionate representation and disparate treatment in child welfare systems, including Native Americans, Latinos/Hispanics, and Asian-Americans/Pacific Islanders (AAPIs). These groups have experienced what observers describe as similarly disparate treatment once identified by child welfare systems, and they continue to be disproportionately represented in many states and counties (Hill 2004, 2011). The scope of child welfare concerns makes a clear case for cooperative efforts between child welfare providers and researchers to provide additional studies of the dynamics that contribute to disproportionality and unequal policy implementation, as well as practices in child welfare service delivery for minority children as a whole and African Americans in particular.

In this chapter we will discuss the issue of disproportionality in child welfare. We start by reviewing definitions of relevant terms and providing an overview of racial demographics in the USA and in the child welfare system. We will then provide a historical context and review the different positions in a debate about disproportionality. Finally, we will discuss cultural competence and cultural humility and their role in working with diverse groups of children and families, followed by a case study intended to improve casework services to minority families and children.

Minority Groups, Disproportionality, and Disparity

How do we describe minority groups, and what role does culture play in their inclusion in formal systems of authority, specifically child welfare systems? When describing a minority group, one must remember that minorities are not defined as such because they are outnumbered in the broader society (e.g., women hold majority status in numbers). Rather, a minority group is defined as such due to the presence of the following five characteristics: unequal treatment, distinguishing physical or cultural traits, involuntary membership, an awareness of subordination, and high in-group marriage (Schaefer 2011). Minority or subordinate groups can also be defined as such due to a range of opportunities that is disproportionately low when compared with their numbers in society at large (Schaefer 2011). Types or categories of minority groups include, but are not limited to, race/ethnicity, gender, religion, sexual orientation or identity, and socioeconomic status. For the purposes of this chapter, and because the largest disproportionality issues in child welfare involve race, we will highlight the experiences of African Americans/ Blacks and Native Americans within the public child welfare system in the USA. Additionally, we will discuss Hispanic/Latino and Asian-American/Pacific Islander (AAPI) children involved in the child welfare system, as some research has shown disparities for these minority groups (and, for Hispanic/Latino children, some disproportionality at the state level).

The terms used to describe differences in participation and in service provision among children and families of different races, minority groups, and ethnicities in child welfare are *disproportionality* and *disparity*. *Disproportionality* refers to the percentage of children of a particular race, ethnicity, or other minority group in the child welfare system compared to the percentage of those same children in the American population (Wells 2011). The term "overrepresentation" is often used interchangeably with disproportionality; however, this not entirely accurate, as underrepresentation is also a form of disproportionality (Chapin Hall Center for Children 2008). *Disparity*, on the other hand, refers to the unequal treatment or outcomes of various racial/ethnic minority groups compared to those of nonminority groups in the child welfare system (Hill 2006; Wulczyn and Lery 2007).

Historical Considerations

Evidence of disparate treatment for minorities is not a new concept. Carp (2002) maintains that child welfare history is scattered with attempts by self-described "child savers" to "liberate" poor, minority, and immigrant children from the assumed dangers related to their familial interactions. Early in the nineteenth century, early child advocates were influenced by their own class and race as they sought to remove children from unfortunate circumstances. Charles Loring Brace, a Protestant minister and early child welfare pioneer, became the most renowned representative of the child rescue movement. He founded the New York Children's Aid Society in 1853 and authored *The Best Method of Disposing of Our Pauper and Vagrant Children* in 1859. Brace and many of his child-rescuing peers considered the poor to be unworthy, degenerate parents, and Brace's religious beliefs strongly influenced his desire to remove the children of poor families from crowded cities and place them in rural Protestant communities with families who espoused his religious beliefs and ideals. From 1854 to 1930, nearly 250,000 impoverished immigrant children were sent by train to midwestern and western states (O'Connor 2001).

The outcomes of these placements, in which a child could be sent to live with almost anyone, were mostly unknown. The letters sent by the agencies to request information about the children after placement were generally unanswered. Many of the children so placed were not orphans, but rather came from families suffering from extreme poverty, inadequate housing, illness, and alcohol abuse. Largely dependent on private, sectarian philanthropy, this social program changed thousands of lives, and until complaints arose about the placement of children of mostly Catholic immigrants with Protestant families (Gordon 1999) it was widely imitated, despite being largely unexamined and unregulated by government.

Brace believed that removing children from "immoral" parents early on would help these children avoid the inferior culture inherent in their biological families and give them an opportunity to live "normal," productive lives. It is not surprising that this ideology, which seemed benevolent and humanitarian to Protestants, earned Brace a reputation as a child stealer rather than a child saver in many Catholic communities. Consequently, many secular groups developed their own social services and child-caring institutions. The orphanage movement gained considerable momentum, and in the late nineteenth century, the Catholic church built numerous institutions designed to provide care for the growing numbers of children abandoned or neglected in the abject poverty of the cities. The Ursuline Convent, founded in 1727, was the first US orphanage; by 1910, there were 110,000 children living in 1,151 orphanages (Crossen-Tower 2010).

While these preparations for the nations' White destitute children were being made, African-American children generally did not receive similar child welfare services until after the civil rights movement expanded equal rights for African Americans as a whole (Galante 1999). Indeed, African-American children, as well as potential African-American parents, were virtually locked out of the public child welfare system for decades (Carp 2002). Furthermore, despite the higher illegitimacy rates among African Americans, the existing facilities that cared for unmarried mothers or their children were almost exclusively for White unmarried mothers (Hill 2004). When early attempts to provide institutions for African-American children did arise, they were initiated by African-American women's organizations, Black churches, and individual Black community organizers. Examples include the Big Sister Home for Girls, the Meigs Reformatory, and the Carrie Steele Orphan Home (Perry and Davis-Maye 2007).

Until the early 1960s, the few African-American children in placement remained in foster care, without much effort to reunify families or to place them in adoptive homes (Edwards 1999). Notwithstanding the high numbers of available Black children, potential Black adoptive parents had great difficulty adopting compared to White potential parents (Roberts 2002). Not until the cost of foster care began to skyrocket did the situation become a public policy issue. At that point the government began to contract with agencies to look for adoptive homes for Black children who were wards of the public court system (Edwards 1999).

In 1973, a class action suit in New York City, the Wilder case, was launched in order to gain equity for African-American children in the city's foster care system (Bernstein 2001). Until that point private sectarian charities, which controlled the area's foster care beds, were legally able to discriminate and to use government funds to facilitate placement of children of their own group's ethnic or religious background while African-American children in care waited for placement.

Over more than 2 decades, with countless delays, the suit succeeded in bringing about a change in the law, but for the years prior to the change and during the progress of the suit through the courts, the right of private agencies to use public funds to treat children unequally was defended by many in New York City's child welfare system.

While federal government intervention was scarce in the lives of most children and families until the early twentieth century, for one group, it was overwhelmingly intrusive. Native Americans had been systematically exterminated, driven from their lands, defeated in war, and finally confined to desolate areas with little possibility of earning a living (Halverson et al. 2002). The result was staggering poverty in Native-American communities. Specific government policy efforts to assimilate the remains of the Native-American population took the form of enforced attendance at distant boarding schools for tribal children (Graham 2008). Hundreds of children were separated from their families for years at a time, forbidden to speak their own languages or practice their tribal beliefs. This separation from parents, siblings, and tribal members was considered critical in making these children "blend" into the dominant White culture (Graham 2008).

In more recent times, the Child Welfare League of America and social workers in many states cooperated with the Federal Bureau of Indian Affairs in placing hundreds of Native-American children for adoption with White families, in what is now recognized as part of a continuing effort to blot out tribal cultures by assimilation of the young (Deserly and Gardner 2011). Then, in 1978, passage of the federal Indian Child Welfare Act (ICWA) established tribal authority in determining child custody. It required states to determine tribal affiliation for children and to give notice to family and tribe members before any legal proceedings could begin. ICWA also made clear the preference that American Indian children be placed with extended kin or in tribally approved placements (Jones et al. 2000; Libby et al. 2007; Matheson 1996). However, thus far, ICWA has not proved successful in stemming the tide of native children placed for care outside their tribes (Fletcher 2009).

Immigration to the USA in recent years has also impacted the child welfare system. Influxes of immigrants from Latin American (the majority of whom are from Mexico), Asia (predominantly from the Philippines, China, India, Vietnam, and Korea), and the Caribbean (primarily from Jamaica, Haiti, and Trinidad and Tobago) have contributed to the growing child population in this country (Landale et al. 2011). More than one in five children in the USA have at least one foreign-born parent; in fact, children of immigrants have accounted for more than 75 % of the growth of the US child population since 1990 (Landale et al. 2011). While immigrant status alone certainly does not warrant involvement with the child welfare system, immigration does bring a unique set of stressors to families, including poverty, isolation, and language barriers, which may contribute to child welfare involvement (Stalker et al. 2009). Further, different cultural norms around family roles, parenting, and discipline may be challenging for immigrant families, as well as child welfare professionals, to navigate (Stalker et al. 2009).

The Child Welfare System and the Overrepresentation Debate

The racial/ethnic makeup of the USA has changed dramatically during the last decade, more dramatically than at any time during the twentieth century. The US population is far more diverse than at any time in recent history, with the Black/African-American population increasing by 12.3 %, Native/Alaskan Americans by 18.4 %, Asian-Americans by 43.3 %, and Native Hawaiian and other Pacific Islanders by 35.4 % from 2000 to 2010 (US Census 2010). Hispanics/Latinos increased their percentage in the population to 16.3 % (an increase of 43 %; US Census 2010); Hispanics will make up 29 % of the US population in 2050. Additionally, nearly 20 % of Americans will be immigrants by 2050. The non-Hispanic White population will increase more slowly than other racial and ethnic groups and Whites will become a minority (47 %) by 2050 (US Census 2010).

Percentages of children in the general population and percentages of foster children by race

Children in (US) population by race and ethnicity	Children	Foster children
Black	14 %	29 %
Hispanic/Latino	24 %	21 %
White	53 %	41 %
American Indian/Native-American	1 %	2 %
AAPI	4 %	1 %
Other[a]	4 %	7 %

[a] Comprises persons with more than one race or ethnicity or unknown
Source: Kids Count Data Center 2012

Given the history of bias and discrimination in our nation, many who are concerned about families and children involved with child welfare services have critically examined the ethnic/racial makeup of children in agency care. The National Incidence Study (NIS) is a federally mandated, periodic endeavor charged with compiling national data regarding the incidence of child abuse and neglect in the USA (Sedlak et al. 2010a, b). NIS-1 was conducted in 1979–1980. The second and third waves (NIS-2 in 1986–1987 and NIS-3 in 1993–1995) showed no race differences in maltreatment incidence, suggesting that the issue was related more to disparity than to disproportionality. Many consumers of that data concluded that the high rates of contact between child welfare and Black children and families were a result of bias in the child welfare system (Bartholet et al. 2011; Chibnall et al. 2010). Dorothy Roberts, whose popular book *Shattered Bonds* (2002) has been widely quoted, placed responsibility for the overrepresentation of African-American children squarely upon child welfare agencies; she blamed lack of training, ambiguous definitions, and caseworker subjectivity (Roberts 2002). Researchers and policy makers called for investigations of agency characteristics (e.g., worker attitudes, worker bias, agency culture) and public policies that may have unintentionally supported disparate responses to Black children and families (Hill 2011).

Findings from NIS-4 (conducted in 2004–2009), however, did show race differences in maltreatment rates. In fact, it showed that maltreatment rates are 73 % higher for Black children than for White children (Bartholet et al. 2011).

These findings have been in part attributed to a larger, more rigorous, and more precise study than in previous waves (Bartholet et al. 2011). However, Drake and Jonson-Reid (2011) contend that findings across NIS waves may not actually be radically different. They point out that NIS-2 and NIS-3 did show racial differences in maltreatment rates similar in magnitude and valence to NIS-4; however, large confidence intervals kept those differences from achieving statistical significance (Drake and Jonson-Reid 2011).

Another national effort to track incidences of child abuse across large populations has been the National Child Abuse and Neglect Data System (NCANDS), which provides yearly counts of child abuse and neglect, rates of victimization, and child welfare services provided (DHHS 2008; Drake and Jonson-Reid 2011). Victimization rates have consistently been higher for Black children than White children. Discrepancies between earlier waves of NIS and NCANDS supported the theory that any disproportionality was due to bias in the child welfare system. However, the more recent NIS-4 is consistent with NCANDS findings, indicating that maltreatment rates are indeed higher for Black children than for White and suggesting that these differences are not necessarily due to bias, but to other underlying issues (DHHS 2008; Drake and Jonson-Reid 2011). We will discuss these potential contributing factors to disproportionality in the next section of this chapter.

Issues of disparity are also evident. According to the *Child Welfare Outcomes 2006–2009: Report to Congress*, there were many states where the percentage of minority children entering foster care was at least one and a half times greater than the percentage of these children in the states' populations; this was true for Black children in 32 states, Native-American children in 13 states, and Hispanic children in 6 states (US Department of Health and Human Services 2010). Not only do children of color enter the foster care system at higher rates than White children, they experience longer lengths of stay in placement, experience more frequent placement changes, and wait greater periods of time to achieve permanency through adoption and legal guardianship (Huebner 2007; Zinn et al. 2006). Black children are less likely to be reunified with their birth families than other children and are also less likely to be adopted than other children (Shaw et al. 2008). Research has also shown that African-American foster parents have less contact with child welfare workers than do White foster parents (Casey Family Programs 2006).

While American Indian/Alaskan-Native children account for only 1 % of the census, they represent approximately 2 % of children in out-of-home care (AFCARS 2012). Rates of disproportionality for this group are even greater in certain states (e.g., Alaska and Minnesota; Carter 2010). Using the National Child Abuse and Neglect Data System (NCANDS) and the Adoption and Foster Care Analysis and Reporting System (AFCARS), Hill (2007) found that compared to all other racial/ethnic groups, American Indian/Alaskan-Native children were the most likely to be in placement. Other research has also found that being of American Indian/Alaskan-Native heritage was predictive of out-of-home placement (Carter 2010; Donald et al. 2003; Fox 2004). American Indian/Alaskan-Native families that come into contact with the child welfare system also receive significantly lower levels of mental health services than do families of other racial/ethnic backgrounds (Libby et al. 2007).

Although studies have not shown child welfare disproportionality for Latino children at the national level, there are some important trends to note for this minority group. The number of Latino children in foster care has more than doubled between 1990 and 2010, growing from 8 to 21 % of the foster care population (Garcia et al. 2012; US Department of Health and Human Services 2010). There is also evidence of disproportionality in 19 states (Dettlaff 2011; Garcia et al. 2012). Research has also shown that Latino children have higher referral rates than White children, are more likely to have an accepted referral, are more likely to be placed in out-of-home care, and stay in care for longer periods of time (Church 2006; Dettlaff and Cardoso 2010; Garcia et al. 2012; Texas Health and Human Services Commission, Texas Department of Family and Protective Services 2006; Washington State Racial Disproportionality Advisory Committee 2010). Further, recent research has highlighted differences between children of immigrant parents and nonimmigrant parents in terms of experiences with the child welfare system. One study showed that more than a third of Latino children who come into contact with the child welfare system have at least one immigrant parent (Dettlaff et al. 2009).

Asian-Americans/Pacific Islanders are disproportionately underrepresented in the child welfare system. While AAPIs represent 4 % of the child population, they represent only 1 % of the children in foster care (Casey Family Programs 2006). Even among immigrant families, AAPI children are underrepresented in terms of their involvement with the child welfare system (18 % in the general population of children of immigrants vs. 7.5 % of children of immigrants in the child welfare system) (Dettlaff and Earner 2010). However, there is a small body of research that highlights the variability among AAPI ethnic groups in terms of involvement with child welfare; this variability is a result of both structural factors (e.g., poverty, language barriers, isolation, discrimination) and cultural factors (e.g., parenting styles, beliefs about physical discipline) (Pelczarski and Kemp 2006). For example, a California study showed that Samoan and Southeast Asian families (i.e., Cambodian, Thai, Vietnamese, and Laotian) were overrepresented in referrals to child welfare, while Japanese, Chinese, and Filipino families were underrepresented relative to their representation in the general population (Pelczarski and Kemp 2006). Another study found that AAPI children in out-of-home care were less likely than Whites to be reunified with their parents, indicating some additional disparity for this group (Hines et al. 2007). The involvement of AAPIs with the child welfare system has not been studied extensively; it is possible that low report rates actually reflect an underlying cultural value of family privacy and/or a lack of familiarity with US child welfare laws (Larsen et al. 2008).

Moving Beyond a Disproportionality Focus

In all areas of life, race and culture play an inescapable role in the way people regard and react to each other. Child welfare systems are no exception, and thus the ability to disregard bias, past experiences, and learned behaviors toward certain racial groups is difficult for many. At every decision point, from reporting suspected abuse and neglect to termination of parental rights and adoption, the race, minority status, and ethnicity of the family as well as the race, status, and ethnicity of the formal authority (e.g., caseworker, judge, mandated reporter, police officer) may be a factor in the outcome of the case, including its duration and disposition.

Contemporary researchers encourage viewing the subject of race and child welfare in context. The connection between race and child welfare outcomes is confounded by the relationship between race and other contributors to poor child welfare outcomes, including poverty, parental substance abuse, mental health and physical health issues, incarceration, and domestic violence (Barth et al. 2001; Chaffin et al. 1996; Courtney, et al 1996; Dworsky et al. 2010). It is imperative that child welfare practitioners, administrators, and researchers understand that these factors pose increased risks for children when present in their family situations. Further, segregated impoverished communities often have higher incidences of child welfare involvement, and both African-Americans and Native Americans are disproportionally living under these conditions (Bartholet et al. 2011). While it is beyond the scope of this chapter to describe each of these comorbid risks in detail, we will highlight a few below, with an emphasis on their relationship with racial disproportionality in child welfare.

Poverty

There is vast evidence that although poverty alone certainly does not cause child maltreatment, maltreatment does occur disproportionately among poor families (Dettlaff et al. 2011; Drake et al. 2009; Drake and Pandey 1996; Freisthler et al. 2007). In fact, the NIS-4 shows that children living in poverty are victims of at least one form of maltreatment more than five times as often as nonpoor children (Sedlak et al. 2010a, b). Among children reported for maltreatment, poor children have worse outcomes than nonpoor children in terms of child welfare and non-child welfare outcomes (Jonson-Reid et al. 2009).

Understanding poverty plays a critical role in comprehending racial disproportionality and disparity in child welfare, as African-American families are more than twice as likely as White families to live in poverty (Moore et al. 2009). Further, African-Americans are in poverty for longer periods of time than Whites and have lower exit rates from poverty than all other racial groups (Corcoran 2001; Dettlaff et al. 2011). According to the National Center for Children in Poverty, in 2010, 64 % of Black children, 63 % of American Indian children, and 63 % of Hispanic children were living in poverty, as opposed to 31 % of White children and 31% of AAPI children (Addy and Wight 2012). Given the disparities seen in the child welfare system for each of these minority groups, it is critical to understand the relationship of poverty to child welfare outcomes.

Immigration status is also an important factor in whether or not a family lives in poverty. Sixty-one percent of children of immigrant parents live in poverty, whereas

41 % of children of native-born parents live in poverty (Addy and Wight 2012). Further, poverty is higher for groups that have a higher proportion of recent immigrants (Takei and Sakamoto 2011). Limited fluency in English and/or illegal immigrant status can contribute to lack of employment (or underemployment), lower income levels, poor health, and poverty (Capps et al. 2003; Stalker et al. 2009).

Substance Abuse

Children whose caregivers abuse substances are almost three times as likely to be abused and four times as likely to be neglected as children whose caregivers do not abuse substances (Wallace et al. 2004). Estimates for prevalence of parental substance abuse for families involved in child welfare range from 60 to 75 %; in most cases, a caregiver's struggle with substance abuse lasts at least 5 years (Brook and McDonald 2009; Wallace et al. 2004). The further into the child welfare system the family is, the more likely it is that substance abuse is involved. For example, at the point of an unsubstantiated report, approximately 40 % of cases involve parental substance abuse, whereas 75 % of cases at the point of out-of-home placement involve parental substance abuse (Brook and McDonald 2009; Young et al. 1998). Children whose families don't receive appropriate treatment for substance abuse are more likely to end up in foster care, remain in foster care longer, and reenter foster care once they return home than children whose families do receive treatment (Brook and McDonald 2009; Wallace et al. 2004).

Poverty plays a significant role in this issue. Black and Hispanic adults are no more likely to use or abuse substances than are White adults. However, substance use is higher among the poor than the rest of the population (across racial/ethnic groups) (Wallace et al. 2004).

Further, although rates of substance abuse are similar across racial/ethnic groups, the consequences are far more negative for minority groups (Burlew et al. 2009; Iguchi et al. 2002). More African-Americans are incarcerated for drug-related offenses than are White offenders (see section on Incarceration below), and more African-American children are removed because of parental substance abuse (Children's Defense Fund 2007; McRoy 2011).

There is evidence that participation in treatment results in positive outcomes, both in terms of sobriety and reunification. Gregoire and Schultz (2001) found a positive relationship between treatment completion and sobriety and treatment completion and child custody. Grella et al. (2009) found that mothers who completed at least 90 days of treatment were almost twice as likely to be reunified with their children than those who did not spend 90 days in treatment. Green et al. (2007) also investigated the role of treatment and found that mothers who entered treatment faster, stayed in treatment longer, and who completed at least one treatment were more likely to be reunified with their children instead of having their children freed for adoption (Choi et al. 2012).

Despite these promising findings, research suggests that minorities are less likely to participate in substance abuse treatment (Substance Abuse and Mental Health Services Administration 2002) and are less likely to describe treatment as helpful (Burlew et al. 2009; Heron et al. 1997; Longshore et al. 1999). Further, other research demonstrates that participation in treatment can actually be a red flag for child welfare-involved families and result in more visibility within the system. One study showed that families participating in a comprehensive substance abuse program actually moved more slowly toward reunification than those not participating and that children from these families were more likely to reenter out-of-home care after reunification was achieved. The authors hypothesized that this was in part due to the difficulty inherent in maintaining sobriety, as well as the heightened scrutiny these families might be under compared to families not dealing with substance abuse (Brook and McDonald 2007). Another study demonstrated that the re-reporting of substance abusing caregivers within 2 months of the initial report was most likely to happen if the report was directly related to substance abuse, if the caregiver was at high risk for criminal behavior, if law enforcement was not already involved with the family, and if the head of household was a single African-American woman (Brook and McDonald 2009; Fuller 2005). Other research showed that re-report was most likely to occur if the caregiver affected by substance abuse received substance abuse treatment during the service period (Barth et al. 2007; Brook and McDonald 2009). Finally, even with treatment, reunification rates for children in care and their substance-abusing parents are quite low. For example, Ryan et al. (2006) found that intensive substance abuse treatment supports increased the likelihood of reunification when compared to treatment as usual. However, even these increased reunification rates were still relatively low: 12 % for those participating in intensive supportive services versus 7 % for those participating in treatment as usual.

The Adoption and Safe Families Act (ASFA) of 1997 requires increased oversight of child welfare cases by caseworkers and the court. Previous policy mandates (The Adoption Assistance and Child Welfare Act of 1980) focused on family reunification and adoption subsidies which often allowed for a protracted length of stay in care and extensive family disruption. However, ASFA implements different timelines, which were designed to decrease foster care drift and prioritize children's safety. These new timelines often conflict with the natural substance abuse recovery process, which can often involve relapse. The quantity and quality of numerous innovative practices are improving client outcomes; however, few have been adopted as standard practice. The child welfare system's answer to substance abuse cannot continue to depend on new programs to which few families have access. Comprehensive improvements are essential if families are to be provided a legitimate opportunity for recovery within ASFA timeframes (National Conference of State Legislatures 2000). Such improvements may include increased residential substance abuse treatment facilities for single mothers, where they are permitted to bring their children. One of the most common reasons for relapse, beyond physical access to a risky lifestyle, is anxiety over the termination of parental rights for dependent children (Rockhill et al. 2007).

Health and Mental Health Limitations of Parent and/or Child

The physical and mental health of both caregivers and children can play a role in child maltreatment. Children with physical disabilities or health concerns are at increased risk for maltreatment (Turner et al. 2011). The NIS-4 found that children who had restricted capacities exhibited significantly lower rates of physical abuse but substantially higher rates of psychological neglect and more serious injuries from maltreatment (Sedlak et al. 2010a, b). Other research shows that children with disabilities are more likely to be placed in out-of-home care than children without disabilities and that more than a quarter of children with physical health problems reentered care within three years of initial reunification (Lightfoot et al. 2011; Courtney 1995). Children with behavioral and mental health conditions are also at increased risk for maltreatment (Jaudes and Mackey-Bilaver 2008; Turner, et al. 2011). In fact, one study found that if a child had a history of abuse before age three and was also diagnosed with a behavioral health condition, the child was ten times more likely to be maltreated again (Jaudes and Mackey-Bilaver 2008). This increased risk among children with physical and/or developmental delays has been attributed to higher levels of stress (either psychological or economical) for parents (Jaudes and Mackey-Bilaver 2008; Turner et al. 2011). The vulnerable status of children with disabilities mandates more scrutiny by child welfare systems when these children come into care.

Caregivers' mental health has also been shown to be associated with child maltreatment. Some research has found relationships between poverty and poor mental health status in African-American women (Chadiha and Brown 2002). Many of these women face multiple issues; they are poor, are frequently single parents, and may experience discrimination and other stressors (Bobo 2001; McRoy 2011). These combinations of challenges may contribute to higher levels of depression, anxiety, and/or stress, which may result in poorer parenting practices, particularly if the mental health issues are not recognized and addressed. Libby et al. (2007) investigated mental health and substance abuse services to parents of children involved with child welfare, with a focus on American Indian parents. They found that American Indian parents were less frequently formally assessed for mental health issues than parents of other racial/ethnic groups. Further, although almost all American Indian parents in the sample were dealing with serious mental or emotional difficulties; less than 20 % of them were referred for mental health services paid for by child welfare and even fewer actually received services as a result of the referral. Conversely, although there were lower than average substance abuse problems for American Indian parents (compared to other racial/ethnic groups), parents were referred to substance abuse treatment far more often than mental health services.

Minority families don't necessarily experience more mental and/or physical health risks; however, they are less likely to have access to appropriate prevention and intervention services, particularly if they are poor (Dettlaff and Cardoso 2010; Wang et al. 2005). Distrust and expectations of mistreatment may discourage access to services. Additional barriers may include cultural values regarding doctors and help-seeking behaviors, cultural differences in understanding children's development and behaviors, and lack of culturally appropriate services (Dettlaff and Cardoso 2010; Wang et al. 2005). Research has shown that AAPIs, in particular, are less likely to seek help for mental health problems than are members of other racial and ethnic groups, instead preferring informal solutions (Chu and Sue 2011). Practitioners would do well to explore some of these potential barriers with families and to work with families to connect them with culturally appropriate services.

Domestic Violence

It is difficult to determine the prevalence of domestic violence; estimates range from 12 to 30 % of the American population, with domestic violence affecting women of all ages, racial and ethnic groups, and socioeconomic strata (Tjaden and Thoennes 2000). However, some research has shown that some minority groups have higher levels of domestic violence. Tjaden and Thoennes (2000) found that American Indian/Alaskan-Native women experienced the highest levels of lifetime victimization, followed by women of mixed race. White and African-American women had similar rates, with rates of African-American women being slightly higher. They found no differences between Hispanic and non-Hispanic women (Tjaden and Thoennes 2000). Rennison and Welchans (2000) also found similar rates for Hispanic and non-Hispanic women. However, they found that African-American women experience intimate partner violence at a rate 35 % higher than White women and approximately 2.5 times the rate of women of other races. They also found that American Indian women were victimized at rates higher than all other groups (Rennison and Welchans 2000). Studies on domestic violence frequently do not include AAPI women, so prevalence data on this minority group is even scarcer. However, a few community samples suggest that prevalence rates could range from 24 to 60 % among AAPI immigrant women (Lee and Hadeed 2009). Additionally, AAPI immigrant women are regularly overrepresented in domestic violence homicides (Asian and Pacific Islander Institute on Domestic Violence 2005; Lee and Hadeed 2009). Racial differences often disappear when social class is accounted for; however, some studies continue to show higher rates for African-American women, even after taking into account social class (and it should be noted that very few studies include American Indian women in their samples). There are also racial and cultural differences in what behaviors are and are not seen as abusive, and cultural values play an important role in whether or not abused women seek assistance (Grossman and Lundy 2007). For example, AAPI immigrant groups may place value on a wife's subservience to her husband and may see domestic violence as normative behavior; further, cultural values prohibiting the disclosure of family problems to outsiders may discourage AAPI women from seeking help (Lee and Hadeed 2009).

Prevalence estimates for domestic violence among families involved with the child welfare system are much higher, ranging from 30 to 70 % (Appel and Holden 1998;

Kelleher et al. 2008). One study suggests that national estimates of families in the child welfare system have a lifetime prevalence of domestic violence of approximately 44 %, with 28 % experiencing at least one episode of violence within the preceding year (Hazen et al. 2004). While in some cases it may be the perpetrator of domestic violence who maltreats children in the family, in other cases, it may be the victim of the violence who maltreats (Casanueva et al. 2009). For example, using a national child welfare sample, Kelleher et al. (2008) found that female victims of domestic violence reported using higher rates of aggressive and neglectful disciplinary behaviors with their children than non-victims. Using the same dataset (National Survey of Child and Adolescent Well-being), Casanueva et al. (2009) found that children of mothers victimized by an intimate partner during the previous year were twice as likely to be re-reported to child protective services as were children of mothers who had not been victims of intimate partner violence. Additionally, re-reports happened almost twice as quickly for children of intimate partner violence victims compared to children of mothers who were not victims of intimate partner violence. Research has also shown that rates of reunification are lower for families experiencing domestic violence than those not living with domestic violence (Hess et al. 1992).

Incarceration

There is significant overlap between risk factors for child maltreatment and for parental arrest and/or incarceration; these include, but are not limited to, poverty, substance abuse, mental illness, and family violence (Phillips and Dettlaff 2009; Phillips et al. 2010). Households where a caregiver has been arrested have higher rates of poverty, substance abuse, and domestic violence than households where caregivers have never been arrested (Phillips and Dettlaff 2009). Research shows that approximately one out of every eight children who are subjects of maltreatment allegations has a primary caregiver (usually a mother) who was recently arrested (Phillips et al. 2004). While incarcerated mothers are proportionately more likely to have children in foster care than incarcerated fathers, there are almost ten times more incarcerated fathers than mothers on any given day (Phillips et al. 2010). There is also some overlap between mothers and fathers in that almost two-thirds of children whose mothers have been arrested also have fathers who have been arrested (Farrington et al. 2001; Phillips and Dettlaff 2009). Additionally, children whose parents have had involvement with the criminal justice system are more likely than other children to spend time in out-of-home care (Phillips et al. 2004, 2007, 2010).

There is vast disparity in arrest and incarceration rates across racial groups, with African-Americans faring the worst. African-American men are incarcerated at a rate more than six times that of White men, and African-American women are incarcerated at a rate more than three times that of White women (Sabol et al. 2007). African-Americans comprise only 12 % of the population and only 13 % of drug users; however, they make up more than a third of individuals arrested for drug offenses and over half of individuals convicted for drug offenses (Wallace et al. 2004).

Using data from the National Survey of Child and Adolescent Well-Being (NSCAW), Phillips et al. (2004) found that almost 13 % of children assessed for maltreatment had parents who had recently been arrested. However, African-American children were overrepresented in this sample: only 28 % of African-American children were subjects of maltreatment reports, yet they constituted 43 % of the children with arrested parents. Almost one-fifth of African-American children in the sample had a parent who had recently been arrested, which was twice the rate for White children and four times the rate for Hispanic children.

Understanding Culture

There must be urgency among child welfare trainers, administrators, and caseworkers to understand how race and ethnicity intersect with poverty and other risk factors in families involved in the child welfare system. It is equally critical that they understand the protective role that culture can have within the families with whom they work. Both types of knowledge will help to inform the culturally proficient engagement skills necessary to work successfully with families and prevent disparities. Practitioners with these skills should, at a minimum, be able to engage in supportive, inclusive dialogue with families in the child welfare system and address families' concerns with respect for their culture, traditions, language, identity, and ethnicity.[1]

When caseworkers are trying to assist families who are part of an unfamiliar minority group or a group different from their own, it is advised that they seek information about the group prior to meeting with the family. Parenting techniques and practices of some minority groups may differ from those of the dominant American culture, or they may appear to be qualitatively opposed to traditional American practices; however, workers have a responsibility to be open to unfamiliar cultures in order to deliver fair and unbiased services to their clients. It is very important to remember that different cultural practices should not be feared or interpreted as negative practices. Caseworkers should hold paramount the safety of children and evaluate family behaviors within the context of culture (Fraser 1997). Caseworkers must consider how individual manifestations of bigotry, prejudice, and stereotypes affect judgment and behaviors toward minorities. They must be cognizant of the role systems and institutions have had in furthering discrimination, particularly for minorities. Finally, caseworkers must have an understanding of the historical context of race in the USA and how it manifests currently. Slavery, immigration, and tribal issues are all important considerations when thinking about race and culture in this country.

---

[1] While we acknowledge that culture encompasses a wide array of beliefs, traditions, behaviors, and identities, for the purposes of this chapter, we will discuss culture only as it pertains to race.

The field of social work has typically taken a *cultural competence* stance toward working with racial and ethnic minority groups. As defined by the National Association of Social Workers (NASW 2001), cultural competence is "the integration and transformation of knowledge about individuals and groups of people into specific standards, policies, practices, and attitudes used in appropriate cultural settings to increase the quality of services, thereby producing better outcomes....Competence in cross-cultural functioning means learning new patterns of behavior and effectively applying them in appropriate settings" (pp. 11–12). Stated differently, cultural competence "denotes the ability to transform knowledge and cultural awareness into...interventions that support and sustain healthy client-system functioning within the appropriate cultural context" (McPhatter 1997, p. 27). Thus, cultural competence involves awareness, knowledge, and skills. In a cultural competence framework, it is the responsibility of the social worker to learn about different cultural groups and be able to apply what she/he has learned when working with individuals from those cultural groups.

As such, researchers and policy makers are advocating for a *cultural humility* approach to working with individuals or families from other cultural groups. Key components of this approach include training workers to be self-aware, particularly about their own cultural lens and the degree to which their culture shapes their world view, complete with recognition of their biases (Ortega and Faller 2011). Further concepts of cultural humility include openness to the experiences of others and the ability to learn from families served. Workers employing cultural humility do not need "to possess expert knowledge about an array of cultural differences. This perspective has the benefit of placing the worker in a learning mode as opposed to maintaining power, control and authority in the working relationships, especially over cultural experiences about which the client is far more knowledgeable" (Ortega and Faller 2011, p. 33). Cultural humility also espouses both a multicultural perspective (i.e., a particular culture is not uniform) and an intersectionality perspective (i.e., individuals simultaneously have multiple cultural identities) (Ortega and Faller 2011).

The effectiveness of child welfare services is dependent on the skill and acumen of the caseworkers who work with the families. Ideally, caseworkers will exhibit a combination of cultural competence and cultural humility in their work with families. While it can be helpful to have a sense of cultural norms for different populations, it is also critical that caseworkers are open to learning from families about their values and traditions, even if (or especially if) they are different from what the caseworker thinks she/he knows. Learning the nuances of the myriad cultures, races, and ethnicities on the American landscape is a lifelong process, and each family will express their own culture in their own way. Collaborative, trusting relationships can only be built when families are treated with dignity and respect, regardless of the caseworker's cultural lens or any cultural differences between the caseworker and family members.

Case Study: Marisol and the Matthews Family

Marisol recently graduated from college and is a new caseworker in the intake unit of the Department of Children, Youth, and Families. Marisol is 22 years old and of mixed Latino/ Caucasian ethnicity. She is asked to meet with the Matthews family, who live in a neighborhood to which Marisol has not yet been; the neighborhood is known to be impoverished and consists primarily of African-American families and older adults. The Matthews family is African-American and has lived in the community for many years. An allegation of neglect was made by the teacher of the two youngest children in the family, Baileigh and Britneigh, both 10 years old. The teacher stated that although the girls were impeccably dressed on the first day of school, they have since only attended school sporadically and have worn ill-fitting clothes since then, which are increasingly inappropriate for the weather. The teacher also noticed that the girls have been asking classmates for extra food during breakfast and lunch.

Marisol is nervous when she arrives at the Matthews home but is determined to appear confident and authoritative. Mrs. Matthews welcomes Marisol into the front room of her home. Marisol observes that the room is beautifully furnished and tidy. Mrs. Matthews has recently turned 62 and is older than Marisol expected and dressed in simple, worn clothing. Marisol learns that Baileigh and Britneigh are Mrs. Matthews' nieces; Mrs. Matthews' youngest sister was killed several years earlier, and Mrs. Matthews became a kinship caregiver for the girls. They have four older siblings, ranging in age from 14 to 17, who live out of state with other family members. Mrs. Matthews has five grown children, lives on a fixed income, and has health concerns that include diabetes and hypertension.

When asked about Baileigh and Britneigh's school attendance, Mrs. Matthews speaks proudly about how the girls looked on the first day of school. However, she is vague when asked about subsequent school attendance and talks about how she sometimes needs the girls' help around the house, especially when she is not feeling well. When Marisol asks to see the rest of the house, Mrs. Matthews seems to feel insulted and insists on Marisol staying in the front room, since that is where "guests are entertained." Marisol is embarrassed that she made Mrs. Matthews feel badly, and although she knows she needs to see the rest of the house, she doesn't know how to proceed.

In order for the visit to conclude successfully, Marisol must think about her own cultural lens as she continues to talk to Mrs. Matthews. What cultural assumptions does Marisol bring with her to this interaction? How might Mrs. Matthews' assumptions differ? What questions can Marisol ask Mrs. Matthews about her cultural beliefs, values, and traditions to learn about these differences? Furthermore, how might Marisol's age and nervousness affect her mannerisms and behavior, and how might these impact her interaction with Mrs. Matthews? By asking questions and approaching the situation from a position of cultural humility, Marisol can learn more about Mrs. Matthews' cultural background, the background in which Baileigh and Britneigh have been raised. If Marisol can acknowledge her own cultural lens and the ways in which Mrs. Matthews' cultural beliefs differ from hers, she will be better able to help find solutions for Baileigh and Britneigh.

Conclusion

In summary, it is incumbent upon child welfare workers to have an understanding of racial disproportionality and disparity in child welfare—their roots and their ramifications. Without understanding the historical context of racial disproportionality and disparity in child welfare, practitioners cannot move toward equal treatment and policy implementation. Further, in order to work effectively with families, child welfare workers must thoughtfully consider how race and culture intersect with social and economic risk factors that contribute to poor child welfare outcomes. Combined with a balance of cultural awareness and humility, this knowledge will enable practitioners to successfully engage with the families with whom they work.

Questions for Discussion

1. What is the difference between disparity and disproportionality? How do other factors (e.g., poverty, substance abuse) affect disparity and disproportionality?
2. What are the strengths and limitations of cultural competence versus cultural humility?
3. What is your own cultural lens? How might that affect how you view and interact with different families?
4. What assumptions do you have about particular racial cultural groups? What steps will you take to combat those assumptions as you encounter families from those cultural groups?

References

Addy, S., & Wight, V. R. (2012). *Basic facts about low-income children, 2010: Children under age 18*. New York: National Center for Children in Poverty.

Appel, A. E., & Holden, G. W. (1998). The co-occurrence of spouse and physical child abuse: A review and appraisal. *Journal of Family Psychology, 12*, 578–599.

AFCARS. (2012). *Preliminary FY 2011 estimates as of July 2012*. Washington, DC: U.S. Department of Health and Human Services, Administration for Children and Families.

Asian and Pacific Islander Institute on Domestic Violence. (2005). *Domestic violence in Asian communities: Factsheet – July 2005*. San Francisco: Author.

Barth, R., Gibbons, C., & Guo, S. (2007). Substance abuse treatment and the recurrence of maltreatment among caregivers with children living at home: A propensity score analysis. *Journal of Substance Abuse Treatment, 30*, 93–104.

Barth, R., Miller, J., Green, R., & Baumgartner, J. (2001). *Toward understanding racial disproportionality in child welfare services receipt*. Paper presented at The Race Matters Forum

Bartholet, E., Wulczyn, F., Barth, R. P., & Lederman, C. (2011). *Race and child welfare*. Chicago: University of Chicago.

Bernstein, N. (2001). *The lost children of Wilder*. New York: Random House.

Bobo, L. D. (2001). Racial attitudes and relations at the close of the twentieth century. In N. J. Smelser, W. J. Wilson, & F. Mitchell (Eds.), *America becoming: Racial trends and their consequences* (pp. 264–301). Washington, DC: National Academy Press.

Brook, J., & McDonald, T. (2007). Evaluating the effects of comprehensive substance abuse intervention on successful reunification. *Research on Social Work Practice, 17*, 664–673.

Brook, J., & McDonald, T. (2009). The impact of parental substance abuse on the stability of family reunifications from foster care. *Children and Youth Services Review, 31*, 193–198.

Burlew, A. K., Feaster, D., Brecht, M., & Hubbard, R. (2009). Measurement and data analysis in research addressing health disparities in substance abuse. *Journal of Substance Abuse Treatment, 36*, 25–43.

Capps, R., Fix, M., Passel, J. S., Ost, J., Perez-Lopez, D. (2003). *Immigrant families and workers: Facts and perspectives*. Brief No. 4. Washington, DC: Urban Institute.

Carp, E. W. (2002). *Adoption in America: Historical perspectives*. Ann Arbor: University of Michigan Press.

Carter, V. B. (2010). Factors predicting placement of urban American Indian/Alaskan Natives into out-of-home care. *Children and Youth Services Review, 32*, 657–663.

Casanueva, C., Martin, S. L., & Runyan, D. K. (2009). Repeated reports for child maltreatment among intimate partner violence victims: Findings from the National Survey of Child and Adolescent Well-Being. *Child Abuse and Neglect, 33*, 84–93.

Casey Family Programs. (2006). *Disproportionality in the child welfare system: The disproportionate representation of children of color in foster care*. Seattle, WA: Author.

Chadiha, L. A., & Brown, G. G. (2002). Contributing factors to African American women caregivers' mental well-being. *African American Perspectives, 8*, 72–83.

Chaffin, M., Kelleher, K., & Hollenberg, J. (1996). Onset of physical abuse and neglect: Psychiatric, substance abuse and social risk factors from prospective community data. *Child Abuse and Neglect, 20*, 191–203.

Chapin Hall Center for Children. (2008). *Understanding racial and ethnic disparity in child welfare and juvenile justice*. Chicago: Author.

Chibnall, S., Dutch, N., Jones-Harden, B., Brown, A., & Gourdine, R. (2010). *Children of color in the child welfare system: Perspectives from the child welfare community*. Washington, DC: U.S. Department of Health and Human Services, Children's Bureau.

Children's Defense Fund. (2007). *America's cradle to prison pipeline*. Washington, DC: Author.

Choi, S., Huang, H., & Ryan, J. P. (2012). Substance abuse treatment completion in child welfare: Does substance abuse treatment completion matter in the decision to reunify families? *Children and Youth Services Review, 34*, 1639–1645.

Chu, J. P., & Sue, S. (2011). Asian American mental health: What we know and what we don't know. *Online Readings in Psychology in Culture, Unit 3*. Retrieved from http://scholarworks.gvsu.edu/orpc/vol3/iss1/4.

Church, W. T. (2006). From start to finish: The duration of Hispanic children in out of home placements. *Children and Youth Services Review, 28*, 1007–1023.

Corcoran, M. (2001). Mobility, persistence, and the consequences of poverty for children: Child and adult outcomes. In S. H. Danziger & R. H. Haveman (Eds.), *Understanding poverty* (pp. 127–161). New York: Russell Sage.

Courtney, M. E. (1995). Reentry to foster care of children returned to their families. *Social Service Review, 69*, 226–241.

Courtney, M., Barth, R. P., Berrick, J. D., Brooks, D., Needell, B., & Park, L. (1996). Race and child welfare services: Past research and future directions. *Child Welfare, 75*, 99–137.

Crossen-Tower, C. (2010). *Understanding child abuse and neglect* (8th ed.). Boston, MA: Allyn & Bacon.

Department of Health and Human Services. (2008). *Child Maltreatment 2006*. Washington, DC: Author.

Deserly, K., & Gardner, J. (2011). Disproportionality of American Indian and Alaska Native children. In D. K. Green, K. Belanger, R. G. McRoy, & L. Bullard (Eds.), *Challenging racial disproportionality in child welfare* (pp. 341–345). Washington, DC: Child Welfare League of America.

Dettlaff, A. J. (2011). *Disproportionality, disparities, and Latino children in the U.S. child welfare system*. Paper presented at ChildLaw Center's 13th Annual Children's Summer Institute, Loyola University, Chicago, IL.

Dettlaff, A. J., & Cardoso, J. B. (2010). Mental health need and service use among Latino children of immigrants in the child welfare system. *Children and Youth Services Review, 32*, 1373–1379.

Dettlaff, A. J., & Earner, I. (2010). *Children of immigrants in the child welfare system: Findings from the National Survey of Child and Adolescent Well-Being.* Englewood, CO: American Humane Association.

Dettlaff, A. J., Earner, I., & Phillips, S. D. (2009). Latino children of immigrants in the child welfare system: Prevalence, characteristics, and risk. *Children and Youth Services Review, 31*, 775–783.

Dettlaff, A. J., Rivaux, S. L., Baumann, D. J., Fluke, J. D., Rycraft, J. R., & James, J. (2011). Disentangling substantiation: The influence of race, income, and risk on the substantiation decision in child welfare. *Children and Youth Services Review, 33*, 1630–1637.

Donald, K. L., Bradley, L. K., Day, P., Critchley, R., & Nuccio, K. E. (2003). Comparison between American Indian and non-Indian out-of-home placements. *Families in Society, 84*, 267–274.

Drake, B., & Jonson-Reid, M. (2011). NIS interpretations: Race and the National Incidence Studies of Child Abuse and Neglect. *Children and Youth Services Review, 33*, 16–20.

Drake, B., Lee, S. M., & Jonson-Reid, M. (2009). Race and child maltreatment reporting: Are Blacks overrepresented? *Children and Youth Services Review, 31*, 309–316.

Drake, B., & Pandey, S. (1996). Understanding the relationship between neighborhood poverty and child maltreatment. *Child Abuse and Neglect, 20*, 1003–1018.

Dworsky, A., White, C., O'Brien, K., Pecora, P., Courtney, M., Kessler, R., Sampson, N., & Hwang, I. (2010) Racial and ethnic differences in the outcomes of former foster youth. *Children and Youth Services Review, 32*, 902–912.

Edwards, J. (1999). *Black cultural issues in adoption. In The Adoption Factbook III.* Waite Park, MN: Park Press Quality Printing.

Farrington, D. P., Jolliffe, D., Loeber, R., Stouthamer-Loeber, M., & Kalb, L. M. (2001). The concentration of offenders in families, and family criminality in the prediction of boys' delinquency. *Journal of Adolescence, 24*, 579–596.

Fletcher, M. L. M. (2009). *The origins of the Indian Child Welfare Act: A survey of the legislative history.* Lansing, MI: Michigan State University College of Law, Indigenous Law and Policy Center.

Fox, K. E. (2004). Are they really neglected? A look at worker perceptions of neglect through the eyes of a national data system. *First Nations Child and Family Review: A Journal on Innovation and Best Practices in Aboriginal Child Welfare Administration, Research, Policy and Practice, 1*, 73–82.

Fraser, M. W. (Ed.). (1997). *Risk and resilience in childhood: an ecological perspective.* Washington, DC: NASW Press.

Freisthler, B., Bruce, E., & Needell, B. (2007). Understanding the geospatial relationship of neighborhood characteristics and rates of maltreatment for Black, Hispanic, and White children. *Social Work, 52*, 7–16.

Fuller, T. (2005). Child safety at reunification: A case–control study of maltreatment recurrence following return home from substitute care. *Children and Youth Services Review, 27*, 1293–1306.

Galante, L.M.C. (1999). Subtle racism in child welfare decision-making. *Digital Dissertations.* (UMI No. 9958390).

Garcia, A., Aisenberg, E., & Harachi, T. (2012). Pathways to service inequalities among Latinos in the child welfare system. *Children and Youth Services Review, 34*, 1060–1071.

Gordon, L. (1999). *The great Arizona orphan abduction.* Cambridge, MA: Harvard University Press.

Graham, L. M. (2008). Reparations, self-determination, and the seventh generation. *Harvard Human Rights Journal, 21*, 47–103.

Green, B. L., Rockhill, A., & Furrer, C. (2007). Does substance abuse treatment make a difference for child welfare outcomes? A statewide longitudinal analysis. *Children and Youth Services Review, 29*, 460–473.

Gregoire, K. A., & Schultz, D. J. (2001). Substance-abusing child welfare parents: Treatment and child placement outcomes. *Child Welfare, 80*, 433–452.

Grella, C. E., Needell, B., Shi, Y., & Hser, Y. I. (2009). Do drug treatment services predict reunification outcomes of mothers and their children in child welfare? *Journal of Substance Abuse Treatment, 36*, 278–293.

Grossman, S. F., & Lundy, M. (2007). Domestic violence across race and ethnicity: Implications for social work practice and policy. *Violence Against Women, 13*, 1029–1052.

Halverson, K., Puig, M., & Beyers, S. (2002). Culture loss: American Indian family disruption, urbanization and the Indian Child Welfare Act. *Child Welfare, 81*, 319–336.

Hazen, A. L., Connelly, C. D., Kelleher, K., Landsverk, J., & Barth, R. (2004). Intimate partner violence among female caregivers of children reported for child maltreatment. *Child Abuse and Neglect, 28*, 301–319.

Heron, R., Twomey, H., Jacobs, D., & Kaslow, N. (1997). Culturally competent interventions for abused and suicidal African American women. *Psychotherapy, 34*, 410–424.

Hess, P. M., Folaron, G., & Jefferson, A. B. (1992). Effectiveness of family reunification services: An innovative evaluative model. *Social Work, 31*, 304–311.

Hill, R. B. (2004). *Overrepresentation of children of color in foster care in 2000.* Rockville, MD: Race Matters Consortium.

Hill, R. B. (2006). *Synthesis of research on disproportionality in child welfare: An update.* Washington, DC: Casey-CSSP Alliance for Racial Equality in the Child Welfare System.

Hill, R. B. (2007). *An analysis of racial/ethnic disproportionality and disparity at the national, state, and county levels.* Seattle, WA: Casey-CSSP Alliance for Racial Equity in the Child Welfare System.

Hill, R. B. (2011). Gaps in research and public policy. In D. K. Green, K. Belanger, R. G. McRoy, & L. Bullard (Eds.), *Challenging racial disproportionality in child welfare* (pp. 101–108). Washington: Child Welfare League of America.

Hines, A. M., Lee, P. A., Osterling, K. L., & Drabble, L. (2007). Factors predicting family reunification for African American, Latino, Asian and White families in the child welfare system. *Journal of Child and Family Studies, 16*, 275–289.

Huebner, R. (2007). *Descriptors, predictors and outcomes of placement stability.* Washington, DC: Presentation at the Casey-CWLA Outcomes Benchmarking Roundtable, March 1, 2007.

Iguchi, M., London, J., Forge, N., Hickman, L., Fain, T., & Reihman, K. (2002). Elements of well-being affected by criminalizing the drug user. *Public Health Reports, 117*, 146–150.

Jaudes, P., & Mackey-Bilaver, L. (2008). Do chronic conditions increase young children's risk of being maltreated? *Child Abuse and Neglect, 32*, 671–681.

Jones, B., Gilette, J., Painte, D., & Paulson, S. (2000). *Indian child welfare act: A pilot study of compliance in North Dakota.* Seattle, WA: Casey Family Programs.

Jonson-Reid, M., Drake, B., & Kohl, P. L. (2009). Is the overrepresentation of the poor in child welfare caseloads due to bias or need? *Children and Youth Services Review, 31*, 422–427.

Kelleher, K. J., Hazen, A. L., Coben, J. H., Wang, Y., McGeehan, J., Kohl, P. L., & Gardner, W. P. (2008). Self-reported disciplinary practices among women in the child welfare system: Association with domestic violence victimization. *Child Abuse and Neglect, 32*, 811–818.

Kids Count Data Center. (2012). *Data across states.* Retrieved from http://datacenter.kidscount.org/data/acrossstates/Default.aspx.

Landale, N. S., Thomas, K. J. A., & Van Hook, J. (2011). The living arrangements of children of immigrants. *Future of Children, 21*, 43–70.

Larsen, S., Kim-Goh, M., & Nguyen, T. D. (2008). Asian American immigrant families and child abuse: Cultural considerations. *Journal of Systemic Therapies, 27*, 16–29.

Lee, Y., & Hadeed, L. (2009). Intimate partner violence among Asian immigrant communities: Health/mental health consequences, help-seeking behaviors, and service utilization. *Trauma Violence Abuse, 10*, 143–170.

Libby, A. M., Orton, H. D., Barth, R. P., Webb, M., Burns, B. J., Wood, P. A., & Spicer, P. (2007). Mental health and substance abuse services to parents of children involved with child welfare: A study of racial and ethnic differences for American Indian parents. *Administration and Policy in Mental Health and Mental Health Services Research, 34*, 150–159.

Lightfoot, E., Hill, K., & LaLiberte, T. (2011). Prevalence of children with disabilities in the child welfare system and out of home placement: An examination of administrative records. *Children and Youth Services Review, 33*, 2069–2075.

Longshore, D., Grills, C., & Annon, K. (1999). Effects of a culturally congruent intervention on cognitive factors related to drug-use recovery. *Substance Use and Misuse, 14*, 1223–1241.

Matheson, L. (1996). The politics of the Indian child welfare act. *Social Work, 41*, 232–235.

McPhatter, A. R. (1997). Cultural competence in child welfare: What is it? How do we achieve it? What happens without it? *Child Welfare, 76*, 255–278.

McRoy, R. (2011). Contextualizing disproportionality. In D. K. Green, K. Belanger, R. G. McRoy, & L. Bullard (Eds.), *Challenging racial disproportionality in child welfare* (pp. 67–71). Washington, DC: Child Welfare League of America.

Moore, K. A., Redd, Z., Burkhauser, M., Mbwana, K., & Collins, A. (2009). *Children in poverty: Trends, consequences, and policy options*. Washington, DC: Child Trends.

National Association of Social Workers. (2001). *NASW standards for cultural competence in social work practice*. Washington, DC: Author.

National Conference of State Legislatures. (2000). *Linking child welfare and substance abuse treatment: A guide for legislators*. Washington, DC: Author.

O'Connor, S. (2001). *Orphan trains: The story of Charles Loring Brace and the children he saved and failed*. Boston: Houghton Mifflin Company.

Ortega, R. M., & Faller, K. C. (2011). Training child welfare workers from an intersectional cultural humility perspectives: A paradigm shift. *Child Welfare, 90*, 27–49.

Pelczarski, Y., & Kemp, S. P. (2006). Patterns of child maltreatment referrals among Asian and Pacific Islander families. *Child Welfare, 85*, 6–31.

Perry, T. E., & Davis-Maye, D. (2007). Bein' womanish: Womanist efforts in child saving during the progressive era: The founding of Mt. Meigs Reformatory. *Affilia, 22*, 209–219.

Phillips, S. D., Burns, B. J., Wagner, H. R., & Barth, R. P. (2004). Parental arrest and children in child welfare services agencies. *American Journal of Orthopsychiatry, 2*, 174–186.

Phillips, S. D., & Dettlaff, A. J. (2009). More than parents in prison: The broader overlap between the criminal justice and child welfare systems. *Journal of Public Child Welfare, 3*, 3–22.

Phillips, S. D., Dettlaff, A. J., & Baldwin, M. J. (2010). An exploratory study of the range of implications of families' criminal justice system involvement in child welfare cases. *Children and Youth Services Review, 32*, 544–550.

Phillips, S. D., Erkanli, A., Costello, E. J., & Angold, A. (2007). Differences among children whose mothers have a history of arrest. *Women & Criminal Justice, 17*, 45–63.

Rennison, C. M., & Welchans, S. (2000). *Intimate partner violence. Bureau of Justice Statistics Special Report*. Washington, DC: U.S. Department of Justice.

Roberts, D. (2002). *Shattered bonds: The color of child welfare*. New York: Basic Books.

Rockhill, A., Green, B. L., & Furrer, C. (2007). Is the Adoption and Safe Families Act influencing child welfare outcomes for families with substance abuse issues? *Child Maltreatment, 12*(1), 7–19.

Ryan, J. P., Marsh, J. C., Testa, M. F., & Louderman, R. (2006). Integrating substance abuse treatment and child welfare services: Findings from the Illinois alcohol and other drug abuse waiver demonstration. *Social Work Research, 30*, 95–107.

Sabol, W. J., Couture, H., & Harrison, P. M. (2007). *Prisoners in 2006. Bureau of Justice Statistics Bulletin*. Washington, DC: U.S. Department of Justice, Office of Justice Programs.

Schaefer, R. T. (2011). *Race and ethnicity in the United States* (6th ed.). Upper Saddle River, NJ: Prentice/Hall.

Sedlak, A. J., McPherson, K., & Das, B. (2010a). *Supplementary analyses of race differences in child maltreatment rates in the NIS-4*. Washington, DC: U.S. Department of Health and Human Services.

Sedlak, A. J., Mettenburg, J., Basena, M., Petta, I., McPherson, K., Greene, A., et al. (2010b). *Fourth national incidence study of child abuse and neglect (NIS-4): Report to congress*. Washington, DC: U. S. Department of Health and Human Services.

Shaw, T. V., Putnam-Hornstein, E., Magruder, J., & Needell, B. (2008). Measuring racial disparity in child welfare. *Child Welfare, 87*, 23–36.

Stalker, C., Maiter, S., & Alaggia, R. (2009). The experiences of minority immigrant families receiving child welfare services: Seeking to understand how to reduce risk and increase protective factors. *Social Work Faculty Publications*. Paper 2. Retrieved from http://scholars.wlu.ca/scwk_faculty/2.

Substance Abuse and Mental Health Services Administration. (2002). *National Study on Drug Use and Health*. Washington, DC: Department of Health and Human Services, Office of Applied Studies.

Takei, I., & Sakamoto, A. (2011). Poverty among Asian Americans in the 21st century. *Sociological Perspectives, 54*, 251–276.

Texas Health and Human Services Commission, Texas Department of Family and Protective Services. (2006). *Disproportionality in child protective services: Statewide reform effort begins with examination of the problem*. Austin, TX: Author.

Tjaden, P., & Thoennes, N. (2000). *Extent, nature and consequences of intimate partner violence: Findings from the National Violence Against Women Survey*. Washington, DC: U.S. Department of Justice.

Turner, H. A., Vanderminden, J., Finkelhor, D., Hamby, S., & Shattuck, A. (2011). Disability and victimization in a national sample of children and youth. *Child Maltreatment, 16*, 275–286.

U.S. Census Bureau. (2010). *National population profile*. Washington, DC: Author.

U.S. Department of Health and Human Services. (2010). *Child welfare outcomes 2006–2009: Report to Congress*. Washington, DC: Author.

Wallace, J. M., Myers, V. L., & Osai, E. R. (2004). *Faith matters: Race/ethnicity, religion, and substance abuse*. Baltimore, MD: Annie E. Casey Foundation.

Wang, P. S., Lane, M., Olfson, M., Pincus, H. A., Wells, K. B., & Kessler, R. C. (2005). Twelve-month use of mental health services in the United States: Results from the National Comorbidity Survey replication. *Archives of General Psychiatry, 62*, 629–640.

Washington State Racial Disproportionality Advisory Committee (WSRDAC). (2010). *Racial disproportionality in Washington State: Report to the legislature*. Olympia, WA: Author.

Wells, S. J. (2011). Disproportionality and disparity in child welfare: An overview of definitions and methods of measurement. In D. K. Green, K. Belanger, R. G. McRoy, & L. Bullard (Eds.), *Challenging racial disproportionality in child welfare* (pp. 3–12). Washington: Child Welfare League of America.

Wulczyn, F., & Lery, B. (2007). *Racial disparity in foster care admissions*. Chicago: Chapin Hall Center for Children.

Young, N., Gardner, S., & Dennis, K. (1998). *Responding to alcohol and other drug problems in child welfare: Weaving together policy and practice*. Washington, DC: CWLA Press.

Zinn, A., DeCoursey, J., Goerge, R., & Courtney, M. (2006). *A study of placement stability in Illinois*. Chicago: Chapin Hall Center for Children.

Chapter 8
Skill-Based Training and Transfer of Learning

Anita P. Barbee and Marcia L. Martin

Abstract There have been great strides in attending to skill-based training and transfer of learning over the past 15 years in the field of child welfare. We know that classroom training builds a foundation that must be reinforced in the field in order to be practiced in day-to-day work with clients. When skills are reinforced through additional practice exercises, coaching, mentoring, and specific feedback on key practice behaviors, both client outcomes and organizational outcomes can be affected and improved. We know that training must go hand in hand with supervision to be effective and that these two areas of the organization must be in concert. Further research is needed to better understand how to engage the practice sector of child welfare agencies in embracing this important role of supervisors and senior frontline workers. In addition, more research is needed on what aspects of classroom training and its reinforcement lead to the changes in behavior that are necessary to impact child and family outcomes. Extending this work to refine our understanding of the transfer process will help to make certain that all families entering the child welfare system throughout the country will find a skilled workforce that is equipped to meet their needs and help them ensure that their children are safe, in permanent homes, and successful in life.

In order to deliver appropriate services to clients, however, simply possessing knowledge and skills is insufficient; a child welfare worker must also be able to translate a sense of knowing and doing into distinct situations. It is the *application* of knowledge and skills that becomes so critical. Furthermore, bringing skills from the classroom and from training into practice does not signify that the worker's learning has reached a place of ultimate meaning. Instead, it represents an unending

A.P. Barbee (✉)
Kent School of Social Work, University of Louisville, Louisville, KY, USA
e-mail: anita.barbee@louisville.edu

M.L. Martin
Graduate School of Social Work and Social Research, Bryn Mawr College,
Bryn Mawr, PA, USA

H. Cahalane (ed.), *Contemporary Issues in Child Welfare Practice*, 183
Contemporary Social Work Practice, DOI 10.1007/978-1-4614-8627-5_8,
© Springer Science+Business Media New York 2013

series of efforts to gain and regain understanding, predicated on multiple shifts in context. Child welfare workers must actively engage as translators in a transfer of knowledge and skills; they must critically reflect on how knowing and doing interrelate, while ultimately recognizing that meaning cannot be transferred whole from one situation to another, but must be shaped by the uniqueness of context. The translation of child welfare knowledge and skills is both responsive and generative and involves reaffirmation and adaptation that simultaneously honors both what is learned in a classroom setting and the ways in which that learning is applied in practice. A transfer of learning is all about building bridges that transport us between knowing and doing, making us translators in the most conscious and deliberate of ways as we engage each new client and each new situation.

Keywords Transfer of learning • Skill-based training • Level three evaluation

Introduction

A 2-month-old child with hydrocephalus was hospitalized because his mother did not feed him enough and he was failing to thrive. The CPS investigative worker substantiated child neglect and removed the child from his home. The case has had three workers across 2 years since the child was placed in a therapeutic foster home. Two years later, a new worker inherits the case. She finds that the child is still in the state's custody in a foster home, but the foster parents, to whom he is attached, do not have plans to adopt him. For him to achieve permanency, he needs to be either returned to his mother or removed from this foster home and moved to a home where someone will adopt him. Such a move will disrupt his attachment to his current foster parents.

The case is made more complex by the fact that the mother was herself neglected and sexually abused as a child. This, along with her IQ of 65, has left her very immature, vulnerable, and emotionally and severely cognitively impaired. Her husband, with whom she lives, is not the father of the child and suffers from bipolar disorder. The child's father has been violent with the mother in the past and is unsuitable to parent the child. The mother continues to see the child's father, however, and does not understand that he is a danger to both her and their son. While she is nice to her son during their weekly visits, the two of them show no signs of attachment to each other. After she plays with her son awhile, she then seeks the attention of the child welfare worker about her own issues.

There have been two separate interventions with family preservation work in the home and six additional months where the new worker has unsuccessfully tried to teach the mother parenting skills so that her child can safely return home. The caseworker has also determined that the home itself has no room for a child and has an unsanitary backyard full of dog feces. Furthermore, none of the adults in the home (a third adult is a veteran with PTSD) have the capacity or desire to care for a young child. Therefore, the worker comes to the conclusion that the mother is incapable of parenting her child safely. She first tries to persuade the mother to do what is in the best interest of the child and give up her parental rights so that he can be adopted. While the mother would like to do that, she fears that others will think she is a bad mother for doing so. Thus, after consultation with her supervisor, the worker is forced to write a petition to the court for a termination of parental rights and movement of the child to a foster-adopt home. What she finds is a judge who is reluctant to terminate the rights of a mentally challenged adult.

At this point, the worker must use the skills she learned in social work practice and research classes to build a case as to the inability of the mother to learn required parenting

skills that will allow her to safely parent a medically fragile child. She goes back to her case visitation notes and creates a chart of all of the skills she sought to teach the mother, how the mother did or did not follow directions each week, and the complete lack of transfer of parenting skills from one week to the next across the 6-month period. She also describes in detail the conditions of the home and the testimony of the two other adults living in the home as to their unwillingness to help the mother raise the child. Because the mother has no natural social supports to help her raise a child, she has begun to visit her own abusive parents and continues to see her abusive lover. The worker adds these new facts to the court report arguing for termination of parental rights. The worker goes back to court and successfully persuades the judge to terminate parental rights and move the child to a permanent home.

A frontline child welfare worker has 15 (if Child Welfare League of America [CWLA] standards are met) to 30 (as is standard in under-resourced states and counties across the nation) cases like this on his or her plate at any given moment. The question this raises is: What knowledge and skills must a child welfare worker possess to handle a complex case like this? Here are some examples we generated:

Knowledge
- Child development
- Attachment theory
- The effects on immediate and ultimate child well-being of removing a child from attachment figures at the age of 2
- The treatment and effects of hydrocephalus
- The role mental handicaps play in a person's ability to parent
- The role that a history of child neglect and sexual abuse has on adult functioning and parenting
- Domestic violence and its effects on parenting, child safety, and child well-being
- Mental illness such as bipolar disorder and its effects on parenting ability

Skills
- How to utilize critical thinking and research skills
- How to assess parenting ability
- How to sort through many facts about a case and determine the best course of action
- How to compassionately engage parents who have maltreated their children
- How to intervene with parents and provide services to parents with severe handicaps
- How to make decisions that lead to the least damage to children
- How to document work in such a way as to build a persuasive argument for the courts in a court report
- How to testify in court
- How to identify adoptive parents who can care for a medically fragile child
- How to educate foster parents about attachment so they can play a role in transitioning the child to the next set of parents in a way that preserves the attachment to the foster parents, while still building a new attachment to the adoptive parents in an effort to reduce further traumatization for the child
- How to work with service providers, foster parents, adoptive parents, and other types of child welfare workers (adoption workers) to move a case along

- How to manage time effectively so that the work of this case and 15–30 others is carried out according to policy
- How to cope with the heart-wrenching situation of having to take a child away from a parent who, through no fault of her own, is incapable of safely parenting her child and who is otherwise a nice human being and a victim herself

Where do child welfare workers learn these types of knowledge and skills? Ideally, as is common in other professions, child welfare workers would have degrees in Social Work or would have completed courses in Child Development, Family (which routinely includes information on parenting and domestic violence), Psychopathology, Child Welfare Policy and Practice, and Research, as well as practice classes that include engagement, assessment, case planning, case documentation, intervention, referral and case closure skills, diversity (including information on people with various cognitive and physical handicaps as well as those from different races, cultures, and religions), social work and the law, and policy. Unfortunately, most state, county, and tribal child welfare agencies do not require a Social Work degree and often not even a related degree. And when child welfare workers have Social Work or related degrees, there are usually pieces of information missing (i.e., Family Studies and Psychology undergrads do not get courses in the case management process, policy, or legal aspects of social work practice, and social work students may not get a specific course on Families and do not always take Psychopathology).

Thus, child welfare agencies rely on a variety of training approaches, such as preservice certification programs that allow social work students to also learn child welfare policy and practice, as well as 3–16 weeks of in-service training to give college graduates with or without related degrees the knowledge and skills they need to work in child welfare (e.g., Fox et al. 2003). While these training academies do not last for a long time, there is research to suggest that with reinforcement of skills in the field through exercises, coaching, and mentoring, and evaluation efforts that verify transfer of learning from the classroom to practice, training can lead to positive outcomes for families and children (Antle et al. 2008a, b; 2010a, b; Antle et al. 2012; Curry 2001; Curry et al. 1994, 2005; Kessler and Greene 1999; Van zyl et al. 2010).

So what is skill-based training and transfer of learning in child welfare, and how can they be used to adequately prepare frontline workers, supervisors, and administrators in the system? *Skill-based training* is training delivered in the classroom or on the web that is reinforced in the field setting. Such training not only teaches the values and knowledge necessary to complete a set of skills but also allows time for learners to observe skills, practice skills, and receive feedback on their skill development and execution, until ultimately they are delivering the skills at a minimally competent level. Over time it is expected that learners will improve on these skills until they have achieved mastery. *Transfer of learning* is a concept used in training evaluation (e.g., Kirkpatrick 1959, 1976, 1994, 2005). According to Kirkpatrick and others (e.g., Parry and Berdie 1999), in training evaluation, there are five areas that can be assessed to determine if training has had the desired impact on learners. These include participant perceptions of the training as being useful, increases in participant knowledge and skills from before to after training, transfer of training concepts and skills to the practice setting, impact of the transfer of skills to organizational outcomes, and impact of the transfer of skills to practice outcomes. In child welfare, transfer of learning is measured in a variety of ways, including assessing intent to transfer and presence of transfer supports upon leaving training (Curry et al. 2011), interviewing or surveying participants some months after the end of training to determine perceived transfer of knowledge and skills to their daily work (Curry et al. 2005), interviewing or surveying supervisors some months after the end of training to determine their observations of skills that should have been acquired in training (Antle et al. 2010a), having coaches or evaluators observe training participants on the job and rate the adequacy of particular skills (Barbee et al. 2013), or interviewing clients about the skills their workers have demonstrated, workers about the skills their supervisors have demonstrated, or supervisors about the skills their managers have demonstrated, depending on who the target of training has been (Courtney 2011).

The Importance of Theoretical Underpinnings and Integration of Knowledge and Skills

The profession of social work, like many other professions, seeks to utilize theory supported by research to inform practice—what might be termed evidence-based and empirically corroborated practice. This inadvertently can create a dichotomy between the profession's systematic body of knowledge and the application of that knowledge through skills and techniques. In a 1989 article, Dennis Saleebey, Emeritus Professor of Social Welfare at the University of Kansas School of Social Welfare, criticized this estrangement of knowing and doing, noting that ultimately it both separates the responsibility for knowing from the responsibility for doing and risks negating other forms of knowing that emerge from intuition and implicit understanding. While the integration of theory and practice might appear to be a resolution, this fails to acknowledge the hierarchical relationship between theory and applied skills/techniques that places theory in the superior position.

Argyris and Schon (1978) recognized this tension in their discussion of theories of action. Argyris and Schon make a distinction between an individual's espoused theory and that individual's theory-in-use. An espoused theory is what one says—and most often actually believes—supports one's actions. A theory-in-use, however, represents what is implicit in one's actual behaviors and actions. For example, a Children and Youth Services (CYS) caseworker may espouse Carl Rogers' concept of unconditional positive regard, in which a client is respected and accepted regardless of any set of behaviors, actions, thoughts, or feelings; in other words, one suspends judgment of a client as a step toward creating a safe environment in which a client can discuss and explore sensitive and even controversial and taboo issues. Yet, when this same CYS worker is videotaped during meetings with clients, she not only fails to suspend judgment in many instances, but is often seen issuing reprimands designed to gain compliance. In other words, there is a significant disconnect between the espoused theory on which she says her behavior is based, and the theory-in-use evident in her actions. The caseworker's espoused theory is one of acceptance, while her theory-in-use reflects judgment and control.

One might ask about the relevance of this discussion to knowledge- and skill-based training and transfer of learning. The simple answer is that theory-guided practice requires congruence between espoused theory and theory-in-use. Such an answer, however, belies the complexity of achieving such consistency while simultaneously acknowledging the role of both evidence-based knowledge and intuition-supported knowledge, and recognizing the need to view theory and skills and techniques through a single lens.

At the beginning of this chapter, we provided a list of information and skills needed to address the complexities presented in achieving permanency for a medically fragile child whose mother was both emotionally and cognitively impaired and whose foster parents, to whom he was attached, were disinterested in adoption. The list was prodigious and required that the caseworker possess not only a wide range of clinical knowledge and skills but also an understanding of human behavior, applicable policies and laws, relevant research, and the effects of trauma. The worker would also need to be adept at maintaining appropriate documentation, testifying in court, and serving as an advocate. Two lists were presented—one for knowledge and one for skills. While such a division is not unusual, and actually may be helpful in discerning the scope of what is required of a CYS caseworker, thinking in such dualistic terms fails to directly tackle the challenges of integration. Knowledge and skills training must forge a connection between these two skill sets in order to ensure that what gets transferred from the training center to the workplace represents coherence between the basis for a caseworker's action and the action itself.

For this and other reasons, there are obstacles to achieving the transfer of knowledge and skills to the field. Broad and Newstrom (1992) in their book on transfer of training, for example, observe that there exists an enormous gap between the investment made in training and the ultimate application of that training to the workplace. In fact, they suggest that trainees recall and use just a small portion (by some estimates as little as 20 %) of what was learned during training. They suggest that what is needed is a "culture of transfer" that provides a context in which a significant amount of the knowledge and skills accrued in the classroom find their way into actual practice. Such a culture relies on a supportive organizational climate in which administrators and supervisors demonstrate their commitment to transfer of knowledge and skills by engaging in activities that include involving staff in determining training needs; introducing trainees to course objectives, content, and processes prior to the training; articulating the potential application of course knowledge and skills to the workplace; providing sufficient time for pre-training preparation, the workshop itself, and post-training implementation and assessment; and building transfer of learning expectations into performance standards (e.g., Curry et al. 2005).

Holton et al. (2000), in constructing their Learning Transfer System Inventory, utilize the term "transfer system" to define aspects of the person, training, and organization that can serve to enhance or obstruct the transfer of learning. In that sense they build on the work of Baldwin and Ford (1988) who, in reviewing research on transfer of learning, noted that the role of trainee characteristics (ability, personality, and motivation), training design (principles of learning, sequencing of programs, and specific content), and work environment (support and opportunity for application) all contribute significantly to the level of transfer. While these factors are in some ways discrete, in order for the transfer of learning to be successful, all three factors must be seen as integral and interdependent. For example, in designing a training program for child protective service caseworkers that focuses on a strength-based, solution-focused intervention process, one needs to determine not only the workers' level of preparation/experience but also the agency's readiness to adopt, support, and apply new strategies to the parallel processes of engagement, data gathering, understanding, and assessment (Barbee et al. 2011). Echoing the thoughts of Broad and Newstrom (1992), this may start with a collaborative planning process and include supervisor preparation; appropriate time allocation; a training model that incorporates didactic presentations, experiential exercises, and actual case material; and the evaluation of ongoing application opportunities. This chapter will discuss the organizational environment needed for effective skill-based training and transfer of learning to take place, and give examples of successful skill-based training in child welfare as measured by transfer of learning.

Systemic Readiness and Organizational Commitment Necessary to Support Skill-Based Training and Transfer of Learning

Each year, nearly 3.3 million reports of child abuse and neglect are investigated by child protection agencies, resulting in close to 900,000 substantiated cases of child maltreatment (Sedlak et al. 2010). Families who come to the attention of the child welfare system frequently face other hardships, such as poverty, incarceration, homelessness, substance abuse, mental health problems, domestic violence, and adolescent parenthood (NIS-4; Sedlak et al. 2010). Furthermore, many of these families are a part of a multigenerational cycle of abuse and neglect (e.g., Pecora et al. 2000). As a result, many victims of child maltreatment are removed from their families. More than 400,000 children are in foster care each year. These numbers remain high despite the change in the laws regarding abuse and neglect (CWLA 1995; GAO 1995). When these children are able to leave care, about 52 % are reunited with their families, about 8 % live with relatives, 20 % are adopted, and approximately 20 % age out of the system at age 18 (US Department of Health and Human Services 2012).

While the problem of child abuse and neglect is a constant in our society, the child welfare systems responsible for protecting and placing children are often overwhelmed and under-resourced (Zlotnik 2003). In the past 15 years, three laws were enacted to support program outcomes in child welfare such as child safety, permanency, and well-being: the Adoption and Safe Families Act (ASFA) of 1997, the Chafee Foster Care Independent Living Act of 1999, and the Fostering Connections

Act of 2008. ASFA includes initiatives to quantify success in the child welfare system, including the federal monitoring and evaluation component, Child and Family Services Reviews (CFSRs). The purpose of CFSRs is to measure states' performance on statewide aggregate data relative to national standards, as well as performance on qualitative criteria related to the delivery of child welfare services. After two rounds of reviews, few agencies fulfill all requirements. However, these reviews do not take into consideration whether or not systems have adequate funding, nor do they require states to maintain manageable caseloads for staff—both of which undergird the ability to do high-quality work. The reviews also do not require standards for the backgrounds of child welfare administrators, supervisors, or frontline staff. But the reviews do take a look at the strength of agencies' training systems, giving some credence to the importance of the workforce in delivering services (e.g., Milner and Hornsby 2004).

Research on high-performing organizations and case studies of child welfare agencies describe certain key factors in creating a healthy, vibrant, and effective training system that supports evidence-based and evidence-informed practice, leading to positive outcomes for families and children (Kanak et al. 2008). Child welfare agencies that are high functioning and that achieve positive outcomes for children have dynamic leadership and well-educated, well-trained frontline supervisors and staff who can make life-determining decisions about vulnerable families (Barbee and Cunningham 2009). Successful leaders of any organization tend to be not only talented and hardworking personally but also humble, visionary, and capable of galvanizing people to be committed to a vision for the organization (Collins 2004). These leaders enhance performance so that organizational goals are achieved (Collins 2004). They seek to reduce red tape, de-emphasize the role of rules to give employees more discretion, and create a learning culture and climate (Kelman 2005) where expertise is valued and date, evaluation, and research are used routinely to ensure continuous quality improvement (Senge 2006). To do this, they also surround themselves with high-quality people, ensure that high-quality people are hired throughout the organization, and ensure that these employees are in the best positions given their talents (Collins 2004; Kotter 1996).

These systems not only hire and train personnel but keep turnover at a minimum. While personnel selection, advancement at all levels of the organization, and low turnover are critical to such success, so is ensuring that all personnel are well trained for the job. When child welfare workers who are prepared for their jobs in terms of motivation, values, knowledge, skills, and abilities are not available or not selected as employees, a strong training system can still help to shape values, instill motivation, and hone the knowledge and skills of workforce members in their particular roles of interacting with clients, supervising frontline staff, and managing the operations of the system (e.g., Yankeelov et al. 2009). It is often the role of the child welfare training system to keep up with advances in the field and introduce leadership to new and emerging evidence-based and evidence-informed practices, as well as to infuse the training curriculum with such cutting-edge knowledge (Kanak et al. 2008). It is also the role of training units to ensure that what is learned in classroom settings is reinforced in the field and actually transferred to daily practice with families and children, supervision of workers, and managing all operations of the system.

Components of a Strong Training and Professional Development System

Strong training systems have strong management/leadership, staff, and resources to support partnerships with the larger organizational leadership team, for example, case practice and policy managers, quality assurance managers, and universities (see Kanak et al. 2008). A number of studies have shown the positive influence of agency-university partnerships in producing high-quality training systems (e.g., Dickinson and Perry 2002). In addition, strong training systems create curricula that are based on needs assessments of staff, evidence-based and evidence-informed practices and knowledge, and values and skill competencies. A strong training system can be key in:

(a) Providing training for top leadership and management in best child welfare practices, state-of-the-art management strategies, and best structures for success
(b) Providing training to frontline supervisors in how to be good administrators, how to supervise good clinical practices, and how to choose good workers. Strong supervisors can add better workers to the pipeline over time and retain good workers as well
(c) Providing training to new and veteran child welfare workers in best practices and stress management
(d) Providing linkages between managers, supervisors, and frontline staff to enhance support for training and learning and transfer of skills to the field
(e) Providing on-the-job training exercises to reinforce classroom training in the field
(f) Providing coaching and mentoring of new and veteran staff to reinforce training
(g) Enacting training evaluation strategies to demonstrate that training is seen as useful to participants, knowledge and skills are gained and enhanced from before to after training, and knowledge and skills are transferred to the field and linked to child welfare outcomes

Examples of Strong Training Systems

Kentucky

In 1981 Kentucky Governor John Y. Brown, Jr. eliminated training in the Cabinet for Health and Human Services as a cost-saving measure during difficult economic times. After a slew of child deaths, in 1983, the training department was reinstated and Kentucky's University Training Consortium (UTC) was founded as a partnership between the state universities and the Department for Social Services (now the Department for Community Based Services, DCBS). DCBS oversees child welfare, and adult protective services, family support, and child care among other social service agencies for the state. While Eastern Kentucky University is the leader of the UTC, all eight public universities (Kentucky State University, Morehead State University, Murray State University, Northern Kentucky University, University of Kentucky, University of Louisville, and Western Kentucky University) in the state are part of the UTC. All deliver training in their respective regions of the state and each has a unique contribution to make to the UTC system.

By the mid-1990s the UTC was fully operational and included a system for developing curricula based on key knowledge, skills, and abilities of the job (DACUM), offering an array of competency-based training for new and veteran workers and resource parents, as well as a full training evaluation program. This program covered everything from trainee reactions to transfer of learning in the field. In 1996 a new Cabinet for Families and Children (CFC) was formed and the Secretary of Social Services sat on the Governor's Cabinet. Because the governor was in office 8 years, the CFC had continuity of leadership for that length of time. The CFC Secretary was an educator who believed strongly in training, research, and learning organization principles. Through a partnership between the state and the UTC, the organizational culture and climate of the Department of Social Services was transformed into a true learning organization through leadership training and supervisory training. A strong economy and federal funding for training and research from UTC's partner universities were two additional factors that contributed to this successful change. These innovations occurred during a time when more frontline workers were hired, pay for child welfare workers and supervisors increased, certification from the Council on Accreditation (COA) was achieved, caseloads were lowered to meet CWLA standards, and a solution-based casework practice model (Christensen et al. 1999) was created. Even when the Cabinet was remerged with health services in 2004, the training innovations stayed intact. The system remains a strong partner with DCBS.

Kentucky learned many lessons during those rapid years of development and beyond about what it takes to achieve successful outcomes for families and children.

Preemployment Training

Between 1996 and 1998 a team developed the Public Child Welfare Certification Program (PCWCP) that was a collaboration between the state agency (particularly the training unit), the UTC, and all accredited Bachelor of Social Work (BSW) programs in the state (now 11). Through extensive evaluation research, the collaborative found that it is important to train social work students in child welfare policy and practice so that they are able to understand the true nature of the work and begin their tenure in public child welfare with many of the competencies needed for the job. This allows them to practice in ways that are more in keeping with family-centered ideals and to remain with the agency longer. Evaluation studies found that PCWCP students are more confident and outperform their peers in intervening more aggressively in cases by investigating more cases and substantiating more cases. They also provide more services, more accurately align risk with substantiation, assign more children to permanency goals, and change more goals to adoption after 12 months of out-of-home care. They place more children with relatives and fewer in residential facilities, place more children in adoptive homes and fewer in emergency shelters (i.e., move children to less-restrictive environments), visit the children in their caseload more regularly, and engage foster parents better so as to receive higher ratings of satisfaction with those visits, as compared with their peers who do not complete a PCWCP (Barbee et al. 2009a, b). One third of all new hires are PCWCP graduates, which may explain why even when some gains in resources were lost in the recessions of the 2000s, the state's outcomes on the CFSR improved tremendously from the first to second round of reviews (Barbee and Cunningham 2009).

Reinforcement of Skills in the Classroom and Field

Classroom and web-based training is not enough to ensure skill building and transfer of learning to the field; additional types of learning must be incorporated into an effective child welfare education program. First, it is essential to include time in the classroom for practice of critical skills. Second, it is essential to space out classroom or web-based training with field assignments and structured observations in the field to allow trainees to practice new skills under the watchful eye of a coach (Yankeelov et al. 2000). Routine training in Kentucky has on-the-job training weeks in between classroom and web-based weeks, to ensure that training concepts and skills are reinforced and practiced and competency is achieved. At one time there was even a field training specialist (FTS) program where:

- All new workers had on-the-job training weeks in between classroom training weeks with a specially trained senior worker who served as a coach.
- In that FTS model, the new workers would have a senior worker who served as their mentor and would work with the coach on the senior worker's cases.
- The mentor and mentee would discuss what was learned in training the previous week.
- Then the mentor would allow the new worker to observe an interaction with a client in that newly learned area (such as intake, investigation, development of a case plan, or managing a case plan) during the ongoing status of the case whether it was an in-home or out-of-home placement.
- The next time, the new worker would interact with a client in that same case process and receive both written and verbal instruction from the coach about his or her level of competency in completing the task.
- This feedback was facilitated by a behavioral anchor rating tool that listed all of the key behaviors in a particular area (such as intake, investigation, adoption) with a description of novice (score of 1–2)—not yet meeting standards of policy and practice; competency (score of 3)—meeting standards of policy and practice

at a minimum level; or excellence (score of 4 or 5)—exceeding the standards of policy and practice.

- The new worker scores over the course of the week and the entire training were shared with supervisors so that not only was the training reinforced but the continuing needs of workers could be identified and addressed through additional training or supervision (Barbee et al. 2013).

When that program became too costly in tight economic times, all supervisors were trained in coaching and mentoring skills so that they could provide similar oversight during training. While that method was less effective, those supervisors that used the behavioral anchor rating tool did continue to find their workers gaining a better grasp of skills compared to others.

Importance of Training Supervisors

Supervisors are essential to ensuring that workers transfer learning from training to the field, and practice with fidelity to the practice model. As a part of one Children's Bureau grant, supervisors received training with their teams on key practice skills of assessment, case planning, and coaching within the framework of the state's child welfare practice model, solution-based casework (Christensen et al. 1999). Supervisors were both recipients of the training and active participants in helping to guide the learning of their staff. For the evaluation, supervisors and their teams receiving the week-long training were compared to a matched sample of supervisors and teams who had not received the training intervention. Both groups were followed for a year. In those teams where supervisors and team members were trained (including training reinforcement sessions back in the field office), casework practice (e.g., assessments, case plans) of staff was superior to that of the comparison teams, and child maltreatment recidivism was half the rate in intervention versus comparison teams. Furthermore, the number of child placements in out-of-home care were fewer, the number of dental visits was higher, and the time between child visits with biological parents was shorter in intervention versus comparison teams (Antle et al. 2008a, b, Antle et al. 2010a; Van zyl et al. 2010). As a result of this research, supervisors currently work with their teams as part of the case review/CQI process each quarter and attend training that is consultation based to hone clinical skills in working with their staff.

In addition to training supervisors in clinical supervision, it is also important to train them in the administrative aspects of the job, such as hiring, creating a team, mitigating stress and secondary traumatization for staff, managing meetings effectively, managing conflict, managing difficult employees, documenting for termination of employment, and following EEOC rules. These skills help supervisors hire and retain better workers and keep morale up when workers face high caseloads and difficult client situations. Research in Kentucky has found that high-functioning supervisors reduce burnout and turnover (Yankeelov et al. 2009).

Importance of Training Leaders and Managers

Supervisors cannot do a good job supporting frontline workers without the support of high-level administrators and managers. Just as frontline workers need supervisors to support them in their work, supervisors need their managers and higher administrators to communicate clearly why new policies or requirements are necessary to achieve desired outcomes, remove barriers from their team so that their job can be manageable, and support their professional development and advancement needs (Antle et al. 2008a). Thus, continual training for leadership on how to maintain a positive organizational culture (even in tough economic times), how to use data to problem solve rather than to oppress staff, and how to manage conflict in the workplace is essential for the continued support of those working with clients. Early in the 2000s Kentucky developed the Human Services Leadership Institute, aimed first at top-level administrators in the central office and regional offices around the state and then at those who reported directly to them (middle managers in both settings). Evaluation of that training found that the more administrators and managers transferred the skills learned in the training (as reported by their staff), the greater staff morale was and the higher the productivity in those units (Fox et al. 2002).

Training of Resource Families

Like child welfare staff and managers, resource families need more than the basic training to fulfill their duties and prevent placement disruptions. Through two federal grants from the Children's Bureau, researchers in Kentucky found that resource parents had fewer problems with children in their care when they learned about the role of strong interpersonal relationships among adults in the family in mitigating child maltreatment and child behavioral problems. Furthermore, when newly adoptive parents learned about how to form families with their newly adopted children and how to build and maintain healthy relationships among the adults living in the home and with natural and foster/adopted children, placement disruptions were reduced (Sar, personal communication). A third federal grant found that engaging resource families can be a key step in ensuring that youth aging out of the system have the skills they need to thrive (Antle et al. 2010c).

Pennsylvania

In Pennsylvania, child welfare services are state supervised through the Department of Public Welfare's Office of Children, Youth, and Families, and administered on the local level by county children and youth agencies. There are 67 different counties, and each county has its own children and youth agency which receives state and federal funding based on the number of children served. All new public child welfare caseworkers in Pennsylvania must complete 3 days of safety assessment training prior to beginning work. In addition, in order to obtain certification as a direct service worker as defined in the Pennsylvania Protective Services Regulations, newly employed child welfare professionals in Pennsylvania must complete Charting the Course Toward Permanency for Children in Pennsylvania, a 120-h competency- and skills-based training course, as well as a 6-h transfer of learning component. Continuing child welfare professionals in Pennsylvania must accrue 20 h of related continuing education annually.

Pennsylvania's Child Welfare Training Program (now the Pennsylvania Child Welfare Resource Center) began in 1992 under the auspices of Shippensburg University, through a contract with the Pennsylvania Department of Welfare (DPW) and in partnership with the Pennsylvania Children and Youth Administrators (PCYA). Funding was provided through Title IV-E and IV-B, and emphasis was on training direct service workers, supervisors, administrators, and foster parents in the provision of services to abused and neglected children and their families. Initially, the focus was on the core competency-based training required of all child welfare caseworkers in Pennsylvania. Transfer of learning (TOL) and organizational effectiveness, while considered, were not emphasized in this early period. In 2001, leadership of the Child Welfare Training Program was assumed by the University of Pittsburgh School of Social Work. Since that time, funding has expanded to include not only Federal Title IV-E, Title IV-B, and the Child Abuse Prevention and Treatment Act (CAPTA) funds but also grants from the John D. and Catherine T. MacArthur Foundation and Casey Family Programs. The program places significant emphasis on supporting transfer of learning (TOL), ensuring organizational effectiveness, modeling best practices, and monitoring Pennsylvania child welfare programs in relationship to Child Family Service Review system outcomes through a continuous quality improvement (CQI) process. In order to better reflect its array of technical, organizational, research, and training initiatives, in 2011, the program became known as the Pennsylvania Child Welfare Resource Center.

During fiscal year 2011–2012, the training program conducted 1,463 workshops that included 16,927 participants. Of those workshops, 649 focused on Charting the Course and included 5,130 h of training over a total of 855 days (PA Child Welfare Resource Center 2012). Charting the Course serves as an example of training that emphasizes theoretical knowledge and skills along with an understanding of policy and best practices. In other words, it provides a context within which to integrate both knowing and doing, and includes transfer of learning activities designed to support the application of learned theoretical knowledge and skills to the practice arena. For example, there is a Charting the Course module that introduces participants to Pennsylvania's child welfare system and includes a consideration of federal and state laws and mandates, another that focuses on skills outlined in Lawrence Shulman's interactional helping model, and a third that explores principles of child development. Each module includes didactic material, exercises, case examples, and transfer of learning activities that articulate the link between the classroom and the field.

In order to reinforce and evaluate this link between classroom and field, the training program has developed three transfer of learning packages that include a ten-step program, a standard program, and a county-specific program. The ten-step program is the most comprehensive, and the steps are as follows:

- An initial meeting between a TOL specialist and participants' supervisors occurs to discuss the TOL process and the role played by supervisors, identify strategies that can be utilized by supervisors to enhance transfer of learning, and conduct an assessment of the current level of performance of participating caseworkers with regard to items specified in an on-the-job assessment tool (OTJA).
- An initial meeting between the TOL specialist and the participating caseworkers occurs to explain the TOL process and provide an opportunity for the caseworkers to complete a self-assessment of their current skill level with regard to items specified in the OTJA tool.
- Prior to the training workshop, participating caseworkers engage in prework activities specifically designed to connect their current work to the upcoming workshop and to provide them with an opportunity to "tune in" to the curriculum.
- Both caseworkers and their supervisors participate in the training. While the actual workshop content is not distinct from that included in the same workshop taken by caseworkers not involved in a TOL-specific process, there is special emphasis on encouraging caseworkers to immediately begin applying the presented knowledge and skills to their job.
- A TOL support session occurs 30 days following the completion of training and is designed to address what has been called a "results dip" and accompanying frustration that often occurs soon after a caseworker attempts to utilize new knowledge and implement new skills. A TOL specialist will review the established learning objectives with the participating caseworkers and supervisors and note progress and address problems associated with the application of new knowledge and skills. The TOL specialist will also review with supervisor strategies they might implement in promoting the TOL process.
- A second TOL support session occurs 60 days after the completion of training. Again, the focus is on identifying the successes and barriers related to the application of new knowledge and skills. Supervisors will be asked to complete an assessment of the current level of performance of participating caseworkers with regard to items specified in the OTJA tool, and caseworkers will be asked to complete a self-assessment of their current skill level with regard to items specified in the OTJA tool.
- A 3-h "booster shot" training conducted by the original trainer occurs a few months following the initial training and provides an opportunity to review the learning objectives of the training. Case studies and other practice exercises and tools are used to continue to address any "results dip" and to further enhance the caseworkers' capacity to apply knowledge and skills to their current work.
- A third TOL support session occurs 5 months following the initial training and, in addition to discussing the knowledge and skill application process, prepares both the participating caseworkers and the supervisors for an upcoming assessment.
- A written assessment occurs 6 months following the initial training and focuses on the learning objectives of the training. The assessment is reviewed by both the

caseworkers and supervisors in what is designed to be a collaborative process. This provides supervisors and caseworkers with an opportunity to not only review caseworkers' knowledge and skill levels but also begin developing the next steps in a specific curricular area.

- A final TOL support session provides the TOL specialist with an opportunity to share with caseworkers and supervisors her/his feedback on the transfer of knowledge and skills and encourages the caseworkers and supervisors to give the training program feedback on the TOL process as they experienced it.

This TOL process serves to identify several factors critical to the achievement and assessment of a transfer of knowledge and skills from training center to workplace. First, organizations must be fully supportive of staff participation in the training process, demonstrating both a commitment to providing these staff with time for the training, follow-up meetings with TOL specialists, and ongoing assessment, and a willingness to support the utilization of knowledge and skills in new or expanded ways. Second, supervisors of participating caseworkers must be involved in the process from the onset; they must acknowledge the need for their support and recognize and accept the expectations that are essential to the training and TOL processes. Third, the TOL process must be introduced as a collaborative process that involves organizational administrators, supervisors, caseworkers, a TOL specialist, and a trainer. Fourth, pre-workshop performance assessments of items specified in the on-the-job assessment (OTJA) tool must be completed by participating caseworkers and their supervisors in order to determine baseline performance and later to judge the level of transfer of knowledge and skills to job performance. In this way knowledge and skills prior to training, knowledge and skills accrued during training, level of trainee self-confidence before and after training, and trainee sense of usefulness with regard to the knowledge and skills gained during training can be measured. Fifth, follow-up support sessions for participating caseworkers and their supervisors should be used to reinforce learning, reintroduce strategies designed to bolster the transfer of learning, and address barriers to the workplace application of knowledge and skills from the workshop. Sixth, assessment tools must be readministered to supervisors and caseworkers at the conclusion of the complete TOL training period in order to evaluate effectiveness as judged by caseworkers' application of knowledge and skills accrued through training.

The training program is involved in an ongoing research study designed to assess the extent of transfer of learning as evidenced in Pennsylvania child welfare services. The study focuses on three questions:

- Do trainees apply new knowledge and skills on the job 1 year after training?
- What agency, individual, and training-related factors are related to TOL 1 year after training?
- Does organizational support for training change in relationship to receiving a TOL-enhanced training curriculum?

The study seeks to compare outcomes of trainees who participate in a TOL-enhanced training workshop as described above with those of trainees who participate in the training workshop only. Study participants complete question-naires at baseline and at 60 days, 6 months, and 12 months post-training.

A pilot study, undertaken in 2008, collected data from one Pennsylvania county child and youth services agency that participated in a TOL-enhanced training work-shop called Strength-Based, Solution-Focused Practice. Over one hundred trainees participated in this pilot study. Participants' knowledge and skill levels were reported before and after the training, and participant and agency characteristics were also identified. For this evaluative purpose, the OTJA tool referenced earlier was utilized, along with an agency environment survey. The OTJA tool includes 38 very specific statements that focus on knowledge and skills and on the extent to which the training affects job performance. In addition, three open-ended questions address practices that may either encourage or hinder the use of new knowledge and skills. Supervisors were asked to complete the tool with regard to their supervisees' performance pre- and post-training, and supervisees were asked to use the same tool to rate their own performance. The focus was on the Strength-Based, Solution-Focused Practice training, and statements included "I (she/he) can identify three reasons why it is important to identify client strengths," "I am confident in my (her/his) ability to apply the solution-focused intervention model," and "Within the past 60 days, I have (she/he has) used a scaling question in my (her/his) work with a typi-cal family or child." The agency environment tool, completed by caseworkers par-ticipating in the training, included 18 statements focusing on how training was viewed at their agency. The statements included, "My colleagues appreciate me using new skills I have learned in training," "My supervisor meets with me to dis-cuss ways to apply training on the job," and "People in my group generally prefer to use existing methods, rather than try new methods learned in training."

In the pilot study, 92 % of participants agreed that the training was important to them and to their abilities; 75 % agreed that they were confident that they would use the training; 82 % agreed that they learned something that could be immediately applied. Only 58 % of participants in this study agreed that they were informed of training goals prior to the training, and 59 % agreed that they were informed of the relevance of the training prior to the training. When queried about supervisor sup-port of the use of new skills, about three quarters of the respondents indicated that supervisors expressed interest in the knowledge and skills they accrued in the train-ing, but only about half of the respondents reported that their supervisors actually discussed the specific benefits and challenges of applying such skills, or encouraged supervisees to set goals for the application of this new learning. As for peer support, not surprisingly, participants who described their peers as "open to change" reported greater use of new knowledge and skills over time than those who saw their peers as "less open to change." Unfortunately, less that 50 % of respondents described their peers as open to change while over 60 % of respondents indicated that their peers preferred to use existing methods (PA Child Welfare Training Program 2009).

This early study of a TOL initiative reinforces the previously cited lessons learned. The support of administrators, supervisors, and peer colleagues is essential; opportunities to apply knowledge and skills are critical; an organizational openness to changing the way things are done is important; the evaluation of effectiveness of both the transfer of learning and the impact on practice of that transferred learning is necessary in assessing the quality of services and in developing and refining specific training initiatives.

Other Examples of Strong Training Systems

Kentucky and Pennsylvania are the states with which we are most familiar, but many states have strong child welfare training units. For example, the California Social Work Education Center (CALSWEC), part of the University of California at Berkeley School of Social Welfare, was founded in 1990 by Harry Specht and led by Nancy Dickinson. Dickinson went on to enhance and strengthen the systems in North Carolina and Maryland, and is Co-PI of the Children's Bureau National Child Welfare Workforce Institute. At CALSWEC, all curricula for frontline workers, supervisors, and resource families are competency based, and these materials are available on the web for use by anyone in the nation. CALSWEC developed a Common Core Curricula for its first Practice Improvement Plan (PIP) in 2003, and since that time has developed transfer of learning materials for each module (Coloma 2010).

The center's IV-E stipend program has been in place for 20 years and has a focus on MSW students, since California is one of the few states that primarily hires Masters-level staff in most counties. CALSWEC, too, evaluates the work of its graduates and is finding interesting results on skill building and practice outcomes. The center also began hosting an annual symposium on human services training evaluation in 1998 and includes the proceedings from those meetings on its website. This symposium has moved the field of training evaluation forward tremendously.

Ohio's Institute for Human Services (IHS) had an early impact on the nation with the development of the first competencies for child welfare work. Over 25 states adopted its curricula or its model of developing competency-based curricula. IHS continues to work with some of those states and to do most of its work in Ohio through five regional training academies that serve 88 counties throughout the state. IHS recently created a stipend program with good results and is expanding its evaluation to demonstrate the effectiveness of its curriculum. It was in Ohio that Dale Curry did his seminal work on training transfer, some of which is cited above.

Conclusion

All in all there have been great strides in attending to skill-based training and transfer of learning over the past 15 years in the field of child welfare. What we know is that classroom training builds a foundation that must be reinforced in the field in order to be practiced in day-to-day work with clients. When skills are reinforced through additional practice exercises, coaching, mentoring, and specific feedback on key practice behaviors, both client outcomes and organizational outcomes can be affected and improved. In addition, we know that training must go hand in hand with supervision to be effective; these two areas of the organization must therefore be in concert. Further research is needed to better understand how to engage the practice sector of child welfare agencies in embracing this important role of supervisors and senior frontline workers. In addition, more research is needed on what aspects of classroom training and its reinforcement lead to the changes in behavior that are necessary to impact child and family outcomes. Incorporating findings from studies conducted thus far and extending this work to refine our understanding of the transfer process will mean the world to clients like those described in the introductory story. Our hope is that all families entering the child welfare system throughout the country will find a skilled workforce that is equipped to meet their needs and help them ensure that their children are safe, in permanent homes, and successful in life.

The case introduced at the beginning of this chapter told the story of a 2-year-old child diagnosed with hydrocephalus who was removed from his home as a result of substantiated child neglect. The case, though it presents enormous complexities, is not itself extraordinary; indeed, it reflects many of the challenges experienced by child welfare workers on a daily basis. What is extraordinary, however, is the breadth of knowledge and skills required to deal with this case; the list of requisite knowledge and skills presented earlier was prodigious but by no means all-inclusive. In order to deliver appropriate services to clients, however, simply possessing knowledge and skills is insufficient; a worker must also be able to translate a sense of knowing and doing into distinct situations. It is the *application* of knowledge and skills that becomes so critical.

Furthermore, even when a child welfare worker brings skills from the classroom and from training into practice, this does not signify that the worker's learning has reached an end in some place of ultimate meaning. Instead, it represents an unending series of efforts to gain and regain understanding, predicated on multiple shifts in context. The task itself seems shrouded in impossibilities. Yet when workers in this most-challenging field of child welfare actively engage as translators in a transfer of knowledge and skills, they must critically reflect on how knowing and doing interrelate, while ultimately recognizing that meaning cannot be transferred whole from one situation to another, but must be shaped by the uniqueness of context. The translation of knowledge and skills, then, is both responsive and generative, and, as such, the transfer of knowledge and skills in child welfare involves reaffirmation and adaptation that simultaneously honor both what is learned in a classroom setting and the ways in which that learning is applied within a practice environment. In the simplest of terms, a transfer of learning is all about building bridges that transport us between knowing and doing, making us translators in the most conscious and deliberate of ways as we engage each new client and each new situation.

Questions for Discussion

1. Review the case example at the beginning of this chapter and consider the key elements of skill-based training and transfer of learning. How might management of this case differ between a worker who received traditional, classroom-based

training only and one who received classroom-based training plus transfer of learning support?
2. What are some common organizational barriers to skill-based training and transfer of learning in an agency?
3. What are some of the unique challenges to training transfer for resource families?
4. How might child welfare authorities better incorporate skill-based training and transfer of learning outcomes into the federal review process?

References

Antle, B. F., Barbee, A. P. & Sullivan, D. J.(2010). Evidence-based supervisor-team independent living training: Kentucky Development and Implementation. Special Issue on Independent Living. A. Barbee & B. Antle (Eds). *Training and Development in Human Services, 5*. 53–66.

Antle, B. F., Barbee, A. P., Christensen, D. N., & Martin, M. (2008a). Solution-based casework in child welfare: Preliminary evaluation research. *Journal of Public Child Welfare, 2*(2), 197–227.

Antle, B. A., Barbee, A. P., Sullivan, D. J., & Christensen, D. (2010a). The prevention of child maltreatment recidivism through the Solution-Based Casework model of child welfare practice. *Children and Youth Services Review, 31*, 1346–1351.

Antle, B. F., Barbee, A. P., & van Zyl, M. A. (2008b). A comprehensive model for child welfare training evaluation. *Children and Youth Services Review, 30*(9), 1063–1080.

Antle, B.F., Barbee, A. P., & Sullivan, D.J. (2010c). Development of Kentucky's Supervisor Training. Special issue on independent living in training and development in human services, 5, 53–66.

Antle, B. F., Christensen, D. N., van Zyl, M. A., & Barbee, A. P. (2012). The impact of the solution based casework (SBC) practice model on federal outcomes in public child welfare. *Child Abuse and Neglect, 36*, 342–353.

Antle, B. F., Sullivan, D. J., Barbee, A. P., & Christensen, D. N. (2010b). The effects of training reinforcement on training transfer. *Child Welfare, 32*(2), 223–230.

Argyris, C., & Schon, D. (1978). *Organizational learning: A theory of action perspective.* Reading, MA: Addison-Wesley.

Baldwin, T. T., & Ford, J. K. (1988). Transfer of training: A review and directions for future research. *Personnel Psychology, 41*, 63–105.

Barbee, A. P., Antle, B., Sullivan, D., Huebner, R., & Fox, S. (2009a). Recruiting and Retaining Child Welfare Workers: Is Preparing Social Work Students Enough for Sustained Commitment to the Field? *Special Issue of Child Welfare, 88*, 69–86.

Barbee, A. P., Christensen, D., Antle, B., Wandersman, A., & Cahn, K. (2011). System, organizational, team and individual changes that need to accompany adoption and implementation of a comprehensive practice model into a public child welfare agency. *Children and Youth Services Review, 33*, 622–633.

Barbee, A. P. & Cunningham, M.R. (2009). Evaluation of the Children's Bureau Training and Technical Assistance Network. Report to the National Child Welfare Resource Center for Organizational Development and the Children's Bureau. Louisville, KY.

Barbee, A. P., Sullivan, D. J., Antle, B. F., Moran, E. B., Hall, J. C., & Fox, S. (2009b). The Public Child Welfare Certification Program: Worker retention and impact on practice. *Journal of Social Work Education, 45*, 427–445.

Barbee, A. P., Yankeelov, P. A., Antle, B. F., Fox, S., Harmon, D., Evans, S. & Black, P. (2013). The importance of training reinforcement in child welfare: Kentucky's field training specialist model. *Child Welfare* (in press).

Broad, M. L., & Newstrom, J. M. (1992). *Transfer of training: Action-packed strategies to ensure high payoff from training investments*. Reading, MA: Addison-Wesley.

Child Welfare League of America. (1995). *The Child Welfare Stat Book*. Washington, D.C.: Child Welfare League of America.

Christensen, D., Todahl, J., & Barrett, W. (1999). *Solution-based casework: An introduction to clinical and case management skills in casework practice*. New York: Aldine DeGruyter.

Collins, J. (2004). *Good to great*. New York: HarperCollins.

Coloma, J. (2010). *Transfer learning guide*. Academy for Professional Excellence. San Diego State University. Retrieved from http://theacademy.sdsu.edu/resources_new/transfer_of_learning_guide_2010%20_v_1_1.pdf

Courtney, M. (2011). *Evaluating large-scale child welfare casework practice models: Ideal and realistic methodologies and evaluation implementation given systems characteristics*. Washington, D. C.: National Child Welfare Evaluation Summit.

Curry, D. (2001). Evaluating transfer of learning in human services. *Journal of Child and Youth Care Work, 15–16*, 155–170.

Curry, D., Caplan, P., & Knuppel, J. (1994). Transfer of training and adult learning (TOTAL). *Journal of Continuing Social Work Education, 6*, 8–14.

Curry, D., Lawler, M., Donnenwirth, J., & Bergeron, M. (2011). Application potential of professional learning inventory- APPLI-33. *Training and Development in Human Services, 6*, 129–139.

Curry, D., McCarragher, T., & Dellmann-Jenkins, M. (2005). Training, transfer, and turnover: Exploring the relationships among transfer of learning factors and staff retention in child welfare. *Children and Youth Services Review, 27*, 931–948.

Dickinson, N. S., & Perry, R. E. (2002). Factors influencing the retention of specially educated public child welfare workers. *Journal of Health and Social Policy, 15*, 89–103.

Fox, S., Barbee, A. P., Harmon, D., Staples, K., & Spang, G. (2002). Leadership: Can it really be developed through training? *Training and Development in Human Services, 2*, 8–16.

Fox, S., Miller, V., & Barbee, A. P. (2003). Finding and keeping child welfare workers: Effective use of Title IV-E training funds. *Journal of Human Behavior in the Social Environment, 7*, 67–82. Also a chapter in *Charting the Impacts of University-Child Welfare Collaboration*. Ed. Katherine Briar-Lawson & Joan Levy Zlotnick. Haworth Social Work Practice Press.

Holton, E. F., Bates, R. A., & Ruona, W. E. A. (2000). Development of a generalized learning transfer system inventory. *Human Resource Development Quarterly, 11*(4), 333–360.

Kanak, S., Baker, M., Herz, L., & Maciolek, S. (2008). *Building effective training systems for child welfare agencies*. Portland, ME: National Child Welfare Resource Center for Organizational Improvement.

Kelman, R. (2005). *Unleashing change: A study of organizational renewal in government*. Washington, D. C.: Brookings Institute.

Kessler, M. L., & Greene, B. F. (1999). Behavior analysis in child welfare: Competency training caseworkers to manage visits between parents and children in foster care. *Research on Social Work Practice, 9*(2), 148–170.

Kirkpatrick, D. L. (1959). Techniques for evaluating programs. *Journal of the American Society of Training Directions, 13*(11), 3–9.

Kirkpatrick, D. (1976). Evaluation of training. In R. L. Craig (Ed.), *Training and development handbook: A guide to human resource development* (2nd ed.). New York: McGraw-Hill.

Kirkpatrick, D. (1994). *Evaluating training programs: The four levels*. San Francisco: Berrett-Koehler.

Kirkpatrick, J. (2005). Transferring learning to behavior. *Training and Development, 59*(4), 19–21.

Kotter, J. (1996). *Leading change*. Boston: Harvard Business School Press.

Milner, J., & Hornsby, W. (2004). Training of child welfare staff and providers: Findings from the Child and Family Service Review. *Protecting Children, 19*(3), 4–14.

PA Child Welfare Resource Center. (2012). *Fiscal Year 2011–2012 Annual Report*. Pittsburgh: University of Pittsburgh, School of Social Work.

PA Child Welfare Training Program. (2009). *On-going Transfer of Learning in Pennsylvania Child Welfare Services*. Pittsburgh: University of Pittsburgh, School of Social Work, Child Welfare Education and Research Programs.

Parry, C., & Berdie, J. (1999). *Training evaluation in the human services*. Washington, DC: American Public Human Services Association.

Pecora, P. J., Whittaker, J. K., Maluccio, A. N., Barth, R. P., & Plotnick. (2000). *The child welfare challenge*. New York: Aldine de Gruyter.

Saleebey, D. (1989). The estrangement of knowing and doing: Professions in crisis. *Social Casework, 70*, 556–563.

Sedlak, A. J., Mettenburg, J., Basena, M., Petta, I., McPherson, K., Greene, A., & Li, S. (2010). *Fourth national incidence study of child abuse and neglect (NIS-4): Report to congress*. Washington, DC: U. S. Department of Health and Human Services, Administration for Children and Families.

Senge, P. M. (2006). *The fifth discipline: The art and practice of a learning organization* (Revth ed.). New York: Currency/Doubleday.

US Department of Health and Human Services, Administration for Children and Families, Administration on Children, Youth and Families, Children's Bureau (2012). *The AFCARS Report. Preliminary FY 2011 estimates as of July 2012(19)*. Retrieved from http://www.acf.hhs.gov/sites/default/files/cb/afcarsreport19.pdf

US General Accounting Office (1995). *Child welfare: Complex needs strain capacity to provide services*. Washington, D. C.

Van zyl, M. A., Antle, B & Barbee, A. P. (2010). The prevention of child maltreatment recidivism through the solution-based casework model of child welfare practice. In Maria Roberts-DeGennaro & Sondra J. Fogel (Eds.), *Empirically Supported Interventions for Community and Organizational Change*.

Yankeelov, P. A., Barbee, A. P., Barber, G., & Fox, S. (2000). Timing isn't everything, but it can be important. *Training and Development in Human Services, 1*, 67–81.

Yankeelov, P. A., Barbee, A. P., Sullivan, D. J., & Antle, B. F. (2009). Individual and organizational factors in job retention in Kentucky's child welfare agency. *Children and Youth Services Review, 31*, 547–554.

Zlotnik, J. L. (2003). The use of title IV-E training funds for social work education: An historical perspective. *Journal of Human Behavior in the Social Environment, 7*, 5–20.

Chapter 9
Stress and Child Welfare Work

Elizabeth A. Winter

Abstract Child welfare workers speak of the satisfaction of knowing they have made a critical difference in children's lives; at the same time, there is also the difficulty of dealing with the stressful aspects of working in this field. Some level of stress is inherent in child welfare work, and this affects both individuals and organizations. Exposure to details of the suffering of maltreated children is a job requirement for child welfare workers as they carefully investigate maltreatment allegations and interact with people who often do not want to see them and who may threaten them or try to hurt them. In addition to their day-to-day responsibilities, child welfare workers may also have to face the news of a child's injury or death that they could not prevent. The combination of all of these factors can certainly be extremely taxing, and severely stressful events can result in negative effects on functioning in child welfare workers, such as traumatic stress, depression, and anxiety.

Child welfare organizations can suffer from traumatic stress in ways that are analogous to the suffering of individuals. Organizations face the stress of using increasingly scarce resources in trying to meet great need. Severe budget cuts and the assignment of additional tasks without receiving additional funds only add to the stress inherent in child welfare work for an already overburdened workforce. In addition, environmental stressors are added to the mix for both individuals and organizations, such as lack of understanding of the work of child welfare by the general public. Child welfare workers are required to protect child and family privacy, so the many successful cases in this field rarely come to public attention in the way that cases involving disastrous outcomes often do. Child welfare administrators are prohibited from speaking about specific cases, such as the death of a child, and

E.A. Winter (✉)
Child Welfare Education and Research Programs, School of Social Work,
University of Pittsburgh, Pittsburgh, PA, USA
e-mail: eaw44@pitt.edu

H. Cahalane (ed.), *Contemporary Issues in Child Welfare Practice*,
Contemporary Social Work Practice, DOI 10.1007/978-1-4614-8627-5_9,
© Springer Science+Business Media New York 2013

can only respond in very general terms. Child welfare workers thus have little voice in addressing public perceptions and cannot explain or defend the decisions they must make.

Workers may have pre-existing risk factors and face the likelihood of both primary and secondary exposure to traumatic stressors in the course of their everyday work. Any resulting traumatic stress is likely to involve significant suffering and potentially affect work quality and staff turnover. Approaches to the problem may occur at the client level, the worker level, and the organizational level. Since the problem affects an entire organizational system and all its members, organizational-level approaches, while time consuming and initially costly, may be the most promising in providing relief from suffering, and may be more cost effective in the long run. Significant research evidence exists concerning the risks for and potential impact of worker traumatic stress and materials providing approaches are becoming increasingly available. Evidence of effectiveness of these approaches is beginning to emerge and will hopefully continue to grow, showing the way forward in dealing with one of the major concerns in the field of child welfare.

Keywords Stress • Trauma • Secondary traumatic stress • Vicarious trauma • Secondary trauma • Compassion fatigue • Compassion satisfaction • Posttraumatic growth • Primary trauma • Organizational culture • Trauma-informed

Case Study

Barbara has worked in public child welfare for about 9 years. She started out with high hopes and a desire to help abused and neglected children. She thought she could stand anything, as long as she knew she was making a difference.

Barbara's first job was in the Intake Department, where she would go out and investigate allegations of child abuse and neglect in her county. She quickly established a reputation as a good worker and was proud of being able to establish a good relationship with children and listen to them empathically. Barbara derived satisfaction from knowing that she was making a difference for many of the children she came into contact with, one child at a time, and believed that her work contributed to the greater good of society.

Still, there were some days when Barbara was horrified by what she found. It was hard for her to believe that some children suffered so terribly at the hands of those who were charged with their care and safety. Barbara remembers that in the early days, she would often go home and cry about what she had seen and heard. It was particularly hard for her when there was simply not enough evidence to justify placing a child in out-of-home care when she truly believed that child to be unsafe. As time went by, Barbara found that some cases seemed to haunt her; she would find herself thinking about a few particularly bad situations over and over again. This was particularly distressing at night, when she could not get these thoughts out of her head as she was trying to go to sleep.

Barbara found that some of her co-workers were sympathetic to her reactions, while others told her that she would (and should) "toughen up" and not let it get to her. At the same time, while Barbara had always tried to see the best in people, she found she was

increasingly suspicious of others, particularly regarding children. If she heard a child cry out, her first thought was that someone was abusing the child. She would find herself watching families she saw in public places, checking whether the children were adequately fed and clothed or whether they appeared to be fearful.

After 4 years of doing investigations, Barbara was feeling more and more hopeless and frustrated about her work. She was becoming more cynical and angry and found herself telling the newer workers that they should toughen up and just "get over it" when they expressed distress about their cases. This alternated with periods of feeling numb, distant, and disinterested in her work. To add to her problems at work, Barbara's relationship with her long-time partner was suffering; he complained that she was distant with him and just seemed like a different person. Barbara started having nightmares in which she was trying to run away from people chasing her; she would wake up frightened and not be able to get back to sleep.

As Barbara became more distressed, her work suffered. Her relationship with her supervisor became progressively more adversarial, and she was written up for not getting her paperwork completed on time. Barbara had always considered herself to be in child welfare for the long haul, but now she began to consider leaving the field. When she was written up again for losing her temper with her supervisor over a disagreement about a case, Barbara received a mandatory referral to the agency's Employee Assistance Program, which in turn referred her for a psychological evaluation. Barbara met criteria for posttraumatic stress disorder and started therapy with another provider when her EAP sessions were completed. During this period, due to staffing changes, she got another supervisor, one who had been trained in process supervision and secondary traumatic stress. Barbara felt immediate relief with a supervisor who validated her distress and frustration about severe cases and took the time to check in with her and see if she was OK. Her new supervisor was also able to help Barbara refocus on situations which turned out well and to get back in touch with her original reasons for feeling satisfaction from her work. Barbara completed her course of therapy and returned from time to time for booster sessions when she had particularly difficult cases.

Several co-workers started a walking group at lunch time, which Barbara joined when she was in the office. She also made a point of spending time with her partner during which she did not talk about her job. As a result of the shift in her work environment, specifically the support she received from her new supervisor and from colleagues, Barbara began to feel less anxious and better able to manage the pressures inherent in child protective services work.

Child welfare workers speak of the satisfaction of knowing they have made a critical difference in children's lives; at the same time, there is also the difficulty of dealing with the stressful aspects of working in this field (CWERP 2012; Stamm 2010). Some level of stress is inherent in child welfare work, and this affects both individuals (Horwitz 1998, 2006; Morrison 1992) and organizations (Bloom 1997; Catherall 1995). Exposure to details of the suffering of maltreated children is a job requirement for child welfare workers. Caseworkers carefully investigate maltreatment allegations, which exposes them to highly distressing information and to interactions with people who often do not want to see them and who may threaten them or try to hurt them (Newhill and Wexler 1997). In addition to their day-to-day work of completing paperwork, meeting deadlines, connecting families and children to needed resources, and preparing for and making court appearances, child welfare workers may also have to face the news of a child's injury or death that they could not prevent. The combination of all of these factors can certainly be extremely taxing, and severely stressful events can result in negative effects on functioning in child welfare workers, such as traumatic stress, depression, and anxiety (Bride 2007; Conrad and Kellar-Guenther 2006; Horwitz 1998, 2006; Morrison 1992).

There has also been growing support for the view that organizations can suffer from traumatic stress in ways that are analogous to the suffering of individuals (Bloom 1997; Herman 1992b; Hormann and Vivian 2005). Organizations face the stress of using increasingly scarce resources in trying to meet great need. Severe budget cuts and the assignment of additional tasks without receiving additional funds (known as "unfunded mandates") only add to the stress inherent in child welfare work for an already overburdened workforce.

In addition to the stresses inherent in the work, environmental stressors are added to the mix for both individuals and organizations, such as lack of understanding of the work of child welfare by the general public. Child welfare work is viewed with ambivalence by society. On one hand, it is recognized as a necessary safeguard for vulnerable children, while on the other hand, it frequently does not receive sufficient funding and is viewed with suspicion and sometimes outright disrespect (Morrison 1992). Child welfare workers are required to protect child and family privacy, so the many successful cases in this field rarely come to public attention in the way that cases involving disastrous outcomes often do. The death of a child (whether or not this child is already involved in the child welfare system) is usually widely reported with questions about the competence of child welfare workers and administrators, to which administrators can only respond in very general terms because they are prohibited from speaking about specific cases (Chenot 2011). Child welfare workers thus have little voice in addressing public perceptions and cannot explain or defend the decisions they must make. This tends to result in a one-sided public view of child welfare work and workers (Chenot 2011; Morrison 1992).

This chapter addresses these questions of satisfaction and stress for child welfare workers and organizations and, in particular, the impact of traumatic experiences. The early part of the chapter describes the concepts of compassion satisfaction and traumatic growth (also called posttraumatic growth), followed by the concepts of stress, burnout, and traumatic stress, both primary and secondary. Traumatic stress will be addressed primarily in the context of Posttraumatic Stress Disorder (PTSD) and the features associated with it at both the individual and organizational levels.

The second section of this chapter examines risk and protective factors related to traumatic exposure and warning signs and symptoms of traumatic stress among child welfare caseworkers, supervisors, and administrators and in child-serving organizations themselves. The third section of this chapter looks at emerging evidence and suggested ways that organizations, administrators, supervisors, and individuals can work toward self-care and provide an environment in which effective trauma-informed (T-I) supervision and administrative practices can flourish. The fourth part of this chapter describes resources and practical tools available to individuals and agencies to maximize their own T-I self-care. Lastly, resources for further information and study are listed at the end of the chapter.

Satisfaction and Growth, Stress, and Burnout

Compassion Satisfaction

As we consider what qualities make child welfare workers satisfied or dissatisfied with their work, Stamm's (1995) formulation of compassion satisfaction is a helpful starting point. Stamm describes the combination of compassion satisfaction and compassion fatigue as dual forces that together form a construct she names the Professional Quality of Life. Compassion fatigue will be discussed in more detail below, but we have already mentioned one example of compassion satisfaction. In the case at the beginning of this chapter, the positive feelings Barbara experienced when she started work fall within the concept of compassion satisfaction. Barbara had the satisfaction of knowing she was making a difference to individuals and perhaps to society as a whole; she had the altruistic sense of being able to make things better for another human being.

Traumatic Growth

Posttraumatic growth, a term coined by Calhoun and Tedeschi (1998), is the growth that occurs following a struggle with a deeply distressing experience. In other words, the same traumatic events that can precipitate posttraumatic stress can also result in posttraumatic growth. Three general domains of perceived growth emerged from the literature, namely, changes in self-perception ("If I can get through this, I can get through anything"), changes in relationships with other people ("I now value the people around me so much more"), and changes in how one views the world, or philosophy of life ("Now I appreciate each moment I am alive") (Calhoun and Tedeschi 1998). As will be seen below, negative changes in these three domains can also occur following traumatic experience, particularly in the context of post-traumatic stress disorder. Woodward and Joseph (2003), in looking at posttraumatic growth in adults who had experienced childhood emotional, physical, or sexual abuse, also identified what they termed "vehicles of change" for posttraumatic growth. These vehicles of change help us to understand a little more about *how* such posttraumatic growth may occur. The vehicles of change include (a) experiencing genuine acceptance by others; (b) the awakening of responsibility, such as realizing one has a choice about taking care of oneself; (c) experiencing love and nurturing, both by self and by others; (d) a sense of liberation and freedom; (e) a sense of mastery and control; and (f) experiencing a sense of belonging and connection. Woodward and Joseph (2003) point out that while previous work stressed the characteristics of individuals in terms of their coping skills and other attributes, their work suggests the importance of social context, noting that it was mostly through relationships that respondents in their study felt accepted, nurtured, and liberated. While we do know that individual characteristics play a part in how people react to traumatic experience, these findings begin to suggest the kinds of social environments that may be more conducive to posttraumatic growth.

Since posttraumatic growth and distress can coexist, the next question that arises is whether posttraumatic growth is associated with fewer PTSD symptoms. Linley, Joseph, and Goodfellow (2008), in their study of 40 people who had experienced severe traumatic events, reported that perceived positive changes were associated with lower levels of PTSD symptoms, as well as less depression and anxiety, at a 6-month follow-up.

Tedeschi and Kilmer (2005) and Joseph (2009) take the view that this growth is not the same construct as resilience. Resilience is usually thought of as the ability to struggle well with adversity, due to a combination of internal factors (such as temperament or a sense of optimism) and external factors (such as the presence of a significant nurturing adult during childhood) that enable the individual to survive well despite the adversity. By contrast, posttraumatic growth, or growth following adversity (another term for posttraumatic growth), involves more than struggling and surviving because of a particular blend of risk or protective factors. It has been described as the positive growth that can emerge from the struggle with the stressor itself and the meaning the experience comes to have for the individual experiencing it (Joseph 2009; Tedeschi and Kilmer 2005). According to this view, resilience enables someone to cope during adverse experience, whereas posttraumatic growth occurs after the trauma itself. An alternate view of resilience in families is given by Walsh (2003), who describes resilience as including growth following adversity. The most practical view may be to see posttraumatic growth as a particular example of growth following (and in part due to) traumatic adversity.

It is important to avoid several erroneous assumptions about posttraumatic growth. While growth is possible following traumatic experience, this does not mean that the impact of traumatic experience can be minimized or that this type of experience should be seen as a "good thing." Secondly, no individual should be blamed for failing to demonstrate this kind of growth (Joseph 2009). There is much more work to be done in this area before it will be possible to suggest what may reliably facilitate this kind of growth, but a focus on the potential for posttraumatic growth as well as posttraumatic stress offers hope for those exposed to trauma routinely during the course of their work.

Stress

The function of the stress response system in humans is to protect us in situations which are or may be dangerous. When the stress response system is activated, a host of hormonal and neurotransmitter responses prepare the body to manage the real or perceived threat. A faster heart rate, sweaty palms, and feeling a little shaky are familiar signs that the stress response system has been activated. When we know that the threat has passed or been managed successfully, the system settles back to normal. When stress is predictable, moderate, and manageable, and followed by sufficient recovery time, our stress response systems become resilient over time. However, when the stress is severe and unpredictable, it can be experienced as overwhelming or traumatic, leading to changes in the stress response and underlying physiology such that the baseline moves and the system no longer returns completely to rest (Perry 2010).

Burnout

In child welfare work, the concept of burnout is often discussed alongside the concepts of stress and traumatic stress; indeed, stress, burnout, and traumatic stress can coexist. Burnout is a syndrome first identified by Maslach in the early 1980s. It is composed of emotional exhaustion, depersonalization, and a diminished sense of personal accomplishment (Maslach 1982). Burnout is generally described as consisting of physical, emotional, and mental exhaustion, brought on by chronic exposure to workplace stressors which wear the person down over time. By contrast, as discussed below, traumatic stress is precipitated by exposure to a severe event or events, known as "traumatic" stressors. The experience of traumatic events is also not confined to the workplace, whereas in the definition of burnout, the stressors are work-related. These work-related stressors may include role conflict, high workloads, and lack of recognition for work and effort. When a caseworker is feeling burned out, he or she may feel a lack of physical and emotional energy and may dread going to work. Interactions with clients may be cold or emotionally detached, and the person may also begin to feel that families and children are "objects" to be managed rather than individuals to engage with. Burnout is frequently accompanied by a decline in feelings of success, competence, and worth. Some of the outcomes of burnout are dissatisfaction with and intention to quit a job and physical and psychological symptoms. Koeske and Koeske (1989) tested a model of job stress with social workers. They found that stress had a strong relationship with emotional exhaustion, which in turn predicted intention to leave the job. However, they did find that social workers who reported higher levels of social support tended to have less intention to quit. These authors also looked at a particular work demand—workload (Koeske and Koeske 1989). Once again, the buffering condition was social support, specifically coworker support.

Traumatic Stress

Traumatic Stressors

As noted above, all stressors are not equal; some are more severe than others. For example, getting paperwork completed on time is probably not as severe a stressor as going to a home where you have previously been threatened, which in turn may not be as severe as seeing a critically injured child in a hospital emergency room.

The most severe stressors include single or multiple events that are termed "traumatic"; in other words, the event or events may overwhelm the stress response system and lead someone to develop a stress-related syndrome, such as Posttraumatic Stress Disorder (APA 2013). While there is not complete agreement about what makes a stressor traumatic, the most recent edition of the Diagnostic and Statistical Manual of Mental Disorders (DSM-5™) states that exposure to death (actual or threatened), serious injury, or sexual violence, in one of a number of specified ways, meets the traumatic event exposure criterion (Criterion A) for Posttraumatic Stress Disorder (PTSD). The ways in which the event may be experienced include directly experiencing it oneself (Criterion A1); witnessing it occurring to others (Criterion A2); learning of it occurring to a close family member or close friend (Criterion A3); and, lastly, exposure to aversive details, with such exposure being either repeated or extreme (Criterion A4). Criterion A4 refers explicitly to those who come into contact repeatedly with details of child abuse; while the DSM-5™ explicitly mentions police officers, by logical extension, this would include child welfare workers (APA 2013).

The traumatic events referred to in the previous paragraph are regarded as severe because exposure to them may result in the development of symptoms of either PTSD or Acute Stress Disorder (APA 2013). Therefore, while seeing a critically injured child in the emergency room may well be a traumatic stressor or event, completing paperwork is not. Going to a home where you have previously been threatened (unless threatened with death), while it may be very worrying, would not, by itself, be a traumatic event.

By analogy, events can also be viewed as traumatic to an organization if they are seriously threatening. For example, severe budget cuts resulting in layoffs, or the death of a child receiving agency services followed by a public outcry for "heads to roll" and subsequent firings, threatens "serious injury" to the organization and its integrity.

Who's on First? Distinguishing Primary and Secondary Traumatic Stressors

Both the DSM-IV-TR and now the DSM5™ descriptions of traumatic events appear to include both primary and secondary traumatic exposure, although this is not always a clear-cut distinction (APA 2000, 2013). When a worker experiences a traumatic event, such as being attacked or threatened with severe injury, this is primary exposure. When the worker hears or views traumatic material (say, a description of abuse during a child interview or perhaps photographs in a medical report), this is regarded as secondary exposure to a traumatic event (Figley 1995; McCann and Pearlman 1990), with the exposure occurring through the empathic bond the worker has with that child. Child welfare workers clearly face exposure to both primary and secondary traumatic stressors (Catherall 1995; Horwitz 2006).

Similarly, organizations can be seen to experience both primary and secondary traumatic stressors. The example above, of severe budget cuts and subsequent layoffs, is a primary trauma at the organizational level. A child death is an example of a secondary trauma for the agency and its staff, while at the same time it can be experienced as a primary trauma by the worker who had worked directly with the family. Catherall (1995) also states that when one person in an organization is exposed to primary traumatic events, everyone in the agency is at risk for secondary traumatic exposure. In any work setting where traumatic events are the day-to-day work of the agency, such as child welfare, firefighting, emergency medicine, or police work, repeated primary exposure for some, and secondary exposure for all, is to be expected.

Secondary Traumatic Stress, Compassion Fatigue, and Vicarious Trauma

In the research on secondary traumatic stress, three terms have been used to describe the exposure to and impact of secondary traumatic stressors. These terms—vicarious traumatization (McCann and Pearlman 1990), compassion fatigue (Figley 1995), and secondary traumatic stress (Figley 1995; Stamm 1995)—have similar meanings.

McCann and Pearlman (1990) coined the term "vicarious traumatization" to describe the potential impact on therapists of their clients' disclosure of traumatic experiences. Saakvitne and Pearlman (1995) described vicarious traumatization as "the transformation of the therapist's or helper's inner experience as a result of empathic engagement with survivor clients and their trauma experience" (p.25). Figley (1995) used the term "compassion fatigue" when referring to the impact of client trauma on workers, calling it "the cost of caring." Compassion fatigue was then further divided into secondary traumatic stress (comparable to vicarious trauma) and burnout. The term Secondary Traumatic Stress (STS) will be used in this chapter to refer to the traumatic impact of secondary exposure to clients' traumatic material.

Empathy is an essential component for good connection with clients, whether they are children or adults. Figley (1995) noted that empathy forms the pathway by which people who work with traumatized clients become vulnerable to compassion fatigue. The impact of STS was described as being similar to PTSD, except that the traumatic exposure was secondary and not primary and that resulting symptoms might not be as severe for the worker as for the client. However, the risk posed by multiple exposures to client traumatic material was noted as increasing the risk for STS. In Barbara's story above, her traumatic symptoms intensified over time as her exposure to the trauma of others built up.

The concept of secondary traumatic stress was developed in the context of psychotherapy, where almost all the traumatic exposure psychotherapists experience is of a secondary nature. Child welfare workers are faced with primary traumatic events in addition to hearing or reading accounts containing traumatic material from clients and others (secondary traumatic events), so that their overall exposure is likely to be higher than that of psychotherapists working in an office setting. The next section explores some of the major risk and protective factors for the development of PTSD.

Risk Factors

Risk factors for PTSD fall into several categories. Some factors relate to the stressor, some to the person experiencing the stressor, and some to the person's environment.

Stressor-Related Risk Factors

There are different types of stressor-related risk factors for developing traumatic stress. These are also referred to as peritraumatic risk factors (APA 2013). Those discussed here include the severity and type of event and whether the stressor is of an interpersonal nature or not. Most people who are exposed to a single traumatic event do not develop PTSD (Kessler et al. 1995). However, not all traumatic stressors have the same probability of resulting in PTSD. Some types of events, such as those involving interpersonal violence (as in childhood sexual abuse), have a much stronger association with PTSD. Additionally, the PTSD symptoms themselves may be more severe for those experiencing interpersonal traumatic events than for those experiencing non-interpersonal traumatic events, such as an automobile accident or a natural disaster (Kilpatrick et al. 2003). Using data from the National Comorbidity Survey, Kessler and et al. (1995) reported that the probability of developing PTSD after a rape is much higher than after a threat with a weapon, which in turn is higher than having witnessed a traumatic event. Deykin and Buka (1997), in a study examining risk factors for PTSD among chemically dependent adolescents, reported that approximately three quarters of both male and female youth met criteria for PTSD following rape.

In both the National Comorbidity Study and the Deykin and Buka (1997) study, females were much more likely to have been raped than males. So it is important to note that while rape may operate similarly as a risk factor for males and females, females have a much higher risk of experiencing rape than do males. This may explain, in part, the higher lifetime prevalence of PTSD in women. The first general population and community studies in the 1980s reported that one fifth to one quarter of women and approximately one sixth of men had experienced sexual abuse during childhood (Finkelhor et al. 1990; Russell 1984). While child maltreatment appears to be quite underreported (Theodore et al. 2005), in 2011, child protective services in the United States reported that a little over 9 % of the approximately 677,000 substantiated reports of child maltreatment involved child sexual abuse (United States Department of Health and Human Services 2012), indicating a substantial number of child sexual abuse victims within public child welfare.

Risk Factors Related to the Individual Exposed

Not everyone is impacted in exactly the same way by a particular stressor, and individual factors account for some of the variability in the probability of developing PTSD following traumatic exposure. Risk factors related to the person exposed include their gender, their relationship to the perpetrator (in the case of interpersonal trauma), the extent of their previous traumatic exposure, and their history of previous mental health problems.

Gender

Gender appears to operate as a risk factor to increase the probability of developing PTSD following certain types of traumatic events. In the National Comorbidity Survey (Kessler et al. 1995), women were significantly more likely to report PTSD symptoms than men after being threatened with a weapon, physically attacked, sexually molested, or physically abused as a child. The overall risk for women exposed to all kinds of traumatic experience of developing PTSD was more than twice as high for women as for men. Similarly, among youth in the Deykin and Buka (1997) study, the overall risk for female youth of developing PTSD following traumatic experience was 1.7 times higher than for male youth. As noted in the previous section, in addition to being more likely than males to develop PTSD following certain traumatic events, women are also more likely to experience events with a high probability of causing PTSD for anyone. In other words, women appear both to have a higher exposure risk to events that cause PTSD and to be more vulnerable to developing PTSD.

The relevance of gender as a risk for the child welfare workforce is that most child welfare workers are women (Levine 2005). Also, child welfare workers are more likely to experience actual or attempted violence than other social services workers (American Federation of State, County, and Municipal Employees 1998; Newhill and Wexler 1997). Newhill and Wexler (1997) reported that children and youth services social workers (including child welfare workers) in California and Pennsylvania were significantly more likely to report having been threatened with violence, or to have experienced an attempted or actual attack, than were social workers in other areas of practice.

Multiple Exposures to Traumatic Events

It matters greatly whether the stressor is experienced once only or on multiple occasions. Terr (1991) formulated the concepts of Type I and Type II childhood trauma, based on a distinction between a single incident and prolonged or repeated childhood suffering. Exposure to traumatic events appears to be relatively common in the United States. In the National Comorbidity Survey (Kessler et al. 1995), 61 % of men and 51 % of women reported having experienced at least one event, while 34 % of men and 25 % of women reported having experienced two or more traumatic events.

Exposure to one or more previous traumatic events increases the risk for PTSD from later traumatic events (Breslau et al. 1999). Additionally, experiencing multiple previous events increases the risk for subsequent PTSD more than a single previous event does, as demonstrated by Breslau and colleagues in a general population study, the Detroit Area Survey of Trauma (1999). This is particularly so for those who experienced assaultive violence in childhood (Breslau et al. 1999). Similarly, Green et al. (2000), in looking at a large sample of female college students, reported that previous exposure to multiple traumatic events was associated with more severe PTSD symptoms and that those with previous exposure to multiple traumatic events which were interpersonal in nature had even worse PTSD symptoms. Early separation from parents has also been reported as a risk factor for developing PTSD (Breslau et al. 1991).

Pearlman and MacIan (1995) found that a personal history of exposure to traumatic events in therapists who worked with trauma survivors predicted more negative effects than no personal history of trauma exposure. Nelson-Gardell and Harris (2003), in the first study of secondary trauma in child welfare workers, found, not surprisingly, that a history of childhood maltreatment was significantly associated with STS and that having experienced more than one type of childhood maltreatment raised the risk for later STS even more. In this study, childhood emotional abuse and emotional neglect emerged as the strongest childhood maltreatment risk factors.

A similar study looking specifically at child welfare workers found that workers who had less frequent and fewer recent traumatic events reported lower levels of distress (Regehr et al. 2004). It should be noted that recent work by Breslau et al. (2008), reporting the results of a prospective cohort study, suggests that subsequent exposures to traumatic events only increase the risk for PTSD if the previous event or events also resulted in PTSD.

Existing evidence suggests that the impact of exposure to traumatic events is cumulative. Contrary to what one might expect, people do not appear to become desensitized or accustomed to trauma, as Barbara's story illustrates. In looking at the effects of traumatic exposure over the previous 3 months on child welfare caseworkers and supervisors, Horwitz (2006) found that direct events were associated with more traumatic effects for caseworkers than for supervisors. However, secondary events during that time period were associated with greater traumatic stress effects for supervisors. Since prior personal and professional trauma histories were not taken into account, it is not possible to determine what effect these histories may have had. Supervisors have their own direct service and personal exposure history; the effects of this history are perhaps compounded by secondary exposure from hearing about cases and the traumatic events impacting their supervisees. Since the empathic bond is regarded as the pathway which makes workers vulnerable to secondary trauma, this may be the equivalent of a superhighway for supervisors. The empathic supervisor/supervisee bond exposes supervisors not only to the events and feelings experienced by their supervisees but also to those supervisees' secondary exposure to events experienced by the many children whose cases they supervise.

In turn, these findings suggest that since child welfare workers face continued exposure to traumatic events, both primary and secondary, it is extremely important for workers to develop good self-care skills and for agencies to provide an environment that mitigates the impact of these multiple exposures, together with access and referrals to supports as needed. Horwitz (2006) calls for the recognition and validation of reactions to secondary as well as primary traumatic events, on the basis that secondary traumatic events may be less obvious than primary traumatic events. Supervision provides an ideal opportunity for such recognition and validation, as well as referral to any needed additional resources, as can be seen in Barbara's case.

Mental Health and Personality Factors

Breslau et al. (1991) reported that neuroticism, preexisting anxiety or depression, and a family history of anxiety were associated with a higher risk of developing PTSD following exposure. Neuroticism, in this context, is a personality trait which involves a tendency to worry, be moody, and to have stronger emotional reactions than a situation is thought to call for (Eysenck and Eysenck 1975). In samples of those already suffering from PTSD, rumination and negative interpretations of intrusive symptoms of PTSD were found to be associated with more severe outcomes (Clohessy and Ehlers 1999; Ehlers et al. 1998). One may also speculate that those who stay in child welfare have a tendency to be independent and self-reliant. Child welfare workers may go alone and unarmed to homes that the police visit in pairs and carrying firearms (CWERP 2012). This self-reliance, reinforced by the nature of child welfare work, may in turn lead to a personal expectation of being able to manage one's own response to traumatic events without seeking help.

Risk Factors Related to Social Environment

In their meta-analysis, Brewin et al. (2000) reported that lack of social support was one of the strongest predictors of PTSD severity. Ullman (2007) reported that in a sample of adult survivors of childhood sexual abuse, the experience of negative reactions to their disclosure in childhood predicted more severe PTSD symptoms as adults. While not established empirically as a risk factor for child welfare workers, Pryce, Shackleford, and Pryce (2007) describe the negative impact of "dismissal and disbelief trauma." These authors relate reports from workers of not being believed by judges, police officers, and attorneys when relating details of abuse. Child welfare workers' experience of disbelief has been compared to that of abused children when they are not believed (Morrison 1992).

Protective Factors

Broadly speaking, protective factors are those which reduce the probability of negative outcomes in a given situation, although there are various models of exactly how protective factors may achieve this and debate about precise definitions (Masten et al. 2009). The narrowest definition of a protective factor restricts the protection to situations involving actual adversity. For example, wearing a life jacket would be protective only if the wearer fell into the water; it is not protective until the adverse situation arises. Other factors which may help mitigate the effects of adversity (in this case traumatic exposure) are known as promotive factors or assets (Masten et al. 2009). These protective and promotive factors help individuals to be resilient, to "struggle well" and persevere in the face of adversity (Walsh 2006). For convenience, the term "protective" will be used in this chapter for both promotive and protective factors.

Individual Protective Factors

Protective factors include having a healthy cognitive coping style. In their work with American male and female Vietnam veterans, King et al. (1998) identified personal "hardiness" as reducing the impact of traumatic exposure. The construct of hardiness has three main elements, namely, a sense of control over one's life (a high internal locus of control), an openness to viewing change as a challenge, and the tendency to commit to or involve oneself deeply in whatever one is doing (Kobasa et al. 1982).

Protective Factors Related to Social Environment

Social support has been identified as a factor which ameliorates the impact of traumatic stress in Vietnam veterans (King et al. 1998). Catherall (1995) recommends that organizations which work with traumatic situations prepare in advance to address traumatic stress by planning appropriately and then educating, empowering, and supporting staff as needed. Catherall (1995) applies to the "family" of the organization the same elements described by Figley (1989) as providing a healing environment for family members affected by traumatic stress. These include recognition that the stressors are real and legitimate so that the problem is acknowledged by the agency (not blamed on the individual), clearly expressed support, a high degree of cohesion (so the individual worker is not isolated), open and effective communication, and an approach to the problem that seeks to find solutions, not assign blame. While there is little research evidence to directly support this approach, it is logically attractive. Indeed, this sounds very much like the strengths-based, solution-focused approach recommended for child welfare clients, applied here, in a parallel process, to workers' traumatic exposure. It is worth noting that Horwitz (2006) did not find that traumatic effects were mitigated by job support or job satisfaction. Building on this work, further research is needed which takes into account long-term traumatic exposure.

Glisson (2007), in describing organizational climate in child welfare agencies, points out that the social context of an agency determines the psychological impact of the working environment on individual workers, as well as the services to children and families. When workers share similar perceptions of the impact of the work environment upon them, this is termed organizational climate. Glisson (2007) describes child welfare agency climates as being either "stressful" or "engaged." In cultures characterized as engaged, workers describe higher levels of personal accomplishment, being able to stay personally involved in their work, and being concerned about their clients. In stressful climates, workers report higher levels of emotional exhaustion, being overloaded with work, experiencing conflicting work demands, and being unable to get everything done (Glisson and Green 2011). Importantly, climate appears to affect not only the workers themselves but also the children they serve. Children served in organizations seen as engaged have significantly better outcomes than children served in organizations described as stressful (Glisson and Green 2011).

Warning Signs and Symptoms

Individual Warning Signs and Symptoms

While traumatic events may have a cumulative effect that eventually leads to acute reactions, more subtle warning signs may sometimes appear before any obvious symptoms of PTSD are evident. Having satisfied the requirements of Criterion A (the event or events), the symptoms of PTSD fall into four main categories, namely, (a) intrusion symptoms, including reexperiencing or reliving of traumatic events (Criterion B), (b) persistent avoidance of reminders of the event or events, (c) negative alterations in cognitions and mood (Criterion D), and (d) alterations in arousal and reactivity (Criterion E) (APA 2013) (see Table 9.1 for details). For a diagnosis of PTSD, these symptoms must persist for more than a month and cause "clinically significant distress or impairment in social, occupational, or other important areas of functioning" (APA 2013, p. 272). In Acute Stress Disorder, the symptoms are similar and must last for at least 3 days, but not more than 1 month (APA 2013).

Criterion D in the DSM-5™ now includes several elements which were included as associated descriptive features in the DSM-IV-TR (APA 2000; APA 2000, 2013). Criterion D includes exaggerated negative beliefs (such as feeling permanently damaged or worthless); persistent guilt, shame, fear, and the like; and persistent distorted cognitions (such as inappropriate self-blame). The addition of Criterion D appears to bring PTSD in the DSM-5™ somewhat closer to Complex Trauma or Complex PTSD, as formulated by Herman (1992a), to take account of the multifaceted effects of prolonged and repeated interpersonal trauma.

Even if someone does not meet full diagnostic criteria for PTSD, suffering caused by subsyndromal symptoms can still be highly distressing and has been found in a population study to increase the risk for suicidal ideation and impairment, even after controlling for major depressive disorder (Marshall et al. 2001). There are various instruments available for assessing the presence of PTSD symptoms.

Table 9.1 Criteria B, C, D, and E of PTSD

B. Presence of one (or more) of the following intrusion symptoms associated with the traumatic event(s), beginning after the traumatic events occurred:

1. Recurrent, involuntary, and intrusive distressing memories of the traumatic event(s)[*].
2. Recurrent distressing dreams in which the content and/or affect of the dream is related to the traumatic event(s)[**].
3. Dissociative reactions (e.g., flashbacks) in which the individual feels or acts as if the traumatic events were recurring. (Such reactions may occur on a continuum, with the most extreme expression being a complete loss of awareness of present surroundings)[***].
4. Intense or prolonged psychological distress at exposure to internal or external cues that symbolize or resemble an aspect of the traumatic event(s)
5. Marked physiological reactions to internal or external cues that symbolize or resemble an aspect of the traumatic event(s)

C. Persistent avoidance of stimuli associated with the traumatic event(s), beginning after the traumatic event(s) occurred as evidenced by one (or both) of the following:

1. Avoidance of or efforts to avoid distressing memories, thoughts, or feelings about or closely associated with the traumatic event(s)
2. Avoidance of or efforts to avoid external reminders (people, places, conversations, activities, objects, situations) that arouse distressing memories, thoughts, or feelings about or closely associated with the traumatic event(s)

D. Negative alterations in cognitions and mood associated with the traumatic event(s), beginning or worsening after the traumatic event(s) occurred, as evidenced by two (or more) of the following:

1. Inability to remember an important aspect of the traumatic event(s) (typically due to dissociative amnesia and not to other factors such as head injury, alcohol, or drugs)
2. Persistent and exaggerated negative beliefs or expectations about oneself, others, or the world (e.g., "I am bad," "No one can be trusted," "The world is completely dangerous," "My whole nervous system is permanently ruined")
3. Persistent, distorted cognitions about the cause or consequences of the traumatic event(s) that lead the individual to blame himself/herself or others
4. Persistent negative emotional state (e.g., fear, horror, anger, guilt, or shame)
5. Markedly diminished interest or participation in significant activities
6. Feelings of detachment or estrangement from others
7. Persistent inability to experience positive emotions (e.g., inability to experience happiness, satisfaction, or loving feelings)

E. Marked alterations in arousal or reactivity associated with the traumatic event(s), beginning or worsening after the traumatic event(s) occurred, as evidenced by two (or more) of the following:

1. Irritable behavior and angry outbursts (with little or no provocation) typically expressed as physical aggression toward people or objects
2. Reckless or self-destructive behavior
3. Hypervigilance
4. Exaggerated startle response
5. Problems with concentration
6. Sleep disturbance (e.g., difficulty falling or staying asleep or restless sleep)

APA 2013, pp. 271–272

[*]*Note*: In children older than 6 years, repetitive play may occur in which themes or aspects of the traumatic event(s) are expressed

[**]*Note*: In children, there may be frightening dreams without recognizable content

[***]*Note*: In children, trauma-specific reenactment may occur in play

One of the best known clinical measures is the Trauma Symptom Inventory (TSI). The TSI is a 100-item instrument, developed for clinical use (rather than research use) to measure traumatic symptoms related to exposure to interpersonal trauma (in childhood or adulthood), combat-related trauma, and nonpersonal traumatic experiences (such as accidents and natural disasters). It has good psychometric properties (Briere et al. 1995) and includes some of the other features now included in Criterion D (referred to above), such as altered beliefs.

A recommended resource for assessing compassion fatigue (or STS), compassion satisfaction, and burnout is the ProQOL instrument, revised by Stamm (2010) from the Compassion Fatigue Self-Test for Practitioners, originally developed by Figley (Figley and Stamm 1996). ProQOL is a self-assessment tool with three subscales, namely, compassion fatigue, compassion satisfaction, and burnout.

Organizational Warning Signs and Symptoms

There has been growing support for the view that organizations and whole societies (as well as individuals) can suffer from traumatic stress in ways that are analogous to individuals (Bloom 1997; Herman 1992b; Hormann and Vivian 2005). These traumatized systems lead to challenging and unsupportive work environments, which can then compound the effects of the work itself. See Table 9.2 below for examples of what signs and symptoms could be present for an individual and what those signs and symptoms might look like for an organization.

One nonproprietary resource for organizational self-evaluation related to trauma-informed (T-I) care is that developed by the National Center on Family Homelessness (NCFH), originally for use in residential settings serving homeless women and children. The Trauma-Informed Organizational Self-Assessment should be completed by every staff member and by consumers in an organization to give information about how the organization operates from all perspectives. The self-assessment is part of an overall organization toolkit intended for use in applying the principles of T-I care for consumers (Guarino et al. 2009). The NCFH has also developed a companion volume addressing whether an organization is trauma-informed and supportive from the workers' perspective (Volk et al. 2008). There are several self-assessment tools that could be used to reflect the perspective of child welfare workers in relation to their own experiences of whether the organization responds to them in a way that is trauma-informed.

Individual Self-Care

In what is often regarded as the classic work on self-care for STS, Saakvitne and Pearlman (1995) asked the question "What transforms vicarious traumatization?" These authors suggest that there are two fundamental modes of addressing STS.

Table 9.2 Examples of warning signs for individuals and organizations affected by traumatic events

Posttraumatic Stress Disorder symptoms, associated features	Examples of warning signs for traumatized individuals	Examples of warning signs for traumatized organizations
Criterion A: Traumatic event(s)	Example: maltreatment death of child served by agency, followed by critical press coverage and community calls for worker and management terminations	
Criterion B: Intrusions	Worker has frequent distressing images of dead child and feels like he/she is reliving the event; nightmares of the event	The death overshadows everything in the agency; feels like working in a "war zone"
Criterion C: Avoidance	Worker avoids talking about event and avoids driving near house where the death happened	No discussion of feelings or reactions (which may be seen as a "luxury"); no reflective supervision; a "task" focus on work
Criterion D: Alterations in cognitions and mood	Worker feels detached and disconnected from others; persistent feelings of guilt ("I should have been able to do something"); worker feels that everyone is dangerous	Exaggerated negative beliefs about parents ("Most people don't deserve children"); work environment feels unsafe; persistent atmosphere of fear and anger in the agency; workforce feels shame, despair, or hopelessness; loss of trust in colleagues, management
Criterion E: Alterations in arousal and reactivity	Worker has outbursts of anger; exaggerated startle response—overreacts to small things; difficulty concentrating	Outbursts of anger by workers/management; firings of those handling the case and their direct superiors; hypervigilance for problems; overreaction to minor errors (adoption of "zero tolerance" policies)

These modes are (a) improving and maintaining self-care and (b) finding ways to transform the negative beliefs, loss of hope, or loss of meaning that can result from the work.

Self-care involves taking care of basic needs such as proper nutrition, exercise, and sleep. Also included here are setting healthy limits (such as being able to say "no" sometimes to requests for help); nurturing oneself; finding time for play, relaxation, and activities that allow one to forget about work; and maintaining positive connections with others. Under the heading of transformation are four types of activity: (a) creating meaning, (b) infusing a current activity with meaning, (c) challenging negative beliefs, and (d) participating in community-building activities. Pearlman and Saakvitne (1995) recommended regular, confidential, professional, and frequent T-I consultation for therapists exposed to client trauma in the course of their work. The child welfare equivalent is T-I-reflective supervision. In a similar vein, Pearlman and Caringi (2009) have also stressed the importance of personal responsibility for self-care and working reflectively.

One introductory resource for self-care is "The Cost of Caring" (Perry 2003), a web-based self-paced learning course giving an introduction to what STS is, including case examples, and how it occurs. Information is included on good supervisory practices and how people who work with traumatized children can take care of themselves, following the principles and recommendations originally laid out by Pearlman and Saakvitne (1995). In "What About You? A Workbook for Those Who Work with Others" (Volk et al. 2008), some of the fundamental recommendations for self-care include proper nutrition, adequate physical exercise and sleep, and relaxation exercises. While this may sound simplistic, it is important to prioritize and schedule self-care. There is always more work, so if self-care is at the bottom of the list, then there is unlikely to be time remaining for it. When self-care is a priority, workers are more likely to have the energy and emotional stamina to manage their stress more effectively.

The Role of Supervisors

Supervisors are in a position to provide work-based social support by acknowledging the difficulty of particular events or situations, showing concern for the worker's distress, and making referrals for more assistance when the need exceeds the role of the supervisor. This presupposes a willingness and ability to provide support, which may be compromised by the supervisor's own traumatic experience, together with the need to comply with the formal requirements of meeting strict timelines, completing paperwork, and preparing for court. In focus groups held with child welfare workers receiving graduate social work education, themes emerged of both the traumatic nature of the work and the lack of recognition and support by supervisors, in part due to a focus on task completion (CWERP 2011). Those students who felt unsupported were also aware of the irony of being asked to provide a strengths-based, solution-focused approach for clients while feeling as though they were denied the same thing as workers.

However, it is important to remember that while supervisors should provide support, they may need to receive support as well. Although supervisors are no longer going out on all the calls that frontline workers are, they are exposed to all the traumatic material brought back by these workers. One implication of this (in addition to the frequent problem of high caseloads) is that supervisors also need a support system in place.

The finding that negative interpretations of intrusive symptoms of PTSD are associated with more severe outcomes (Clohessy and Ehlers 1999; Ehlers et al. 1998) suggests a need for assistance in normalizing and reinterpreting intrusive symptoms. While this can certainly be addressed in the realm of individual therapy, supervisors can also play a role in child welfare by normalizing workers' reactions to traumatic exposure on the job. Supervisors are ideally placed to check in with workers to address issues of traumatic exposure and stress in the course of regular supervision. Symptoms of traumatic stress are not always obvious to others, so it is important to have this become standard procedure. Supervisors can validate workers' responses, support them in appropriate self-care strategies, and also act as gatekeepers in suggesting referrals to clinical care when STS threatens to overwhelm the worker's ability to function in the workplace. In the Horwitz (2006) study, experienced workers reported that they received less support from inside their agency than inexperienced workers did. Given the cumulative nature of traumatic exposure, supervisors would be well advised to provide continued support to their more experienced workers, who may not show obvious signs of distress.

One of the risks for child welfare workers experiencing STS is that their judgment may be clouded because of previous experience and altered belief systems. In these instances, where the supervisor is aware of a worker's rush to judgment based on faulty assumptions (perhaps because of reminders of previous severe cases), the supervisor may use reflective supervision techniques to help the worker become aware of his or her own thinking errors or biases. One recent study (Regehr et al. 2010) reported that child welfare caseworkers with greater exposure to traumatic events tended to assess child abuse risk as lower than workers with less traumatic exposure. Workers with more traumatic symptoms assessed risk as lower on one, but not all, of three standardized measures of risk used in the study. This is a highly concerning report, suggesting the possibility that children who are at risk for abuse may not be accurately identified (by those with more traumatic exposure) or alternatively that children with a lower risk for abuse may be inaccurately identified as being at higher risk than they actually are (by those with less traumatic exposure). Again, further research is needed to investigate how assessment instruments behave according to raters' traumatic exposure, as well as the many other factors which are relevant to the assessment of child risk. (Please see Chap. 10 for a fuller description of reflective supervision.)

Organizational Approaches

Organizational approaches to trauma may be best understood as existing along continua at three levels, depending upon how the organization defines "the problem." The problem, namely, trauma, may be organizationally viewed as existing at one or more of the following levels: (a) the client level, (b) the worker level, or (c) the organizational level (see Table 9.3). When trauma-related issues are not recognized at a particular level, then the organization may be said to be "trauma blind" at that level. An organization may see the problem as relating just to clients or just to clients and workers. In these cases, the responsibility for providing T-I services to clients or for workers' self-care typically resides with the worker, and a comprehensive organizational approach is likely to be lacking. When problems arise, they are likely to be seen as related to the individual worker's performance; in this situation, analysis of the problem as belonging to the organization collectively is less likely to occur. When an organization sees the problem as relating to the entire organizational culture, then both client and worker well-being are more likely to be taken into account, and the organization is more likely to take responsibility for the organizational changes that will best support the well-being of both clients and workers.

Table 9.3 Organizational responses to traumatic stress at three levels

	Trauma blind	Trauma aware	Organizational changes	Responsibility level	Quality assurance
Client-level problem	No action	Planning/ preparing	Workers trained on client trauma; T-I service development	Caseworker, supervisor, program	Client services
Worker-level problem	No action	Planning/ preparing	Workers trained on own trauma and self-care	Individual worker	None
Organizational culture problem	No action	Planning/ preparing	Comprehensive trauma training and transfer of learning; T-I services developed; T-I supervision and management mechanisms developed	Organization	Client services; supervisory processes

A Client-Level Problem

When the problem is seen only as one of client behavior, the organizational response is likely to initially be one of trauma blindness. Client behaviors are then not seen in the context of traumatic experience ("What happened to you?"), but rather as intentional and conscious actions ("What is wrong with you? What are you thinking?"). An example of this might be when a youth in residential treatment with a history of repeated sexual assault at night becomes violent when it is time for the lights to go out at bedtime. A trauma-blind program might interpret this as oppositional, "acting out" behavior rather than a person being triggered by a potent reminder of a traumatic experience.

The first step toward more compassionate and effective care for a trauma-blind organization is to train staff about traumatic stress as it relates to clients, in the hope that this will translate into a T-I response to clients. This relies on individual workers, who will vary in their ability and motivation to transfer what they learned into their practice behaviors. (Please see Chap. 8 for more information on how learning is transferred into practice.) The next phase for an organization which perceives trauma as a client-level problem is to develop T-I services. Responsibility may be viewed as existing at the program level, with frontline workers, supervisors, and the program manager being responsible for implementing T-I services and possibly reporting trauma-related client outcomes to management and/or funders.

A Worker-Level Problem

The implementation of T-I services for clients does not, of itself, recognize or address the issue of STS for the organization's workforce. If trauma is recognized as a worker-level issue, though still not embraced as an organizational-culture-level concern, then training may be offered to workers. Informal support networks are likely to exist already, and more formal peer support meetings may also be arranged when worker STS is recognized by the organization (CWERP 2011). At this level of attention, the problem of worker STS is addressed by the organization, but still "belongs" with individual workers and supervisors. So in Barbara's case, the organization recognizes her traumatic exposure and may also recognize the evidence of her STS, but still sees it only as her responsibility to get the help she needs, perhaps by accessing an Employment Assistance Program (EAP) so that she can function appropriately and effectively. At this level of recognition, organizational culture changes are not considered or implemented.

An Organizational-Level Problem

Once an organization recognizes that its culture impacts not only client services but also the well-being and effectiveness of workers, then the organization may consider comprehensive organizational culture change. Such change goes beyond adding a new program or sending staff to trainings; it impacts every person, every system, and every program in the organization. It requires leadership commitment, modeling, and allocation of sufficient resources to implement a new philosophy about how all employees and clients come into contact with each other (Bloom 1997; Farragher 2011). The organization takes responsibility for cultural change and workers share in responsibility for change; appropriate services are provided and self-care is encouraged. Ideally, such cultural change includes continuous feedback mechanisms and quality assurance mechanisms to support safety for clients and the workforce.

There are various resources available to support the development of T-I services; these often include information on workers' self-care. A recommended list is included in Table 9.4. Another resource is the National Center for Trauma-Informed Care (NCTIC), which is located within the Substance Abuse and Mental Health Services Administration. The mission of the NCTIC is to provide technical assistance, build awareness of T-I care, and promote implementation of T-I practices in programs and services (NCTIC n.d.).

The National Child Traumatic Stress Network provides detailed training resources; the Child Welfare Trauma Training Toolkit (National Child Traumatic Stress Network 2008) is designed for use by all child welfare workers to increase their knowledge about the impact of traumatic stress on child-welfare-involved children. The toolkit includes case vignettes and activities and is intended for use with administrators, clinicians, caseworkers, and other direct service staff. Module 6 of the toolkit, Managing Personal and Professional Stress, addresses STS and covers

Table 9.4 Recommended resources

Name and web address	Available materials
ProQOL http://compassionfatigue.org/ pages/ProQOLManualOct05.pdf	Measure of compassion satisfaction, compassion fatigue, and burnout (individual)
National Child Traumatic Stress Network (NCTSN) http://www. nctsn.org	Impact of traumatic experience on children ("Child Welfare Trauma Training Toolkit." Click on "Products," then "NCTSN Products"); self-care materials for workers (Module 6)
National Center for Trauma-Informed Care (NCTIC) http://www.samhsa.gov/nctic	Information and technical assistance on trauma-informed practices in programs and organizations
The ChildTrauma Academy http://www.childtrauma.org	Impact of traumatic experience on children; self-care materials for individuals; ("The Cost of Caring." Click on "Training," then "CTA University")
The Sanctuary Model® http://www.sanctuaryweb.com	Materials relating to creating a trauma-informed organizational culture
The National Center on Family Homelessness http://www.homeless.samhsa.gov http://www.familyhomelessness.org http://www.familyhomelessness.org/ media/90.pdf 508.center4si.com/SelfCareforCare Givers.pdf	Materials for developing T-I services for clients (Trauma-Informed Organizational Toolkit); self-care materials for workers. (*What About You?: A Workbook for Those Who Work with Others*)

the following key learning points: The child welfare profession has the potential for STS, STS is distinct from burnout, child welfare workers may experience similar reactions to the traumatized children with whom they work, STS can affect workers' ability to manage stress, and lastly, workers need to have their own plan for addressing STS. The training includes self-care strategies and skills and is free of charge when downloaded from the website.

The Trauma-Informed Organizational Toolkit (Guarino et al. 2009) provides tools for organizational self-assessment and program adaptation. A "User's Guide" is included, giving more information about the provision of T-I care. Lastly, a "How-To Manual for Creating Organizational Change" is included, giving concrete, step-by-step instructions. Although the Trauma-Informed Organizational Toolkit was written for organizations which provide services to homeless families, these agencies face many of the same challenges as child welfare agencies and may share the same clients. This resource is also available free of charge as a download.

Addressing all three levels described above is the Sanctuary Model® (Bloom 1997), which is an emerging practice model based on trauma theory. The model is designed to help organizations build a T-I organizational culture for both clients and staff and addresses four fundamental domains which are impacted in a traumatized person's or organization's life. These domains are (a) safety, (b) emotions, (c) loss, and (d) future, for which the acronym SELF is used. One of the assumptions of this model is that any problem arising in a treatment setting will fit into one of these domains and that accurately defining the problem is one of the first steps in making that problem manageable.

In addition to the potentially traumatic nature of day-to-day child welfare work, individual critical incidents, such as a widely publicized child death, may impact the agency and all its workers. Dickinson and Comstock (2009) recommend a Critical Incident Response (CIR)-style intervention following such discrete incidents. Attridge and Vandepol (2009), in reviewing both published studies and anecdotal accounts of CIR, describe the potential financial benefits of using CIR responses, including reductions in the cost of health care, disability, and workers' compensation claims and reduced worker turnover.

One example of CIR is the SAFE-R Model, based on principles of CIR developed by Everly and Mitchell (1997) and described by Dickinson and Comstock (2009). The goals of this intervention are stabilization and return to duty or referral for more assistance. The steps of the model are (a) removing the worker from the **S**timulus; (b) **A**cknowledging the situation, in terms of both the facts and the person's reactions; (c) **F**acilitation of understanding, including normalizing the person's responses; (d) **E**xplanation, including psychoeducation concerning stress and stress management; and (e) **R**estoration of independent function or **R**eferral for more assistance. Use of this model would not preclude ongoing organizational or supervisory attention to STS in the form of training and social support.

Conclusion

Traumatic stress, including STS, is an ongoing reality in child welfare work for both clients and workers. Workers have individual risks and face the likelihood of both primary and secondary traumatic exposure in the course of their everyday work. STS involves significant distress and is likely to affect the quality of work, as well as staff turnover. Approaches to the problem may occur at the client level, the worker level, and the organizational level. Since the problem affects an entire organizational system and all its members, organizational-level approaches, while time-consuming and initially costly, may be the most promising in providing relief from suffering and may be more cost-effective in the long run. Ample research evidence exists concerning the risks and impact of STS, and materials providing approaches to STS are becoming increasingly available. Evidence of effectiveness of these approaches is beginning to emerge and will hopefully continue to grow, showing the way forward in dealing with one of the major concerns in the field of child welfare.

Tips for Workers: New and Old
- Prioritize self-care. When you do, you are better prepared to meet the challenges of your work. It is never too late to start taking care of yourself, even if you have not always done so.
- From time to time, check on how well you are taking care of yourself. You can use a resource such as the Self-Assessment Tool: Self-Care or the Self-Care and

Relationships Checklist from *What About You?* on pages 10 and 23, respectively (Volk et al. 2008).

- Recognize that your work is emotionally taxing and that deep feelings are appropriate and to be expected.
- Know that the best way to manage these intense feelings is with self-care and appropriate support rather than by losing the empathy that makes you a good child welfare professional.
- Be familiar with the symptoms of PTSD and Acute Stress and seek appropriate support, including professional care, when acute stress symptoms do not resolve within a few weeks. You can use the ProQOL instrument to find out if you are experiencing symptoms of Acute Stress or PTSD (Stamm 2010).
- Spend time with colleagues, friends, and family who support your self-care efforts. See the tips on page 28 of *What About You?* (Volk et al. 2008).
- Minimize your time with colleagues or others who are not supportive of or are hostile to your self-care efforts.

Tips for Supervisors

All of the above, and:

- Check in with your supervisees about their well-being during supervision and acknowledge particularly difficult situations as they occur. Remember to include more experienced workers as well as those who don't show any outward signs of distress.
- From time to time, take a few minutes to find out how you may be perceived by supervisees. If your organization does this with a regular assessment of agency climate process, then this information may be available to you from this source, if collected by unit. You can also use a self-check resource such as the consumer version of the Organizational Assessment developed at the National Center on Family Homelessness (Guarino et al. 2009). As a supervisor, this tool enables you to assess your organization around domains such as support for staff development, creating a safe and supportive environment, assessing and planning services, and involving consumers.

Tips for Administrators

All of the above, and:

- At regular intervals, assess what your organization does to support self-care and provide appropriate support to the workforce, as well as how workers feel about the climate of the workplace. You can use a resource such as the Organizational Self-Care Checklist from *What About You?* (Volk et al. 2008) or the Children's Services Survey (Glisson and Hemmelgarn 1998).
- Examine agency climate in relation to staff turnover and client outcomes.
- Ensure that the information from assessments is used for supervisor and manager evaluations.
- Initiate or continue an agency-wide process of moving toward being a T-I agency at all three levels.

Questions for Discussion

1. Does Barbara shows signs of secondary traumatic stress and/or burnout?
2. How would you help Barbara become aware of her compassion satisfaction and/ or posttraumatic growth?
3. What are the barriers for organizations in implementing fully trauma-informed cultures?
4. What steps do organizations need to take in order to maintain a trauma-informed culture?

References

American Federation of State, County and Municipal Employees. (1998). *Double jeopardy: Caseworkers at risk helping at-risk kids.* Washington, DC: Author.
American Psychiatric Association. (2000). *Diagnostic and statistical manual of mental disorders (Revised* (4th ed.). Washington, DC: Author.
American Psychiatric Association. (2013). *Diagnostic and statistical manual of mental disorders* (5th ed.). Arlington, VA: Author.
Attridge, M., & Vandepol, R. (2009). The business case for workplace critical incident response: A literature review and some employed examples. *Journal of Workplace Behavioral Health, 25,* 132–145.
Bloom, S. L. (1997). *Creating sanctuary: Toward the evolution of sane societies.* New York, NY: Routledge.
Breslau, N., Chilcoat, H. D., Kessler, R. C., & Davis, G. C. (1999). Previous exposure to trauma and PTSD effects of subsequent trauma: Results from the Detroit Area Survey of Trauma. *American Journal of Psychiatry, 156*(6), 902–907.
Breslau, N., Davis, G. C., Andreski, P., & Peterson, E. (1991). Traumatic events and posttraumatic stress disorder in an urban population of young adults. *Archives of General Psychiatry, 48*(3), 216–222.
Breslau, N., Peterson, E. L., & Schultz, L. R. (2008). A second look at prior trauma and the posttraumatic stress disorder effects of subsequent trauma: A prospective epidemiological study. *Archives of General Psychiatry, 65*(4), 431–437.
Brewin, C. R., Andrews, B., & Valentine, J. D. (2000). Meta-analysis of risk factors for posttraumatic stress disorder in trauma-exposed adults. *Journal of Consulting and Clinical Psychology, 68*(5), 748–66.
Bride, B. E. (2007). Prevalence of secondary traumatic stress among social workers. *Social Work, 52*(1), 63–70.
Briere, J., Elliott, D. M., Harris, K., & Cotman, A. (1995). Trauma Symptom Inventory: Psychometrics and association with childhood and adult trauma in clinical samples. *Journal of Interpersonal Violence, 10*(4), 387–401.
Calhoun, L. G., & Tedeschi, R. G. (1998). Beyond recovery from trauma: Implications for clinical practice and research. *Journal of Social Issues, 54*(2), 357–372.
Catherall, D. R. (1995). Preventing institutional secondary traumatic stress disorder. In C. F. Figley (Ed.), *Compassion fatigue: Coping with secondary traumatic stress disorder in those who treat the traumatized* (pp. 232–247). New York, NY: Brunner/Mazel.
Chenot, D. (2011). The vicious cycle: Recurrent interactions among the media, politicians, the public, and child welfare services organizations. *Journal of Public Child Welfare, 5,* 167–184.
Child Welfare Education and Research Programs, School of Social Work, University of Pittsburgh. (2011). *2010–2011 Annual Report.* Pittsburgh, PA: Author.

Child Welfare Education and Research Programs, School of Social Work, University of Pittsburgh. (2012). *2011–2012 Annual Report*. Pittsburgh, PA: Author.

Clohessy, S., & Ehlers, A. (1999). PTSD symptoms, response to intrusive memories and coping in ambulance service workers. *British Journal of Clinical Psychology, 38*(3), 251–265.

Conrad, D., & Kellar-Guenther, Y. (2006). Compassion fatigue, burnout, and compassion satisfaction among Colorado child protection workers. *Child Abuse & Neglect, 30*(10), 1071–1080.

Deykin, E. Y., & Buka, S. L. (1997). Prevalence and risk factors for posttraumatic stress disorder among chemically dependent adolescents. *American Journal of Psychiatry, 154*(6), 752–757.

Dickinson, N., & Comstock, A. (2009). Getting and keeping the best people. In C. C. Potter & C. R. Brittain (Eds.), *Child welfare supervision* (pp. 241–261). Oxford University Press: New York.

Ehlers, A., Mayou, R. A., & Bryant, B. (1998). Psychological predictors of chronic posttraumatic stress disorder after motor vehicle accidents. *Journal of Abnormal Psychology, 107*(3), 508–519.

Episode 77—Brian Farragher: The Sanctuary Model: Changing the Culture of Care—It Begins with Me (part 1 of 2). (2011, August 8). *Living Proof Podcast Series*. [Audio Podcast] Retrieved from http://www.socialwork.buffalo.edu/podcast/episode.asp?ep=77

Everly, G. S., & Mitchell, J. T. (1997). *Critical Incident Stress Management (CISM). A new era and standard of care in crisis intervention*. Ellicott City, MD: Chevron Publishing.

Eysenck, H. J., & Eysenck, S. B. G. (1975). *Manual of the Eysenck Personality Questionnaire*. London: Hodder & Stoughton.

Figley, C. R. (1989). *Helping traumatized families*. San Francisco, CA: Jossey-Bass Publishers.

Figley, C. R. (Ed.). (1995). *Compassion fatigue: Coping with secondary traumatic stress disorder in those who treat the traumatized*. New York, NY: Brunner/Mazel.

Figley, C. R., & Stamm, B. H. (1996). Psychometric review of Compassion Fatigue Self Test. In B. H. Stamm (Ed.), *Measurement of stress, trauma, and adaptation*. Lutherville, MD: Sidran Press.

Finkelhor, D., Hotaling, G., Lewis, I. A., & Smith, C. (1990). Sexual abuse in a national survey of adult men and women: Prevalence, characteristics and risk factors. *Child Abuse and Neglect, 14*, 19–28.

Glisson, C. (2007). Assessing and changing organizational culture and climate for effective services. *Research on Social Work Practice, 17*(6), 736–747.

Glisson, C., & Green, P. (2011). Organizational climate, services and outcomes in child welfare systems. *Child Abuse & Neglect, 35*(8), 582–591.

Glisson, C., & Hemmelgarn, A. (1998). The effects of organizational climate and interorganizational coordination on the quality and outcomes of children's services systems. *Child Abuse and Neglect, 22*(5), 401–421.

Green, B. L., Goodman, L. A., Krupnick, J. L., Corcoran, C. B., Petty, R. M., Stockton, P., & Stern, N. (2000). Outcomes of single versus multiple trauma exposure in a screening sample. *Journal of Traumatic Stress, 13*(2), 271–286.

Guarino, K., Soares, P., Konnath, K., Clervil, R., & Bassuk, E. (2009). *Trauma-informed organizational toolkit*. Rockville: MD: Center for Mental Health and Substance Abuse Services Administration, and the Daniels Fund, the National Child Traumatic Stress Network, and the W. K. Kellogg Foundation. Retrived from http://www.homeless.samhsa.gov and http://www.familyhomelessness.org

Herman, J. (1992a). Complex PTSD: A syndrome in survivors of prolonged and repeated trauma. *Journal of Traumatic Stress, 5*(3), 377–391. doi:10.1002/jts.2490050305.

Herman, J. (1992b). *Trauma and recovery*. New York, NY: Basic Books.

Hillesum, E. (1985). *An interrupted life: The diaries of Etty Hillesum 1941–43*. New York, NY: Washington Square Press.

Hormann, S., & Vivian, P. (2005). Toward an understanding of traumatized organizations and how to intervene in them. *Traumatology, 11*(3), 159–169.

Horwitz, M. (1998). Social worker trauma: building resilience in child protection social workers. *Smith College Studies in Social Work, 68*(3), 363–377.

Horwitz, M. J. (2006). Work-related trauma effects in child protection social workers. *Journal of Social Service Research, 32*(3), 1–18.

Joseph, S. (2009). Growth following adversity: Positive psychological perspectives on posttraumatic stress. *Psychological Topics, 18*(2), 335–344.

Kessler, R. C., Sonnega, A., Bromet, E., Hughes, M., & Nelson, C. B. (1995). Posttraumatic stress disorder in the National Comorbidity Survey. *Archives of General Psychiatry, 52*, 1048–1060.

Kilpatrick, D. G., Ruggiero, K. J., Acierno, R., Saunders, B. E., Resnick, H. S., & Best, C. L. (2003). Violence and risk of PTSD, major depression, substance abuse/dependence, and comorbidity: Results from the National Survey of Adolescents. *Journal of Consulting and Clinical Psychology, 71*(4), 692–700.

King, L. A., King, D. W., Fairbank, J. A., Keane, T. M., & Adams, G. A. (1998). Resilience-recovery factors in post-traumatic stress disorder among female and male Vietnam veterans: Hardiness, postwar social support, and additional stressful life events. *Journal of Personality and Social Psychology, 74*(2), 420–434.

Kobasa, S. C., Maddi, S. R., & Kahn, S. (1982). Health and hardiness: A prospective study. *Journal of Personality and Social Psychology, 42*(1), 168–177.

Koeske, G. F., & Koeske, R. D. (1989). Construct validity of the Maslach Burnout Inventory. *Journal of Applied Behavioral Science, 25*(2), 131–144.

Levine, L. (2005). *The child welfare workforce: An overview*. Washington, DC: Library of Congress, Congressional Research Office. Retrieved from http://congressionalresearch.com/RL32690/document.php?study=The+Child+Welfare+Workforce+An+Overview

Linley, P. A., Joseph, S., & Goodfellow, B. (2008). Positive changes in outlook following trauma and their relationship to subsequent posttraumatic stress, depression, and anxiety. *Journal of Social and Clinical Psychology, 27*(8), 877–891.

Marshall, R. D., Olfson, M., Hellman, F., Blanco, C., Guardino, M., & Struening, E. L. (2001). Comorbidity, impairment, and suicidality in subthreshold PTSD. *American Journal of Psychiatry, 158*(9), 1467–1473.

Maslach, C. (1982). *Burnout: The cost of caring*. New York: Prentice-Hall.

Masten, A. S., Cutuli, J. J., Herbers, J. E., & Reed, M.-G. (2009). Resilience in development. In C. R. Snyder & S. J. Lopez (Eds.), *The Oxford handbook of positive psychology* (2nd ed.). New York, NY: Oxford University Press.

McCann, I. L., & Pearlman, L. A. (1990). Vicarious traumatization: A framework for understanding the psychological effects of working with victims. *Journal of Traumatic Stress, 3*(1), 131–149.

Morrison, M. (1992). The emotional effects of child welfare work on the worker. *Practice, 4*, 253–271.

National Center for Trauma-Informed Care (n.d.). Retrieved from http://www.samhsa.gov/nctic/

National Child Traumatic Stress Network (2008). Child Welfare Trauma Training Toolkit. Retrieved from http://www.nctsn.org/products/child-welfare-trauma-training-toolkit-2008

Nelson-Gardell, D., & Harris, D. (2003). Child abuse history, secondary traumatic stress, and child welfare workers. *Child Welfare, 82*(1), 5–26.

Newhill, C. E., & Wexler, S. (1997). Client violence towards children and youth services social workers. *Children and Youth Services Review, 19*(3), 195–212.

Pearlman, L. A., & Caringi, J. (2009). Living and working self-reflectively to address vicarious trauma. In C. A. Courtois & J. D. Ford (Eds.), *Treating complex traumatic stress disorders: An evidence-based guide* (pp. 202–224). New York: Guilford.

Pearlman, L., & MacIan, P. (1995). Vicarious traumatization: An empirical study of the effects of trauma work on trauma therapists. *Professional Psychology, Research and Practice, 26*(6), 558–565.

Pearlman, L. A., & Saakvitne, K. W. (1995). Treating therapists with vicarious traumatization and secondary traumatic stress disorder. In C. R. Figley (Ed.), *Coping with secondary traumatic stress disorder in those who treat the traumatized* (pp. 150–172). New York: Taylor & Francis.

Perry, B. D. (2010). *Surviving childhood: An introduction to the impact of trauma*. Houston, TX: Child Trauma Academy. Retrieved from http://www.childtrauma.org.

Perry, B. D. (2003). *The cost of caring: Secondary traumatic stress and the impact of working with high-risk children and their families.* Houston, TX: Child Trauma Academy. Retrieved from http://www.childtrauma.org.

Pryce, J. G., Shackleford, K. H., & Pryce, D. H. (2007). *Secondary traumatic stress and the child welfare professional.* Chicago, IL: Lyceum Books.

Regehr, C., Hemsworth, D., Leslie, B., Howe, P., & Chau, S. (2004). Predictors of posttraumatic distress in child welfare workers: a linear structural equation model. *Children and Youth Services Review, 26,* 331–346.

Regehr, C., LeBlanc, V., Shlonsky, A., & Bogo, M. (2010). The influence of clinicians' previous trauma exposure on their assessment of child abuse risk. *The Journal of Nervous and Mental Disease, 198*(9), 614–618.

Russell, D. E. H. (1984). *Sexual exploitation: Rape, child sexual abuse, and sexual harassment.* Beverly Hills, CA: Sage.

Saakvitne, K. W., & Pearlman, L. A. (1995). *Transforming the pain: A workbook on vicarious traumatization.* New York, NY: Norton.

Stamm, B. H. (Ed.). (1995). *Secondary traumatic stress: Self-care issues for clinicians, researchers, and educators.* Lutherville, MD: Sidran.

Stamm, B. H. (2010). *The Concise ProQOL Manual* (2nd ed.). Pocatello, ID: ProQOL.org.

Tedeschi, R. G., & Kilmer, R. P. (2005). Assessing strengths, resilience, and growth to guide clinical interventions. *Professional Psychology: Research and Practice, 36*(3), 230–237.

Terr, L. C. (1991). Childhood traumas: An outline and overview. In G. S. Everly & J. M. Lating (Eds.), *Psychotraumatology: Key Papers and Core Concepts in Posttraumatic Stress* (pp. 301–320). New York, NY: Plenum.

Theodore, A. D., Chang, J. J., Runyan, D. K., Hunter, W. M., Bangdiwala, S. I., & Agans, R. (2005). Epidemiologic features of the physical and sexual maltreatment of children in the Carolinas. *Pediatrics, 115*(3), 331–337.

Ullman, S. E. (2007). Relationship to perpetrator, disclosure, social reactions, and PTSD symptoms in child sexual abuse survivors. *Journal of Child Sexual Abuse, 16*(1), 19–36.

U.S. Department of Health and Human Services, Administration for Children and Families, Administration on Children, Youth and Families, Children's Bureau. (2012). *Child Maltreatment 2011.* Retrieved from http://www.acf.hhs.gov/programs/cb/research-data-technology/statistics-research/child-maltreatment.

Volk, K. T., Guarino, K., Grandin, M. E., & Clervil, R. (2008). *What about you? A workbook for those who work with others.* Newton Centre, MA: The National Center on Family Homelessness. Retrieved from http://508.center4si.com/SelfCareforCareGivers.pdf.

Walsh, F. (2003). Family resilience: A framework for clinical practice. *Family Process, 42*(1), 1–18.

Walsh, F. (2006). *Strengthening family resilience.* New York, NY: Guilford.

Woodward, C., & Joseph, S. (2003). Positive changes processes and posttraumatic growth in people who have experienced childhood abuse: Understanding vehicles of change. *Psychology and Psychotherapy: Theory, Research and Practice, 76,* 267–283.

Chapter 10
Reflective Practices in Supervision: Why Thinking and Reflecting Are as Important as Doing

Mary Elizabeth Rauktis and Tammy L. Thomas

Abstract The professionals who work in the child welfare system make critical decisions that have long-term impacts on the lives of children and families, and these case-level determinations must be made with careful consideration. Given the high stakes nature of child welfare work, there is tremendous pressure to "do" something at all times. There is a demand for child welfare workers and supervisors to *act* but less focus on the actual *thinking* about cases. Case decisions must be grounded in information secured from multiple sources of data. This task is notably difficult, time consuming, and complex due to high levels of uncertainty. Decisions at all critical junctures in the child welfare system are made with incomplete, insufficient and, at times, contradictory information. In the face of uncertainty, practices that assist workers in improving their decision making are both desirable and appreciated.

The process of reflective supervision and other reflective practices holds promise for addressing the needs of caseworkers and promoting child- and family-centered practice. These practices help workers manage the stressful nature of the work by providing a space to reflect on their own thoughts and feelings. Supervision that is less focused on compliance with discrete, concrete tasks and more on thoughtful decision-making provides an opportunity to move child welfare work beyond the narrow focus on investigation of abuse to a holistic assessment of child and family needs. It also increases the potential for keeping committed, compassionate, and well-educated workers in the field of child protection as abuse and neglect are complex issues and difficult to address. Moving child welfare to a point where thinking, problem-solving, and exploring emotions is part of standard practice has the potential

M.E. Rauktis (✉)
Child Welfare Education and Research Programs, School of Social Work,
University of Pittsburgh, Pittsburgh, PA, USA
e-mail: mar104@pitt.edu

T.L. Thomas
School of Social Work, University of Pittsburgh, Pittsburgh, PA, USA

H. Cahalane (ed.), *Contemporary Issues in Child Welfare Practice*,
Contemporary Social Work Practice, DOI 10.1007/978-1-4614-8627-5_10,
© Springer Science+Business Media New York 2013

to improve decisions that are made when working with children and families. The evidence for reflective practice, while still emerging in social work, has shown early positive outcomes in Early Head Start programs serving families and young children in the community. Continued research into how to implement reflective practices and ongoing examination of the results at the child, family, and organizational level is called for so that we can improve the lives of children, families, and the individuals who are charged with their safety.

Keywords Social work supervision • Reflective supervision • Critical thinking

Introduction

Cleaver and Freeman (1995) wrote that working in child welfare requires the skills of Machiavelli, the wisdom of Solomon, the compassion of Augustine, and the hide of a tax inspector. A great deal has been written previously about the inherently stressful nature of the work and the role that supervision plays in making the job manageable for workers. Rycraft (1994), in her study of retention of public child welfare workers, found that supervision was an important factor in creating a tolerable environment. More recent studies have also confirmed that supervision is critical to worker satisfaction and the retention of caseworkers (APHSA 2005; Cahalane and Sites 2008; Collins 1994; Collins-Camargo and Groeber 2003; Conway et al. 2003; Dickenson and Perry 2002; Ellett et al. 2004; McCarthy 2003; Rauktis and Koeske 1994; Westbrook et al. 2006). In an evaluation of the Pennsylvania Professional Title IV-E Education Program (Child Welfare Education and Research Programs 2009), a social work graduate disclosed her anxiety and ambivalence about remaining on the front lines as a child welfare worker:

> I am very grateful to be employed and I take my responsibilities very seriously. However, the grave seriousness of protecting children while working with families/parents/generations who have deeply ingrained problems with drugs, alcohol, mental health, overall dysfunction, neglect, etc., can be very emotionally taxing on the family of course, but also on the child welfare worker. Sometimes, I don't think it's a very healthy job to work in for a long time. What would convince me to stay? I'm not sure what could be changed about child welfare social work that would alleviate my anxiety about the job. Often I feel "damned if I do, damned if I don't" and face pressure from parents, extended family members, drug and alcohol counselors, therapists, and school staff who all think you should be doing different things for a family. It's a lot of pressure and a very serious responsibility that can in turn be emotionally taxing on the people in my own life…

This quote exemplifies the challenges that child welfare workers face. What can be done to help child welfare workers such as this woman manage the stress of the work? How can the child welfare system keep committed, compassionate, and well-educated workers in the field of child protection? Can supervision move child welfare work beyond the narrow focus on investigation of abuse to a holistic assessment of child and family needs? In this chapter, we propose that the process of reflective supervision and other reflective practices holds promise for addressing the needs of caseworkers and promoting child- and family-centered practice. We describe reflective supervision and other reflective practices, using examples from a qualitative study of caseworker decision making, and propose that these practices help workers manage the stressful nature of the work by providing a space to reflect on their own thoughts and feelings. In the last section of this chapter, we discuss the challenges and the benefits of implementing these practices and the process for doing so in agencies.

Review of the Literature on Reflective Supervision Practice

Those working in public child welfare systems are under tremendous pressure to "do" something at all times. Gillian Ruch writes that "concrete manifestations of the emphasis on 'doing' in social work abound in the burgeoning of procedures and audit requirements that represent an increasingly technical-rational understanding of practice. A further, all too familiar source of pressure arises from other professionals exhorting social workers to *do* something" (Ruch 2007b, p. 371). There is increased pressure for child welfare workers and supervisors to *act*, but less focus on the actual *thinking* about cases. In the past, the most common supervision approach was a three-part model of accountability, development, and support (Kadushin 1992), but increasingly supervisors must focus on accountability and performance-monitoring functions in supervision rather than on reflection (Jones and Gallop 2003). Simultaneously, caseworkers have limited time to think about their work. Too much to do in too little time results in less time to reflect about the families they are working with and generate ideas about the nature of these families' problems. This can have negative consequences for the children, youth, and families being worked with, as well as for the workers themselves. Not only may they make decisions that fail to take into account all the complexities of the situation, they may also become disengaged from the children and families, viewing interventions with them as another "checkoff" in a list of tasks.

Supervisors can encourage caseworkers to think about the families they work with and to practice family-centered casework within the regulatory culture of child welfare (Conway et al. 2003). For example, a caseworker might react in a certain manner in dealing with an individual or a family without a conscious understanding of why or what is influencing him or her or how this impacts the safety, permanency, and well-being of the children in the family. Without a supervisory "space" (Randall et al. 2000) or a forum in which to not only discuss reactions, thoughts, and ideas and examine feelings but to also receive guidance and generate hypotheses (Jones et al. 2002), workers can arrive at less-than-ideal solutions without fully understanding the meanings and intentions behind their actions. Research from other fields such as medicine (Croskerry 2003), education (Ashraf and Rarieya 2008; Weiss and Weiss 2001), and public health (Parker et al. 2009) tells us that taking the time to "think about our thinking and our feelings" is a valuable use of time. Reflective supervision and other reflective practices that help people to think and reflect have the potential to help workers to manage stress and feel supported, as well as think critically about their practice.

What is reflective supervision? Emily Fenichel defined reflective supervision as a relationship for learning with three essential elements: regularity, collaboration, and reflection (Fenichel 1992). *Regular* supervision is not an "on the fly" or "in the hallway" conversation but a routinely scheduled time on the calendar that is protected by both the supervisor and the supervisee. It is *collaborative* because the supervisor is not correcting or evaluating the supervisee in this process. Although structurally the supervisor has the power in the relationship, in the reflective process the supervisor deliberately takes a "one down" position, not directing the process but sharing it with the supervisee. In other words, as Gilkerson (2004) observes, "the best supervisory relationships become true partnerships" (p. 427). Lastly, *reflection* is asking about both the doing and the feeling with questions such as "What did you do?" and "How do you feel about what you did?" (Gilkerson 2004, p. 428). The intent of asking these two questions is to connect feelings and emotions to action and to highlight that the inner world of the caseworker both impacts and is impacted by the outside work world. It also has a cognitive component in that the caseworker is reflecting on his or her own thinking—thinking about ideas and actions and interactions with others. Similarly, Ruch writes that the operational definition of reflective practices is "triadic—thinking, feeling, and doing" (Ruch 2002, p. 200).

What does reflective supervision look like, and how has it been used? McAllister and Thomas (2007) analyzed the experiences of an Early Head Start (EHS) program in adopting and implementing an Infant Mental Health approach. They found that reflective supervision was one of the critical elements to a successful adoption and implementation of a family-centered approach. In the EHS program, reflective supervision involved the supervisor helping the workers to look more holistically at the relationships within the families they were working with, as well as encouraging introspective self-reflection, helping the workers to understand their own feelings and reactions. The EHS workers felt that the most valuable aspect of reflective supervision was the opportunity it provided to think about the lives of the families they worked with from different perspectives and thereby construct a tailored and family-specific working plan. Similar to the EHS research, a study of Pakistani teachers (Ashraf and Rarieya 2008) found that, while important, creating time for reflective work was challenging. Without an established infrastructure to support the reflective practice on a regular basis, it became an add-on that could be easily discarded. Weiss and Weiss (2001) describe a reflective supervision model for students who are training to be teachers. In this model, reflective supervision practices included a large range of activities such as supervisory conferences, reflective practice exercises, on-site seminars, and collaboration and mentoring with experienced teachers in group settings. They found that meaningful reflective supervision required changing the top-down hierarchical structure, which usually placed student teachers at the bottom, acting as passive recipients, and principals at the top, as unquestioned authorities. Instead, students were required to take an active role in their learning. Additionally, principals, teachers, and students had to come together as collaborative learners.

Much of what has been written about reflective supervision practices in child welfare comes from Australia (Gibbs 2001) and the United Kingdom (Jones and Gallop 2003; Ruch 2002, 2007a, b). In Britain, a widely publicized child death resulted in an examination of child casework practices. A subsequent report, the Laming Inquiry (Department of Health 2003), resulted, recommending that casework practices in child protection include both "doing" and "thinking" activities (Ruch 2007a). Although opinions differed as to the best methods for increasing reflection in caseworker practice (Jones and Gallop 2003; Ruch 2007b), a learning culture was believed to be critical to improving outcomes for children in need and their families (Jones and Gallop 2003, p.105). As this review of the literature shows, reflective supervision has a great potential for supporting child welfare workers in what is a challenging yet critical and rewarding position. This next section reviews a recent study in which supervisors and child welfare caseworkers discussed their own reflective and supervisory practices.

Perceptions of Reflective Practice

These findings are part of a larger mixed-methods study that aimed to determine the extent and causes of racial disproportionality in a child welfare system in Northwestern Pennsylvania. As such, the aim was to better understand the decision-making processes of child welfare workers. Eleven individuals were interviewed between January and November of 2008. The interviewees represented the broad spectrum of those working in child welfare, including program directors; family services supervisors; an intake supervisor; caseworkers each from foster care, independent living, and family support services; two intake workers; and one family advocate. The majority of the 11 participants were female and white. This was an experienced group, having an average of 6 years experience in their current positions; two individuals had over 10 years experience in child welfare. Seven of those interviewed had Master's Degrees in Social Work, three had Bachelor's or Associate's Degrees, and one individual held a Doctorate in Social Work.

All interviews were conducted in the offices of the interviewees and lasted approximately 60–90 min. Following a semi-structured format of open-ended questions, the interview explored child welfare workers' perceptions of how they obtain information, the process of making decisions, and what role race plays in their decisions. Individuals were also asked to discuss case examples where decisions were both easy and difficult to make. Additionally, they were queried about how supervision impacted their work and decision-making processes. A consistent set of probes was used to encourage "thinking out loud." All interviews were recorded, transcribed verbatim, and analyzed.

These findings reconfirmed that those who work in child welfare make critical decisions that have long-term impacts on the lives of children and families and that workers make decisions about cases with careful consideration. The participants described the many ways they make decisions grounded in information secured from multiple sources of data. Decisions concerning this work are notably difficult, time-consuming, and complex due to high levels of uncertainty. Decisions at all critical junctures in the child welfare system are made with incomplete, insufficient, and, at times, contradictory information. In the face of uncertainty, practices that assist workers in improving their decision making are both desirable and appreciated. Child welfare workers from all levels in the system discussed the importance of not making decisions in isolation; rather, they preferred to seek support from supervisors and colleagues. In some instances, caseworkers would call or meet with their supervisor to discuss a case, seek guidance, and obtain feedback; other practices included convening a group of colleagues to discuss a case and establishing regular meetings to solicit feedback and guidance from colleagues and supervisors. The findings suggested that supervisors and caseworkers do engage with other workers in some types of reflective practice.

Supervisor Perspectives

Research on decision making has found that people make various types of "thinking shortcuts" due to cognitive biases (Arnott 2006; Croskerry 2003). Child welfare workers' decisions were often influenced by these "thinking shortcuts." In particular, preliminary case information, in the form of referral information or screening information, was very influential in how workers thought about the cases. Supervisors noted that the caseworker often formed a picture of the family he or she was working with even before meeting them. There was concern that these pre-formed ideas about the case would influence what information the workers would see and focus on in their investigation. In fact, supervisors shared examples of cases where early information was not correct, yet caseworkers were building their thinking around these "facts" despite not having verified the information.

Since reflective practices were not standard agency procedures, they occurred differently across regional offices. One director talked about how at her office the intake workers meet as a group with the supervisor in order to set the stage for what workers should be evaluating when they go out to meet a family referred for investigation: "whenever these [referrals] come over, we get together with the intake worker. There's a group of us that get together to outline what kind of things the intake worker needs to look at and what specific things based on the complaint." Another director said it was important to set up ways of thinking broadly and ask questions of her staff early on during the intake process, so she would individually meet with her intake workers: "Don't just rely on the other person who took the call. Because sometimes what my staff likes to do, and we all do it, you know, we pick up a record and we think we're reading the Bible or the Koran or something and its gospel." Both directors recognized the need to reflect with the caseworkers about the information they have and about how to investigate their cases in ways that allow them to evaluate the merits of what they are seeing and hearing in the field and from collateral sources.

Reflective practices occurred both formally and informally. In formal situations, supervisors used reflective supervision as part of their supervision with workers. This happened individually with the supervisor and the child welfare worker meeting to discuss cases. In some instances, the supervisor encouraged the worker to talk about the thinking process and where they were going with the cases. One supervisor described her process of reflective supervision:

> I just ask a lot of questions and really try to get them to find out why they made that judgment. They might come in and say to me, "Well I just don't like her." And I say, "Why?" It might be someone having an issue with their past criminal [history] or their style of talking… you have to get to where you can communicate with them effectively. Some people just turn off or instantly get defensive about it. I had this one lady [client] who calls me sweet pea because it annoys me and I can't stop being annoyed about it because she says it really mean, like, "sweet pea" [says in a mean voice]. And I don't know what it is that annoys me about it, but it does and it showed on my face one time because she loves to do it when she's mad at me. But she ranted and you just keep being respectful. I have a few caseworkers and we're working on it not being personal.

She then emphasized the need to help her staff understand how they react and respond to clients and how this shapes their decisions:

> Yes. We're trying to get to the point to when they don't feel personally attacked. Cause I'm like, "Why are you taking this personally?" And they're like, "But I didn't do anything…" So just why they react a certain way. Cause there's some people who just, if you can get them to stop screaming, they have a lot of good stuff to say. I said to this client, "You have a lot of good things to say, but the way you say it, I don't listen because you're screaming and bringing in all kinds of stuff that doesn't make sense." And I said, "Why don't you write this stuff down?" And it's just different ways of dealing with it because some caseworkers get to the point where they're loudly talking back. And it's like, "You did it." "No, I didn't do it, blah blah blah." You know, you did what you did. Why are you getting into it? So we talk about that stuff all the time. There's a lot of stuff about personal space. Some of the caseworkers have a hard time when parents are talking loudly at them. But I think that's cultural too.

Another supervisor related the type of individual discussions he has with his staff in order to help them think about how and why they make their decisions and how to connect their feelings about a family to the potential actions they may take.

> Sometimes as a supervisor…I've told folks that it's not good if you don't like someone and you hold it against them, and it's just as bad is if you really like someone and you want to give them extra. Those are both bad. They're equally bad. Be objective. That's my job to let them come in here and air it out, their stuff, not just the case stuff, but their own stuff.

Supervisors discussed assisting their staff with the process of thinking through why they are reacting to individuals in a certain way. The child welfare worker may be unaware of how individuals cause emotional responses in them and how this in turn impacts their thinking about the family and consequently their decisions. Bringing these thoughts, feelings, and reactions to the surface can help the worker respond to individuals and families in ways that may ultimately be more productive. Supervisors, as in the cases above, can draw upon their own previous experiences in order to model for their staff how to develop awareness of their own feelings and thinking processes. One supervisor talked with his staff about his own "soft spot" for grandparent caregivers and how his feelings and beliefs could bias his decisions in cases when caregiving grandparents are protesting the reunification of children with birth parents. His awareness of this potential bias helps him when making decisions and recommendations. Using his own experiences in supervising his staff normalized this process of self-examination for biases and provided a safe environment for his staff to examine how their own experiences could impact their decisions.

Reflective practices can also occur in a group format. A reflective group practice, where a group of colleagues from various disciplines and ranks come together to think through cases, was valued by supervisors as a tool to promote stronger and more accurate decision making and recommendations, as well as minimizing personal bias:

> So when we do that we work on a recommendation for the court. [This] is always an agency recommendation, not my workers'—not mine, not anyone else's. We sit in this room and decide what we're going to do. We put everybody's mind to it and that way it does get away from some of those personal feelings.

These group meetings help to mitigate situations where one person holds all of the decision-making power. Child welfare workers not only are relieved from feeling the sole responsibility for making critical decisions but also are able to feel they are part of a system invested in making thoughtful decisions.

In addition to the bias-reducing benefits of group reflection, supervisors felt reflective processes supported caseworkers in doing quality work by reducing their feelings of grief, frustration, and isolation. Caseworkers, often young and inexperienced, work in highly emotional situations and have to make decisions that hold significant consequences; reflection can help them process and deal with those emotions. One supervisor shared:

> And especially with the young people, in their twenties. Three of my four people are in their twenties, and they really want to do a good job and they really want to see people do well, and they're devastated too…

The high turnover rates in the child welfare field can make doing this reflective work challenging but necessary. Having workers frequently leave and be replaced with new staff requires time for supervisors to understand the set of assumptions and personal experiences of each of the new caseworkers they supervise. One supervisor spoke of the challenges of assessing caseworkers' abilities to make decisions and determining what factors may influence those decisions when the caseworker and supervisor had not worked together previously: "Yes, and it's nice I've had all my caseworkers for over a year now, which is amazing. So I do know them because it's hard too if you don't know people, of what they're making judgments on." She shared an example of how assumptions can infuse the decision-making process. In this instance, a worker had an underlying assumption about grandmothers being virtuous and the preferred caregiver of children removed from parental care. Due to preconceived ideas, he neglected to question a grandmother's appropriateness as a caregiver in a particular case. The supervisor challenged him to think outside of his own values and comfort zones: "Just cause grandma's there doesn't mean it's good… Is grandma on drugs herself?" A close working relationship and efforts to understand how caseworkers make decisions provide supervisors with an understanding of how to engage with each of their staff, so those staff members can work optimally.

Permanency planning is another area where supervisors find reflective practice to be useful in decision making. These planning meetings have been described as formal as well as informal and generally include supervisors, caseworkers, and directors. In these meetings, long-term placement goals for children are discussed, and the reflective process allows for voicing a range of opinions valuable to decision making. These meetings also serve to support those who need to make critical decisions about the future of children and families by allowing for the gathering and processing of the most relevant information about a case. One supervisor said:

> I think my staff finds them very helpful. And usually what we do is if we're at the point of... we're mandated to do them if we think a child's at risk and we need to consider removal. Prior to actually removing, we convene staff in the office kind of on the spot. Grab... it's really just grabbing people and going into somebody's office. The caseworker, supervisor; we have caseworker IIIs here that we'll pull in and other supervisors. We usually have about four or five, six people. Sometimes if our attorney's available or our resource coordinator and we'll just basically, you know, present the case and brainstorm and come up with recommendations. We're mandated to do it when we're looking at removal, but I think my staff uses them for almost any reason. You know, if you have a complicated situation or you're just not sure which way to go. We do at times, but not all the time, pull in other professionals that will be on the phone. If we need to, we'll invite, you know, family to them as well. But because in any given day... well sometimes in the morning, you know, we might do four or five of them. So they're really pretty spontaneous.

Supervisors who valued and utilized a reflective practice continued to develop and grow professionally in this process by staying abreast of what is happening in the field and learning from others. The merit of learning from each other and not "standing" on hierarchy is demonstrated in this comment from a supervisor regarding learning from his supervisees:

> It's not even that I have more ideas or more resources, sometimes my other workers who I think are very good, they'll know how to get a bed and I'll ask them. So I learn from my workers and interns. I think it's a really good go-around and a teaching thing for both of us. And it's part of the ongoing training as far as I'm concerned. So we talk about each of these and sometimes it takes longer and to discuss where are we going and what do we need to do next.

Supervisors spoke to the necessity and usefulness of utilizing reflective practices in the child welfare arena. The next section features the perspectives of caseworkers on this topic.

Caseworker Perspective

Caseworkers also value informally meeting with colleagues to discuss cases. As one worker in the intake department said, it "never hurts to get a second or third set of eyes" on a case. Caseworkers described often taking the lead to initiate small group meetings. One caseworker described the process and significance of gathering a group of colleagues to discuss cases and collaborate:

> We'll go out, we'll do assessments, and we'll come together. You know, it might take like one or two people on my unit and say I went out there and I got this kind of feeling, what do you think? I mean we'll chew stuff around together amongst co-workers to get different angles, different points of view.

In discussing the worth of these sessions, another participant said talking with others can help caseworkers to think about possibilities and ideas they may have neglected to think about on their own. This is especially true during crisis situations when time is of the essence.

Reflective practice is also utilized in formal settings, where child welfare workers are regulated by policy to collaborate on cases. Preplacement meetings provide an opportunity to use reflective group processes. In the preplacement discussion, colleagues and supervisors assist the caseworker in thinking through the options and consequences of placements, whether the children in question are remaining/returning home or going on to some version of out-of-home placement. Many child welfare workers attested to the benefits of these meetings. One shared: "And I really do appreciate our preplacement meetings because certain values I have in picking a foster home might not be the same that other people have, so we can work off of each other." The process of discussing cases and challenging assumptions (conscious or unconscious) helps to advance the best possible decisions for children and families. One caseworker said:

> I do appreciate it when we have more people to really discuss them out. We've been a pretty stable office for a while and I know what [name of worker] is going to say, or [name of worker] is going to say. I never know what [name of worker] is going to say, but that's why I like having her there. And we have such a wide range of experience and points of view. I do think it's nice to hash it out.

Caseworkers appreciate having support in the decisions they make and being able to engage with other colleagues in order to promote their best work.

Facilitating Reflection in Supervision

In the previous section, we explored the perspectives of workers and supervisors as they described their own use of reflective supervision and practice, including how they use it and why they find it useful. In this final section, we discuss the organizational and individual challenges and benefits of implementing reflective supervisory practices and some techniques that are constructive in the reflective process. These suggestions are not intended to be prescriptive; rather, they are to be used as a starting point for developing these reflective approaches in child welfare practice.

Creating the Culture

First and foremost, it is imperative to have leadership commitment to the reflective processes. This practice requires time and energy on the part of workers and supervisors, commitment to meeting consistently, and patience, since the results may not be immediately or readily apparent in terms of measurable outputs (e.g., forms signed, plans completed). Therefore, agency directors and supervisors must see the value of reflective practices, communicate this to others, and hold everyone accountable to the practice—not just those who may be inclined to practice reflection. In other words, there needs to be an agency culture that supports reflection as a necessary component of child welfare work. A commitment must also be made to creating an environment with safe space where staff can reflect and talk about ideas, thoughts, and feelings. This type of environment values reflective practices even in the face of other seemingly "more important" required tasks.

Organizational commitment is demonstrated by including reflective practice expectations in supervisory and caseworker roles, incorporating it into policy and job descriptions, and also designating these practices in the work schedule. This affirms that these practices are not treated as a "luxury" that can be easily discarded when schedules become hectic. Having high-level administrators model reflective supervision with their own supervisees reinforces the importance of this practice. A supportive, reflective culture also promotes openness and does not stand on unquestioned authority. Instead, it encourages frontline workers to pose questions, challenge current thinking, and offer new solutions (Ashraf and Rarieya 2008). As illustrated in the findings, supervisors must be open to new ideas and appreciate other perspectives as well as be able to understand how individuals express their feelings and frustrations. They must be able to do this in a supportive, nonpunitive way, building trust with frontline workers. Finally, they need to be willing to suspend their positions of power and authority and work collaboratively as professionals.

Caseworkers will also need help and support to be reflective. Not all caseworkers are trained to be aware of their thoughts and emotions or are naturally comfortable asking for help or talking about their feelings. They may experience anxiety due to the uncertainty and ambiguity that individual or group discussions may generate, since such discussions may lead to more questions than solutions. McAllister and Thomas (2007) found that some home visitors expressed confusion about the purpose of reflective supervision and discomfort talking about feelings. One of the home visitors in their study expressed not knowing if she or he was "saying things they want to hear or if I was completely off the subject" (McAllister and Thomas 2007, p. 206). Finally, workers may need to be coached simply because they are not used to thinking in a reflective way. Osmond (2001) found that child welfare workers reported difficulty with reflective case discussions because they were not used to thinking about their practices in this manner. They found the process to be hard.

Finally, it is important to remember that organizations, like individuals, may be affected by traumatic events and that reflection may be a productive way to deal with this trauma. For example, a maltreatment death of a child in agency care is a traumatic event that will impact the entire organization. When an organization becomes traumatized after such an event, that trauma may overshadow everything in the agency, and it may be unsafe for the workers to discuss their feelings or reactions. The focus of future work may move to tasks rather than reflection, as workers and managers attempt to numb and avoid feelings associated with this event. (See Chap. 9) for more detailed information about traumatized organizations.) While it would be difficult to initiate reflective practices in this culture, doing so would be a therapeutic intervention for the agency. The Laming Inquiry Report following the death of a child in care recommended that reflective practices be instituted in the agency as a potential intervention (Ruch 2007b).

Although creating a receptive climate for reflection, whether for an entire organization or for individual caseworkers, requires time and energy and is both professionally and personally challenging, much of what was reported by the caseworkers, supervisors, and directors in the study suggests that it is worth the effort. Given the potential for long-lasting impacts on families, reflective practices bring a unique opportunity to improve decision making and judgment. Not only do workers avoid making decisions in isolation, they continually develop skills through sharing ideas and discussing cases. Workers also feel they make more informed decisions when they are able to, as one of our participants shared, "air their own stuff out" in individual supervision and in groups. A sense of collegiality is built which can enhance the overall work setting. With a more equitable power balance between caseworkers and supervisors, working relationships can be more fruitful. The reflective process can also bring about a more respectful working environment. Both staff and supervisors might develop a comfort level in dealing with emotions. Additional benefits to the work environment include an enhanced sense of curiosity and a setting in which supervisors can be more in touch with what is happening in the field and exercise their own skills. Given the high rates of turnover and the potential for burnout and secondary trauma in child welfare, reflective practices—when done well—can provide the support and relief workers need. This is beneficial to the entire system: agencies, supervisors, caseworkers, and children and families.

Techniques for Facilitating Reflection

The techniques discussed below offer guidance to those interested in integrating reflective practices into a child welfare setting. These techniques result from our research, Osmond and Darlington's (2005) suggested techniques for facilitating reflection, and the work of Parker and colleagues (2009). See Tables 10.1 and 10.2 for dialogue examples of reflective supervision.

Referral, Intake, and Investigation

Our research identified how reflective practices can be instrumental in countering the problem of unquestionable acceptance of information provided prior to

Table 10.1 Intake/referral

Reflective questions	Dialogue
What are the objectives—what do you want to accomplish in going to the family home?	Worker: First, I want to find out if the children are in a home situation that is unsafe. Coming to school without clean clothes and unwashed and tired suggests that something bad is going on in the home that caused this change, but what exactly is going on and if it puts them at risk for greater harm isn't clear from the information. So what I want is to gain additional information to make this determination
What do you know now? What will be the sources of information? Sources of uncertainty? And how do you think that you will get the information you need?	I know only that the teacher has reported a change in their appearance and behavior. Amy and Adam are sources of information, although they are five, and so they may not be able to fully tell me what is happening. So I'll be looking for clues that may explain some of what the teacher observed, e.g., is there food in the house, are there food wrappers, is there electricity, and running water since they are unwashed and commented about lack of food. The teacher may be another source of information. Their parents will be an important source, and I'll need to be able to quickly get their cooperation. Some other sources could be neighbors. I am also going to look in our database to check if they are known to us, and if so, who was their caseworker and what happened to the case. This could be another source of information
What did you find out?	I checked in our database, and they had an open case two years ago with us but it was closed. The parents were reported by the neighbors for neglecting the twins. I looked at the record and talked to the worker who investigated them. She said that the house was a mess and that the parents were really "spacey" but that they couldn't find evidence of supervisory or other neglect. They put some in-home services in place and then closed the case after 90 days. I also talked to the teacher. She said that the kids have been "a wreck." I'm thinking that what is going on in the home is drug abuse and the children are being neglected

(continued)

Table 10.1 (continued)

Reflective questions	Dialogue
Have you gone out to the home?	No
What makes you think this is neglect due to the parents' substance abuse?	Well, the previous worker said the parents were spacey, and the teacher said that the twins were a mess…they have a history. It sounds a lot like the case I had last month with the Murphy family where the children were found wandering the streets and their parents were stoned
The Murphy family case sticks in your mind, doesn't it….	It made the paper and those kids could have been hit by a car or taken by strangers and it would have been our fault
When we talked earlier, you said that your goal was "to gain more information to make this determination." It sounds like you have made your determination before seeing the home and talking to the children. So why the change?	I guess that the teacher and the other intake worker and the record….well, I guess it made me think of the Murphys…I still feel bad about those kids
Yes, I know, and that is a normal feeling. We all want to prevent bad things from happening to children, but sometimes we remember our worst case and that colors what we see in the present. I do think that while you have some information about this situation, you need to go back to your first plan—which was "Amy and Adam are sources of information, although they are five, and so they may not be able to fully tell me what is happening. So I'll be looking for clues that may explain some of what the teacher observed, e.g., is there food in the house, are there food wrappers, is there electricity, running water since they are unwashed and commented about lack of food. The teacher may be another source of information. Their parents will be an important source and I'll need to be able to quickly get their cooperation. Some other sources could be neighbors." Then we can talk again after you have talked to the children, observed their parents and the home. You are a very observant person and I know you will be able to figure this out	Ok (laughs). Thanks for "talking me down from the ledge." I'll check in with you later today

As an intake worker, you are given the following information about a referral that came from a teacher. Amy and Adam, 5-year-old twins, have been coming to school unkempt (i.e., clothes are dirty; children are unwashed) and without proper clothing for the weather. They told the teacher "Mommy says that we have no food." The twins have been acting differently in school—Amy has been sleeping in class and cries easily, and Adam alternates between crying and acting out. They both are having a hard time concentrating. The teacher is concerned about these changes in their appearance and behavior and calls the child abuse hotline to make a report

Table 10.2 Ongoing services

Reflective question	Dialogue
Who is involved with this family?	CYS of course, the D&A provider working with the parents, the school that the boys attend, their parents, the Smiths, the foster care provider that employs the Smiths. There are aunts and uncles but they have not been actively involved with the boys since their placement
What are our objectives or goals in our intervention?	My immediate goal is to make sure that Michael and Sean have a safe and stable placement and emotional security so they can continue a normal developmental course. I also want them to continue to have contact with their parents in a safe and controlled way because the boys do love them, even though their parents can't safely care for them
How do you feel that the Smiths feel about the boys and this situation?	Mrs. Smith is the primary caregiver and calls Michael and Sean "her boys." She has been supportive of their visits with the parents and the boys' attachment to their parents. She seems to enjoy caring for them, saying that they "keep her young." However, since Mr. Smith has been ill, she has had to miss appointments for the boys. She has not said anything, but she often looks tired and older in the past few months
	Up until his illness, Mr. Smith was an involved co-parent. His recent illness (congestive heart failure) has resulted in several hospitalizations and home care. He isn't able to drive now and can't play with the boys. He seems to enjoy their company, but he is easily tired out
What do we know? What don't we know?	There are several sources of uncertainty. First, we don't know if the parents are going to show enough progress on their plan and stop using drugs within the time frames mandated by the court. We don't know the judge and the attorney's perspective
	We don't know the course of Mr. Smith's illness and whether he will recover his former vigor. We don't know how Mrs. Smith feels about being the sole caregiver of both the boys and her husband. We don't know what sources of support she potentially has from her family or church or the foster care agency or extended family
What information do we need to reduce uncertainty?	I need to find out some information: (1) How do the Smiths feel? (2) What is the medical prognosis for Mr. Smith? (3) What assistance are they getting from their agency, friends, and family, and who are other potential sources of help? (4) What is the legal perspective of this situation? (5) How do the boys feel about living with the Smiths?
Do you have a "favorite" position or option?	I guess I'd like to see Michael and Sean stay with the Smiths. For the last year, they have made good progress because they have had a stable home, consistent parenting, and a routine. They are starting school soon, with Michael going into first grade and Sean into kindergarten. I'd like them to have some stability in school. The Smiths have provided good care (although not high energy), and they have helped the boys maintain ties with their parents. I think this contact is a motivator for their parents to work toward their service plan goals

(continued)

Table 10.2 (continued)

Reflective question	Dialogue
How can this impact how you go about resolving uncertainties?	I'll have to be careful that I don't influence the Smiths into telling me that everything is "OK," i.e., ignore information that suggests that they want the boys to be moved. I have to keep in mind that finances may be a problem for them and that they may need the income from foster care to supplement their retirement income. I also need to be neutral when talking with Michael and Sean about the Smiths. I'm frustrated with the parents—why can't they get it together? I guess that I'll have to watch that too!

In this example, the ongoing services caseworker uses a group reflective process to assist in thinking about the placement status of Michael and Sean, two brothers in foster care. She is considering the longer term consequences of the boys remaining in their current foster care placement. Participating with her in the group are her supervisor, a parent advocate, the paralegal who works within her division, the adoption supervisor, and three other caseworkers and a supervisor. Her supervisor starts off the group by asking a general question: "Tell us about the case."

"Michael (age 6) and his brother Sean (age 5) have been in foster care with the Smiths for a year. As their caseworker, I am monitoring their placement and I support the Smiths, as well as support the parents as they work on their service plan goals. However, their progress on the plan goals in the past 12 months is slow since both parents are still using drugs. As a result, I am concurrently working on two permanence goals—reunification or adoption. While the Smiths are providing adequate care for Michael and his brother, they are older (65 and 67), and Mr. Smith has been in and out of the hospital in the past 6 months, requiring his wife to assume primary caretaking of the boys and caring for her husband. They are not asking me for a placement change, but looking into the future, and with the possibility of a permanence goal change to adoption, I am wondering if I should consider a new foster care placement for the boys. The boys are quite active, and while they have been safe in the home, I wonder if they need more physical activities than the Smiths have been able to provide. However, the boys seem to be happy with the Smiths and call them "Grampy" and "Grammy." As I am preparing for the next court hearing, I am thinking about a placement change."

The supervisor then poses the reflective questions to the group investigation of a case. This "thinking shortcut" may likely be due to a priming effect of early information—early written or verbal information about a referral can shape how it is perceived, what information is collected, and what decision is made. Reflective practices used to offset this preferably would help child welfare workers identify their preconceived ideas, encourage their sense of curiosity, and assist them in being open to alternative information. In practice, either individually or in a group, the supervisor would meet with the caseworker between the time of case assignment and the caseworker going out into the field. Together or as part of a larger group, the documented information from the referral, previous case records, and any other collected data would be reviewed. The caseworker then would go into the field after having a discussion based on the following questions, which are designed to prime the caseworker with a "neutral" frame of reference:

1. What are the objectives? What do you want to accomplish?
2. What do you know now? What do you anticipate will be sources of uncertainty, and how do you anticipate that you will get the information you need?

This approach is in contrast to what is typically discussed at this juncture, which often consists only of reviewing the family's history and problems.

The supervisor or the group would follow up with the worker shortly after the investigation with another series of reflective questions adapted from Osmond and Darlington (2005):

1. What are your thoughts now after seeing the child(ren) and family?
2. How is this different from before meeting with them, and why? How did you come to this understanding? What was influencing your thoughts before that may not be now?
3. Was there anything you observed or heard that brings up any reactions or feelings for you?

Ultimately, the goal is for caseworkers to internalize this process and use it as part of their own reflective self-practice in their work. Additionally, caseworkers will become more adept at using this process in helping their colleagues.

In addition, the following set of questions and probes, valuable to group reflection during the intake and investigation phase, is based on our research findings and the work of Osmond and Darlington (2005) and Parker et al. (2009):

1. Are the right people in this group? Should others join us?
2. What are the objectives or goals in investigating this family—what do we want to accomplish? (*Not* just typically required data, such as what are the family's history and problems, and not just the standard answer of safety, permanence, and well-being.) What will it look like if all goes well?
3. Who is involved with this case/situation? (Draw an ecomap.)
4. What do we know? What are the sources of uncertainty? What/who don't we know about?
5. What information do we need to get to reduce uncertainty?
6. Do we have contradictory information or information that challenges our favorite positions?

7. What may be the cause(s) of abuse and/or neglect in this family? How do you, as the caseworker, understand or explain the issues/situation?
8. What are the options for action? Are there policies that assign "weight" to certain pieces of information (e.g., child age) or to certain options (e.g., kinship is preferred to non-kin)? What are the consequences to the options and what could go wrong?
9. What would a "good decision" look like at this point in time?
10. How do you feel about the family? Did anything affect you on a personal level?

In the early stages of investigation, when overfocusing on one factor or holding to a firmly held belief may keep the caseworker from seeing the big picture, the process of "exploring differences and other contingencies" is useful because it helps to identify the factors caseworkers may be primarily considering (Osmond and Darlington 2005, p. 6). Then, by asking questions such as "what if the children were younger?" or "what if the children were older?", the supervisor or group can help the caseworker identify if certain factors may be assuming dominance and if these are impacting the decisions made by the caseworker. Thus, this process can help caseworkers reflect on why certain factors are weighing more heavily upon their thinking (Ruch 2007b).

Finally, the responsibilities required in the intake and investigation stages of child welfare work can be stressful and anxiety inducing. Time frames for decisions are short and situations are potentially dangerous. Caseworkers serve as the "front line," and their decisions lead to serious consequences. For example, the failure to remove a child from an unsafe situation can result in harm or death for the child. Additionally, circumstances necessitating investigation, such as physical and sexual abuse and neglect, are emotionally challenging. Osmond (2001) found caseworkers perceived having little opportunity in supervision to consider the emotional reactions that emerged from undertaking such challenging work. Child welfare workers need a space and time to reflect and share their feelings. Reflective processes serve to validate feelings and assist workers in developing an understanding of how their feelings link to their perceptions and actions.

Family Services/Foster Care/Independent Living

While child welfare workers charged with ongoing supervision of families in treatment or children in out-of-home care do not have the same pressures as experienced by intake and investigative workers, they have their own unique challenges. In our study, child welfare caseworkers in family services had to determine whether placement situations promoted the well-being of children or if children needed to move to more appropriate care, if possible. Caseworkers interacted with families struggling with mental health issues, addiction, and interpersonal violence, as well as families unable to meet the goals on their family plans, sometimes resulting in the termination of parental rights. While attempting to maintain their alliance with the parents, caseworkers built collaborative relationships with families and then had to remove children. The caseworkers and supervisors who were interviewed expressed feelings of sorrow and sadness about the circumstances families face. Those who participated in group and individual reflective practices believed these types of thoughtful and supportive interventions promoted their ability to identify and manage emotions, and that this in turn opened up thinking which made them feel more confident about their decisions.

Additionally, caseworkers engaged in the family services area talked about a group process in which they would bring in a variety of people and discuss what was happening with a family, particularly when there was a decision point or a problem. For example, a group would convene when it appeared a foster home placement was in jeopardy or when a parent was not making progress on family plan goals. The goal would be to engage people in a group discussion, including people who were likely to have different opinions or perspectives (i.e., not just people who work together in a unit). Having a diverse group of individuals participate in a discussion is valuable because each individual looks at the situation from a different perspective.

A group discussion could be organized around reflective questions or prompts informed by our findings, as well as those of Osmond and Darlington (2005) and Parker et al. (2009). These reflective questions are the same as those discussed earlier for referral and intake, but include reference to the care providers involved in a case in order to evaluate the degree of systems collaboration that is (or should be) present. These probes and questions are valuable because they help workers systematically reflect and then talk about their knowledge, which further assists in identification of gaps and allows others to raise questions and contribute differing opinions (Osmond and Darlington 2005).

In our study, caseworkers and supervisors who used group methods identified the value of having others critically appraise their ideas, opinions, and decisions. In addition, having others involved in the discussion helped to identify when a caseworker was using personal rather than empirical information. In this process, the role of the group facilitator (often a supervisor) is to stimulate the reflection by posing questions as well as monitoring the tone of the discussion, focusing on both what is said and what is not said. It is not the role of the facilitator to make a decision, to "solve a problem," or to simply "sign off" on a decision. An example is presented in Table 10.2 above.

Osmond and Darlington (2005) also suggest a "case analysis" process that could be done in either a group or an individual setting. A set of reflective questions can promote critical thinking about a case by encouraging people involved in the case to examine their perspectives. This could be particularly valuable in family services, since problems in care often occur due to differences in perception about what is happening in the family. For example, workers talked about how placement issues often became problematic between grandparents and parents or different sets of parents. The questions that a case analysis would use can be modified, but Osmond and Darlington suggest the following list (Osmond and Darlington 2005, p. 5), which would be used as part of a supervisory session or a small group discussion. A supervisor poses these questions and facilitates the discussion. In this example, the caseworker is asked to consider the perspective of the parent of a child, but any individual could be substituted, e.g., foster parent or child:

1. Tell us about the case.
2. Who is involved with this family?

3. How do you think the parent (or another individual) felt/feels about the incident/issue/situation?
4. Where do you think the parent generated their ideas or explanations from?
5. How do you feel about the specific incident/issue/situation?
6. How do you understand or explain the incident/issue/situation?
7. Where do you think you have generated your ideas and explanations from?

Osmond and Darlington suggest that this set of probes be repeated for each of the persons involved in the case, such as the parents, workers, and children. These probes are about thinking and feeling aspects, and because they systematically consider everyone involved, quick decisions or rushing to a solution before fully understanding the problem may be less likely to happen.

Another reflective practice technique that Osmond and Darlington (2005) report as useful is "think-aloud." A supervisor in a one-on-one session would ask a caseworker to talk aloud while solving a problem that she or he is experiencing with a family. This method reveals the cognitive processes and the knowledge utilized when trying to work through a problem or situation. In our study, we used the thinking aloud process to try to uncover social workers' decision making related to investigating a child maltreatment referral. The child welfare workers said that while this process was being used as part of a research study, they could see that it would be useful in supervision as well.

Conclusion

Abuse and neglect are complex issues and difficult to address. Moving child welfare to a point where thinking, problem-solving, and exploring emotions are part of standard practice has the potential to improve decisions that are made when working with children and families. The evidence for reflective practice, while still emerging in social work (Ruch 2002, 2005, 2007a, b), has shown early positive outcomes in Early Head Start programs serving families and young children in the community (McAllister and Thomas 2007). Continued research into how to implement reflective practices and ongoing examination of the results at the child, family, and organizational level is called for so that we can improve the lives of children, families, and the individuals who are charged with their safety.

Questions for Discussion

1. Think about a family that you have been working with and apply one of the techniques for facilitating reflection. Then do this again with a coworker or a group of coworkers. Did you come to any different decisions as a result of this process?
2. If your case decision remains the same, what factors did you consider as you thought through the case again?

3. What aspects of the case did you think about differently as a result of using a reflective process?
4. How might you approach this case differently?

Acknowledgement Special thanks to the caseworkers who participated in this study.

References

American Public Human Services Association. (2005). *Report from the 2004 child welfare workforce survey: State Agency Findings*. Washington, DC: APHSA.

Arnott, D. (2006). Cognitive biases and decision support systems development: A design science approach. *Information Systems Journal, 16*(1), 55–78.

Ashraf, H., & Rarieya, J. F. (2008). Teacher development through reflective conversations—possibilities and tensions: A Pakistan case. *Reflective Practice, 9*(3), 269–279.

Cahalane, H., & Sites, E. W. (2008). The climate of child welfare employee retention. *Child Welfare, 87*(1), 91–114.

Child Welfare Education and Research Programs. (2009). *2008–2009 Annual Report, School of Social Work, University of Pittsburgh*. Pittsburgh: University of Pittsburgh.

Cleaver, H., & Freeman, P. (1995). *Parental perspectives in cases of suspected child abuse*. London: HMSO.

Collins, P. M. (1994). Does mentorship among social workers make a difference? An empirical investigation of career outcomes. *Social Work, 39*(4), 413–419.

Collins-Camargo, C., & Groeber, C. (2003). Adventures in partnership: Using learning laboratories to enhance frontline supervision in child welfare. *Professional Development: The International Journal of Continuing Social Work Education, 6*(1), 17–31.

Conway, P., Shaver, C., Bennett, P., & Aldrich, A. (2003). *I can't get no satisfaction: Exploring the relationship between supervision, job satisfaction and turnover in two rural child protection agencies*. Paper presented at the Annual Program Meeting of the Council on Social Work Education, Atlanta, GA.

Croskerry, P. (2003). Cognitive forcing strategies in clinical decision-making. *Annals of Emergency Medicine, 41*(1), 110–120.

Department of Health. (2003). *The Victoria Climbie Inquiry: Report of an Inquiry*. London: Her Majesty's Stationary Office.

Dickenson, N., & Perry, R. (2002). Factors influencing the retention of specially educated public child welfare workers. *Journal of Health and Social Policy, 15*(3/4), 89–103.

Ellett, A. J., Ellett, C. D., Ellis, J., Westbrook, T., & Dews, D. (2004). *A state-wide qualitative study of 385 professionals: Toward a greater understanding of employee retention and turnover in child welfare*. Paper presented at the Society for Social Work Research, New Orleans, LA.

Fenichel, E. (1992). *Learning through supervision and mentorship to support the development of infants, toddlers and their families: A sourcebook*. Washington DC: Zero to Three.

Gibbs, J. A. (2001). Maintaining front-line workers in child protection: A case for refocusing supervision. *Child Abuse Review, 10*, 323–335.

Gilkerson, L. (2004). Irving B. Harris Distinguished Lecture: Reflective supervision in infant-family programs: Adding clinical process to nonclinical settings. *Infant Mental Health, 25*(5), 424–439.

Jones, J., & Gallop, L. (2003). No time to think: Protecting the reflective space in children's services. *Child Abuse Review, 12*, 101–106.

Jones, J., Treseder, J., & Glennie, S. (2002*). An exploration of participation within an Action Research Project designed to improve service delivery to a small group of families with* *complex needs in an English new town*. Paper presented at the Conference on Action Research Constructivism and Democracy, Stockholm.

Kadushin, A. (1992). *Supervision in Social Work* (3rd ed.). New York: University of Columbia Press.

McAllister, C., & Thomas, T. (2007). Infant mental health and family support: Contributions of Early Head Start to an integrated model for community-based early childhood programs. *Infant Mental Health Journal, 28*(2), 192–215.

McCarthy, M. (2003). *Workforce retention research in New York State*. Paper presented at the meeting of the Council on Social Work Education, Atlanta GA.

Osmond, J. (2001). *The practice of knowledge use: A study of explicit and tacit understandings of Practitioners*. Ph.D. Thesis. The University of Queensland.

Osmond, J., & Darlington, Y. (2005). Reflective analysis: Techniques for facilitating reflection. *Australian Social Work, 58*(1), 3–14.

Parker, A., Nelson, C., Shelton, S. R., Dausey, D. J., Lewis, M. W., Pomeroy, A., & Leuschner, K. J. (2009). *Measuring crisis decision making for public health emergencies*. Prepared for the U.S. Department of Health and Human Services Office of the Assistant Secretary for Preparedness and Response. RAND WR-577-DHHS.

Randall, J., Cowley, P., & Tomlinson, P. (2000). Overcoming barriers to effective child care practice. *Child and Family Social Work, 5*, 343–352.

Rauktis, M. E., & Koeske, G. (1994). Maintaining social worker morale: When supportive supervision is not enough. *Administration in Social Work, 18*(1), 39–59.

Rycraft, J. R. (1994). The party isn't over: The agency role in the retention of public child welfare caseworkers. *Social Work, 39*(1), 75–80.

Ruch, G. (2002). From triangle to spiral: Reflective practice in social work education, practice and research. *Social Work Education, 21*(2), 199–216.

Ruch, G. (2005). Reflective practice in contemporary child-care social work: The role of containment. *British Journal of Social Work, 37*, 659–680.

Ruch, G. (2007a). Case discussion in child care social work. *Child and Family Social Work, 12*, 370–379.

Ruch, G. (2007b). 'Thoughtful' practice: Child care social work and the role of case discussion. *Child and Family Social Work, 12*, 370–379.

Weiss, E. M., & Weiss, S. (2001). Doing reflective supervision with student teachers in a professional development school culture. *Reflective Practice, 2*(2), 125–154.

Westbrook, T. M., Ellis, J., & Ellett, A. J. (2006). Improving retention among public child welfare workers: What can we learn from the insights and experiences of committed survivors? *Administration in Social Work, 30*(4), 37–62.

Chapter 11
Organizational Effectiveness Strategies for Child Welfare

Phil Basso, Helen Cahalane, Jon Rubin, and Kathy Jones Kelley

Abstract Child welfare agencies are dynamic, multifaceted organizational structures that exist by statute and are driven by bureaucratic policies and procedures. These complex, hierarchical social structures often function within a larger human services system and are influenced by a myriad of social, political, economic, and environmental factors. As with all social systems, child welfare agencies vary in effectiveness. Some are highly functioning, others struggle to meet professional standards, and many fall somewhere in between. Practice models exist for promoting organizational effectiveness within child welfare agencies, and draw from applied work in organizational development, performance management, quality improvement, organizational learning, and leadership. One such model is DAPIM™ which is a systematic approach to organizational effectiveness that enables work teams to drive continuous improvement using learning-by-doing methodology. The model provides a sequential process of activities directed toward helping organizations leverage their strengths, address areas where performance does not meet established goals, and continuously improve across all areas of work.

The "DAPIM™" model involves **defining** priority improvements in operational terms; **assessing** specific and observable strengths and gaps and identifying root causes and general remedies for priority gaps; **planning** quick wins, mid-term

P. Basso • J. Rubin
Organizational Effectiveness Department, American Public Human Services Association, Washington, DC, USA

H. Cahalane (✉)
Child Welfare Education and Research Programs, School of Social Work, University of Pittsburgh, Pittsburgh, PA, USA
e-mail: hcupgh@pitt.edu

K.J. Kelley
Merced County Human Services Agency, Merced, CA, USA

H. Cahalane (ed.), *Contemporary Issues in Child Welfare Practice*,
Contemporary Social Work Practice, DOI 10.1007/978-1-4614-8627-5_11,
© Springer Science+Business Media New York 2013

improvements, and longer term improvements; **implementing** action plans while managing communication and capacity; and **monitoring** progress, impact, and lessons learned for accountability and ongoing adjustments. The process is best conceptualized as a continuing cycle of quality improvement, not as a series of linear stages with a beginning and end. A compelling aspect of organizational effectiveness interventions and models such as DAPIM™ is their usefulness in addressing real world problems for child welfare agencies in real time.

Using organizational effectiveness approaches to target organizational system change provide distinct advantages for child welfare agencies. These include a lens through which agency culture can be observed and shifted, a basis for improving training and quality assurance systems design, a basis for improving staff supervision practices, and a parallel process between organizational leadership and frontline practice. Child welfare organizations are vibrant social structures ripe with opportunities to positively impact children, families, and the professionals who dedicate their careers to improving the lives of young persons. Organizational effectiveness and effective frontline practice reinforce and complement one another as agencies build, test, refine, and implement their plans for continually improving services, their capacity to deliver these services, the caliber of the staff they employ, and the outcomes of the children, families, and communities they serve.

Keywords Organizational effectiveness • Continuous quality improvement • Performance management • Organizational change • Learning by doing • DAPIM

Introduction

Child welfare agencies are dynamic, multifaceted organizational structures. They exist by statute, are driven by bureaucratic policies and procedures, and are influenced by a myriad of social, political, economic, and environmental factors. While the outcomes of child welfare services are often defined in global terms (i.e., assuring safety, permanency, and well-being) and are subject to local implementation, there is little disagreement that providing services to vulnerable children and families is a monumental responsibility. The qualities that are most central to highly functioning organizations—structure, power and authority, communication exchange, decision making, strong leadership, and a well-trained and skillful workforce—are often the same characteristics that make change and innovation within child welfare agencies a complicated endeavor. The child welfare organization is a complex, hierarchical social structure often functioning within a larger human services system. It is also a vibrant social structure ripe with opportunities to positively impact children, families, and the professionals who dedicate their careers to improving the lives of young persons.

As with all social systems, child welfare agencies vary in effectiveness. Some are highly functioning, others struggle to meet professional standards, and many fall somewhere in between. The shift across all human services toward the adoption of evidence-informed practices and the measurement of outcomes requires child welfare systems to analyze their internal functioning in order to improve their ability to meet the needs of children and families in their care. This focus is supported by evidence showing the influence of organizational characteristics on the quality and outcomes of child welfare services (e.g., Aarons and Palinkas 2007; Glisson and Hemmelgarn 1998; Yoo et al. 2007). The work of Glisson and others (e.g., Cahalane and Sites 2008; Glisson et al. 2008b; Mallak et al. 2003) has demonstrated the profound impact of organizational culture and climate on commitment and job satisfaction within the workforce and on the successful implementation of service programs and practices (e.g., Hemmelgarn et al. 2006; Glisson et al. 2008a).

Successful child welfare organizations devote attention to the structural context in which the work of the organization takes place. This requires a focus on the internal functioning of the organization, such as working climate, communication processes, leadership and authority, problem solving, strengths, and limitations. It also means that the organizational leadership team must make a commitment to ongoing improvement and change. Huse (1978), Jackson (2006), Marguiles and Raia (1972), and other scholars have described this focus on planned change as organizational development. In applying an organizational development framework to child welfare services, Curry et al. (2011) note that using behavioral science knowledge can enhance an organization's effectiveness and efficiency.

This chapter describes a practice model for promoting organizational effectiveness within child welfare agencies. The approach draws from applied work in organizational development, performance management, quality improvement, organizational learning, and leadership to delineate a set of key strategies designed to enhance agency functioning, capacity, and ability to meet client outcomes. Defined globally as *organizational effectiveness* (OE), the model provides a systematic approach to continuous quality improvement that emphasizes learning by doing at the team and system level of the child welfare organization. The approach involves a sequential process of activities directed toward helping organizations leverage their strengths, address areas where performance does not meet established goals, and continuously improve across all areas of work (American Public Human Services Association 2010, 2011).

Continuous quality improvement is an organizational process, a supervisory responsibility, and a frontline service delivery skill that must be mastered. Expertise in engagement, assessment, collaborative planning and decision making, facilitation, and evaluation is essential in both micro and macro social work practice arenas. The parallels between intervention with individuals, groups, families, and communities and the process of organizational effectiveness within child welfare agencies will be presented through case examples.

Theoretical and Conceptual Framework

Organizational effectiveness interventions emanate from numerous conceptual frameworks and theoretical approaches. Curry et al. (2011) observe that, while the conceptual models most prominent in strategic organizational change initiatives do

Table 11.1 Key concepts of systems theory

Open systems	The flow of energy and exchange of information between the system and the environment
Subsystems	Interrelated parts or elements of the whole
Inputs and outputs	The dynamic flow of energy and communication from (input) and to (output) the environment or other subsystems
Boundaries	The division or delineation between parts of a system or between the system and the environment
Goal seeking	The values, objectives, purpose, and function of individuals, subsystems, and the larger system
Entropy, negative entropy, and differentiation	The tendency of a system to move toward deterioration and the counteracting forces toward growth and transformation
Dynamic equilibrium, homeostasis, and steady state	The tendency of a system to achieve a state of balance among the system components
Roles and rules	The predictable patterns of functioning among parts of the system and the mechanisms to achieve the purpose of the system
Equifinality and multifinality	The achievement of results through many different conditions, activities, and methods

Adapted from Holden and Holden (2000), Kast and Rosenzweig (1972), Netting et al. (2012). Used with permission

not represent a unified theoretical approach, these models come from the related disciplines of organizational science, behavioral psychology, and the systems concepts adopted by both biological and social scientists. Several of these theoretical and conceptual frameworks are briefly described in the following section.

Systems Theory, Cybernetics, and Systems Thinking

The formative work of Ludwig von Bertalanffy (1968) introduced general systems theory (GST) as a framework for understanding the complex interactions between multiple components of a structure or organism that are joined together through relationships. A biologist by training, Bertalanffy proposed a theory to explain the intricate behaviors and characteristics of systems that bridged biological and social science. He emphasized that to understand phenomena, one must consider the interrelated components of the larger system rather than looking at one part in isolation. Many key concepts of GST have been described in the literature (e.g., von Bertalanffy 1968, 1972; Easton 1965; Parsons 1951) and have been applied to business and management in order to understand how organizations are structured, how they function, and how they are maintained over time (Broedling 1999; Kast and Rosenzweig 1972; Schein 1970). Several fundamental concepts of GST are described in Table 11.1.

Early work in the social psychology of organizations (e.g., Kast and Rosenzweig 1970, 1972; Katz and Kahn 1978) applied general systems theory to the empirical study of human service organizations. Questions regarding the ability of organizations to meet the needs of clients led these early investigators to consider issues such as how efficiently a system functioned, how it used its resources, and how effective it was at benefitting the larger society. Broadly defined, behaviors required for organizational effectiveness (OE) were identified as commitment, dependability in role performance, and participation in innovation. These elements of OE are present in contemporary approaches to human service program accountability, such as performance-based contracting that ties provider payment to child and family outcomes (Hannah et al. 2010).

In application, GST and cybernetics (the study of feedback within a system) are conceptualized as systems theory. Applying systems theory to child welfare services allows for a greater understanding of why organizations function as they do; of the dynamic interplay of individual, group, and organizational factors within systems; and of the connection between organizational performance and the quality of services provided to individuals, families, and communities. Systems theory also forms the basis for many models of family therapy, as well as the multidimensional approach to assessment and intervention used by social work practitioners (Hepworth et al. 2010).

The use of systems thinking to guide problem solving within an organization is grounded in the principles of systems theory described above. It requires a shift in thinking from linear causality (causality based in the individual) to one that considers the interactions of subsystems (the team, unit, workgroup, or department) and the broader organizational context (the agency, community, and the larger sociopolitical environment). The literature on systems thinking is vast and can be found in the disciplines of economics, education, engineering, evaluation, and physics (National Implementation Research Network, n.d.). Just as social workers would not think about working with a child without considering the impact that child's family, friends, and community have on the child's day-to-day functioning, organizations must be considered in a similar type of context.

Continuous Quality Improvement

Mary (2005) describes the movement across human services administration and leadership toward the adoption of new management models that focus on processes and results for clients. Management by objectives (MBO), total quality management (TQM), continuous quality improvement systems (CQI), and results-based accountability frameworks all have the common goal of increasing organizational capacity and performance (Patti 2009; Hannah et al. 2010). Many of these approaches use sequential steps or questions to implement and manage the quality improvement process.

Although relatively new within the array of human services, continuous quality improvement systems in the USA have their origins in industry and date to the beginning of mass production efforts during the Industrial Revolution. Early work during the 1930s introduced the Shewhart Cycle (Deming 1982), an approach to integrating

Table 11.2 Core principles of continuous quality improvement

• Quality is a continuous effort by all members of the organization to meet customer needs and expectations (Laffel and Blumenthal 1989)
• Customers are purchasers or recipients of the product of the organization
• Customers include every person or group, internal or external to the organization
• Top management must endorse and commit to the continuous improvement of quality
• All individuals want to perform to the best of their ability and will do so when given appropriate resources and support
• Processes, not individuals, are the unit of focus
• Every individual must be dedicated to quality and assume a sense of ownership and responsibility for success
• A multidisciplinary, nonhierarchical team with knowledge and authority to implement change must be formed

Adapted from Decker (1992). Used with permission

new standards of quality also known as the plan–do–check–act (PDCA) cycle. The highly successful work of Deming and Juran in introducing quality improvement methods to Japanese industry after World War II led to a resurgence of the CQI movement within the USA. The core principles of CQI are noted in Table 11.2.

While widely accepted in industry, CQI principles and management systems are not uniformly incorporated in all human service organizations, including child welfare (Decker 1992). Quality assurance systems in child welfare have been adapted from models in business and finance. An initial focus on compliance with federal and state requirements led to a history of child welfare agencies focusing on achieving minimal regulatory obligations versus best practice standards. More recent evaluation and monitoring efforts have progressed toward measuring the process and quality standards known to influence a broad range of child well-being outcomes. Organizational capacity is recognized as a critical variable in leveraging child welfare agencies toward more rigorous performance improvement and monitoring (Wulczyn et al. 2009). A recent Information Memorandum (ACYF-CB-IM-12-07) issued by the Administration for Children and Families provides child welfare agencies with guidance to establish and maintain CQI systems (U.S. Department of Health and Human Services 2012).

Organizational Readiness for Change

Implementing meaningful and sustained change within a system requires adaptation at multiple levels of the organization. The literature on organizational readiness for change provides a useful perspective and grounding for understanding the complexity of adopting new ways of conducting business within child welfare agencies. Based on the classic field theory of Lewin (1951), change within an agency can be understood as the interplay between driving and restraining forces. Further empirical work by Lewin and others (Lewin 1958; Schein 1987, 1992) identified three stages involved in behavioral change: awareness of the need for change, development of new behaviors, and integration of these new behaviors into everyday practice. These stages of readiness apply to both organizations and individuals. Studies by Prochaska and colleagues (e.g., Prochaska and Norcross 2010) have illustrated stages of change among individuals seeking treatment for a range of behavioral health problems. At the organizational level, the stages of change readiness can be seen as agencies determine strategic priorities and work toward quality improvement initiatives.

Subsequent scholars (Kelman 2005; Lehman et al. 2002; Fuller et al. 2007; Saldana et al. 2007; Weiner 2009) added to the conceptual foundation of organizational readiness for change by describing the conditions important for change (e.g., motivation, resources, climate, staff attributes) and the shared commitment and confidence necessary to implement new knowledge, skills, and innovation within an organization. The work of the Society for Organizational Learning (Senge 2006; Senge et al. 2005, 2008) identified factors central to sustaining change. These include leadership, opportunities for skill application, and an agency environment characterized by trust, support, and mutual learning.

Organizational Learning

Learning in an organization is a dynamic process that occurs over time as experience is converted into knowledge and that knowledge influences the cognitions, practices, or performance of the organization (Argote and Miron-Spektor 2011). Interest in organizational learning has increased over the past decade as teams and organizations have become more cognizant of learning as a collective process that occurs at the individual, team, larger group, and system level (Bunderson and Reagans 2011). Researchers have approached the study of organizational learning by measuring cognitions (e.g., McGrath and Argote 2001), behaviors (e.g., Huber 1991), and processes (e.g., Jackson 2006). Central to any organizational change as a result of new knowledge and experience is the context of the learning environment itself. Factors such as agency climate, the degree to which creativity and motivation are supported, how knowledge is retained, and the mechanisms for transferring new learning to practice all impact learning within an organization.

Learning Circles: Practice-Level Organizational Change

The creation of Learning Circle teams in child welfare agencies is an approach for bringing supervisors and workers together in a participatory problem-solving process and is one component of a larger organizational change initiative. Teams build a learning culture through biweekly meetings over the course of a year that focus on improving practice, organizational climate, and outcomes. Learning Circles are useful in building supervisory skills and in establishing an organizational culture of learning through experiential, applied approaches to best practice at the team level (Brittain and Morales 2010).

Experiential Learning

Experiential learning theory emerged from the works of Dewey, Lewin, and Piaget. Lewin's model of action research emphasized the importance of concrete experiences and feedback processes for goal-directed learning. Dewey explicitly noted that learning is developmental in nature and emphasized the integration of ideas, experience, and action. Piaget's cognitive development theory identified stages of cognitive growth and the processes that shape adult learning. Taken together, these theoretical foundations form a holistic model of experiential learning (Kolb 1984).

Experiential learning theory operates from the assumption that learning is a continuous process in which knowledge is created through experience (Kolb 1984). Kolb and colleagues (Kolb et al. 2001; Mainemelis et al. 2002) posit that individuals learn best through a cycle of experience, reflection, thought, and active experimentation. Experiential learning is closely aligned to the concept of "learning by doing" (Arrow 1962), a process first described in economic theory to explain innovation within a workforce. Kolb's (1984) typology of individual learning styles added to this body of knowledge regarding the acquisition and use of new information and technology by workers within an organization.

Empowerment

Principles of empowerment theory are found at both the individual and organizational levels. Zimmerman (1990) describes individual empowerment as including participatory behavior, motivations to exert control, and feelings of efficacy. Organizational empowerment is characterized by shared leadership, opportunities to develop skills, and effective community influence. Community-level influence encompasses the opportunity to participate in decision making and tolerance for multiple perspectives and solutions. In social work practice, empowerment is operationalized as the ability of individuals to control their environment, connect with resources, and negotiate problems by mobilizing strengths and addressing structural inequalities (Gibson 1993). The underlying principles of empowerment are applicable to practitioners working in child welfare agencies and their ability to impact organizational change, supervisors working with their staff, and to clients served by the child welfare system.

A Model for Organizational Effectiveness in Child Welfare

Child welfare agencies are organizational systems comprised of a number of dynamic and interrelated parts. Thinking about the child welfare agency from a systems perspective is analogous to the social-environmental view that guides social work practice with families. Rather than focusing on individuals in isolation, family systems interventions emphasize the interdependency of family members and their community context. As multidisciplinary team members and leaders in child welfare agencies, social workers are positioned to apply the principles of systems thinking to their work environment. Organizational effectiveness strategies build on systems theory by applying the principles of systems thinking to agency practice improvement efforts.

Drawing from successful business strategies and systematic methodologies used in corporations (e.g., Antony and Banuelas 2002; Collins 2001; Goleman 2000, 2004; Harry and Schroeder 2000; Kwak and Anbari 2006), the American Public Human Services Association (APHSA) developed an organizational systems model for facilitating a continuous quality improvement process within child welfare and other human service organizations. The model defines the following interconnected, moving parts of an organization:

- *Strategy*: the aim of the organization, shared and seen as important by staff and stakeholders external to the organization
- *Inputs*: resources put into the organization to achieve the strategy
- *Performance capacity*: the organization's ability to advance toward outcomes using available resources
- *Performance actions*: activities of the organization toward outcomes
- *Outputs*: results of system performance
- *Outcomes*: changes in lives as a result of system performance
- *Feedback from the environment*: feedback from clients, staff, partners, other key stakeholders, and the community about how well the organization is achieving its desired outputs and outcomes

Each component of the organizational system must be interconnected with others in order to achieve desired outcomes.[1] A strategy defines the desired outcomes, and the achievement of those outcomes is measured through feedback. Feedback creates the opportunity to evaluate achievements and is used to identify areas needing improvement if the outcomes are not being attained.

The diagram below illustrates the organizational systems model (Table 11.3).

Ideally, strategy drives the system (i.e., what the agency wants to achieve and the development of resources, capacity building, and programs). In "real-life" practice, however, many external demands impact the child welfare system and influence changes in strategy. Policy changes involving safety assessment, for example, necessitate a new or revised strategy and a modification in inputs, capacity, and performance. A reduction in resources may also drive a change in strategy; for example, there may be staffing changes as a result of hiring freezes or the elimination of positions because of budget cuts. Agency leaders must be prepared to adjust some of the goals in their strategy based on changes in workforce capacity.

---

[1] *Outputs* and *outcomes* are distinct entities that are sometimes confused. An example of an *output* in child welfare service is the number of child and family visits that a worker performs; the *outcome* of those visits is whether the child is safer as a result.

Table 11.3 Defining the organizational system

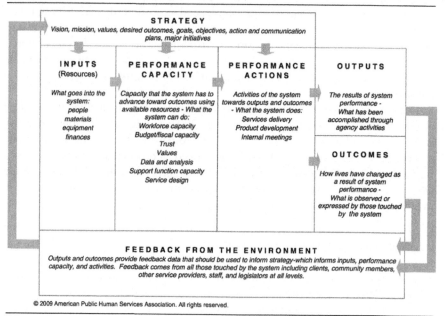

The seven interconnected parts of the organizational system contain within them many discrete tasks involving individual and group areas of work. Strengths are areas in which the agency has expertise, experience, knowledge, and skill to achieve the strategy. These can include strong leadership, the caliber of staff, community support, and recognized expertise in a certain service or program. Challenges are conceptualized as "gaps" which may reflect underdeveloped skill in agency management, less than optimal communication among staff, lack of resources, an atmosphere of distrust, or external relationships that have not been cultivated and that impact the ability to achieve desired outcomes.

The goal of OE is to help an agency create alignment of inputs, capacity, and actions with their strategy; leverage their system strengths; close their gaps; and continuously improve across all areas of work. Alignment with agency strategy is critical; it is not sufficient, for example, to have an abundance of resources if they are not configured to support the agency's core mission. A full staffing complement cannot produce good outcomes if that staff is not prepared to perform to the strategic goals of the organization, and having too few exceptionally performing staff does not allow for larger systems impact.

Components of an Organizational Systems Assessment

Reflective and Critical Thinking

The concept of reflective thinking was introduced by Dewey (1933) to describe learning that arises from the active consideration of ideas, meanings, and possible outcomes. Reflective thinking is often used synonymously with the terms "critical thinking" and "problem solving," although there is a distinction between these concepts. Reflective thinking involves persistent questioning of assumptions, values, and alternative explanations, while critical thinking leads to decisions and next steps. Much as organizational leaders can benefit from reflective and critical thinking, this process also supports the exploration of solutions with individuals and families in casework practice.

Organizational effectiveness interventions begin by engaging teams within an agency in reflective thinking about the agency as an organizational system. Using a basic set of questions to conduct a high-level assessment, teams gain a clear view of their agency: its current state, desired state, significant strengths and gaps, and key strategic priorities for reaching desired outcomes. Critical thinking helps an agency move systematically toward solutions and decide where to pursue continuous improvement. Targeted improvements can be small or large in scale. A broad-based approach is recommended for an agency seeking to drive comprehensive system reform that fundamentally changes the way the organization serves clients (i.e., services integration). A targeted approach directs continuous improvement in particular areas that have persistently needed improvement and/or have high endorsement ("buy-in") from staff and external stakeholders.

Many times change in child welfare systems is driven by crisis. Unfortunate circumstances such as a child death, a lawsuit, or less than optimal performance in a federal services review can precipitate a closer look at a child welfare agency's operation. These crises offer an opportunity to connect the benefits of OE interventions to the child welfare system. The use of reflective and critical thinking allows for a solution-focused process that is not centered on blaming individuals, finding scapegoats, or assigning punishments. Rather, the focus is on seeking systemic root causes for gaps and supporting improvements that limit the potential for future occurrences of the problem. Organizational effectiveness strategies can be used to address real-world problems for the child welfare agency in real time.

Regardless of a broad-based or targeted approach, reflective and critical thinking engages an agency in a systemic and systematic assessment of the following areas of work:

- Vision, mission, and values
- Environmental challenges and opportunities
- Client analysis and desired practice model
- Desired organization structure, culture, and leadership
- Organizational strengths, gaps, and capacity to change
- Strategic goals, objectives, and initiatives

- Major projects or work plans and commitments
- Performance measures, timeframes, and governance

Applying Reflective and Critical Thinking: A Case Example

After assessing each of the seven components of their organizational system, a child welfare agency came to the realization that although they were competent or above in many areas of performance, their overall family and child outcomes were not meeting quality standards. This was because their resources (inputs), design of services (performance capacity), and delivery of services (performance actions) were not connected by a well-defined, clearly articulated strategy for staff. While the agency had what looked like a strong training department, it was not designed to train staff to perform to the vision of leadership, resources were not utilized in the best way to achieve that vision, and actions by staff were not fully aligned to agency goals. This affected performance outcomes and outputs.

To correct this and to begin the process of having the whole staff think systemically, the agency developed a child welfare practice model that described the values of the organization and outlined the skills needed to achieve standards of practice. The agency then moved forward with redesigning its training unit to help staff develop the skills needed to achieve the strategy (performance capacity). Further, the agency committed resources (inputs) with a specific goal of achieving the outcomes of the practice model, including the development of staff with organizational effectiveness skills. Finally, the agency committed to continuously improving the specific behaviors (performance actions) of staff by working with supervisors to demonstrate the values and skills outlined in the practice model.

By engaging in systems thinking, the agency began to perform more systemically, starting with an organizational strategy and then connecting the rest of their work to that strategy with the goal of improving outcomes for the children, youth, families, and communities it served.

Reflective Thinking Questions

- Can you think of a time when you engaged a family in overcoming challenges by identifying strengths and supports for their family system? How did reflecting on the entire family system—including resources, family, friends, churches, and community groups—support the family with their challenges? How might this "systems thinking" be applied to a child welfare agency?
- In looking at the organizational systems model, how do you think child welfare agencies might better address the challenges faced by individuals, families, and communities?

Readiness for Change

An individual or group's readiness for change will impact how fast they can change, how many things they can change at once, and how much support they'll need in making a change. In social work practice, an assessment of readiness helps to inform initial goal setting and case planning. This is parallel to when a caseworker engages a family in safety planning by exploring a continuum of risk and safety factors to identify strengths and areas of concern for the family that will lead to a plan for assuring child safety. Essentially, social workers are assessing the family's capacity to provide for the safety of their child. If that capacity is low or the child is not safe, they must assess the family's "readiness for change" in order to successfully develop and implement a plan with the family. Similarly, child welfare organizations, like individuals and families, must be ready to take on the changes needed to improve their overall effectiveness and service outcomes. In assessing readiness, both strengths and challenges are recognized. Readiness capabilities, such as motivation, cooperation, open communication, and trust, can be used to overcome barriers. Because the values and practices of OE and child welfare are closely aligned, organizational interventions and direct work with children and families can be viewed through similar lenses. Both seek to "meet clients where they are" and start with the principles of engagement and an assessment of readiness for change. Clients (organizations or children/families) are helped to fully recognize and understand their situation and their larger context before moving forward.

Plans are most effective when readiness is assessed prior to their development. Readiness issues may also arise during implementation, or at the completion of a continuous improvement project, and should be dealt with at that time. The "Readiness Assessment Tool" (American Public Human Services Association 2011) has been used successfully to help agency leaders and staff identify areas of strength, prioritize areas for continuous improvement, and determine gaps in performance. The factors of system readiness for change identified in the assessment are shown in Table 11.4.

The Readiness Assessment Tool can be particularly helpful for determining if any foundational issues need to be addressed prior to implementation of plans. For example, an agency initiative may be dependent upon a technical infrastructure that is not fully developed, such as data and information technology. In order for the larger change initiative to be successful, that infrastructure must be prioritized. Readiness assessment is a precursor to organizational effectiveness intervention and informs decisions regarding how fast to drive a continuous improvement project, how much improvement work to take on at once, and how much support executive leaders and continuous improvement teams will need.

Applying Readiness for Change: A Case Example

A midsize child welfare agency used the Readiness Assessment Tool to identify the focus and general approach to an organization-wide, multiyear effort to improve the agency's culture. A team of supervisors, along with teams from five other state and local agencies, participated in a four-session, 8-month learning-by-doing institute to apply national guidance in driving continuous improvement. The team reflected on organizational readiness to identify areas in which the agency was generally strong and not as strong. The gap areas the team identified included teamwork across divisions, communication, and decision making. The team decided to focus on improving organizational culture in order to work more effectively across departments in delivering services to clients, recognizing that if the organizational culture was not first improved, plans for improving teamwork, communications, and decision making would ultimately not succeed as the environment would not allow for positive change.

The team used the readiness tool to identify what it would focus on and how it would go about its work. The team provided behavioral descriptors in recommending a focus on

Table 11.4 Factors of system readiness for change

Organizational readiness	Performance history
	Momentum for system improvement
	Organizational climate
	Organizational posture related to continuous improvement
	Clarity of roles and responsibilities
Leadership readiness	Expectations of the organization from leadership
	Posture toward obstacles
	Posture toward feedback
	Decision making
	Time for continuous improvement efforts
	Leadership stability
Staff readiness	Expectations of the organization from staff
	Employees' attitudes toward their work and clients
	Teamwork
General capacity to improve and innovate readiness	Aim of the organization (strategy)
	Data/information technology
	Communications/public relations
	Strategic support functions (human resources, training/staff development, policy, budget/financial management, development/fundraising, quality assurance)
Resources	Staff time
	Shifting of line items in existing budget
	Third-party funding

organizational culture to their executive team. Once its recommendation was accepted, the team drew upon its readiness assessment in deciding to use staff focus groups to define what "culture" specifically meant for them, what the desired culture would be, and what their current strengths and gaps were in respect to that desired culture. This approach contrasts with a "business as usual" approach which would have seen the team itself defining culture with input from executive sponsors or for the sponsors or an outside consultant to define it for them.

Reflective thinking using the readiness model guided the team in defining areas for continuous improvement and determining an approach to assessment that laid a foundation for successful, sustained improvements. One year later, the agency reported increased collaboration between departments, greater consistency across the agency in the way work is done, and improvements in its internal and external performance measures.

Readiness for Change: Reflective Thinking Questions

- Can you think of a time when you worked with a family that demonstrated a low readiness to make changes to assure the well-being of their child? What strategies did you employ to engage the family in planning for their own needs, as well as those of their child? How might these lessons be applied to your work in the child welfare agency?
- How can an assessment of readiness factors be used to support an agency in making forward movement when leading continuous improvement projects?
- How can an understanding of readiness for change assist you in preparing to supervise staff, manage a department, or lead an agency initiative?

Participation and Structure for Change

Social workers in child welfare settings routinely engage families, as well as others important in the family's social network, to facilitate problem solving and planning. Engagement and intervention approaches, such as such as Family Team Conferencing and Family Group Decision Making (see Chaps. 3 and 5), share common elements of participation, voice, and collective decision making. This same practice philosophy also guides organizational effectiveness work by acknowledging that collective input by those most impacted by the continuous improvement plan generally leads to solutions that are more effective and will enjoy greater commitment and follow-through by the participants.

Generating the expertise, buy-in, and ongoing support needed to make positive changes within an organization requires involving people who have an in-depth understanding of the agency and a sense of ownership for its mission and goals. Empowerment for organizational effectiveness work occurs when the executive leadership in an agency establishes clear boundaries, direction, and support for the change efforts at hand. The executive team of the agency functions as the "sponsor group" and is tasked with defining the higher-level vision, specific priorities, and outcomes for the continuous improvement efforts.

Child welfare practice and the organizational effectiveness approach both embrace participation and empowerment as core values. This consistency of values differentiates the approach described here from continuous quality improvement (CQI) initiatives that use outside observers to make recommendations based upon their own experiences and not the experiences of the agency members and clients. In OE, the values of participation and empowerment are reflected in three organizational roles that individuals perform in teams: sponsor groups, continuous improvement teams, and work teams. Although each of the roles is distinctive, membership on the teams is fluid, and oftentimes individuals participate in more than one group or team. This is particularly the case in smaller child welfare agencies.

As the sponsor group, the executive management of the agency sets the parameters for the quality improvement work, participates with staff in defining goals and objectives, and establishes the ground rules for working together. The sponsor team also gives work groups authority for problem solving and provides the resources (time, structural support, policy, training, data, technology) needed for the CQI project. The terms and conditions of the work are formulated into a written document known as a project charter. The charter serves as a project management tool and reference for approval. When the scope of work is clear, resources are allocated, and timelines are delineated; groups can then generate innovative solutions with the confidence that they will be supported by those in authority.

A continuous improvement (CI) team assumes hands-on responsibility for the improvement efforts and should include those whose expertise and buy-in are needed for the change effort to succeed. Usually consisting of 10–15 members drawn from all major departments and across staff positions, the CI team has primary accountability for implementing, monitoring, and sustaining the improvement effort. CI teams make recommendations to senior leaders, oversee work teams, and model continuous improvement work for others in the organization. In smaller organizations, a CI team can consist of three to five members.

A work team is focused on a particular area of improvement and works within a specified timeframe. Work teams are formed when the CI team identifies a particular area for which a new product, policy, or work process is needed. They are typically chartered by the CI team, and members are responsible for implementation and follow-through on specific commitments. The formation of sponsor teams, CI teams, and work teams promotes inclusion of all levels of the organization and helps in creating system-wide support for new ways of providing service.

Applying Participation and Structure for Change: A Case Example

A large, urban child welfare agency developed an enhanced practice model based on principles of teaming and family engagement. As the agency moved forward to implement its new and improved model for practice, it soon realized that it had not established a structure for implementation. As a result, the new model initially resulted in very slow progress and, in some cases, was even counterproductive. Different supervisors and caseworkers were interpreting the family teaming practices in their own ways with little direction or support, and some were making no changes at all. A number of agency staff were not even aware that a new model for practice had been created and were therefore in no position to lend their support. Stakeholders such as community advocacy groups and the court system were confused about the intentions of the rumored changes. Agency leadership became frustrated that staff was being resistant to change and progress, while staff became frustrated that no one seemed to take into account the time and training required for implementation to occur.

The agency leadership realized that they needed an organizational practice model that was parallel to the child welfare practice model they had just designed. As the sponsor group, the executive director and agency managers set the guidelines and worked with staff to define the goals and objectives for the project. They proceeded to form CI teams that included representatives from administrative support, contract management, and human resources, as well as community members, the court, and private service providers. Specific work teams were eventually formed to develop new policies, procedures, multidisciplinary training plans, and transfer of learning activities to support the desired practices. Over time, the agency began to strengthen both its internal and external "family engagement" capacity and performance. Teaming began to be implemented more consistently within the agency, and there was a unified practice approach among the supervisors that served to reinforce the principles of teaming and engagement for the frontline staff. Community providers were included in the development of policies and procedures that impacted their work with the child welfare agency, and cross-training was provided to agency staff and the community partners.

Participation and Structure for Change: Reflective Thinking Questions

- Can you think of a time in your agency when a decision was made or a problem was addressed but those most impacted by the decision were not participants in its creation? What happened as a result? Was the decision or solution the best one possible? Was there sufficient support for the decision or solution for it to be effectively implemented? Did it achieve its objectives?
- Are group decision-making approaches always needed? Are there times when the required expertise and required buy-in for a good decision are very limited?
- If you were part of a family that was seeking help, and you were engaged by a social worker who involved you directly in decision making that resulted in a plan that you felt made sense, would you be more likely to follow through on it? What might be different if the social worker told you what to do without your input?

Active Problem Solving/Systematic Learning by Doing

Adults learn and grow by applying well-ordered critical thinking techniques to solving their real-world problems. When they do so, they find great benefit in recognizing both task- and relationship-oriented reasons for their problems as well as in the ways to solve them. Research on adult learning suggests that the best way to strengthen professional skills and performance for frontline practitioners and agency leaders is through immediate application of new concepts and techniques to real work challenges (Antle et al. 2008; Kolb et al. 2001; Mainemelis et al. 2002). Many state child welfare training systems include comprehensive transfer of learning support to assure opportunities for on-site application of knowledge and skills (See Chap. 8). The use of coaching, mentoring, and guidance to encourage and reinforce learning is supported by implementation science research showing the increased effectiveness of training combined with transfer of learning compared to standard training alone (Fixsen et al. 2005).

Experiential learning researchers have found that adults learn best by having concrete experiences and reflecting on the results (see Mainemelis et al. 2002). These reflections allow learners to identify where they did and did not achieve desired results and think about how to approach similar experiences more effectively in the future. Organizational effectiveness practices apply principles of problem solving, experiential learning, and systematic "learning by doing" (Arrow 1962) by engaging agency work teams in a process of exploration to identify challenges they face in the workplace, potential solutions, and the pathways to enhance service outcomes.

Informed by adult learning research, APHSA developed a systematic approach to staff development that is based on applied learning by doing. The following are core elements of this facilitated approach for engaging work teams in problem solving by using their individual and team knowledge and experiences.

These elements are applicable at the organizational level, the supervisory level, and the casework practice level:

- Working directly with intact teams who perform together day to day
- Building safe, high-trust, team-oriented learning environments
- Encouraging teams to tackle real-life challenges through creativity and experimentation
- Facilitating continuous improvement for aspects of performance of greatest significance to the teams themselves
- Building the capacity of participating teams to handle new and emerging challenges as an ongoing way of doing business
- Using participants' expertise and insight about their own challenges to determine which interventions to introduce and when to introduce them
- Using an organizational needs assessment to determine developmental priorities in alignment with organizational goals and objectives
- Measuring success by identifying concrete improvements to learners' performance on the job and to the lives of the organization's clients

As in child welfare practice, this systematic, learning-by-doing approach is designed to help in real situations and uses planning techniques such as benchmarking and setting deadlines to support achievement. Monitoring is used to maintain accountability and progress toward outcomes.

DAPIM ™: A Method for Promoting Organizational Learning by Doing

We now describe the "DAPIM™" model (APHSA 2008), a systematic approach to organizational effectiveness developed by APHSA that enables work teams to drive continuous improvement using learning-by-doing methodology. This approach resembles the total quality management framework successfully used in industry (Harry and Schroeder 2000) and the classic plan-do-check-act (PDCA) cycle developed by Shewhart and Deming (Deming 1982). DAPIM™ involves **defining** priority improvements in operational terms; **assessing** specific and observable strengths and gaps and identifying root causes and general remedies for priority gaps; **planning** quick wins, midterm improvements, and longer-term improvements; **implementing** action plans while managing communication and capacity; and **monitoring** progress, impact, and lessons learned for accountability and ongoing adjustments. The process is best conceptualized as a continuing cycle of quality improvement, not as a series of linear stages with a beginning and end.

The diagram below demonstrates how the model operates, with each step of DAPIM™ resulting in specific and unique work products. A brief description of each step in this ongoing process follows. We first apply the DAPIM™ model to organizations and then apply these same concepts to direct practice, illustrating the parallel processes that take place in organizational effectiveness and in practice with children and families receiving child welfare services.

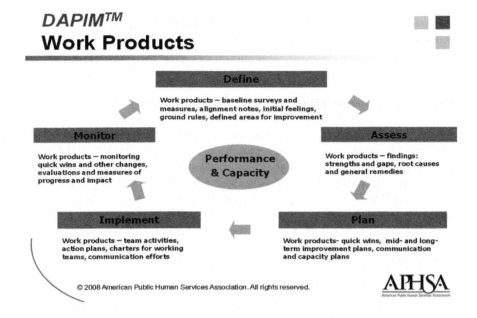

DAPIM™
Work Products

Define
Work products – baseline surveys and measures, alignment notes, initial feelings, ground rules, defined areas for improvement

Monitor
Work products – monitoring quick wins and other changes, evaluations and measures of progress and impact

Performance & Capacity

Assess
Work products – findings: strengths and gaps, root causes and general remedies

Implement
Work products – team activities, action plans, charters for working teams, communication efforts

Plan
Work products– quick wins, mid- and long-term improvement plans, communication and capacity plans

APHSA
American Public Human Services Association

Applying the DAPIM™ Approach to Organizations

Define

Defining the aim for improvement is the first step. Teams first define what they are going to focus on in observable, measurable terms, in line with the agency's core mission and strategic priorities. Defining a team's aim provides a clear, defined, and agreed-upon goal. Similar to the elements of effective service planning with children and families, goals should be specific, concrete, and behaviorally defined. By focusing on a common definition of the areas to target, teams can minimize any bias or prejudgments that might otherwise serve as barriers to good solution-focused planning.

Assess

A comprehensive appraisal of the agency's current state in comparison to the desired state is the next step in the process. Strengths and gaps in services, practices, and the organization (i.e., communication, staffing, policy, resources) are identified, and priority areas needing improvement are determined. Assessment results in specific and observable findings about the current situation (both strengths and gaps) that the team would like to improve. Because team membership consists of individuals from various levels of the organization and across departments, a holistic set of findings is developed that does not include only one perspective. Teams analyze and monitor their findings for improvement over time.

Building the Bridge to Planning: Root Causes and Remedies

Once teams are confident with the findings, they build a bridge from assessment to planning. This work involves group input, brainstorming and dialogue to determine the priority order of identified gaps and root causes of gaps, and general remedies to address the root causes. Root causes can be identified by continually asking "and why is that?" until actionable remedies for the problem emerge. Group input in determining the level of importance for each identified need enables the agency to approach the CQI efforts in a thoughtful manner and is likely to yield the best results for sustained improvement.

General remedies typically take one of three actionable forms:

1. Recommendations: remedies not in the team's control that must be referred to others in the organization for consideration
2. Decisions and commitments: remedies within the team's sphere of control that will allow for relatively easy implementation and advancement of the work
3. Team activities: remedies that require development of new tools and/or processes to implement and may involve chartering a work team or committee to gather additional information or advance the work

Using these general remedies as a guide, root cause analysis that drives planning ensures that time, energy, and other resources are targeted to address fundamental causes for gaps, not just to respond to symptoms of bigger and more important issues. Teams are challenged to think along two dimensions in the root cause analysis: the task dimension (how the work of the organization gets done, policies, procedures) and the relational dimension (group interactions, behaviors, communication, trust, power).

Plan

Planning begins after the root causes of gaps, their remedies, and prioritization for work have been established. There are essentially three types of continuous improvement planning: "quick wins," midterm improvement plans, and long-term improvement plans. Quick wins are changes that can be implemented immediately to resolve crises or pressing issues and generate energy and capacity for longer-term efforts. These immediate solutions are symbolically powerful and can build involvement and trust that lays a foundation for longer-term planning.

Midterm improvement plans include areas that can be changed within the next 30–90 days, and longer-term plans target changes over longer periods of time. Mid- and long-term improvement plans must be easily linked to the definition of the problem(s) to be solved and the root causes for those problems. The focus during these phases of the CQI effort is on building sustainable change and increasing the agency's capacity for problem solving. These planning strategies parallel those used in direct work with children and families. To facilitate a meaningful change process, social workers function as coaches by helping clients set reachable goals, take small steps, and build skills over time to meet future challenges.

Implement

After solid written plans have been developed, the implementation phase begins. At this step, the team and broader organization take increasing ownership of improvement efforts. Team members and others who are involved in implementation activities complete tasks specified in their plans and practice new ways of interacting, providing service, and connecting with outside resources. Implementation is usually thought of as actually doing the work of the CQI plan. It also, however, involves identifying barriers that prevent the team from succeeding and adjusting the improvement plan as work is completed and/or circumstances change. Changing circumstances are identified through monitoring (described below). Implementation and monitoring operate together as mutually reinforcing processes.

Monitor

Monitoring focuses on accountability and continuous adaptation based on what has been learned through the CQI work. Monitoring is accomplished through both qualitative and quantitative means and should bring focus to how the agency is changing as it moves toward its desired future state. Team members can determine how they are progressing and what shifts in tasks and relationships are occurring as they begin to improve their capacity, performance, and impact on others. Through careful review of what went well, what didn't go well, and what should be done differently, agencies are able to adjust their improvement plans and learn from experience. Effective monitoring considers both plan progress and the impact of changes compared to what was expected, ensuring that both outputs and outcomes are considered. Quantitative data (e.g., length of time in care, exits to permanency, reunification rates) and qualitative observations (e.g., interactions among co-workers, coaching, teaming) should be collected and documented.

Monitoring also includes acknowledging the progress that is occurring. When accomplishments are recognized and celebrated within the agency, a culture of success and positive reinforcement is created. Ultimately, monitoring can serve as a motivator within the agency. Systematic monitoring measures the impact of actions from the continuous improvement plan to know what efforts have been successful, what objectives have been achieved, and what remains to be accomplished.

Applying the DAPIM™ Approach to Direct Practice

Define

In direct practice, the definition of problems and development of goals that are meaningful to the client form the foundation for solution-focused work and a context for change (Berg and Kelly 2000). Problems must be identified collaboratively, be defined clearly, and have relevance to a client's daily life. Selekman (2010) notes that properly defining the problem at the outset is just as important as finding its solution. Solution-based casework models (e.g., Antle et al. 2010, 2012; Barbee et al. 2011; Christensen et al. 1999) start with a detailed definition of the problem, requiring caseworkers to identify when the problem occurs, who is involved, who does what and when, what occurs prior to the problem, and how problem behavior is defined.

Assess

Multiple life domains must be considered in order to accurately identify the needs of children and families who are referred for child welfare services. First and foremost, the current safety and risk of future maltreatment requires rapid assessment when children are referred for suspected abuse and neglect. A number of standardized decision-making tools have been developed to determine the presence or imminent likelihood of harm (e.g., Children's Research Center 2008; Coohey et al. 2013; Johnson 2011) and are used widely. Beyond the initial determination of child safety and risk, caseworkers must also consider a multitude of life circumstances and systemic factors that impact the child and family, such as poverty, oppression, substance abuse, mental illness, intimate partner violence, and traumatic events.

A thorough assessment of needs and capabilities requires the caseworker to consider the developmental, educational, social, and cultural dimensions of the child and family in order to develop a strategy for intervention. The assessment is also informed by the family's history and psychosocial context, including previous experiences with child welfare services, the presence of protective capacities and strengths, and community supports. Lietz (2009) notes that caseworkers must often reconcile conflicting information in order to integrate a multitude of details and develop a logical and well-informed plan of action.

Plan

The child welfare system has moved away from deficit-based practice approaches that view families as the problem and toward strength-based approaches that view parents as a primary part of the solution and as experts in defining their own needs and those of their children (Center for Human Services 2009). Family teaming models (e.g., Family Group Decision Making, Family Team Conferencing, Team Decision Making) are one approach used by child welfare agencies to actively engage families in case planning and decision making (see Chaps. 3 and 5). These approaches to practice encourage families to take more active roles in the development of their case plans and in determining the path for accomplishing their goals (U.S. Department of Health and Human Services 2010).

Implement

Caseworkers provide support to children and families as they put behaviorally specific plans into action. Targeted areas often include improving child supervision, assuring safety within the household, enhancing positive communication, and promoting skill in managing everyday life situations. Individuals and families are helped to meet challenges and develop new ways of problem solving, as well as recognize skills that may have been untapped. Caseworkers assist children and families in recognizing obstacles and barriers to progress and developing alternative ways to solve problems (Antle et al. 2010).

Monitor

Work with children and families requires frequent adjustments of service plans over the course of time. New or revised goals often arise from challenges, unanticipated events, or changing conditions. By revising plans at every contact, child welfare workers can make interventions with children and families responsive to real-life needs. Recognizing and celebrating success is a key element of monitoring. Child welfare clients, as well as caseworkers, can often become discouraged by the nature of the problems they are addressing. By paying attention to small signs of progress, children, families, and caseworkers reinforce a focus on solutions and change.

Applying the DAPIM™ Approach: A Case Example

A county Department of Human Services (DHS) system implemented a cross-system, on-call crisis service to meet the needs of the community outside of normal business hours. The crisis service was designed to address an array of needs including child protection, aging, juvenile justice, behavioral health, and disability. After providing mandatory training, the DHS director developed and implemented a system that was based on individual staff performing on-call duties for a week at a time. Management and frontline staff across service lines voiced many concerns about the crisis system, and there was little consensus regarding how it should operate. The director observed signs of low morale among the majority of staff assigned to the on-call service.

The DHS director and the senior-level managers formed a sponsor group to define the parameters for improving the crisis system. A CI team, composed of cross-system staff, supervisors, managers, and the DHS director, was engaged in a learning-by-doing process using the DAPIM™ approach. The team was given authority to problem-solve and define changes for the crisis on-call system. A root cause analysis by the team identified problems in communication, role identification, and knowledge of the various human service divisions. Quick wins were implemented, such as upgrading the resource kit for crisis workers, coordinating meetings with law enforcement, and developing protocols for each area of service. The team developed a plan for implementing system improvements, including a crisis on-call system manual and coaching provided by more experienced staff. Monitoring mechanisms were put in place that included tracking not only the number of crisis calls that were handled but also the outcome of the calls and the collaborative efforts between law enforcement and the on-call crisis workers.

Focus groups were held with staff regarding their experience during on-call assignments. These facilitated discussions focused on the workers' comfort with procedures, knowledge of resources for the service populations, and their experience with mentoring. Supervisors and managers also participated in focus groups to offer their perspectives, and a random sample of clients were asked about their experience with the crisis service. Incremental improvements in the on-call system were highlighted publically across the DHS organization and on the department's website.

After implementing the revised procedures, staff reported feeling engaged in designing and planning a system that met the needs of the community and addressed their concerns due to the empowerment they experienced being involved in the process. The staff, management team, and DHS director observed a higher level of support for the new system, including improved collaboration with law enforcement. Staff and managers across the human service organization reported being more comfortable and familiar with other departments. Ongoing monitoring of the on-call system resulted in the systemic collection of outcome data to measure the effectiveness of the service in providing timely and appropriate crisis responses across the client populations. The problem-solving skills gained through the DAPIM™ approach were applied to other improvement initiatives within the human services organization.

Building the Evidence Base for Organizational Effectiveness Interventions

The DAPIM™ model is designed to be flexible, and it is not yet known what effect differences in the scope and focus of OE work might have on its effectiveness. The identification of elements of the model that are associated with targeted organizational outcomes is a first step toward defining the processes necessary to implement the model with fidelity. Preliminary results from a national evaluation study of the DAPIM™ model in public child welfare agencies suggest that the achievement of a range of organizational outcomes, including the attainment of short- and mid- to long-range goals and increased functional capacity of the organization, is significantly correlated with several factors. These include higher ratings of initial readiness to undertake OE work, the intensity and dosage of the OE intervention, having monitoring procedures in place for improvement plans, high-quality facilitation and technical assistance, agency commitment of staff and resources, and sustained leadership support for the OE work. Results also suggest that a supportive agency context is a key factor of the change process. Widespread endorsement and participation of staff, open communication, clear roles, accountability, and a culture that supports learning are essential elements of a supportive agency context. Preliminary evidence also indicates that the higher achievement of goals related to client outcomes is related to higher readiness to undertake OE work and to having agency staff designated as internal OE facilitators (C.F. Parry, personal communication, June 5, 2013).

Conclusions

Broader Implications of Organizational Effectiveness

Organizational effectiveness is a systemic and systematic approach to continuously improving an organization's capacity, performance, and outcomes for those it serves (American Public Human Services Association 2008, 2011). A compelling aspect of OE work is that it can be used to address real-world problems for child welfare agencies in real time. There are several overall themes to consider when using the OE approach to target organizational change. In conclusion, we summarize them here.

Organizational Effectiveness Is a Lens Through Which to Observe Agency Culture

An OE approach becomes a "way of doing business" for agencies that employ it over time. This way of doing business translates into an agency culture that can be described as:

- Taking a systems view and thinking reflectively
- Focusing on readiness for change
- Emphasizing participation and empowerment
- Asserting clear and healthy boundaries
- Working systematically to continuously improve
- Learning by doing and solving problems proactively
- Emphasizing effective facilitation of groups
- Valuing support functions
- Balancing safety and accountability
- Evaluating for impact

Organizational Effectiveness Is a Basis for Improving Training and Quality Assurance Systems Design

While OE strategies and techniques, such as the DAPIM™ approach, serve to complement traditional staff development and quality assurance approaches, they also provide a basis for critically evaluating the strengths and gaps of those approaches. Common improvements to these approaches that OE helps to identify include:

- Addressing all of the moving parts of the organizational system
- Clearly and operationally defining the desired future state
- Using root cause analysis to develop remedies for gaps in performance
- Gauging readiness for change when planning developmental efforts
- Engaging real-world teams versus individuals from them
- Working through a facilitated learning-by-doing process
- Embedding reflective thinking and systematic critical thinking
- Concurrently building the capacity and performance of the training or QA functions
- Focusing on outcomes and not outputs in program evaluation

Organizational Effectiveness Is a Basis for Improving Daily Staff Supervision

While many of the OE strategies described above are used to implement continuous improvement plans for the entire agency, or to improve the execution of a single project, many of the principles can be used by supervisors as they work with their staff each day. Examples of this include helping staff:

- Reflect on their work with a bigger picture perspective
- Connect their work to agency strategy and practice models
- Become more self-aware about their readiness for change
- Learn how to employ effective structures and processes
- Understand the broader culture within which they work
- Demonstrate a greater level of collaboration with others
- Operate with clear and healthy boundaries
- Make effective use of planning and monitoring tools
- Learn new things as needed and when they can be immediately applied
- Operate more in a learning zone versus a zone of anxiety, apathy, or comfort
- Respect the role of support functions and the help they can provide
- Focus on the impact of their efforts versus checking things off on a list
- Use mistakes or gaps in performance as a basis for systematic continuous improvement
- Use DAPIM™ as a performance management process, allowing for a staff evaluation process that focuses on improved performance without being blaming or judgmental

Organizational Effectiveness Is a Parallel Process with Effective Frontline Practice

Throughout this chapter, the connection between OE interventions and the principles of effective practice with children and families have been illustrated. Engagement, empowerment, participatory decision making, problem solving, collaboration, and continuous improvement are central elements of these macro and micro approaches to best practice in child welfare. Organizational effectiveness and effective frontline practice are not just analogous—they serve to reinforce and complement one another as agencies build, test, refine, and implement their plans for continually improving services, their capacity to deliver these services, the caliber of the staff they employ, and the outcomes of the children, families, and communities they serve.

Questions for Discussion

1. Can you think of a time when you engaged a family in a learning-by-doing approach? What strategies did you employ to engage the family in defining the changes they would like to make and planning for their own needs? How might these lessons be applied to your work in a child welfare agency?
2. How can the DAPIM™ approach to problem solving be used in your agency? What challenges facing the agency can be addressed with a learning-by-doing change strategy?
3. How might DAPIM™ be applied to casework supervision?
4. What are some of the ways that agency leaders can integrate organizational effectiveness practices into the day-to-day work of child welfare staff?

References

Aarons, G. A., & Palinkas, L. A. (2007). Implementation of evidence-based practice in child welfare: Service provider perspectives. *Administration and Policy in Mental Health and Mental Health Services Research, 34*(4), 411–419.

American Public Human Services Association. (2008). *DAPIM™: An approach to systematic continuous improvement.* Washington, DC: Author. Available at www.aphsa.org.

American Public Human Services Association. (2010). *A guidebook for building organizational effectiveness capacity: A training system example.* Washington, DC: Author. Retrieved from http://www.aphsa.org.

American Public Human Services Association. (2011). *Organizational effectiveness handbook.* Washington, DC: Author.

Antle, B. F., Barbee, A. P., Christensen, D. N., & Sullivan, D. (2010). The prevention of child maltreatment recidivism through the Solution-Based Casework model of child welfare practice. *Children and Youth Services Review, 31*(12), 1346–1351.

Antle, B. F., Barbee, A. P., Sullivan, D. J., & Christensen, D. N. (2008). The effects of training reinforcement on training transfer. *Child Welfare, 88*(3), 5–26.

Antle, B. F., Christensen, D. N., van Zyl, M. A., & Barbee, A. P. (2012). The impact of the Solution Based Casework practice model on federal outcomes in public child welfare. *Child Abuse and Neglect, 36*(4), 342–353.

Antony, J., & Banuelas, R. (2002). Key ingredients for the effective implementation of Six Sigma program. *Measuring Business Excellence, 6*(4), 20–27.

Argote, L., & Miron-Spektor, E. (2011). Organizational learning: From experience to knowledge. *Organization Science, 22*(5), 1123–1137.

Arrow, K. J. (1962). The economic implications of learning by doing. *Review of Economic Studies, 29*(3), 155–173.

Barbee, A. P., Christensen, D., Antle, B., Wandersman, A., & Cahn, K. (2011). Successful adoption and implementation of a comprehensive casework practice model in a public child welfare agency: Application of the Getting to Outcomes (GTO) model. *Children and Youth Services Review, 33*(5), 622–633.

Berg, I. K., & Kelly, S. (2000). *Building solutions in child protective services.* New York: Norton.

Brittain, C. and Morales, J. (2010). Learning Circles: An introductory manual. Denver, CO: Western Workforce Initiative, Butler Institute for Families, University of Denver. Retrieved from: http://www.ncwwi.org/resources/library.

Broedling, L. A. (1999). Applying a systems approach to human resource management. *Human Resource Management, 38*(3), 269–278.

Bunderson, J. S., & Reagans, R. E. (2011). Power, status, and learning in organizations. *Organization Science, 22*(5), 1182–1194.

Cahalane, H., & Sites, E. (2008). The climate of child welfare employee retention. *Child Welfare, 87*(1), 91–114.

Center for Human Services. (2009). *A strengths-based approach to working with youth and families: A review of research.* Davis, CA: University of California.

Children's Research Center (2008). The structured decision making model: An evidenced-based approach to human services. Available at: http://nccdglobal.org/sites/default/files/publication_pdf/2008_sdm_book.pdf

Christensen, D. N., Todahl, J., & Barrett, W. C. (1999). *Solution-based casework: An introduction to clinical and case management skills in casework practice.* New York: Aldine De Gruyter.

Collins, J. (2001, January). Level 5 leadership: The triumph of humility and fierce resolve. *Harvard Business Review,* pp. 1–11

Coohey, C., Johnson, K., Renner, L. M., & Easton, S. D. (2013). Actuarial risk assessment in child protective services: Construction methodology and performance criteria. *Children and Youth Services Review, 35*(1), 151–161.

Curry, D., Basso, P., & Kelly, K. J. (2011). Organizational development and effectiveness in human services. *Training and Development in Human Services, 6*(1), 8–19.

Decker, M. D. (1992). Continuous quality improvement. *Infection Control and Hospital Epidemiology, 13*(3), 165–169.

Deming, W. E. (1982). *Out of the crisis.* Cambridge, MA: Massachusetts Center for Advanced Engineering Study.

Dewey, J. (1933). *How we think: A restatement of the relation of reflective thinking to the education process.* Boston: Houghton Mifflin.

Easton, D. (1965). *A systems analysis of political life.* New York: Wiley.

Fixsen, D. L., Naoom, S. F., Blase, K. A., Freidman, R. M., & Wallace, F. (2005). *Implementation research: A synthesis of the literature.* Tampa, FL: University of South Florida, Louis de la Parte Florida Mental Health Institute, The National Implementation Research Network (FMHI Publication #231).

Fuller, B. E., Rieckmann, T., Nunes, E. V., Miller, M., Arfken, C., Edmundson, E., & McCarty, D. (2007). Organizational readiness for change and opinions toward treatment innovations. *Journal of Substance Abuse Treatment, 33*(2), 183–192.

Gibson, C. M. (1993). Empowerment theory and practice with adolescents of color in the child welfare system. *Families in Society, 74*(7), 387–396.

Glisson, C., & Hemmelgarn, A. (1998). The effects of organizational climate and interorganizational coordination on the quality and outcomes of children's service systems. *Child Abuse and Neglect, 22*(5), 401–412.

Glisson, C., Landsverk, J., Schoenwald, S., Kelleher, K., Hoagwood, K. E., Mayberg, S., Green, P., & The Research Network on Youth Mental Health. (2008a). Assessing the organizational social context (OSC) of mental health services: Implications for research and practice. *Administration and Policy in Mental Health and Mental Health Services Research, 35*, 98–113.

Glisson, C., Schoenwald, S. K., Kelleher, K., Landsverk, J., Hoagwood, K. E., Mayberg, S., Green, P., & The Research Network on Youth Mental Health. (2008b). Therapist turnover and new program sustainability in mental health clinics as a function of organizational culture, climate, and service structure. *Administration and Policy in Mental Health and Mental Health Services Research, 35*, 124–133.

Goleman, D. (2000, March). Leadership that gets results. Harvard Business Review, 1–13. Available at www.hbr.org

Goleman, D. (2004, January). What makes a good leader? Harvard Business Review, 1–12. Available at www.hbr.org

Hannah, G., Ray, M., Wandersman, A., & Chien, V. H. (2010). Developing performance-based contracts between agencies and service providers: Results from a Getting to Outcomes support system with social service agencies. *Children and Youth Services Review, 32*, 1430–1436.

Harry, M. J., & Schroeder, R. (2000). *Six Sigma: The breakthrough management strategyrevolutionizing the world's top corporations.* New York: Doubleday.

Hemmelgarn, A. L., Glisson, C., & James, L. R. (2006). Organizational culture and climate: Implications for services and interventions research. *Clinical Psychology: Science and Practice, 13*(1), 73–89.

Hepworth, D. H., Rooney, R. H., Rooney, G. D., Strom-Gottfried, K., & Larsen, J. (2010). *Direct social work practice: Theory and skills* (8th ed.). Belmont, CA: Brooks/Cole.

Holden, J. C., & Holden, M. J. (2000). The working system. *Training and Development in Human Services, 1*(1), 34–38.

Huber, G. P. (1991). Organizational learning: The contributing processes and the literature. *Organization Science, 2*(1), 88–115.

Huse, E. F. (1978). Organization development. *Personnel and Guidance Journal, 403–406.*

Jackson, J. C. (2006). *Organization development: The human and social dynamics of organizational change.* Lanham, MD: University Press of America.

Johnson, W. (2011). The validity and utility of the California family risk assessment under practice conditions in the field: A prospective study. *Child Abuse and Neglect, 35*(1), 18–28.

Kast, F. E., & Rosenzweig, J. E. (1970). *Organization and management theory: A systems approach.* New York: McGraw-Hill.

Kast, F. E., & Rosenzweig, J. E. (1972). General systems theory: Applications for organization and management. *Academy of Management Journal, 15*(4), 447–465.

Katz, D., & Kahn, R. L. (1978). *The social psychology of organizations* (2nd ed.). New York: Wiley.

Kelman, S. (2005). *Unleashing change: A study of organizational renewal in government.* Washington, DC: Brookings Institute.

Kolb, D. A. (1984). *Experiential learning: Experience as the source of learning and development.* Englewood Cliffs, NJ: Prentice Hall.

Kolb, D. A., Boyatzis, R. E., & Mainemelis, C. (2001). Experiential learning theory: Previous research and new directions. In R. J. Sternberg & L. F. Zhang (Eds.), *Perspectives on cognitive, learning, and thinking styles* (pp. 193–210). NJ: Lawrence Erlbaum.

Kwak, Y. H., & Anbari, F. T. (2006). Benefits, obstacles, and future of six sigma approach. *Technovation, 26*(5–6), 708–715.

Laffel, G., & Blumenthal, D. (1989). The case for using industrial quality management science in healthcare organizations. *Journal of the American Medical Association, 262*, 2869–2873.

Lehman, W. F., Greener, J. M., & Simpson, D. (2002). Assessing organizational readiness for change. *Journal of Substance Abuse Treatment, 22,* 197–209.

Lewin, K. (1951). *Field theory in social science: Selected theoretical papers* (1st ed.). New York: Harper.

Lewin, K. (1958). Group decision and social change. In E. E. Maccoby, T. M. Newcomb & E. L. Hartley (Eds.), *Readings in social psychology* (pp. 197–211). New York: Holt, Rinehart & Winston.

Lietz, C. A. (2009). Critical theory as a framework for child welfare decision-making: Some possibilities. *Journal of Public Child Welfare, 3*(2), 190–206.

Mallak, L. A., Lyth, D. M., Olson, S. D., Ulshafer, S. M., & Sardone, F. J. (2003). Culture, the built environment, and healthcare organizational performance. *Managing Service Quality, 13,* 27–38.

Mainemelis, C., Boyatzis, R., & Kolb, D. A. (2002). Learning styles and adaptive flexibility: Testing the experiential theory of development. *Management Learning, 33*(1), 5–33.

Marguiles, N., & Raia, A. P. (1972). *Organizational development: Values, process, and technology.* New York: McGraw-Hill.

Mary, N. L. (2005). Transformational leadership in human services organizations. *Administration in Social Work, 29*(2), 105–118.

McGrath, J. E., & Argote, L. (2001). Group processes in organizational contexts. In M. A. Hogg & R. S. Tindale (Eds.), *Blackwell handbook of social psychology: Group processes* (pp. 603–627). Malden, MA: Blackwell.

National Implementation Research Network (n.d.). Systems thinking annotated references and links. Available at http://nirn.fpg.unc.edu/resources/systems-thinking-annotated-references-and-links

Netting, F. E., Kettner, P. M., McMurtry, S. L., & Thomas, M. L. (2012). *Social work macro practice* (5th ed.). Boston, MA: Allyn and Bacon.

Parsons, T. (1951). *The social system.* New York: Free Press.

Patti, R. J. (2009). Management in the human services. In R. J. Patti (Ed.), *The handbook of human services management* (2nd ed., pp. 3–27). Thousand Oaks, CA: Sage.

Prochaska, J. O., & Norcross, J. C. (2010). *Systems of psychotherapy: A transtheoretical analysis* (7th ed.). Stamford, CT: Cengage Learning.

Saldana, L., Chapman, J. E., Henggeler, S. W., & Rowland, M. (2007). Organizational readiness for change in adolescent programs: Criterion validity. *Journal of Substance Abuse Treatment, 33*(2), 159–169.

Schein, E. (1970). *Organizational psychology (rev.ed.).* Englewood, NJ: Prentice-Hall.

Schein, E. H. (1987). *Process consultation: Its role in organization development.* Reading, MA: Addison-Wesley.

Schein, E. H. (1992). *Organizational culture and leadership* (2nd ed.). San Francisco: Jossey-Bass.

Selekman, M. D. (2010). *Collaborative brief therapy with children.* New York: Guilford.

Senge, P. M. (2006). *The fifth discipline: The art and practice of a learning organization* (Revth ed.). New York: Currency/Doubleday.

Senge, P., Scharmer, C. O., Jaworski, J., & Flowers, B. S. (2005). *Presence: An exploration of profound change in people, organizations, and society.* New York: Doubleday.

Senge, P., Smith, B., Kruschwitz, N., Laur, J., & Schley, S. (2008). *The necessary revolution: How individuals and organizations are working together to create a sustainable world.* New York: Doubleday.

U.S. Department of Health and Human Services. (2010). *Family involvement in the Improving Child Welfare Outcomes through Systems of Care Initiative. Administration on Children and Families.* Washington, DC: U.S. Government Printing Office.

U.S. Department of Health and Human Services (2012, August 27). *Continuous Quality Improvement in Title IV-B and IV-E Programs.* Information Memorandum ACYF-CB-IM-12-07. Washington, DC: Department of Health and Human Services, Administration on Children and Families.

von Bertalanffy, L. (1968). *General systems theory: Foundations, development, applications*. New York: George Braziller.

von Bertalanffy, L. (1972). The history and status of general systems theory. *Academy of Management Journal, 15*(4), 407–426.

Weiner, B. J. (2009). A theory or organizational readiness for change. *Implementation Science, 4*(67), 1–9.

Wulczyn, F. H., Orlebeke, B., & Haight, J. (2009). *Finding the return on investments: A framework for monitoring local child welfare agencies*. Chicago: Chapin Hall at the University of Chicago.

Yoo, J., Brooks, D., & Patti, R. (2007). Organizational constructs as predictors of effectiveness in child welfare interventions. *Child Welfare, 86*(1), 53–78.

Zimmerman, M. A. (1990). Taking aim on empowerment research: On the distinction between individual and psychological conceptions. *American Journal of Community Psychology, 18*(1), 169–177.

Chapter 12
Managing for Outcomes in Child Welfare

Megan Good, Erin Dalton, and Marc Cherna

Abstract Child welfare organizations are increasingly held accountable for the work they perform through the evaluation of performance data. *Outcome measures* are designed to evaluate the result of a service or intervention, while *process measures* track adherence to critical procedures rather than focusing on the end result. Without numbers, there is no objective method for knowing where to target quality improvement efforts. It is by evaluating data that potential problems may be identified and analyzed to see whether or not there truly are problems that must be addressed. Since numbers cannot tell the whole story, this information is supplemented with qualitative information such as subject matter knowledge and feedback, case file reviews, and interviews with clients and community stakeholders.

At the first mention of "outcomes" and "data," some child welfare professionals become wary. They may be uncomfortable with technology or data and fear that the information that is collected and analyzed will not adequately represent the work they do with children, families, and the courts. An additional concern is that the nature of child welfare case management does not lend itself to outcome monitoring because the situation of each child and family is unique, and child welfare staff have no control over the issues and challenges that a family may have when they present for service.

Child welfare services demand accountability, and in an increasingly data-driven environment, staff of child welfare agencies are being held accountable to outcome-based performance more than ever. Performance tools and data serve a purpose beyond just reporting and monitoring. Data can be used to inform and improve practice, with the ultimate result of improving outcomes for children. Agencies with cultures that embrace continuous improvement and feedback from all levels of the organization will be most able to utilize information to their advantage and respond to changes in their environment.

M. Good (✉) • E. Dalton • M. Cherna
Allegheny County Department of Human Services, Pittsburgh, PA, USA
e-mail: megan.good@alleghenycounty.us

H. Cahalane (ed.), *Contemporary Issues in Child Welfare Practice*,
Contemporary Social Work Practice, DOI 10.1007/978-1-4614-8627-5_12,
© Springer Science+Business Media New York 2013

Keywords Outcome measure • Process measure • Performance measure • Continuous quality improvement • Data-driven decision making • Trend • Operational data • Administrative data • Qualitative research • Quantitative analysis • Performance management • Accountability • CFSR • Indicators

Introduction

Individuals and organizations are increasingly held accountable for the work they perform through the evaluation of performance data. Measures are developed to evaluate performance relative to both outcomes and processes. *Outcome measures* are designed to evaluate the result of a service or intervention (e.g., percentage of youth reunified with family). *Process measures* are commonly lumped together with outcome measures in everyday language, but they differ in that they track adherence to critical procedures rather than focusing on the end result (e.g., meeting minimum monthly visitation standards).

At the first mention of "outcomes" and "data," some child welfare professionals become wary. They may be uncomfortable with technology or data and fear that the information that is collected and analyzed will not adequately represent the work they do with children, families, and the courts. They may think that, as pieces of information, outcomes are not that important, because they do not actually capture what is achieved in their daily work; the quality of their work "cannot be put into numbers." Or it may be that the data themselves appear confusing and not easily comprehensible. An additional concern is that the nature of child welfare case management does not lend itself to outcome monitoring because the situation of each child and family is unique, and child welfare staff have no control over the issues and challenges that a family may have when they present for service.

These concerns are important to consider on the path to achieving improved outcomes, but they must not be permitted to remain barriers to the use of information to improve services for children and families. Without numbers, there is no objective method for knowing where to target quality improvement efforts. It is by evaluating data that potential problems may be identified and analyzed to see whether or not there truly are problems that must be addressed. Since numbers cannot tell the whole story, this information is supplemented with qualitative information such as subject matter knowledge and feedback, case file reviews, and interviews with clients and community stakeholders.

The goals of this chapter are to provide readers with a greater understanding of how performance is measured and monitored in child welfare, as well as to illustrate some processes that local agencies can utilize to improve their practice. To achieve these goals, the chapter is organized into three sections. The first section provides an overview of federal accountability and performance measurement, and a schema for evaluation at the local level. The second section discusses principles necessary to implement continuous quality improvement and manage for performance within a child welfare framework. Finally, the chapter concludes with a case study which demonstrates how a local agency could use these principles and performance measures in concert to improve outcomes for children.

> **CFSR Outcome Measures**
>
> Section I – Safety
>   Outcome S1: Children are, first and foremost, protected from abuse and neglect.
>   Outcome S2: Children are safely maintained in their homes whenever possible and appropriate.
>
> Section II – Permanency
>   Outcome P1: Children have permanency and stability in their living situations.
>   Outcome P2: The continuity of family relationships and connections is preserved for children.
>
> Section III – Child and Family Well-Being
>   Outcome WB1: Families have enhanced capacity to provide for their children's needs.
>   Outcome WB2: Children receive appropriate services to meet their educational needs.
>   Outcome WB3: Children receive adequate services to meet their physical and mental health needs.
>
> http://www.acf.hhs.gov/programs/cb/cwmonitoring/tools_guide/sumfinding.htm

Fig. 12.1 CFSR outcome measures

Understanding Outcomes

Accountability

The children served by child welfare agencies are particularly vulnerable. For this reason, child welfare agencies are held accountable at all community levels for outcomes for the children and families they serve—by the federal and state governments, foundations that fund innovative efforts, and community leaders. The agency responsible for oversight at the federal level is the Children's Bureau within the Administration for Children and Families (ACF), an office of the US Department of Health and Human Services (HHS). Established in 1912, the Bureau's formal push for accountability really began following the 1994 Amendments to the Social Security Act (SSA), which authorized HHS to review state programs to ensure substantial conformity with requirements in the SSA (ACF n.d.).

A new review system was established in 2000, known as the Child and Family Services State Plan Review (CFSR). The CFSR expanded upon previous efforts by moving beyond strictly monitoring procedural compliance through reviewing case file documentation, to ensuring states' conformity with federal requirements, determining how children are actually faring in the child welfare system, and assisting states to enhance their capacity to improve outcomes (ACF n.d.).

The CFSR is a two-stage process that consists of a statewide assessment and an onsite review. The assessment is completed through the submission of data by each state for a number of indicators, which are then compared to the national standard as determined by the Children's Bureau (ACF n.d.). The three categories of outcomes included in the CFSR reflect the three commonly accepted goals in child welfare: safety, permanency, and well-being. The CFSR outcomes for each category are listed in Fig. 12.1 (ACF 2007). Some of the outcomes have a number of *indicators* to measure how well a locality is performing. Indicators are more specific instruments used to measure performance relative to an outcome. While the outcomes themselves are widely accepted among child welfare agencies, the precise measures and methodology for calculating the indicators are widely disputed.[1] The CFSR process is also subject to feedback from the states and from academics. There have been two major changes to the CFSR measures, and at the time of this writing, there are proposals for a new set of wide-ranging improvements to the measures and indicators.

The onsite reviews include case record reviews, interviews with families engaged in services, and interviews with community stakeholders. This process is facilitated by a review team comprised of both federal and state agency staff. At the end of the review process, states that are found not to be in substantial conformity with each area of the assessment are required to develop and implement program improvement plans (PIP). After the first review in 2004, each state and territory in the USA was required to implement a PIP (ACF n.d.). Many state PIPs incorporate some of the principles and methodologies presented here. Following the second wave of reviews, each state once again used the review as the basis for ongoing program improvement, as no states had achieved the CFSR goal of substantial conformity in six of the seven outcome areas (ACF 2011).

In order to achieve the outcomes specified above and carry out the strategies for improvement that are outlined in the state plans, states and localities rely on greater amounts of information and more in-depth analyses to inform their decision making than occur at the federal level. This shifts accountability to the local administrators of child welfare services. The remainder of this section discusses how outcomes are monitored at the local level.

Types of Measures

The two primary forms of performance measures are outcome and process measures. Each of those forms can be used to measure performance across a number of different types of services. Services are grouped here into referrals and case progression, case management, family services, and placement services. This categorization mirrors some families' pathways through the child welfare system, though not all families referred for service subsequently receive case management and additional non-placement and placement services. Measures within each of these categories are tied to best practices and service patterns that have been shown to impact a child or family's well-being. A sampling of these common measures is provided in Table 12.1. When evaluating case practice or the effectiveness of an intervention, youths' outcomes are compared whenever possible to those of youth who possess similar characteristics (e.g., age, care type, service involvement).

---

[1] For more information on this, see Administration for Children and Families (ACF) April 5, 2011 Federal Register announcement: Federal Monitoring of Child and Family Service Programs; Request for Public Comment and Consultation Meetings.

Table 12.1 Sampling of common performance measures

(a) Process measures
Timeliness to investigation
Completion of monthly contacts in a timely manner
Completion of case plans and safety assessments in a timely manner
Families actively participating in family team meetings
Concurrent planning for children in placement
Frequent visitation with birth families and siblings for children in placement
Placement with siblings
Placement stability
Progress towards adoption for children in care for an extended period of time

(b) Outcome measures
Families re-reported who were previously investigated
Recurrence of maltreatment
Recurrence of maltreatment in foster care
Rates of entry into out-of-home care
Rate of reentry into care
Length of time spent in out-of-home care
Children reunified with parents
Exits to permanency
Fatalities/near fatalities of children known to child welfare agency

Referrals and Case Progression

Monitoring referrals and investigations provides a wealth of information about how children and families are coming to the attention of child welfare agencies and how agencies handle the initial interactions with them. Common pieces of information (including process and outcome measures) tracked during these early stages of system involvement include referral reasons, the number of referrals (for a child, family, neighborhood, or the whole agency), and the timeliness to investigation. The referral information can be used to identify areas where prevention efforts can be more heavily focused (e.g., adequate housing, early childhood programs). Timeliness to investigation is a closely monitored process measure because the responsiveness of an agency after an allegation is made (measured by the time it takes for someone to visit the child) has significant implications for how well the agency may be protecting the safety of children in their homes. Qualitative information may also supplement the review of administrative data. For example, an agency may review the quality of the safety assessments conducted during the investigation stage of a case to ensure that the agency is doing everything it can to ensure child safety.

From the point of referral, agencies are also able to track the progress of a case, from referral to investigation to case opening to non-placement services to out-of-home placement. Not all cases will progress to the next level at each step, and by examining patterns in case progression, administrators are able to better understand how referrals relate to caseloads and placements, as well as to identify where changes may need to be made to improve the timeliness, type, or level of services provided.

Case Management

Once a case is accepted for service, child welfare professionals must adhere to many standards of case practice. Perhaps the most often discussed case management requirement is monthly caseworker visitation. This may refer to face-to-face contact made with children by their caseworker or to family visits between children in out-of-home placement and their parents or siblings. In accordance with the Child and Family Services Improvement and Innovation Act [Public Law (P.L. 112–34)],[2] all child welfare agencies must require regular visitation as a key component to assessing and ensuring child safety and must report data from monthly caseworker visits with children in foster care to the Children's Bureau. P.L. 112–34 built upon evidence from the first CFSR rounds showing an association between caseworker visits and positive ratings on child and family outcomes (Administration for Children and Families n.d.) and requires the use of consistent data reporting methodology by states. From a qualitative perspective, it is important to track the substantiveness of caseworker visits with children and families. The use of mixed methods (e.g., quantitative and qualitative) allows for an analysis of the regularity and timeliness with which these visits occur, as well as an assessment of the performance of the child welfare agency and the caseworker in building relationships with families focused on both protection and support (National Conference of State Legislatures 2006).

Several other requirements that are common to all agencies, and are often monitored for compliance, include timely completion of service plans, safety assessments, permanency planning conferences, physical health checks, and education status reviews. Beyond these, additional data of interest may be more idiosyncratic to the state or agency and often include measuring how often particular interventions are applied. For example, some jurisdictions require a court review every 3 months for children in out-of-home care. Where this requirement exists, agencies should measure if the reviews are occurring as they should and, in the event they are not, determine the cause of this shortcoming and how the cause can be addressed.

Many of these measures are focused on activities occurring at the individual case or caseworker level. Agency-wide, caseload size is an important variable that is frequently monitored. If caseworkers have too many children and families on their caseload, they may be unable to meet the demands of quality case practice, including engaging families in collaborative efforts to help them manage crisis, build upon strengths, and better meet the needs of their children. Since there are so many demands on caseworkers, tracking caseload size and other case management metrics not only assists with quality improvement efforts but can also assist caseworkers in managing their workloads effectively and making improved case decisions.

---

[2] Title IV-B of the Social Security Act as revised by the Child and Family Services Improvement and Innovation Act [Public Law (P.L. 112–34)] was signed into law by President Obama on September 30, 2011.

Family Services

Many families access services that are designed to provide support for families, improve child development, and strengthen family functioning. Often these services are paid for by the child welfare system. Such services include but are not limited to parenting programs, counseling, home visitation, truancy prevention, and substance abuse treatment services. From the perspective of child welfare outcome analyses, these services have the potential to perform two different primary functions: *prevent system involvement* and *preserve families*.

The services have the potential to be *preventive* if the family is not actively served by child welfare or if their child has not been removed from the home. In this circumstance, the services accessed may prevent the family from requiring any, or greater, intervention by the child welfare agency. In this circumstance, the outcomes monitored often include the prevention of referrals to child welfare, active cases with child welfare, and out-of-home placements.

The services have the potential to *preserve families* if they are accessed following intervention by a child welfare agency that results in a child being removed from the home. In this case, the opportunity for prevention has been missed, but the services accessed by the family may allow the child to safely return home to the family, thereby preserving the family unit. Outcomes frequently monitored for children falling into this category include increased rates of returning to their families, short lengths of stay in care, placement stability, and decreased rates of reentry into care.

For either group of families, other relevant outcomes of service provisions may include an increase in parenting skills or confidence levels, parents developing a better understanding of their children, improved child development, or other indicators of well-being that reflect what the services are designed to achieve. Success relative to these types of outcomes is often the most difficult to measure, and the development of these indicators is often dismissed in favor of measuring outcomes strictly related to out-of-home placement. However, measures that evaluate programs' effectiveness in delivering these services must be included. While rhetoric may reflect that family services are a priority, in an increasingly data-driven environment, what an organization chooses to measure implicitly places more value on that activity (Tilbury 2007). Therefore, failing to measure an activity that truly is valued by an organization may unintentionally diminish its perceived significance. For family services, this is particularly important since the majority of children in the child welfare system are receiving family-focused services, while only a portion of the population are represented in the evaluation of placement outcomes.

Part of the challenge in the early stages of performance measurement is determining how to measure performance appropriately. This challenge should be recognized and addressed through the continuous evaluation of measurement tools themselves, but should not prevent efforts at evaluation, accountability, and prioritization of services (Tilbury 2007).

Table 12.2 Placement indicators

Measure	Description
Removal reason (or placement reason)	The reason(s) a child is removed from the home and placed in an out-of-home placement
Placement setting (care type)	The type of environment in which a youth resides while in out-of-home care. Placement settings include shelter care, kinship care, foster care (or stranger care), congregate care (e.g., group homes), and independent living
Safety in placement	The absence of abuse or neglect while in out-of-home care
Placement stability	The number of placement settings in which a child lives while placed out of the home—often referred to as the number of moves or transfers a child experiences
Length of stay (duration)	The amount of time a child spends in out-of-home care. If the child moves between placement settings, the length of stay refers to the total time in care, not his/her time in just one of those settings
Exit destination	Where a child goes when he or she leaves an out-of-home placement. Potentials exit destinations include, but are not limited to, the birth family, adoption, permanent legal custodianship, reaching majority age, and running away
Reentry	Entry into an out-of-home placement after an exit from a previous placement episode

Placement Services

Children for whom the greatest number of outcomes are tracked are those who have been removed from the home and are in an out-of-home placement. Monitoring the experiences of these youth is critical, since it is vital to their well-being that they remain safe and achieve permanency in a timely manner. As with any other service, the specific measures and outcomes that are tracked will vary by locality or organization, but there are several measures related to placement that are widely accepted and used across the USA. The measures are listed in Table 12.2, along with a brief description of each measure.

Measuring and Understanding Performance

Developing a comprehensive understanding of an entity's performance on a certain indicator is a complex process. No one way of measuring or evaluating an outcome can explain what is happening, why it is happening, and what needs to be done to address any shortcomings. Yet, if each of these elements is not understood, an individual or organization will not be able to effectively create change. There are four methods a locality may use to understand these outcomes and implement efforts for improvement:

- Analyzing trends
- Examining variations in performance across operational units

- Performing qualitative research
- Identifying data needed for operational use

The four methods should be performed in concert, with stakeholders communicating about each method, using the results of one to inform the processes of others. Not only do these methods need to be considered together for a specific outcome, but performance on outcomes and processes must be reviewed holistically because goals may conflict. For example, short lengths of stay and low rates of reentry are both positive outcomes for youth in placement. However, evidence shows that youth with shorter lengths of stay in placement are more likely to experience a reentry into care. Therefore, improving the organization's performance on one outcome (by shortening children's length of stay) may worsen the organization's performance on another (by increasing the percentage of children who reenter placement). In this situation, one would not want to focus on improving one outcome while losing sight of the other. It is important to find balance among the many indicators of successful outcomes and performance.

Analyzing Trends

The most common form of outcome analysis is trend analysis, which entails examining the performance of an indicator at different points in time to see how performance has changed over time. Such analyses commonly include the examination of trends by subsets of the population because experiences will often vary by certain child characteristics. While these subsets are often based on demographics (such as age and race), youth are also grouped by other characteristics, including care type and their length of time in care.

An additional consideration when performing trend analysis is how to select the population of children for whom outcomes are examined. For any analysis, there are three primary ways of establishing this group of children (Center for State Foster Care and Adoption Data 2010).

1. *Point in time*—Youth who are all *actively* participating in a service or activity at a point in time or in a certain period of time (e.g., day, week)
2. *Entry cohort*—Youth who all *entered* a program or began to receive a service within a certain period of time (e.g., month, year)
3. *Exit cohort*—Youth who *exited* or stopped receiving a service within a certain period of time (e.g., month, year)

Each method has pros and cons that make it preferable for different types of analysis, and it is important to understand these differences and carefully select the population that will be used when measuring performance.

One example of a time of when these methods matter is when an agency wants to better understand the age distribution of youth receiving a certain non-placement service. Figure 12.2 shows how this distribution will change significantly depending on how the population is defined.

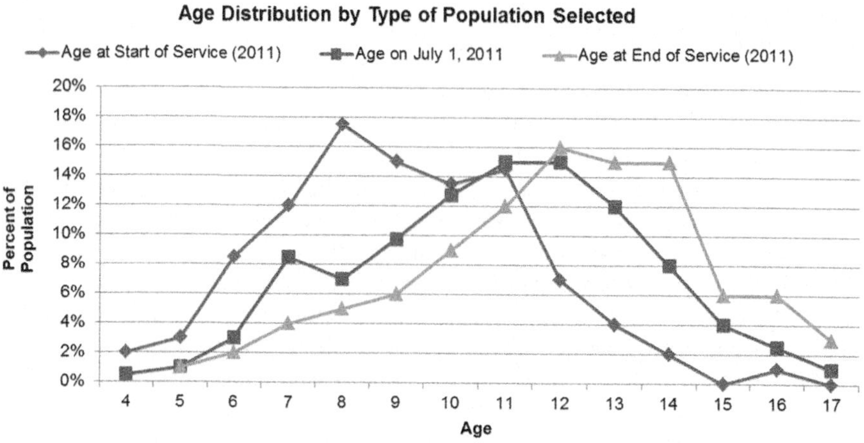

Age Distribution by Type of Population Selected

Fig. 12.2 Age distribution by type of population selected

Examining Variations in Performance Across Operational Units

Within an agency, performance may vary by operational units. Depending on the structure of the agency, these smaller units may include counties, regional offices, and/or contracted provider agencies. It is important, and often useful, to break down the high-level analysis of outcomes to these lower levels in order to determine if the overall outcomes are the result of agency policy, the structure of the systems of care, cultures within different agencies, supervision, the communities served, or other factors.

It is important to begin this analysis by reviewing the underlying populations served by the different units. It would not be appropriate, for example, to expect the same results from a unit serving a population with a high concentration of poverty and a unit serving a population with a substantially lower rate of poverty. After this analysis is completed, if outcomes are the same across all geographies or providers, then it is likely that the results are driven by policy, the system structure, or overall agency culture. If results vary, then it is likely that they are influenced by the culture or supervision style of the smaller units, different interpretations of policy, or other characteristics of the communities served by different units.

The presence or absence of variation in outcomes across an agency's smaller units assists in narrowing the scope of further efforts to understand and investigate the causes of system outcomes. This narrowing is particularly useful for informing and guiding qualitative research.

Performing Qualitative Research

Research is *qualitative* if it seeks to describe human behavior or attitudes and provide explanations as to *why* things occur. This answering of "why" and "how" things happen is what differentiates it from the other forms of analysis described above. Qualitative research relies on communication with individuals who possess knowledge relative to the subject, rather than analyzing statistics (referred to as *quantitative research*) (Engel and Schutt 2013).

Qualitative information can be gathered in multiple ways. Some forms of qualitative research include case reviews, surveying caseworkers, interviewing families, and holding focus groups with supervisors to better understand their experiences related to a specific aspect of service delivery. For example, if we know that youth who are reunified with their parents after being in care for 3–6 months are very likely to reenter placement, speaking to caseworkers or families about what is happening during those transitions can inform how changes to policies or practice may improve permanency for those youth. The importance of such methods is recognized not only by local agencies, but by federal and state government agencies as well.

A common practice at the state level is to engage in Quality Service Reviews[3] (QSRs). The QSR is a self-evaluation tool that promotes practice standards and accountability by engaging all organizational levels within an agency and by tying performance to core components of individualized and participatory practice: engagement, assessment, planning, implementation, and results (Center for the Study of Social Policy 2003; Morris-Compton et al. 2011). QSRs utilize trained teams of reviewers to conduct in-depth evaluations of a sampling of cases. These evaluations include interviews with all case participants and the examination of case records. Following the review, the teams meet with the supervisors and caseworkers to provide feedback and suggestions for improvement. The information from all cases is then evaluated as a whole and used to identify themes related to strengths and areas for improvement across the system (Center for the Study of Social Policy 2003).

Identifying Data Needed for Daily Operations

The three methods discussed so far will shed light on what is occurring and why it is happening, but *operational data* must be available in order to put this information to use. Operational data will inform the day-to-day functions of caseworkers, supervisors, and administrators. The data are available in real time, are reliable, and can be used to monitor progress and, ultimately, implement change. For this information exchange to occur, agencies must develop mechanisms to communicate relevant information to the appropriate people.

For example, let us return to the previous illustration of monthly caseworker visits. Regulatory standards specify that caseworkers must meet minimum monthly visitation requirements for the children on their caseloads who are in federally

---

[3] Quality Service Reviews were developed, at least in part, in response to the federal CFSR qualitative review process, demonstrating the power the federal government has to encourage change at the state and local level.

defined foster care placement (U.S. Department for Health and Human Services, Administration for Children and Families 2012). Operational data that would assist them in meeting these requirements include a report detailing which children on their caseload require visits in the current month. In contrast, operational data that would be valuable to administrators may include a dashboard that tracks their units' performance and activities on a number of key case functions, ranging from timeliness of investigations to the quality of comprehensive permanency plans for children turning 16 who may need to be connected to services for transition-age youth.

Improving Performance

Improving outcomes requires more than understanding and evaluating them. Improving outcomes requires an organizational culture that values the use of processes that use available information to improve practice in ways that will impact outcomes. Such processes are most often referred to as *continuous quality improvement* (CQI). CQI is not time limited, but is rather an ongoing process by which organizations make decisions and evaluate their progress (see Chap. 11; Casey Family Programs & NCWRCOI 2005; PPCWG 2011).

Continuous Quality Improvement

A basic CQI process is cyclical, and its components include defining core outcomes, establishing a baseline, setting goals and a plan for how to achieve them, implementing the plan, monitoring progress, and adjusting the strategy based on progress and feedback throughout the process (American Public Human Services Association 2008; Barbee et al. 2011; Casey Family Programs & NCWRCOI 2005; O'Brian and Watson 2002; PPCWG 2011; Wulczyn 2007). The entire process will be driven, shaped, and defined by the organization's vision, values, and workplace culture (Casey Family Programs and NCWRCOI 2005). Chapter 11 provides a comprehensive overview of DAPIM™, a CQI model for human service organizations that has been adopted by many state child welfare systems.

Implementing and sustaining CQI processes requires dedicated staff, strong leadership, and sustained effort over time (Casey Family Programs and NCWRCOI 2005). Such a process begins from the top level of the organization but necessitates the development of a bottom-up approach with meaningful engagement by all levels of staff and stakeholders (American Public Human Services Association 2008; Casey Family Programs and NCWRCOI 2005; O'Brian and Watson 2002; PPCWG 2011). Figure 12.3 illustrates the CQI process.

Fig. 12.3 Continuous quality
improvement process

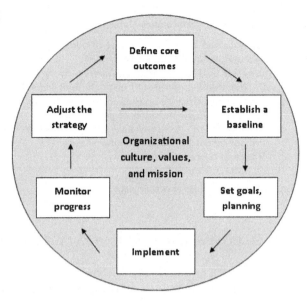

Key Principles of Performance Management

Several principles of *performance management* should accompany the implementation of a CQI process. Adherence to these principles will influence an organization's culture and work processes in ways that determine the extent to which staff at all levels are able to embrace and make the most of a CQI process. Highlighted in Fig. 12.4, each of the principles is explained below.

Top- and Middle-Level Managements Embrace a Culture of Outcome-Driven Quality Improvement

Implementing an agency-wide CQI process requires significant changes to the way work is performed and decisions are made. In order for the process to be implemented, strong and sustained leadership is required at all levels of management (American Public Human Services Association 2008, 2011; O'Brian and Watson 2002; Wells 2006; Wells and Johnson 2001). Even if frontline staff have the tools they need to use information to evaluate practice and identify areas for improvement, evidence suggests that changes do not occur without a culture change (Casey Family Programs and NCWRCOI 2005; Collins-Camargo et al. 2011). Staff need to know that the commitment to a new process will be sustained and that efforts to engage will be both expected and taken seriously.

Key Principles of Performance Management

1. Embrace and champion a culture of outcome-driven quality improvement (both top- and middle-level managers)
2. Integrate CQI process into all aspects of work
3. Provide training for all staff on continuous quality improvement
4. Support participatory decision making
5. Select appropriate measures of performance
6. Use information to inform how to improve performance, not to penalize
7. Provide all workers access to information
8. Review progress regularly

Fig. 12.4 Key principles of performance management

Integrate CQI Process into All Aspects of Work

In time, the CQI process should become central to the operations of the agency; it should not be performed as a task that is separate and additional to normal work processes (Casey Family Programs and NCWRCOI 2005). Reaching this level of integration will require the culture shift discussed above, and it will be a signal of an organization that truly values constant improvement and active engagement from all levels of staff.

Provide Training for All Staff on Continuous Quality Improvement

Providing training to all levels of staff is a key component of implementing continuous quality improvement and the use of information to drive decision making. Child welfare caseworkers and supervisors may not be accustomed to the terminology, techniques, or data used to review and evaluate progress related to outcomes. This lack of knowledge and understanding may be a barrier that might prevent them from being able to fully contribute. However, since their expertise is vital to the CQI process, providing training becomes increasingly important for both understanding of and support for the improvement efforts (Casey Family Programs and NCWRCOI 2005; Wells 2006; Wells and Johnson 2001). Providing training is also a signal of the organization's commitment to the process.

Support Participatory Decision Making

Any time change is introduced in an environment, the degree to which individuals are involved in the information gathering and decision-making processes significantly impacts their openness to the change. Developing methods to engage in, listen to, and learn from frontline staff and other stakeholders about their ideas throughout the entire CQI process will increase buy-in and better inform the process and results (American Public Human Services Association 2008, 2011; Casey Family Programs and NCWRCOI 2005; Collins-Camargo et al. 2011; NCWROI 2007; Wells 2006; Wells and Johnson 2001). This may lead to more staff acting as partners rather than adversaries, easing the change process (Wells 2006).

Select Appropriate Measures of Performance

A common challenge that organizations and individuals face with the creation of performance measures is using them appropriately. We will not go into great length here on how to develop appropriate measures, but it is a complex task. It is important to keep the measurement of data in context and remember that data and the measurement of outcomes are not ends in themselves (Casey Family Programs and NCWRCOI 2005). There must be an appropriate linkage to service provision; programs or services should not be held accountable for outcomes they could never reasonably be expected to achieve. At the same time, outcomes should not be so narrow that they only focus on one element of a service when there are several critical components. In most cases, outcome measures should be coupled with process measures in order to control for the unquantifiable aspects of service delivery (Tilbury 2007; Wells 2006; Wells and Johnson 2001). If outcomes are inappropriate to the service provided, yet agencies or individuals are held accountable for them, there is the potential for the measures themselves to have a detrimental impact on service provision and ultimately on child and family outcomes. This could occur if service providers focus too heavily on performing well on measures that are not central to their mission; through processes which are not best practices; or at the expense of performance in other, equally important areas (Morris-Compton et al. 2011; Tilbury 2007).

Use Information to Learn How to Improve Performance, Not to Penalize

Data related to outcome and process measures can be used to monitor performance and penalize individuals who are performing poorly. While monitoring performance is an important task, supervisors must be conscious of the proper role and dosage of monitoring. If information is consistently used as a means to control or reprimand employees, they will view outcome measurement as something negative—a situation to be avoided. It is only natural for employees to resist the implementation of a tool that they believe will be used against them. This belief may stem from previous experiences with similar efforts at data-based decision making or from an organizational culture that does not value bottom-up feedback from frontline workers.

However, through appropriate framing and use, outcome and process information can be used to help caseworkers, supervisors, and administrators alike work towards common goals. Individuals working in the child welfare field want to perform well and improve the experiences of those they serve. If data related to outcomes and processes are used to help staff members improve their efficiency and the results of their efforts, they may embrace the tools and methods more readily (Casey Family Programs and NCWRCOI 2005). Communication patterns are very important: caseworkers perceive supervisor support as critical to their work, and the nature of the relationship they seek is one in which the supervisor serves in a consultative rather than a monitoring role (Wells 2006). Data can be used as an effective tool to facilitate such a relationship.

Provide All Workers Access to Information

As demands for accountability increase, so do the demands on agencies to have higher quality data and greater amounts of it. Agencies consistently rely on frontline staff to provide more information, whether on paper or in an information system. Caseworkers often feel that they are entering this information and filling out paperwork for no apparent reason (Wells 2006); this is caused by a lack of communication with them about who is using the information, how it is used, and why it is important, and often results in poorer data quality. In reality, this information is often used extensively, but by the limited number of people—usually administrators—who have access to it in a useable format.

Much outcome and process information could be useful to caseworkers and supervisors themselves. In a growing trend, states and localities are now implementing information management systems that improve the access frontline workers and managers have to this information—both by granting them greater access to the information and by presenting it in an easy-to-use manner. Such access is critical to data quality and staff engagement, since it allows staff to see information that is useful to them, see what they are being held accountable for, and better understand the link between their work, data entry, and outcome monitoring (Casey Family Programs and NCWRCOI 2005; Center for Study of Social Policy 2003; O'Brian and Watson 2002; NCWRCOI 2007).

Review Progress Regularly

The regular review of progress is key to both managing culture change and sustaining CQI efforts until they become fully integrated into the work process (Casey Family Programs and NCWRCOI 2005; Wells 2006). The nature of the information being reviewed regularly will vary by job function, but it is the continuous use of updated information that will help frontline staff and administrators use information proactively to inform their work and quickly identify areas for improvement.

Case Example: Timeliness to Permanency

Parsley County contains a metropolitan center with surrounding suburban communities and is located in a state with a county-administered child welfare system. Two years ago, Parsley County Department of Child and Family Services (DCFS) secured funding for technical assistance to develop a CQI process. An internal CQI group, consisting of staff at all levels of the child welfare agency, was established as part of that process. Each year, the group selects one specific practice area on which to focus its efforts. This year, members of the group suggested concentrating on improving timeliness to permanency for youth who have been in care for an extended period of time. This decision was informed by reviewing the agency's performance according to federal outcomes and discussing anecdotal knowledge of their child welfare system.

One indicator on which Parsley County performed poorly was the following federal CFSR measure:

C3.1: Of all children who were in foster care for 24 months or longer on the first day of the target year, what percent were discharged to reunification, relative care, guardianship, or adoption prior to their eighteenth birthday by the end of the target year?

While the county agency's performance was similar to that of other counties and the state through 2009, local performance declined and plateaued over the following 2 years while it was improving among comparable populations. Figure A shows Parsley County aggregate numbers for all similar size counties in the state and the statewide numbers for permanent exits from care.

To begin to understand why the county's trends were not keeping pace with other localities, analysts reviewed the data more closely. Figures B and C below provide some additional information used in taking a closer look at Parsley County's youth in care. The data showed that one of the potential causes for the stagnation in exits to permanency in Parsley County was the sharp increase in youth in kinship care as a proportion of youth in care (Fig. B). In fact, there was very little change in the percentage of youth exiting to permanency over the previous few years by care type (Fig. C). Rather, the shift towards a placement type where legal permanency took longer to achieve made it appear as though exits to permanency for these youth had decreased. The shift towards kinship care was celebrated as a positive outcome for these youth. Nevertheless, the team agreed that timely permanence

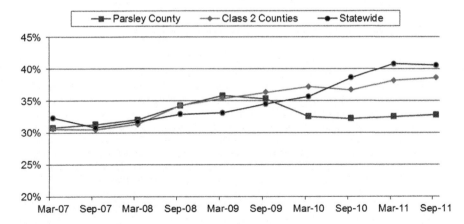

Fig. A Long stayers with permanent exit by end of target year

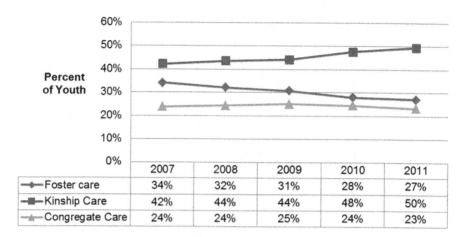

Fig. B Long stayers on first day of target year, by care type

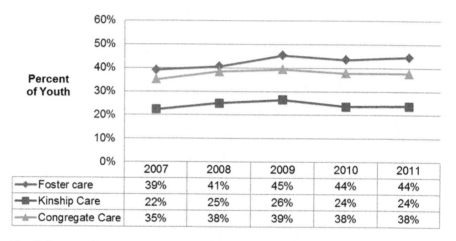

Fig. C Long stayers with permanent exit by end of target year, by care type

for all youth is critical. Recognizing that making a systemic impact on permanency outcomes for youth in care for long periods of time would require long-term commitment, a team member recommended assembling a permanency roundtable, as other child welfare agencies had recently formed. Permanency roundtables are forums for dedicated professionals to engage in ongoing, structured case consultation designed to expedite permanency for youth in care through creative thinking, use of best practices, and breaking down systemic barriers (Casey Family Programs 2012; National Conference of State Legislatures 2010).

The CQI team partnered with DCFS leadership to form a roundtable that included key stakeholders. The CQI team committed to support the department's efforts and charged the stakeholders to focus the first phase of their work on permanency for long stayers in kinship care. In collaboration with roundtable members, the CQI team collected more data to inform their efforts by investigating if there had been any units in the organization or service providers with greater success than others. They also began to identify the particular barriers to permanency for youth in kinship care.

Organizational Variance

DCFS has three regional offices and holds contracts with several community providers to provide out-of-home care for children. Analysis of patterns of exits to permanency for youth in care for over 24 months revealed that the rates were fairly consistent across regions and across providers; there were also no significant differences in the populations served. Therefore, the lack of variance implies that the barriers to permanency are systemic and are not specific to service providers.

Qualitative Analysis

Caseworkers and supervisors serving youth in kinship care for 24 months or longer completed a survey to provide specific information on the challenges to achieving permanency in these cases. The survey results revealed that the kinship care cases are difficult to move to permanency because reunification is not in the best interests of the child, there is hesitancy to move towards adoption or legal custodianship because it could cause tension within the family, and child welfare staff do not push these cases because the child is safe and living with family members. These findings were not novel and reaffirmed the assertions of CQI team members.

However, a significant finding did emerge from the survey: several casework staff expressed concern that children remained system-involved significantly longer than necessary and that agency policies did not provide adequate solutions for providing these youth with the family permanency they needed by allowing for child welfare involvement to end without formal legal permanency. The permanency roundtable immediately responded by prioritizing case reviews for these cases.

Operational Data

Simultaneous to the case reviews, the roundtable worked to develop reports that would assist staff members in their efforts to move children to permanency. The first report was designed as a monthly report for supervisors, to help guide their supervision and consultation with their caseworkers. The report lists youth who are in stable placements with kin, defined as living with the same person for 2 years or longer. The report includes other pertinent case details, such as permanency goals and progress towards achieving them. Additionally, a second report was developed to track key information for all youth in care for 3 years or longer. Initially, the reports were used by supervisors to lead case reviews with teams of caseworkers and supervisors to discuss how to move these youth to permanency. Within 3 months, staff at all levels of the agency began to review the reports regularly.

Now, after 1 year, DCFS has processes in place to assist casework staff in their planning for permanency, continually provide recommendations for action on specific cases, and address systemic barriers. In its early stages, the permanency roundtable has identified areas for collaboration between child welfare leadership, policy experts, and family court judges as they work to safely remove barriers to permanency for youth. These stakeholders will continue to meet and use the information available to them to improve outcomes for children in their care.

Conclusion

Child welfare services demand accountability, and in an increasingly data-driven environment, staff of child welfare agencies are being held accountable to outcome-based performance more than ever. Performance tools and data serve a purpose beyond just reporting and monitoring. Data can be used to inform and improve practice, with the ultimate result of improving outcomes for children. Agencies with cultures that embrace continuous improvement and feedback from all levels of the organization will be most able to utilize information to their advantage and respond to changes in their environment.

Questions for Discussion

1. Improvement on one outcome may correspond with poorer performance on another. Discuss two or three examples of when this might occur and what this means for performance management.
2. Give an example of a performance measure for which a point-in-time sample may be a more appropriate population to examine than an entry or exit cohort.
3. Imagine you are a caseworker. Discuss a concern you may have about your performance being monitored. How would some of the principles of performance management address this concern?
4. Choose an outcome and identify four data-driven methods you could use to measure, better understand, and/or improve performance on that outcome.
5. What else might Parsley County do to increase permanency outcomes of children in care for longer than 24 months?

References

Administration for Children and Families. (2007). *Child and Family Services Reviews Summary of Findings Form.* Retrieved from http://www.acf.hhs.gov/programs/cb/cwmonitoring/tools_guide/sumfinding.htm.
Administration for Children and Families (2011). Children's Bureau. *Federal Child and Family Services Reviews Aggregate Report Round 2 Fiscal Years 2007–2010.* Retrieved from http://www.acf.hhs.gov/programs/cb/cwmonitoring/results/fcfsr_report.pdf.
Administration for Children and Families (n.d.). *General findings from the Child and Family Services Reviews, 2001–2004.* U.S. Department of Health and Human Services. Retrieved from: http://www.acf.hhs.gov/sites/default/files/cb/findings_from_the_initial_cfsr.pdf
Administration for Children and Families. (n.d.). *Child and Family Services Reviews fact sheet.* Retrieved from http://www.acf.hhs.gov/programs/cb/cwmonitoring/recruit/cfsrfactsheet.htm#.
American Public Human Services Association. (2008). *DAPIM™: An approach to systematic continuous improvement.* Washington, DC: Author. Available at http://www.aphsa.org.
American Public Human Services Association. (2011). *Organizational effectiveness handbook.* Washington, DC: Author. Available at http://www.aphsa.org.

Barbee, A. P., Christensen, D., Antle, B., Wandersman, A., & Cahn, K. (2011). Successful adoption and implementation of a comprehensive casework practice model in a public child welfare agency: Application of a Getting to Outcomes (GTO) model. *Children and Youth Services Review, 33*(11), 622–633.

Casey Family Programs (2012). *Permanency roundtables*. Retrieved from: http://www.casey.org/Resources/Initiatives/PermanencyRoundtables/

Casey Family Programs & National Child Welfare Resource Center for Organizational Improvement. (2005 May 17). *Using Continuous Quality Improvement to improve child welfare practice: A framework for implementation* [notes from expert meeting]. Retrieved from http://muskie.usm.maine.edu/helpkids/rcpdfs/CQIFramework.pdf

Center for State Foster Care and Adoption Data. (2010 April 29–30). *Longitudinal data analysis using administrative data* [seminar]. Chapin Hall at the University of Chicago. Chicago, IL.

Center for the Study of Social Policy. (2003). *Quality Service Reviews: A tool for supervision. Safekeeping.* Retrieved from http://www.cssp.org/publications/child-welfare/community-partnerships-for-the-protection-of-children/safekeeping-winter-2003.pdf

Collins-Camargo, C., Sullivan, D., & Murphy, A. (2011). Use of data to assess performance and promote outcome achievement by public and private child welfare agency staff. *Children and Youth Services Review, 33*(2), 330–339.

Engel, R. J., & Schutt, R. K. (2013). *The practice of research in social work* (3rd ed.). Thousand Oaks, CA: Sage.

Morris-Compton, S., Noonan, K., Notkin, S., Morrison, S., Raimon, M., Torres, D. (2011). *Counting is not enough: Investing in qualitative case reviews for practice improvement in child welfare.* Retrieved from http://www.aecf.org/~/media/Pubs/Topics/Child%20Welfare%20Permanence/Other/CountingisNotEnoughInvestinginQualitativeCaseReviews/QCR_vFINAL_R9.pdf

National Child Welfare Resource Center for Organizational Improvement (2007). Strengthening child welfare supervision. *Child Welfare Matters.* Retrieved from http://muskie.usm.maine.edu/helpkids/rcpdfs/cwmatters6.pdf

National Conference of State Legislatures (2006, September). *Child welfare caseworker visits with children and parents.* Retrieved from: http://www.ncsl.org/Portals/1/documents/cyf/caseworkervisits.pdf

National Conference of State Legislatures (2010, August). *Permanency roundtables.* Retrieved from: http://www.ncsl.org/issues-research/human-services/child-welfare-legislative-policy-newsletter-a939.aspx

O'Brian, M., Watson, P. (2002). A framework for quality assurance in child welfare. Retrieved from http://muskie.usm.maine.edu/helpkids/rcpdfs/QA.pdf

Positioning Public Child Welfare Guidance. (2011). *Key processes: The Continuous Improvement (CI) Process.* Retrieved from http://ppcwg.org/change-management-key-processes.html

Tilbury, C. (2007). Shaping child welfare policy via performance measurement. *Child Welfare, 86*(6), 115–135.

U.S. Department of Health and Human Services, Administration for Children, Youth and Families (2012, January). Title IV-B, Subpart 1 of the Social Security Act as revised by the Child and Family Services Improvement and Innovation Act, P.L. 112–34, ACYF-CB-PI-12-01.

Wells, R. (2006). Managing child welfare agencies: What do we know about what works? *Children and Youth Services Review, 28*(10), 1181–1194.

Wells, S. J., & Johnson, M. A. (2001). Selecting outcome measures for child welfare settings: Lessons for use in performance management. *Children and Youth Services Review, 23*(2), 169–199.

Wulczyn, F. (2007). *Monitoring child welfare programs: Performance improvement in a CQI context.* Retrieved from http://www.chapinhall.org/sites/default/files/old_reports/339.pdf

Chapter 13
Conclusions and Future Directions

Helen Cahalane

Abstract Social workers who practice in child welfare must be confident, committed and courageous. They must possess a shared sense of values that emphasize service, honesty, accountability, respect, engagement, and diversity. They must be proficient in engaging youth and families in a helping relationship, have knowledge of diverse client populations, and utilize evidence-informed interventions and approaches that help to reach across cultural divides caused by differences in race, class, culture, and sexual orientation.

Child welfare organizations have their own set of imperatives: establishing visionary and committed leadership, supporting middle managers and supervisors, assuring that reflective, trauma-informed supervision and oversight is provided to caseworkers, and creating agency performance standards that are transparent, clear, and used to drive positive system change.

Future directions for child welfare practice should include a focus on the following key areas: integration among child-serving systems of care; establishing well-defined practice models; developing training and transfer of learning programs that build bridges between knowing and dong; incorporating evidence-driven interventions as standard practice; promoting inclusive practices; including the voice and perspective of youth and families in service delivery and evaluation; assuring that middle managers are proficient in reflective, trauma-informed supervision practices; supporting child welfare organizations in implementing continuous quality improvement initiatives; using data to inform practice; and demonstrating the impact and cost-effectiveness of interventions delivered in the community. Social workers are in a unique position to contribute to the quality and effectiveness of the child welfare system as caseworkers, supervisors, middle managers and agency leaders.

Keywords Systems of care • Practice models • Leadership • Supervision

H. Cahalane (✉)
Child Welfare Education and Research Programs, School of Social Work,
University of Pittsburgh, Pittsburgh, PA, USA
e-mail: hcupgh@pitt.edu

H. Cahalane (ed.), *Contemporary Issues in Child Welfare Practice*,
Contemporary Social Work Practice, DOI 10.1007/978-1-4614-8627-5_13,
© Springer Science+Business Media New York 2013

The contributing authors of this volume have summarized a wide range of literature on child welfare practice and integrated a realistic perspective of the field informed by direct work with children, families, and organizations. While broad in scope, the compilation of topics contained here is by no means inclusive of the entire range of practice imperatives in child welfare. Attempting to offer concluding remarks to a volume focused on a field as diverse as child welfare is akin to trying to summarize the myriad roles a social worker can assume in contemporary society. Overall summary comments are complicated at best and are inadequate in capturing the work of the many talented and dedicated professionals who contributed to this volume.

Nonetheless, there are some primary goals and values that we can identify as being essential to child welfare work. Social workers who practice in child welfare must be confident, committed, and courageous. They must possess a shared sense of values, prizing service, honesty, accountability, respect, engagement, and diversity (PA Child Welfare Resource Center 2012). Given that the child welfare system is charged with serving society's most vulnerable members, the need for a skilled workforce that is equipped to meet family needs, ensure that children are safe, establish supportive connections, promote permanency, and bolster success in life is no small feat. Social workers in child welfare must understand and help to integrate the array of child-serving systems, must consider both youth and caregiver perception and voice, and must be knowledgeable about the policies and practices that promote permanent options for youth. They must be able to engage families in a helping relationship by sharing power and avoiding coercive and adversarial encounters. Social workers practicing in child welfare must have knowledge of diverse client populations and of the evidence-informed interventions and approaches that help to reach across cultural divides caused by differences in race, class, culture, gender, and sexual orientation.

Training, transfer of learning to the field, and the effective application of knowledge and skill within the context of distinct situations are critical in meeting the demand for competence in child welfare practice. Social workers must address the stress and trauma, both primary and secondary, that accompany child welfare work, by practicing self-care and contributing to an organizational culture that is trauma informed and supportive. Supervision is a key factor in determining whether child welfare workers balance the rewards and the challenges of their work or are discouraged from doing so. At the agency level, effective functioning requires a commitment across all levels of the organization to engage in continuous quality improvement and change strategies. In an increasingly data-driven environment, child welfare agencies must use both process and outcome evidence for decision making, as well as for demonstrating that the services they provide to children and families make a difference in these clients' lives and are connected to observable life outcomes.

Child welfare organizations have their own set of imperatives: establishing visionary and committed leadership; supporting middle managers and supervisors who are empowered to make change and who assure that reflective, trauma-informed supervision and oversight is provided to caseworkers on the front lines of child welfare; and creating agency performance standards that are transparent, clear, and used to drive positive system change. Most importantly, child welfare finance reform is desperately needed in order to direct resources toward early intervention, services that maintain the bonds of connection between children and families whenever possible, and community solutions for assuring the safety and well-being of all youth and their caregivers.

In summary, future directions for child welfare practice should include a focus on the following areas:

1. Integrating child welfare among the child-serving systems of care, recognizing that the children, youth, and families receiving child welfare services have a high likelihood of involvement in other human service systems and that cross-systems integration is one way to help a fragmented and troubled family begin to find common ground
2. Establishing well-defined practice models that embrace core features of effective engagement, partnership, solution building, and motivation for change
3. Developing training and transfer of learning programs that are about building bridges between knowing and doing, making social workers translators as they engage in understanding, challenging, and supporting the difficult changes youth, families, and workers themselves must make
4. Incorporating evidence-informed and evidence-based interventions as standard practice in child welfare systems, implementing them to fidelity, and adding to the evidence base by evaluating whether these interventions are effective at the child, family, and organizational level
5. Promoting practices that are inclusive of differences in race, class, culture, gender, spiritual belief, and sexual orientation among clients and social workers, and among other professionals who deliver and oversee child welfare services, such as agencies, courts, public and private providers, advocacy organizations, and family support programs
6. Including the voice and perspective of youth and families in shaping, defining, and evaluating services that are centered on permanence for youth, support for families and providing protection for children without sacrificing familial connections
7. Assuring that middle managers and direct supervisors are proficient in reflective supervision practices that are supportive and trauma informed, and not primarily focused on the completion of task assignments and compliance with policy requirements
8. Supporting child welfare organizations and agency leaders in implementing continuous quality improvement initiatives that are inclusive of all levels of the organization and directed toward establishing a culture of learning and change
9. Using data to inform practice and challenge assumptions of what works and what does not, for whom, when, and under what conditions
10. Demonstrating the impact, outcomes for children and families, and cost-effectiveness of community-based interventions delivered by social workers in child welfare settings

Practicing in child welfare is challenging, rewarding, and full of opportunities to impact the lives of children and families. It comes with tremendous responsibility and requires a skill set that includes critical thinking, a systemic perspective, and the compassion and courage to help vulnerable youth and families make life-determining decisions. Child welfare practice is not for the faint of heart, and those who dedicate themselves to careers in this field must be prepared to deal with the stressful aspects inherent in the work. Social workers are in a unique position to contribute to the quality and effectiveness of the child welfare system, whether as caseworkers on the front lines of service, as supervisors and middle managers, or as agency leaders. The recommendations provided here only begin to touch the surface of this multifaceted and specialized area of social work practice.

Reference

PA Child Welfare Resource Center (2012). *About CWRC. Child Welfare Education and Research Programs*, University of Pittsburgh School of Social Work. Retrieved from http://www.pacwrc.pitt.edu/AboutUs.htm

Index

H. Cahalane (ed.), *Contemporary Issues in Child Welfare Practice*,
Contemporary Social Work Practice, DOI 10.1007/978-1-4614-8627-5,
© Springer Science+Business Media New York 2013

CPSIA information can be obtained
at www.ICGtesting.com
Printed in the USA
LVOW04*1840081216

516418LV00011B/170/P